THE GROWTH OF THE BIBLICAL TRADITION

THE GROWTH
OF THE
BIBLICAL TRADITION
The Form-Critical Method

by
KLAUS KOCH

Translated from the second German edition
by S. M. Cupitt

CHARLES SCRIBNER'S SONS
New York

CONTENTS

46066

INTRODUCTION

On October 30th, 1954, G. von Rad wrote to me asking whether I could 'write a small guide to form criticism for our students'. This suggestion fell on fruitful ground, for in the group discussions I had been taking I had very much regretted the lack of anything comprehensive on Old Testament form criticism. So some months later, when von Rad was visiting the pastor's house at Jena-Priessnitz, the idea took firmer shape. If I had known the extent of such an undertaking I would never have attempted it. But once I had begun I wanted to carry it through, despite the many interruptions occasioned by my travels around Germany. The 'small guide' has become a full-length book, and I now hand it over to my patiently waiting publisher, only too conscious of its limitations.

It is intended therefore as a guide for students, as an introduction to form-critical research, the evidence for which has gradually accumulated in innumerable articles on the Old Testament, some of them now almost unobtainable. The more I studied the literature, the more I became aware that there were many problems of method which would need to be pondered. So much has been written under the name of form criticism that the reader sometimes feels that this field of exegesis should be kept within some sort of bounds. It is hardly surprising that many exegetes tread with caution. Thus I found the emphasis more and more laid upon problems of method, which in the ensuing pages will be seen to be very much in the foreground. In the present state of things it did not seem advisable to attempt a summary of all form-critical investigations. On many points we are still far from having achieved convincing results, and indeed there are many parts of the Bible which have not as yet been studied from the form-critical point of view. Hence I have limited myself to a few examples, choosing only the focal points in this field of research: the early narratives, hymns, songs of lamentation from the Psalter, prophetic sayings and—as examples to illustrate the first sections of the book—the Decalogue and the New Testament Beatitudes.

In the first section I have also allowed myself one or two excursions into the New Testament, in an attempt to bring out the relationship between the two and to show that the methods which are discussed are by no means only applicable to the Old Testament and the Hebrew language. These brief references to the New Testament are not intended to be by any means exhaustive, but only to provide the arguments with greater breadth, for if they had been restricted to the Old Testament alone their basis would have been too narrow. Historically it is quite proper that the subject should be extended to cover the New Testament. The first advocates of form criticism, Gunkel and Gressmann in particular, were convinced that

Old Testament form criticism and New Testament form criticism should not in any way be isolated from each other.

These fathers of form criticism are mentioned very often in this book. In my attempt to present the principles of form-critical exegesis I found that it was the most venerable father of them all, Hermann Gunkel, who provided me with the most information. All that was produced on this subject during the period of his activity appeared under his auspices alone, and since his death very little more has appeared in print about the principles of form-critical work. His name therefore crops up far more frequently than that of any other writer.

The deficiency of material on the origins of form criticism has meant that I have repeatedly had to insert paragraphs for specialists in this field. But in order that the book may be first and foremost a guide for beginners in theology I have consigned many comments to the footnotes and have occasionally used small type in the text. For it must be emphasised that this book is primarily one for students, specially for those who are beginning theological studies. Also the division and arrangement of the material has been done with the student in mind. Anyone who is taking part in an exegetical discussion for the first time will, as I see it, find chapters 1–5 of most help. If the discussion concerns a narrative book, chapter 6 will also be useful, and for poetic texts and units of speech chapter 8. Chapters 7 and 9 are intended for more advanced students, for they attempt a general survey of biblical exegesis. So much for the first part. The second is concerned only with Old Testament problems. Whether the student uses the first, second or third chapter of this part will depend on whether he is concerned with narrative, poetic or prophetic passages. Of course I like to think that there will also be readers who will read the book through from beginning to end. However, chapters 6–9 are quite distinct from the others and can be read without reference to the rest of the book.

A note about the references. I have not aimed at completeness, for this would only tempt the beginner to dispense entirely with other literature. I have given details of what would be useful for further research into biblical literary types and their construction. For the sake of simplicity any literature which was mentioned at the head of a chapter, section or sub-section is referred to afterwards by the author's name only. I beg the reader to refer back to the heading of the chapter in question. A key to the abbreviations can be found on p. xiv.

Many readers will ask: but why 'New Paths in Biblical Exegesis'?[1] What with literary criticism and its emphasis on accuracy, and the more attractive aspects of the 'positivist' tendency of the last century, haven't we enough? Isn't form criticism a rather superfluous exercise, inspired only by aesthetic considerations? It is enough to say that each new epoch of biblical scholarship in the western world has striven after a new understanding of the sacred writings. And it has never been to their detriment. One need only think of the Reformation, and its influence upon Evangelical and Catholic exegesis. Hence the present desire to study the history of

---

[1] *Neue Wege der Bibelexegese*, the sub-title of the German edition.

the form of biblical texts has by no means arisen out of a desire for innovation. It is not intended simply to supersede all previous methods of research. It has arisen out of the recognition that we are faced here with a view of things which can provide us with a deeper understanding of the ancient texts, and which could make contact with them relevant to our own times. In my opinion this is because form criticism brings out the link between literature and life, between the biblical text and the history of God's people, in a way hitherto unimagined.

My wife and my assistant Vikar W. Klatt relieved me of the trouble of correcting the proofs. Mr. Klatt also compiled the indexes. My colleague U. Wilckens provided me with many important suggestions for New Testament problems. To them I extend my sincerest thanks.

Hamburg, August 31st, 1963   KLAUS KOCH

TRANSLATOR'S NOTE

In translating the footnotes I have omitted material which is available only in German and is not referred to directly in the text.

I should like to thank the Rev. B. A. Hardy for his comments on this translation, and also Mr. William Horbury for his work on the Greek and Hebrew.

S. M. C.

AUTHOR'S NOTE TO THE ENGLISH EDITION

For many decades form-critical methods were used in biblical exegesis only by Protestant theologians on the Continent. In English speaking countries they were considered to be merely odd theories held by extremists among scholarly critics of the New Testament in Germany, and were not generally accepted. Today this is changing. Form-critical studies are now appearing in English, in the field of the New Testament as well as the Old. And so it is to be expected that the study of the basic methods of form criticism will find its way into biblical hermeneutics in England and America. I hope that this book will contribute something towards this.

If things are as they seem at present theologians generally and exegetes in particular will need to look more carefully than they have hitherto into the questions of philology and linguistics. The theology of the last century talked much about 'the Word', but unpardonably neglected the importance of speech. Form criticism is an attempt to discover the principles underlying the language of the Bible. This does not and must not imply a mere structural and generic linguistic study. Linguistics still starts from the notion that the sentence is the unit of human speech; but speech is not in fact restricted to the utterance of sentences: it takes the form of the larger unit of the *literary type* of speech, which has a definite sociological function. This applies not only to the human word, but also to the Word of God as it is found in the Bible. Thus we come to the underlying purpose of this book: to try to discover what lies behind the speech of God in the Bible.

While the first edition of this book was being translated it was found necessary to prepare a second German edition, which involved a thorough revision of the entire text. Thanks are due to the translator and publisher for the trouble they took completely to revise the original text. At the same time some bibliographical references which had relevance only for the German reader have been taken out, and here and there reference inserted to available literature in English. This gives a better order to the book. The translation of form-critical terms is not always simple, but a rendering has on the whole been found which will be intelligible to the English reader.

Hamburg, July, 1968   KLAUS KOCH

ABBREVIATIONS

AcOr = *Acta Orientalia* (Copenhagen)

ALT I–III = A. Alt: *Kleine Schriften zur Geschichte des Volkes Israel* Vol. I–III, 1953/59. See p. 27, n. 1, for E.T.

ANEP = *The Ancient Near East in Pictures relating to the Old Testament*, ed. J. B. Pritchard, 1954

ANET = *Ancient Near Eastern Texts relating to the Old Testament*, ed. J. B. Pritchard, ²1955

ANV(A)O = *Avhandlinger utgitt av Det Norske Videnskaps-Akademi i Oslo* (Kristiania)

ATD = *Das Alte Testament Deutsch*, ed. V. Herntrich and A. Weiser

ATLANT=*Abhandlungen zur Theologie des Alten und Neuen Testaments*, ²1968

BEvTh = *Beiträge zur Evangelischen theologie*, ed. B. Reicke and L. Rost

Bentzen: Introduction = A. Bentzen: *Introduction to the Old Testament*, ⁴1958

BHH = *Biblisch. Historisches Handwörterbuch*, ed. B. Reicke and L. Rost

BHTh = *Beiträge zur historischen Theologie*

BK(AT) = *Biblischer Kommentar, Altes Testament*, ed. M. Noth

BRL = Galling, *Biblisches Reallexikon*, 1937

Bultmann: Tradition = R. Bultmann: Die Geschichte der synoptischen Tradition, FRLANT 29, ²1931, ⁴1958, E.T. *The History of the Synoptic Tradition*, 1963

BWANT = *Beiträge zur Wissenschaft vom Alten und Neuen Testament*

BZAW = *Beihefte zur Zeitschrift für die alttestamentliche Wissenschaft*

Dibelius: *From Tradition to Gospel* = M. Dibelius: *Die Formgeschichte des Evangeliums*, ²1933, ³1959, E.T. *From Tradition to Gospel*, 1934

Diss = (Evang. theol.) *Dissertation*

DVfLG = *Deutsche Vierteljahrsschrift für Literaturwissenschaft und Geistesgeschichte*

Eissfeldt: Introduction = O. Eissfeldt: *Einleitung in das Alte Testament*, ¹1934, ²1956, E.T. *Introduction to the Old Testament*, 1965

ET = *The Expository Times*

EvTh = *Evangelische Theologie*

FRLANT = *Forschungen zur Religion und Literatur des Alten und Neuen Testaments*

GuB = H. Gunkel—J. Begrich: *Einleitung in die Psalmen*. Supplementary volume to HKAT 1933

Gunkel: Genesis=H. Gunkel: Genesis, HKAT ³1910, ⁵1922, E.T. The Legends of Genesis 1964 (London, Bailey; New York, Schocken).

Gunkel: GrPro = H. Gunkel, Introductions to H. Schmidt: Die grossen Propheten, SAT II, 2, ²1923

Gunkel, KdG = H. Gunkel: Die israelitische Literatur, in *Die Kultur der Gegenwart*, ed. by Hinneberg, I, 7, ²1925

Gunkel: Schöpfung = H. Gunkel: *Schöpfung und Chaos in Urzeit und Endzeit* ²1921

HAT = *Handbuch zum A.T.*, ed. O. Eissfeldt

HdO = *Handbuch der Orientalistik*, ed. B. Spuler

Hempel: *Literatur* = J. Hempel: *Die althebräische Literatur und ihr hellen-istisch-jüdisches Nachleben, Handbuch der Literaturwissenschaft*, ed. Walzel, 1930

HKAT = *Handkommentar zum A.T.* ed. W. Nowack

HUCA = *Hebrew Union College Annual*

JBL = *Journal of Biblical Literature and Exegesis*

JNES = *Journal of Near Eastern Studies*

JTS = *The Journal of Theological Studies*

KAT = *Kommentar zum A.T.*, ed. E. Sellin

KHC(AT) = *Kurzer Hand-commentar zum A.T.*, ed Marti

MeyerK = *Kritisch-exegetischer Kommentar über das N.T.*, founded by H. A. W. Meyer

Mowinckel: Prophecy = S. Mowinckel: Prophecy and Tradition, ANVAO 1946, 3

Mowinckel: PIW = S. Mowinckel: *The Psalms in Israel's Worship*, 1962

N.S. = New Series

Noth, GS = M. Noth: Gesammelte Studien zum A.T. *Theologische Bücherei* 6, ²1960

Noth, ÜGP = M. Noth: *Überlieferungsgeschichte des Pentateuch* 1948

Noth, ÜGS = M. Noth: *Überlieferungsgeschichtliche Studien* I, ¹1943

NTD = Das Neue Testament Deutsch

von Rad, GS = G. von Rad: Gesammelte Studien, *Theologische Bücherei* 8, 1958

von Rad: Theology = G. von Rad: *Theologie des A.T.*, 1957 ff., E.T. *Theology of the Old Testament*, 1962

PSBA = *Proceedings of the Society of Biblical Archaeology*

RB = *Revue Biblique*

RGG = *Die Religion in Geschichte und Gegenwart*, ²1927 ff., ³1957 ff.

SAT = *Die Schriften des A.T. in Auswahl übersetzt und erklärt*, by H. Gunkel and others

SgV = *Sammlung gemeinverständlicher Vorträge und Schriften aus dem Gebiet der Theologie und Religionsgeschichte*

SNVAO = *Skrifter utgitt av Det Norske Videnskaps-Akademie i Oslo* (Kristiania)

StTh = *Studia Theologica*

ThLZ = *Theologische Literaturzeitung*

ThR = *Theologische Rundschau*

ThW = *Theologisches Wörterbuch zum N.T.*, ed. G. Kittel and G. Friedrich

UT = C. H. Gordon: Ugaritic Texts, *Analecta Orientalia* 35, 1955

UUÅ = *Uppsala Universitets Årsskrift*

VT = *Vetus Testamentum* 1950 ff.

VTS = Supplements to *Vetus Testamentum*

WA = Luther, *Werke*: Weimar edition

WMANT = *Wissenschaftliche Monographien zum Alten und Neuen Testament*, ed. G. Bornkamm and G. von Rad

WZ = *Wissenschaftliche Zeitschrift*

ZAW = *Zeitschrift für die alttestamentliche Wissenschaft*

ZThK = *Zeitschrft für Theologie und Kirche*

PART I

The Methods

Section One: Fundamentals

On Old Testament methods: H. Gunkel: Die Grundprobleme der israelitischen Literaturgeschichte, RuA 29–38. Deutsche Literaturzeitung XXVII, 1906, 1797–1800. 1861–1866. J. Muilenburg: The Gains of Form Criticism in Old Testament Studies, ET 71, 1959, 229–33.

On the New Testament: The introduction to M. Dibelius: *Die Formgeschichte des Evangeliums* ¹1919 ²1933 ⁵1966; *From Tradition to Gospel*, 1934 (London, Nicholson & Watson; New York, Scribner). R. Bultmann: Geschichte der synoptischen Tradition, FRLANT N.S. 12, ¹1921 ⁶1964; ET.; *History of the Synoptic Tradition*, 1963 (Oxford, Blackwell; New York, Harper & Row). R. Bultmann and Karl Kundsin: *Form Criticism—Two Essays on New Testament Research*, 1962 (Harper & Row).

1. LITERARY TYPES AND FORMULAS

A. *A Note on Modern Language Usage*

What is form criticism? The German word *Formgeschichte* appears as a technical term for the first time in 1919 in the book title *Die Formgeschichte des Evangeliums* by M. Dibelius,[1] and quickly established itself as the name of a recognised method of biblical exegesis. Dibelius had been inspired by Hermann Gunkel, who had introduced form-critical methods of biblical scholarship as much as twenty years earlier, although under the name of *Gattungsforschung* (research into literary types), or *Literaturgeschichte* (history of literature). Gunkel is the real pioneer of this branch of literary research.

How Gunkel's achievements concern us can be seen from a very commonplace example from our own times. From the flood of printed matter which comes to us daily through the post I select a sample from a firm dealing in weed control:

> We feel sure that this year you will again wish to eradicate the weeds from the paths and terraces in your garden. For this we recommend our well-proved, extra-potent weedkiller Muramor,[2] manufactured from chloric acid.

[1] The existence of 'forms' in literature has long been recognised, although undefined. In 1865, in his *Geschichte des Volkes Israel* II, p. 139, H. Ewald traced 'the history of the style (form) of commandments', and F. Overbeck could write: 'A literature has a history in its forms; hence a proper history of literature will be a history of forms' (Über die Anfänge der patristischen Literatur, *Historische Zeitschrift*, 1882, pp. 417–72, reprinted 1954, p. 12). The classical philologist E. Norden gave his book *Agnostos Theos*, 1913, the sub-title, 'Studies in the history of religious speech forms'. The German *Formgeschichte* (lit. form history) implies two things: the history of linguistic forms, as well as the historical examination of this history. The meaning of the English *form criticism* is more limited, for it is concerned only with the second of these.

[2] The name has been changed.

This spring there has been a particularly vigorous growth of weeds. Why not order your Muramor now and use it at once! Our much reduced prices are now as follows . . .

We would be grateful if you would use the enclosed form for your order, and remain, yours faithfully, N.N.

This, of course, is an advertising circular, one of dozens pushed through letter boxes every day. It is easy to make out its specific characteristics. An advertising circular is always remarkable for its particularly courteous style, aimed to compensate for the necessarily impersonal form of address (We feel sure that . . . you will again wish; we would be grateful . . . for your order). It will of course be shown that I, the recipient, am in dire and immediate need of the recommended product (This spring . . . a particularly vigorous growth). The scientifically proved method of manufacture, so asserts the company, ensures success (Our well-proved, extra-potent weedkiller, manufactured from chloric acid). Finally, but not of least importance, my attention is drawn to favourable prices.

These characteristics are common to hundreds of such letters. Thus the advertising circular can be seen as a current, standardised type of literature which, despite all variation in detail, cannot be avoided by anyone advertising his goods by post. Also the outward appearance of the letter is in accordance with the literary type. Such letters are not hand-written, but printed, in a style which is aimed to please. They are often in colour, and show painstaking variations in type sizes.

Similar examples of fixed written forms can be found in abundance in our everyday life. From the essay to the telegram, from the drama or novel to forms of writing such as the bill (which can hardly yet be called a work of literature), in short, anything which is written or printed will show specific characteristics of form in its basic construction and in its outward appearance. Anyone who wishes to succeed as a writer must use an established literary type. A company's advertising copy-writer will choose a style which has already proved successful. If a playwright wishes to see his play produced he cannot submit it to the theatre in the shape of an essay. It is just as unlikely for a civil servant to send a request to his headquarters in the form of a poem; he is bound to use the language of bureaucracy. Even something as intimate and personal as a love letter abounds in established expressions (and not only in the opening and the conclusion), which will leave no doubt as to the literary type of the letter. Each individual literary unit which we use today evinces the characteristics, whether intentionally or unintentionally, of a recognisable literary type.

Everything which is written or printed falls into literary types so naturally that we are hardly aware of it. Nevertheless, it is a fact of great consequence. In anything that we read we habitually assimilate not only the sense of the individual sentences but also the particular style of language which is used. When we take up a novel we expect a description of the life of one or more people, a study of their inward and outward struggles; but we know also from the outset that it is an imaginative work and not a record of actual happenings. The recipient of an advertising circular knows that it has been prompted by commercial interests and that the eulogy on the quality and cheapness of the recommended product must not be taken too literally. The literary type therefore determines the scope of the contents in advance and restricts them to a particular function as a communication. For instance, no one would think of looking for searching thoughts about God, mankind and the world in an advertising circular, just as a religious tract would not usually indicate market price developments. Therefore the nature of the form which the literary type takes determines its content from the start. But we must emphasise right from the beginning that the word *form* in the phrase *form criticism* must not be understood in too narrow a sense. The mere type of language used is insufficient to constitute a literary type. Besides this there must be a common 'fund of thoughts and feelings.'[3]

The spoken word also, whether formal or informal, falls into fixed literary types, or should do so if it is to make sense. The first example the theologian thinks of is of course the sermon. The opening, with the quotation from a biblical text, and the address to the congregation, are as characteristic of the literary type as is the amen at the close. But the sermon is not exceptional. Every speech makes use of established forms of expression suitable to the occasion. A fairy story told to children will begin 'Once upon a time'. Formal conventions even determine the shape of such commonplace phenomena as words of greeting or farewell. We say, 'Good morning, Mr So-and-So, how are you?' 'Goodbye', and so on. However, in unofficial communication between people fixed literary types are less easy to distinguish because the forms of expression in day-to-day language tend to be confused.[4] Such speech is characterised more by *formulas*. A formula is a short form of a literary type. It is often used as an introduction or as a mark of identification for a more elaborate literary type. 'How are you?' can trigger off a long conversation.

Thus a literary type is indicated by the typical characteristics of an individual linguistic unit, whereas a formula is a set of connecting words, which, though they can indeed convey a meaning in themselves, usually consist of only one sentence and are used in association with a greater literary type. The transition from one to another, from formula to literary type, is of course scarcely noticeable.[5]

---

[3] Gunkel, ZAW N.S. 1, 1924, p. 182; also ALT I, 284 f.: Form criticism is a process by which 'form and content are studied at one and the same time'.

[4] But does this justify the thesis that 'A loose conversation in which one word leads on to another does not aim at any unity' (W. Kayser, *Das sprachliche Kunstwerk* [3]1954, p. 156)? Only speech described pejoratively as chatter, nonsense, etc., has no unity or form.

[5] Though the difference between formulas and types is an important one, it is useless to try to differentiate between 'type' (*Gattung*) and 'form' (*Form*). What is form? Is a type not a form? Or are there forms of literary units other than types and formulas? How could this be? 'There is no adequate distinction between "form" (*forme*) and "literary type" (*genre littéraire*). The only difference is that form designates a means of concrete expression, a formula of style that is more or less fixed through usage, whereas a type is characterised by a certain number of these means of expression. . . . The form is that by which a gospel unit is connected to a particular literary type; therefore by specifying the forms of a text it is possible to determine the literary type to which it belongs.' J. Dupont, *Les Béatitudes*, pp. 20 f. and elsewhere.

B. *New Testament Example: The Beatitudes*

There is as yet no exhaustive survey of the biblical blessing (i.e. *makarismos*). Isolated passages can be found in Bultmann, *Tradition*. The section on 'The Form of the Jewish and Greek Beatitudes' of J. Dupont's great work *Les Béatitudes*, [2]1958, has unfortunately not yet appeared. On Old Testament prehistory: C. Keller: *Les 'béatitudes' de l'A.T.*, in maqqél shâqédh, Hommage à W. Vischer 1960, 88-100. J. M. Robinson: The Historicality of Biblical Language, in: *The Old Testament and Christian Faith*, 1963 (London, S.C.M. Press; New York, Harper & Row).

Hence the written and the spoken word alike fall into established literary types. In practice a literature or a language does not exist as such: they are found in particular forms in particular circumstances. What consequences does this conclusion have for the exegesis of the Bible? Earlier generations did not subject the Bible to any close analysis and regarded the book, or more accurately, collection of books, as the Canon of Scripture, in fact, as a dogmatic treatise. That meant that each book, and indeed each verse of the Old and New Testament were considered to be of entirely equal standing. In the last 250 years historical research has proved that the Bible is not a unit with a single literary form, and that the idea of the Canon must be more carefully defined. Indeed, the book contains a most remarkable assortment of literature: narratives, some crude, some highly sophisticated, prophetic sayings, proverbs, cultic songs, long letters, apocalyptic visions. The use of words, the style and construction follow correspondingly varied principles, and all these must be considered before a text can be accurately interpreted. This is form criticism.

As a New Testament example I shall take the Beatitudes from Matt. v. 3-12, which introduce the Sermon on the Mount. For centuries church tradition has taken these blessings to be the fundamental definition of the virtues which a Christian should practise in his daily life. Is this confirmed by form-critical evidence?

Blessed are the poor in spirit: for theirs is the kingdom of heaven.
Blessed are they that mourn: for they shall be comforted.
Blessed are the meek: for they shall inherit the earth.
Blessed are they that hunger and thirst after righteousness: for they shall be filled.
Blessed are the merciful: for they shall obtain mercy.
Blessed are the pure in heart: for they shall see God.
Blessed are the peacemakers: for they shall be called the sons of God.
Blessed are they that have been persecuted for righteousness' sake: for theirs is the kingdom of heaven.
Blessed are ye when men shall reproach you, and persecute you, and say all manner of evil against you falsely, for my sake.
Rejoice, and be exceeding glad: for great is your reward in heaven: for so persecuted they the prophets which were before you.

The fact that the Church uses the Beatitudes out of context proves that they are self-sufficient. The reader is given the sensation of being faced with a complete unit, and this is confirmed by a glance at the Lucan parallels. There (vi. 20–23) the Beatitudes are given in an entirely different context. If the Evangelists can place these words of Jesus in different surroundings then they viewed the passage as an independent unit. Also the repeated use of the introductory words, 'Blessed are they', clearly lifts the Beatitudes out of their written context.

But this introductory clause is not otherwise completely unknown. Blessings of this kind are to be found in many places in the Bible and elsewhere. The Greek has its own word for this form: *makarismos*. In Israel and early Christianity a blessing [6] is a poetic [7] saying which can crop up in a variety of connections, although not in any situation. In fact, it is just what we term a formula. But in the Bible as a whole there are two forms of the blessing. First, it appears in Old Testament wisdom sayings, often as a conclusion to a chain of sentences (e.g. Prov. iii. 13; cf. the familiar prologue to Ps. i), or as the logical conclusion to a wisdom argument (e.g. Prov. viii. 32 f; Ecclus. xlviii. 11; l. 28). In this form its subject is worldly well-being. Blessing is conferred upon those who live in conformity with the principles prescribed by God and the wise. Secondly, there is the *apocalyptic blessing*, which is quite different. It is directed at those who will be saved in the Last Judgment and who will participate in the new world because they have remained true to their faith. Here the formula is used as the crowning conclusion to eschatological teaching or to apocalyptic songs (Dan. xii. 12; Eth. Enoch lxxxi. 4, lxxxii. 4; II Bar. (Syr.) x. 6 f., xi. 6, liv. 10; Tob. xiii. 14; Pss. Sol. iv. 26; xvii. 50; xviii. 6; Luke i. 45; James i. 12; Rev. xiv. 13; xix. 9; xx. 6, cf. II Esdras vii. 45). The blessing can also appear as a literary type complete in itself, usually in the form of a series, as in the wisdom texts (Ecclus. xxv. 7–11), and also in the apocalyptic texts (II Enoch (slav) xlii. 6–14; lii. 1–16). In such a series it occasionally includes a motive clause:

> Blessed is he who sows the seeds of righteousness, *for* he shall reap sevenfold (II Enoch xlii. 11)

When it is used the blessing is more than a mere flourish: it is a formal assurance of salvation, 'a weaker form of the benediction (*Segen*)[8]'.[9] What does this tell us about the blessing formulas of the Sermon on the Mount? Jesus obviously uses the literary type of the *apocalyptic* [10] blessing. In fact, a close look reveals that in Matt. v two series of blessings have been linked together: verses 11–12 are differently constructed from the previous verses. They consist of only one saying, with a when-clause, and a longer, different motive clause. They address the audience in the second person, whereas v. 3–10 use the third person. The series of the first eight is very rigidly constructed, and is rounded off as a unit by the first and last line ending with the same exhortation, 'For theirs is the kingdom of heaven'. Moreover

---

[6] *Seligpreisung*. A declaratory rather than a performative formula is intended.
[7] See chapter 8, section C.
[8] See above note 6.
[9] L. Brun, Segen und Fluch im Urchristentum, SNVAO, 1932, no. 1, p. 39.
[10] In the time of the New Testament the blessing (*makarismos*) was also used in Rabbinic texts, but conspicuously seldom, and with no eschatological significance. Hence although the literary type was occasionally borrowed by the Rabbis its roots were not there, and Jesus will hardly have taken it from this source.

it appears that this series too is arranged into two parts, the first four Beatitudes concerning suffering, the last four concerning human conduct in daily life.

The factual content confirms this formal relationship to *eschatological teaching*. Previously the Beatitudes were seen as a vehicle for setting out the virtues ordained by God for man, but now it is quite clear that phrases such as 'poor in spirit', 'those that mourn', are 'meek', 'hunger and thirst after righteousness' are merely different aspects of an attitude to a world nearing its close, an attitude of lasting patience and hope. It is not the virtues which are important so much as the promise of salvation conveyed by the 'blessed' at the beginning as well as by the motive clause in the second half of each line. The motive clause is intended to be strictly eschatological: be comforted, inherit the earth (transformed by God), be filled with righteousness, see God: all this would happen at the Last Judgment and the consummation of the world. The second section, v. 11, is also clearly eschatological. These few observations will show how a form-critical analysis provides a helpful framework for the interpretation of individual sections of the Bible.

C. *Old Testament Example: The Decalogue*

A. Alt=Die Ursprünge des israelitischen Rechts 1934=ALT I, 1953, 278 ff. esp. p. 315–32. J. J. Stamm and M. E. Andrew: *The Ten Commandments in Recent Research*, 1967 (London, S.C.M. Press).

The same can be seen from our second example, this time taken from the Old Testament. I select a well known passage, the Decalogue, or Ten Commandments (given here in a shortened form):

I am the Lord (=Jahweh), thy God.

Thou shalt have none other Gods before me.

Thou shalt not make unto thee a graven image, nor the likeness of any form that is in heaven above, or that is in the earth beneath, or that is in the water under the earth: thou shalt not bow down thyself and serve them: for I the Lord thy God am a jealous God, visiting the iniquity of the fathers . . .

Thou shalt not take the name of the Lord (=Jahweh) in vain; for the Lord will not hold him guiltless that taketh his name in vain.

Remember the sabbath day, to keep it holy (. . . for in six days the Lord (=Jahweh) made heaven and earth . . . and rested the seventh day.).

Honour thy father and thy mother: that thy days may be long upon the land which the Lord thy God giveth thee.

Thou shalt do no murder.

Thou shalt not commit adultery.

Thou shalt not steal.

Thou shalt not bear false witness against thy neighbour.

Thou shalt not covet thy neighbour's house.

Thou shalt not covet thy neighbour's wife, nor his manservant, nor his maidservant, nor his ox, nor his ass, nor anything that is thy neighbour's.

It is obvious that we are faced with a unit here. This is confirmed by the church custom of using the Ten Commandments with no reference to

their biblical context. What literary type is it? Traditionally it has been
held that the Decalogue summarised the noblest moral obligations con-
fronting man, confirming his inherent natural rights. What fresh interpretation does a form-critical analysis yield us? The same sort of series of
brief commandments in the negative, using the second person, can be
found elsewhere. The ban on unlawful sexual intercourse in Lev. xviii. 6 ff.
is similarly worded, as is the instruction for judges in Exod. xxiii. 1–9, and
the precepts laid down in Exod. xxii. 18, 21 f., 28 for relations with those
who are to be respected or shunned. Other series of similar construction
are directed against the admission of unsuitable, and in particular alien,
people to the Israelite national and cultic community (Deut. xxiii. 1–8), or
against wrong conduct in the community (Lev. xix). The Decalogue
belongs, therefore, to a much used literary type, and one which is by no
means only used to express general moral principles and the upholding of
natural rights. For instance, a prohibition such as the one in Deut. xxiii. 3,
forbidding the Jahwistic cultic community to receive an Ammonite in their
midst, is certainly not motivated by a desire for natural rights. The formula,
too, by which God announces himself, 'I am the Lord thy God', speaks
against such an interpretation. It pictures a God associated solely with
Israel. What is the significance of this particular form, and what meaning
does it give to the Decalogue? The translation, 'Thou shalt not', is not
entirely satisfactory, for the Hebrew text, with the particle always preceding
a verb in the imperfect, expresses a particularly forcible negative which
would be more accurately translated, 'It is absolutely impossible for you
to do this or that'. In the Hebrew this construction is the same as an
indicative statement in the future: 'You will not do this or that.'[11] Alt
called this literary type *apodictic law*, and this has become the recognised
term. But how far it concerns law has become a matter for debate. Moreover, Alt includes other forms under this title.[12] It is better to call the
Decalogue and similar forms *apodictic series of prohibitions*. There is a
Hebrew name for it: *debarim*, or the 'words' as in Exod. xx. 1; Deut. v. 22;
Ps. 1. 17; cf. Exod. xxxiv. 1, 28.[13] But the Hebrew דָּבָר means more than the
English rendering; not every use of the English 'word' has this sense. דָּבָר
only applies where a divine or human utterance has the power to bring

---

[11] As is well known the usual negative imperative in the Hebrew is אַל, followed
by the jussive. It is a notable fact that the series of prohibitions never appear in this
form. Therefore it is against everything that *form* criticism stands for when, as in
E. Gerstenberger's Wesen und Herkunft des apodiktischen Rechts in WMANT 20,
1965, cf. JBL 84, 1965, 38–51; such negative jussives (which in the O.T. are also
placed in the mouth of God) are put on a level with apodictic commandments, the
combination of which is made into an abstract form of the general prohibition
(similarly S. Gevirtz, VT XI, 1961, 156).

[12] Alt also includes the apodictic decrees of death (as in Exod. xxi. 12: 'He that
smiteth a man, so that he die, shall surely be put to death.') and series of curses (as
in Deut. xvii. 15–26). But despite the similarity of content to the apodictic commandment it is a matter here of three different literary types, each of which must be
studied independently of one another, and which Alt perhaps too quickly
assumes to be one.

[13] Series of ten prohibitions are made distinct from other apodictic prohibitions
by the heading עֲשֶׂרֶת הַדְּבָרִים (Exod. xxxiv. 28; Deut. iv. 13, x. 4).

about a reality. The word could also be roughly interpreted as 'affair, event'. Thus a knowledge of the literary type tells us that these are forceful words, capable of bringing about events. Such a series of commandments apparently not only conveys a moral appeal to Jahweh's adherents, but also the word itself provides the ability to accomplish what is asked.

A brief prohibition not specifying punishment is therefore the main characteristic of this literary type. Another characteristic is the introductory formula by which God announces himself [14]: 'I am the Lord thy God' (followed by 'who brought you out of the land of Egypt'). It precedes the commandments as a statement of the sovereignty and grace of a God who has been trusted throughout the course of the nation's history. To the modern mind this introductory formula seems hardly in keeping with the strictness of the prohibitions which follow it; but in any form-critical study the exegete is required to distance himself firmly from his own language and to involve himself completely in the language he is studying. The formula is used so regularly in series of prohibitions that it must belong to the literary type (Exod. xx. 2; Deut. v. 6; Lev. xviii. 6, xix. 4 ff.; Ps. l. 7, lxxxi. 11, cf. Exod. xxxiv. 6). Grammatically it is a nominal sentence, a kind of adverbial clause to the following verbal clauses. It could well be translated, 'Because I am Jahweh, your God . . . it is out of the question for you to have other gods before me'.[15] Accordingly apodictic prohibitions can be seen as divine law, and in such a rigid sense that they are applicable only in association with the God of Israel. A third characteristic is the *motive clause*, beginning with 'for', which justifies the prohibition by referring to God's past or future historical guidance (Exod. xxiii. 7–9, xxii. 20; Lev. xviii).[16] In this series these clauses only occur in prohibitions which are directly concerned with the relationship to God.[17] Thus a study of the literary type reveals the essential structure of a passage and lays the basis for an accurate exegesis.

These are merely two examples of the type of conclusions which can be drawn from a form-critical study of a biblical text. Any interpretation of a passage which does not take these points into consideration cannot help but miss the mark. 'To study a writer without defining the literary types he uses is to start building a house with the roof.'[18] Form criticism not

---

[14] It has been thought that this 'I am'-formula originally represented the self-conception of a god in a polytheistic society, as it is used elsewhere in the Ancient Orient. But the Israelite had known no other god but Jahweh for a very long period, and will certainly have understood this formula very differently.

[15] Reventlow, *Gebot und Predigt im Dekalog* 1962, pp. 26–28, attempts to prove that the first part of the second commandment is a statement rather than a commandment, for it is in the third, not the second person (cf. Ps. lxxxi. 10 and its absence in Exod. xxxiv. 14 ff.). In his opinion the series of commandments begins with the prohibition on graven images. The attempt is interesting in that it shows that the Indo-Germanic differentiation between the future indicative and the negative imperfect is insufficient to comprehend the meaning of a Hebrew *tempus*.

[16] B. Gemser, The Importance of the Motive Clause in O.T. Law, VTS I, 1953, 50–66. Here also this element of the literary type is acribed to the 'profane' casuistic law.

[17] A further characteristic of apodictic series of prohibitions is the series of *ten* (Exod. xxxiv; Lev. xviii. 6–17, xix; Ezek. xviii were once also), whose symbolism is no longer known.

[18] Gunkel, SAT[2] II, 2, pp. xxxv f.

only helps to bring order into the discussion of ambiguous passages, but also makes it possible to understand how the oft-lamented lack of continuity arose in such books as the Tetrateuch, the Psalter, books of the prophets,[19] synoptic Gospels, and the Revelation of St John, and to discover behind this lack of continuity more ancient logical units; for in such books literary types which were originally independent were merely strung together, and this has obscured the essential purpose of the book as a whole.

D. *The Bounds Imposed by the Literary Type, Literary Originality, and the Inspiration of the Bible*

Although it is of course important in a study of modern literature to define the literary types which are being used, in an interpretation of the Bible it is a good deal more so. This is not only because the passage of time has made interpretation less easy, but also because in the ancient world the spoken and the written word kept far more closely to the established literary types than is usual today. Not only in pre-Christian Israel but throughout the whole pre-Christian world (in particular in the Ancient Oriental and Hellenistic cultures) the inclinations of the individual were much more controlled than they are in the West today. His entire life, from birth until death, was strictly regulated by custom and practice.[20] 'And it must also be recognised that literary types play a far greater role in the writings of an ancient people than they do today, and that whereas in modern literature the personality of the writer is everything, or appears to be everything, in those days it was kept in restraint in a way which almost surprises us. This is because of the nature of the intellectual life of the ancient cultures. In those days the individual was far more bound by custom and did not have the distinction he has today.'[21] Although it could be said that this would result in a lack of free creativity there was of course no widespread reading public with tastes which could have appreciated

[19] Luther on the books of the prophets: 'They have a strange manner of speaking, as if they maintain no particular order but throw all manner of things together, so that it is impossible to grasp their meaning or to accept what they say' (WA XIX, p. 350). Well known is Goethe's remark about the 'highly regrettable and incomprehensible redaction' in the Pentateuch.

[20] That daily speech among the Arabs of the Near East is still firmly fixed in form today is shown from a report by W. Thesiger, who travelled through South Arabia between 1945–50 (*Arabian Sands*, 1959, London, Longmans; London and New York, Penguin Books Ltd. 1964, pp. 101–2). He describes a meeting in the desert: 'When they were a few yards away Mahsin, whom I identified by his lame leg, called out "Salam alaikum", and we answered together "Alaikum as salam". Then one behind the other they passed along our line, greeting each of us with the triple nose-kiss, nose touching nose on the right side, left side, and again on the right. They then formed up facing us. Tamtaim said to me, "Ask their news"; but I answered "No, you do it. You are the oldest." Tamtaim called out, "Your news?" Mahsin answered, "The news is good". Again Tamtaim asked, "Is anyone dead? Is anyone gone?" Back came the immediate answer, "No!—don't say such a thing".' Question and answer were as invariable as the responses in the Litany. No matter what had really happened, they never changed. They might have fought with raiders; half their party might have been killed and be lying still unburied; their camels might have been looted; any affliction might have befallen them—starvation, drought, or sickness, and still at this first formal questioning they would answer, 'The news is good'.

[21] Gunkel, SAT² II, 2, p. xxxv.

such freedom. Those who read were members of established circles of tradition who read for professional reasons and passed their knowledge on, like the prophets or the disciples.

The fact that there are very few terms for literary types to be found in the Old and New Testament does not contradict this. Presumably by no means every literary type then in use had been given a name. In the ancient word many forms are used as vaguely and indiscriminately as the grammatical forms, which also had no name.

Once the diversity of writing in the Bible is recognised, it is not surprising to find as well as literary types which are 'religious' in the very narrowest sense others which have comparatively little relation to the sphere of religion. A wisdom saying in the Book of Proverbs concerned with behaviour at table has naturally much less to do with the religious side of life than has a psalm sung by a dying man, or a saying by Jesus. Similarly, the annals of the Jerusalem court, some of which have been taken up into the books of the Kings, have less to do with faith in Jahweh than does, for instance, a speech by a prophet. All this must be taken into account. But it would be a mistake for a theologian to concern himself only with the 'religious' literary types, for everything in the Old and the New Testaments must have some bearing on religion, because in Israel and in the early Christian world every aspect of life was regarded as a manifestation of the guiding hand of God. From this point of view the New Testament is more of a unity, because it gives witness to the story of Jesus Christ and his followers rather than to the diffuse history of a people. But here too, for instance in the Epistles, there are passages concerned with private matters rather than specifically religious reflections (e.g. II Tim. iv. 9–13).

A serious objection raised against the study of literary types is that it disregards entirely the individual in literature, and in the Bible in particular. Is it not possible to give undue prominence to form and to lose sight of the originality of the individual prophets and apostles? Is it possible to grasp the essential meaning of the sayings of an Isaiah or a Jeremiah, or even the logia of Jesus, if they are considered from the point of view of the prevailing forms of speech? This critical question is justifiable in so far as it is obvious that the individuality of a biblical writer cannot disappear entirely behind the generalities of literary types. Naturally it depends upon the intellectual level of the writer himself. A modern novel, one written by Günter Grass for instance, takes the recognised literary type of the novel much further than does a cheap paperback bought from a bookstall. Comparable differences in quality are to be found in the biblical writings, where Isaiah reveals a far greater originality than the other prophets, as does John of the Evangelists, and Paul of the Apostles. The nature of the type which is used is also important, for in some there is no scope at all for an expression of the individuality of the writer, whereas in others he has greater freedom, such as in the New Testament Epistles, or in the books of the prophets. But the Old Testament wisdom sayings and legal precepts, on the other hand, give little evidence of who has written them. It would be a mistake to restrict an interpretation either to the expression of the individual or to the literary type. In fact, once the reader has a knowledge of the background to a passage, i.e. of the literary type, he will find it much easier to perceive its originality, for a literary type is bound up with the cultural and linguistic life of the community. Form criticism does not, then, deny the originality of the individual but refuses to overrate 'creative' personalities. This indeed had been the failing of biblical scholarship in the last century.

The theologian, seeking the truth behind biblical statements, may be surprised or even aghast that any interpretation of the Bible should depend upon literary types, and the more so when he discovers that an analysis of types is indispensable for an accurate exegesis. Up till the present he has heard only of prophets, evangelists and apostles, but now he is faced with such things as blessings and apodictic prohibitions. The biblical writers seem to have adapted themselves to the literary patterns which were available to them. Does this conclusion detract from the truth of their writings? Surely the mere variety of the types they used, the fact that they did not restrict themselves to the grey uniformity of doctrine, is a proof of their strength. Surely it shows the profound extent to which the divine word has adopted the human language (and by doing so has extended and transformed it), and has made it its own. What theology terms 'inspiration' is not only a matter of the individual 'enlightenment' of the biblical writers, but it also concerns the overall historical development of the language, by which those literary types were evolved which were able to give expression to the biblical message. For centuries the dogma that the Bible is the Word of God has been understood in far too rigid a sense. A form-critical approach permits us to discover afresh the vitality of God's Word.[22]

E. *The Problem of Literary Types in General Literary Scholarship*

I. Behrens: Die Lehre von der Einteilung der Dichtkunst vornehm-lich vom 16.–19. Jahrhundert. Studien zur Geschichte der poetischen Gattungen. Beih. z. Zeitschrift f. roman. Philologie 92, 1940. The most impressive attempt at a 'form-critical' approach outside the biblical field is A. Jolles: *Einfache Formen* [2]1956; cf. also R. Petsch: Die Lehre von den 'einfachen Formen', DVfLG X, 1932, 335 ff. Also informative is the article presented at the opening of the 3rd Congrès International d'Historie Littéraire by P. van Tieghem: La question des genres littéraires, Helicon I, 1938, 95–101.

The idea of literary types (Ger. *Gattung*, L. *genus*, Gr. *eidos* or *charakter*) dates back to antiquity. Soon after Aristotle, Greek grammarians began to define verse metres and to differentiate between tragedies, epics and others. The same happened in the field of rhetoric.[23] However, until the nineteenth century the study of literary types was very much restricted to poetry. Anything in prose was assumed to be unpoetical and was dismissed as such. Even Schiller considered the novelist to be the poet's very poor relation. The Romantics were the first to bring about a revolution and to classify not only

---

[22] On the consequences for the much disputed problems about the objectivity of statements Zimmerli points out: Gunkel 'dimly recognises that any statement not only contains facts but also something of the writer's situation and his own conception of the problem, and that it is questionable to accept any statement as "objective", as not being in some way or other determined by the originator of the statement', *Das Alte Testament als Anrede*, 1956, p. 11.

[23] Cicero: '. . . poematis enim tragici, comici, epici, melici etiam ac dithyrambici . . . *suum cuiusque est*, diversum a reliquis' (quoted in Behrens 19, see section C).

certain forms of prose, such as the novel, but also the products of folk-lore, such as legends and fairy-tales, as literary types. But although the field had thus been widened, it was still restricted to imaginative literature.

Just as the philosophy of the ancients has affected the development of Christian dogmatics, so the Hellenistic methods of literary analysis have affected biblical exegesis. It is therefore not surprising to find the idea of literary types cropping up frequently in connection with the Bible, and particularly with regard to those books of sacred writings which could be described as poetic. For example, the Venerable Bede knew of three literary types: the *dramatic*, evident in Virgil's Eclogues and in the Song of Songs; the *descriptive*, such as in Lucretius or in the Proverbs of Solomon; and a third, *genus micton*, as evident in Ecclesiastes and the Psalms as in Homer and Job.[24] Luther was convinced that 'Job was as fine a drama as Terence's Comedies'.[25] Later, with the growth of historical analysis, scholars such as J. G. Eichhorn[26] analysed the literary types governing Hebrew poetry. And Herder's influence resulted in a search for folk-lore in the Old Testament. After 1830, however, such scholarly preoccupations were dropped in favour of the search for sources: sources for the history of Israel, or for the life of Jesus. Interest waned in the more poetic books such as the Psalter.[27]

After a lapse of several decades Gunkel brought the idea of literary types back into repute, but only the idea of it as expanded by the Romantics, so that the study of literary types was chiefly concerned with the descriptive, prose forms of literature. He proved that consideration of the literary type was essential to the validity of any exegetical statement, and he succeeded in freeing such discussion from the bonds of classical-medieval scholarship. The definition of literary types in the Old and New Testament was no longer a study of the more obvious divisions between the epic, ode, elegy, and so on, but rather a thorough study of language forms.[28] But the main advance which Gunkel, almost unconsciously, made was to do away with the idea that literary types were to be discovered purely in conjunction with the poetic, whether of the individual writer or in folk-lore. Gunkel commented on legal rulings, the teaching of the priests, and on genealogies. To him it was apparent that all parts of the Old and New Testaments were merely linked literary types, that man expresses himself in stereotyped images, whether written or oral. Thus it was not merely a question of poetic forms. What a writer consciously creates is rather an inherited method of expression. Literary types are units of expression into which all human utterances, if they wish to be intelligible, naturally break down.[29] Today Gunkel's widened view of form seems so self-evident that few form critics realise its restricted origin.

Literary scholarship has of course advanced since Gunkel's day. Above all Jolles attempted a morphological study of the simple forms, such as myths, legends, riddles, aphorisms, case, memorabile, fairy tales, and jokes. This

---

[24] Behrens, pp. 36 f.

[25] H. Bornkamm, *Luther und das Alte Testament*, 1948, p. 30.

[26] *Einleitung ins Alte Testament* I, 1780, p. 13.

[27] Such as the very depreciatory study of the Psalter by B. Duhm, a prominent literary critic.

[28] As at any turning point in theological thought, Gunkel's plan was not without its precursors, as he himself often said (GuB, p. 8 or KdG 99). However, the only genuine precursor, E. Meier, *Geschichte der poetischen National-literatur der Hebräer*, 1856, came to Gunkel's notice only late.

[29] In his early writings it is true that Gunkel occasionally still said that it was entirely a matter of 'the creation of works of art through the word', KdG, p. 55; but this was more in the nature of a concession to the thinking of his period, and perhaps also to his own aesthetic disposition. In fact, even in the study from which this quotation comes Gunkel ranged far outside the narrow scope of poetry. His New Testament pupils assumed as a matter of course that 'we no longer treat the Gospels as if they were poetic or philosophical writings', M. Dibelius, *Botschaft und Geschichte* I, p. 83.

benefited Old Testament form criticism in many ways (see for instance G.
von Rad). With Jolles the study of form broke the bounds of literary scholarship. With Petsch also: 'All known types of formal literature are of recent
origin. They are highly complicated and interwoven versions of such linguistic images (the simple forms), much revised and very often biassed.'[30] Van
Tieghem even advocated 'Genology' as a literary discipline. But since the
Second World War a counter-movement has been in progress. The influence
of phenomenalist philosophy has led to a search for the pure linguistic
composition which is complete in itself, and if the idea of literary types is used
at all it is limited to the three so-called natural forms of literature: the lyric, the
epic and the drama. The search for characteristics of form, their construction
and stratification, has become superfluous. Now the search is for the principle
underlying a text, for the fundamentals. At present it is the English literary
scholars who show most interest in the problem of form criticism.[31]

F. *The Determination of Literary Types and Style Criticism*

Since Hellenistic times poetic and rhetorical literary types have been
studied in connection with *figures of speech*, and this is still so in the study of
style today. Biblical exegesis, too, has always taken figures of speech into
account. The use of alliteration has been studied,[32] ingenious methods of
repetition discovered,[33] and, of great importance with regard to the Old
Testament, the use of *word play* has been examined, whereby the sound of a
word indicates a play upon its meaning. There are many other kinds besides
these: *litotes*, for example, where a statement is made positive by means of a
double negative; or the *metaphor*, where words and expressions are used
figuratively. The figures involved in the classical theory of style have been
compiled by E. König, in his interesting and original, if unhistorical work,
Stilistik, Rhetorik, Poesie, 1900.[34] Many modern studies take the matter further,
using the Indo-European languages as a basis. Semitic characteristics are now
being studied.[35] What relation does this study of style have to the study of
literary types? To begin with, reservations must be made against the usual
method of studying stylistic details, for figures of speech do not occur
regularly in the Old and New Testaments, and where they do occur they are
not always of equal significance. They cannot therefore be approached
unqualifiedly. A play upon words in a prophetic saying, for instance in
Jeremiah's vision of the almond tree where he says, 'I see a rod of an almond
tree', and the voice of the Lord answers, 'I watch over my word to perform
it', (Jer. i. 11 f.), has another, more forcible meaning; just as in Phil. iii. 2,
where the apostle makes a pun on the operation for circumcision.[36] Hence

---

[30] p. 336.
[31] W. Kayser, *Das sprachliche Kunstwerk* [1]1948, [10]1964, p. 16, quotes the Cam-
bridge History of English Literature: The study of literature comprises 'the literature of science and philosophy, and that of politics and economics . . . the newspaper
and magazine . . . domestic letters and street songs; accounts of travel and records
of sport'.
[32] O. S. Rankin, Alliteration in Hebrew Poetry, JTS 31, 1930, 285–331.
[33] J. Muilenburg, A Study of Hebrew Rhetoric: Repetition and Style, VTS I,
1953, 97–111.
[34] M. Weiss: Einiges über die Bauformen des Erzählens in der Bibel, VT XIII,
1963, 456–7, presents examples of 'experienced speech' (*Erlebte Rede*) in the
OT. However, I am not convinced that the OT. narrators used this style 'in complete
awareness' (p. 469).
[35] W. M. W. Roth, The Numerical Sequence X/X+1 in the O.T., VT XII,
1962, 300–11.
[36] H. von Campenhausen: Ein Witz des Apostels Paulus, in: Neutestamentliche
Studien for R. Bultmann, BZNW 21, 1954, 189 f. Even Paul is still far removed
from the present-day conception that a play upon words is humorous and should
be interpreted as a joke.

style-critical considerations cannot be ignored in a study of literary types, for this would result in an unbalanced interpretation of the passage. Indeed, for its own part the study of literary types has a great interest in the choice of words, manner of expression and sentence construction, for these have some significance for the literary type in question or for whole groups of literary types, such as the prophetic units. A great part of the material involved in the study of literary style is therefore of great importance for form criticism, because it brings out the individual characteristics of a literary type. Every type has therefore a style of its own. Perhaps it is best, however, to avoid the term 'style' when referring to the figures of speech in a literary type.[37]

On the other hand there are ways of expression and methods of sentence construction which are relatively independent of a literary type and are particular to one writer. Even the biblical books have a most definite style of their own, which is unmistakeable in such powerful writers as Isaiah, or Paul, and in many others. Once the type has been determined a study of the *personal style* of such writers is well worth while.

The tendency in modern literary scholarship is to avoid any emphasis on personal style and to regard the interpretation of the *style of the piece as a whole* as the essential duty of a critic of style. A work of literature should be finally interpreted with no reference to the personality of the writer. It should be regarded as an entity in itself, and all characteristics of style should be allied to the principle which underlies it. However, with regard to the Bible (and to Ancient Oriental writings generally), this form of style criticism is only applicable to a limited extent, for the complete individuality of a literary work, which it presupposes, does not exist. Indeed, stylistic analyses of biblical passages are possible and useful,[38] but they will never attain the style-critical heights that Germanists believe.

Others have tried to interpret 'style' entirely historically as the style of a period, as in the history of art. The search for an *epochal style* [39] is certainly of some importance in connection with pre-exilic and post-exilic Israel and with the Palestinian and Hellenistic early Christian communities. But for this much preliminary work is needed, and this has hardly yet begun. There will be further discussion of this in the section on the history of literature.

2. THE HISTORY OF LITERARY TYPES

A. *Changes Undergone by the Blessing*

Cf. Section 1B bibliography. A. George: La 'Forme' des Béatitudes jusqu' à Jésus, in Mélanges bibliques . . . A. Robert (1958), 398–403.

Let us consider the advertising circular again. To the present day observer it seems a very serviceable form of literature, but it is clear that it is by no means one which would be usual at all times and in all languages. Its existence is easy to explain in the light of the modern mass circulation of printed matter and the structure of our economy. The form itself is not much more than a hundred years old. It has changed greatly within this

[37] It is misleading to assume that style is only 'the manner of utterance . . . which belongs to the literary type' (as in Dibelius, *From Tradition to Gospel*, p. 7).
[38] G. Gerleman, The Song of Deborah in the Light of Stylistics, VT I, 1951, 168–80.
[39] P. Böckmann calls this study 'form criticism' in his *Formgeschichte der deutschen Dichtung*, 1949.

period, adapting itself continuously to our increasing knowledge of psychology. But even forms of literature many centuries old are not the same as they were. As everyone knows, modern drama differs from the drama of Goethe's and Schiller's time, and even more so from the tragedies and comedies of ancient Greece. It is easy to see from these two examples that no form of literature remains unchanged for long. The fact that a prophet of the eighth century speaks differently to a prophet of the sixth century, or that an Old Testament Apocalypse has characteristics which differ from those of a New Testament Apocalypse, is not only because of the individuality of the different writers, but also because of the changes which the literary type has undergone. For literary types, or groups of literary types (narratives, or songs, for instance), change 'according to certain inherent laws which are not merely dependent upon the individual writer' (Dibelius). Thus a study of the literary type leads inevitably to a study of its history.

Even a form as simple as the New Testament Beatitudes has a clearly discernible origin in history. And now the literary type has disappeared. No one utters such sentences except as a biblical quotation. They were known in Israel before the time of Jesus. But the blessing, i.e. *makarismos*, is not to be found in the earlier books of the Old Testament, and is quite foreign to Ancient Oriental cultures.[1] It arose in the Israelite world as a single sentence, not as a series, praising the prudent man, in a participial or relative clause. The wisdom psalms also extol a constant trust in Jahweh: 'Blessed are they that put their trust in him' crops up frequently (Ps. ii. 12, xxxiv. 8; cf. also lxxxiv. 5, Isa. xxx. 18). The form is used right up to the time of the New Testament (Luke i. 45; John xx. 29). Such blessings were often used as greetings between wise men (Ps. cxxvii. f., cxxxiii). As they found fresh strength in the late Israelite period they were extended to form a series. In the Apocalyptic writings the phrase 'Blessed is he who . . .' is often followed by a motive clause (Tob. xiii. 14; I Enoch lviii. 2, xcix. 10, II Enoch xlii. 11); and here such blessings are contrasted by woes (II Enoch lii, cf. also I Enoch ciii. 5; II Bar. x. 6 f.).[2] No longer is it a general matter of trust in God, but belief in the coming of the end of the world, in the eschatological hope.

Blessings in this extended form abound in the synoptic Gospels and in the Revelation of St John. The eschatological blessings uttered by Jesus and his contemporaries nearly always have a motive clause, which is sometimes emphasised by the phrase, 'Verily I say unto you' (Matt. xiii. 15 f., xvi. 17, xxiv. 46 f.; Luke i. 45, xii. 37, 43; xiv. 14 etc.). Contrasting woes appear in Luke vi. 20 ff. (also vi. 5 (cod. D)), and also in the Revelation of St John where fourteen woes are placed in opposition to seven blessings (see also Did. i. 5). The early Christian blessings therefore continue the tradition of the late Israelite Apocalyptic. This is not merely a matter of formality: Jesus and his followers had obviously taken up the

---

[1] J. Dupont, B 47, 1966, 185–222, has proved the existence of the blessing in ancient Egypt.

[2] In the OT there is a motive clause in Prov. ii. 13 f. (secondary), viii. 34 f. (Ps. cxxvii. 5 f.); but cf. the LXX in Gen. xxx. 13; Isa. xxxi. 9; Ecclus. xxviii. 19, xlviii. 11. The curse as contrast to the blessing is completely unknown (other than Eccles. x. 19 LXX).

3

apocalyptic call to disclose the eschatological story and to confront their contemporaries with an inescapable either-or. However, the literary type of the eschatological blessing was not used long in the Christian world; and it does not seem to have established itself in early Hellenistic Christianity. Thus from form-critical observations it is surprisingly easy to discover the origin of the Beatitudes in Matt. v.

The synoptic blessings take us further than their apocalyptic prototypes in that they repeatedly emphasise the paradox behind the eschatological hope. The consummation of the world will bring with it a complete reversal of all circumstances: he who is poor shall be rich; he who hungers (after righteousness) shall be filled (and not only in the Evangelists but also in sayings such as in I Peter iii. 14, iv. 14; Rev. xiv. 13). Also new is the use of the direct address form which is sometimes to be found in the Gospels and in the second section of the blessings quoted above. Previously in Old Testament blessings the address was purely rhetorical: the audience was never directly spoken to, even though the second person was used.[3]

What is surprising is that a complete form-critical survey reveals that a similar literary type existed in Greece, and that it evidently arose quite independently of those examples which are to be found in the Old Testament. In epitaphs, songs of triumph and mystery rites a man is blessed (*makar, olbios, eudaimon*) if he can elevate himself above the troubles and sorrows of day-to-day existence. 'Such blessings are frequently to be found in Greek poetry and prose over the centuries, and they reflect the pains and needs, wishes and ideals of ancient Greece.'[4] The Greek often uses the formula 'Thrice blessed . . .', thus intensifying his description of a man's, or even a god's, bliss. This would be impossible in the Old Testament. The Greek blessings also seem to have no motive clause, so that the synoptic Beatitudes would appear to have been modified from those in the Old Testament, and not to have been influenced by Greek examples. On the other hand there are clear signs of Greek influence in the blessings in the New Testament text, where God himself is praised (I Tim. vi. 15); and this influence grows stronger on the Apostolic fathers.[5] Thus it is within the framework of the historical and linguistic development and decline of the literary type of the blessing that the words of Matt. v have their place, and it is as part of this process that they should be studied.

B. *Changes Undergone by Apodictic Series of Prohibitions*

The historical position of the Matthean Beatitudes has been effectively determined as coming somewhere between the late Israelite Apocalyptic and early Christian Greece. But a form-critical approach of this kind is of even greater consequence when applied to the Decalogue. Before form-critical exegesis was known it was impossible to make an even moderately reliable

---

[3] Deut. xxxiii. 29; Isa. xxxii. 20; Ps. cxxviii. 3 (cf. verse 2); Eccles. x. 17.

[4] ThW IV, 366, 30–32.

[5] In Greek examples the direct address form is often used. Is this the source of it in the synoptic gospels? Cf. the notable transition to the third person in the blessing in Luke i. 45, which was previously part of a Semitic tradition.

historical classification of these important prohibitions. The date was fixed anywhere between pre-Mosaic and late post-exilic times, according to the subjective opinion of the scholar. But a study of the history of the literary type can give us a more accurate idea of when and how it came into being. Apodictic series of prohibitions already occur in the earliest parts of the Old Testament, in the work of the Jahwist (Exod. xxii. 17, 20 ff., xxiii. 1 ff., xxxiv). Hence they were already known in the pre-monarchical period (before 1000 B.C.). On the other hand it is difficult to trace them back to the time before the conquest of Palestine and hence to Moses. To begin with it is unlikely that the tribes which subsequently became the Israelites already spoke Hebrew in the wilderness; and the prohibitions definitely belong to the Hebrew language. Moreover the earliest series of prohibitions presuppose a rural community such as that which existed after the Israelites were permanently established (Exod. xxii. 20, 24, 28, xxxiv. 25). As regards the latter stages of the literary type, in the late monarchical period the 'thou shalt not' sentences were incorporated into the Deuteronomy sections concerning the law, thus losing their independence (Deut. xii. 4 f., 8 f., 17 f., xxiv. 3 ff., etc.). The plural address form came to be used (Deut. i. 17 etc.). In the post-exilic period no further series of this kind arose, as far as we can see. The classical Decalogue, rich in interpretations, but with its construction still clearly defined by the dominating use of the negative imperfect, is obviously a late stage in the development of the form, although not the last. Already the contents have been much elaborated by later reflection. They attempt to regulate day-to-day existence as well as the great gatherings for cultic festivals. Their tendency to cover all aspects of life sets them apart from the other apodictic series of commandments, which are concerned with only one particular side of life. Thus the Decalogue, in its present form as a series of ten, cannot be placed at the beginning of the history of the literary type, and will therefore not have existed as far back as the pre-monarchical period; but neither can it be placed at the end, and therefore will hardly have first arisen in the post-exilic period.[6]

But could *some* of the commandments be older? As well as the literary type of series of apodictic prohibitions there are also prohibitions expressed in single-sentence formulas, such as that in the book of the covenant:

Thou shalt not suffer a sorceress to live (Exod. xxii. 17).[7]

There are similar prohibitions in other collections of laws which also take the form of single-sentence formulas and which are apparently of ancient origin (e.g. Lev. vi. 6 P; Deut. xiv. 3 D). It is usually considered that formulas of this kind and apodictic series of prohibitions are one and the same literary type. However, an accurate study of them proves this not to be so.

[6] The student of theology could well be shocked when he first learns that the Decalogue did not come from Moses: surely this affects the truth of the sacred writings? But this truth can only effectively be seen as divine and human utterance in one when the reader grasps the implication of its gradual linguistic development. Only then is it possible to link it convincingly with the present. See section 9.

[7] To piece together an ancient series of commandment from this verse and other individual commandments (verses 20, 27) as Alt suggests, is very hypothetical.

This does not mean that the literary type of the series of prohibitions could have not once arisen out of formulas collected for a particular purpose. In this case, as with the blessing, the rigid uniformity of the series would be 'the result of a longer development and elaboration'.[8]

In the Decalogue itself the series of prohibitions in the negative is interrupted by the presence of *commandments*, concerning parents and the sabbath, taking a *positive* form. They are not in the usual imperative, but in the stricter infinitive construction (or with a following imperfect). That the form was well established can be seen most clearly from cultic commandments such as that in Exod. xiii. 2:

> Sanctify unto me all the first-born.[9]

In the course of time formulas of this kind will have been appended to apodictic series of prohibitions to provide a positive conclusion to them (Lev. xix. 9 f., 35 f.; Deut. xxv. 13–15; Ezek. xviii. 8 f., 17). Thus it is possible that what is commonly called the 'first table' of the Decalogue, comprising those prohibitions dealing with duties to God, is, together with the positive fourth commandment, part of an earlier stage of development, making those prohibitions dealing with human relationships a later addition to the series (see section 4). Thus the Decalogue is not a single example of a literary type long existing in Israel, but, like the Beatitudes, part of a linguistic movement. An analysis of this kind of Old or New Testament texts reveals that not only do they belong to established literary types but also to some particular stage in the development of that type.

Whether we are dealing with prophetic sayings or kerygmatic formulas, Old Testament historical writing or New Testament epistles, *the difference between passages in the Bible of the same literary type is not merely the result of the personality of the writer but is determined to a far greater degree by the stage of development the literary type has reached at that particular time.* Thus as soon as the literary type of the text has been established, the exegete must turn to the history of that literary type.

C. *A Look at Other Languages of the Ancient World*

Just as with the Beatitudes (p. 18), a study of any biblical literary type involves a glance at the neighbouring languages of the ancient world. This aspect of research has resulted in a lively dispute over the origin of apodictic series of prohibitions, some scholars seeing them as arising out of the ancient oriental wisdom precepts which were widely used. An Egyptian wise man (Merikare, before 2000 B.C.) admonished:

> Quiet the weeper; do not oppress the widow.[10]
> Supplant no man in the property of his father.[11]

---

[8] S. Mowinckel, Zur Geschichte der Dekalog, ZAW N.S. 14, 1937, 218–35.
[9] Variant in Num. iii. 13 (with introductory formula by which God announces himself); Exod. xxii. 29, xxxiv. 20.
[10] Cf. Exod. xxii. 22.
[11] ANET 415.

And an example of Babylonian (wisdom?) instructions for sacrifice:

> You shall not eat the omentum, neither shall you drink blood. [12]
> Commit no crime . . . slander no one.
> Do no evil.[13]

But likeness to these admonitions, which are so inextricably part of a quite different context, could be accidental. The suggestive force of the modern translation must also be considered. The words translated as 'not', 'you shall', are quite often very different in the original. It cannot be proved that series of prohibitions were at all commonly used.

Other scholars point to the state treaties by which the Hittite kings made agreements with their vassals (in the second millennium) as the prototype for series of prohibitions.[14] A treaty of this kind always took the form of (a) a title 'Thus (saith) the sun NN, the great king, king of Hatti land, the valiant'. This is reminiscent of the formula in series of prohibitions by which God announces himself, 'I am Jahweh (your God)'. There then follows (b) a historical prologue, setting out at length the previous benefits granted the vassal's dynasty by the king. This corresponds to the historical apposition, 'which brought thee out of the land of Egypt', although this is much briefer and only to be found in the Decalogue. It is followed by (c) a declaration of principles, with resulting commandments: 'So honour the oath to the king and the king's kin; then I, the king, will be loyal towards you . . . and the tribute which was imposed upon your father and upon your grandfather . . . you shall present them likewise.' Here also there are prohibitions which have an apodictic ring to them:

> Do not turn your eyes to anyone else; your fathers presented tribute to Egypt; you (shall not do that).[15]

The agreement closes with (d) details about the provision of weapons and legal assistance in the casuistical if-style, (e) a call for divine witness and (f) curse and blessing; three parts which do indeed have affinity with other parts of the Old Testament but which do not help our study of apodictic series of prohibitions. Although the Hittite prohibitions are very much bound to their context in the treaty and can by no means be seen as independent formulas, the great similarity between sections a-c and series of prohibitions makes it quite possible that the Old Testament series were originally based on the form taken by Hittite state treaties. The god Jahweh makes the same sort of agreement with his vassal Israel, in the same unconditional terms, as the Hittite king. It seems therefore that the

---

[12] Gen. ix. 4; Lev. iii. 17, xvii. 12, 14.

[13] W. G. Lambert, *Babylonian Wisdom Literature*, 1960, p. 247 (London and New York, Oxford University Press).

[14] G. Mendenhall, *Law and Covenant in Israel and the Ancient Near East*, 1955 (also: *The Biblical Archaeologist*, vol. xvii, 1954). D. J. McCarthy, Treaty and Covenant, Analecta Biblica 21, 1963. The term 'state treaty' is an inadequate modernism. The Hittites spoke of 'oaths' and saw the whole as decrees of the king, cf. G. M. Tucker, Covenant Forms and Contract Forms, VT XV, 1965, 487–503.

[15] ANET 204 (cf. 183 note 24). A list in McCarthy, p. 49; series of imperatives in the second person singular are conspicuously more often used in Hittite language than in Akkadian. Also, pp. 35–37.

literary type of the apodictic series of prohibitions was inspired by non-Israelite prototypes. But it was only in Israel that the tendency arose to form a series. And it was only there that motive clauses came to be included, to make the prohibitions intelligible.[16] A particular need was felt to use sentences of this kind to free as many aspects of life as possible from any sort of defilement, and thus avoid disturbances within the community. The history of the literary type of the apodictic series of prohibitions reveals that Israel adopted a form which had originated in the Ancient Orient and through this form gave expression to her own particular experience of God.

Archeological excavations and the deciphering of ancient texts have helped enormously with the interpretation of texts. Oriental studies and the study of the ancient world bring much to bear on form criticism. Even nearer to Israel than the great powers was the Canaanite culture, which the Israelites found in Syria and Palestine and which they partly adopted. We can get a particularly good picture of their literature from the texts of the ancient Canaanite city of Ugarit (Ras Shamra), which were excavated in 1929.[17] For the New Testament types, too, there are parallels, in particular in the Greek minor literature. This is not surprising, for the intellectual life of that time was dominated by a high regard for the miracle worker as *theios aner*, and the popular philosophies and the mystery cult were spread by the itinerant preacher. However, of particular importance is the Jewish community of the day and its literary types, for this was already well on the way to becoming a missionary community, out of which early Christianity was gradually to emerge as an independent culture.

A comparison with the literary types of antiquity will of course also indicate how and to what extent Israel and early Christianity differed from their neighbours. Magic, with rituals and incantation, was very common in Egypt, Babylon, and in Hellenistic papyri, but was almost entirely absent in Israel. Death and burial rites were of much less significance, if they were not entirely unknown. There are only small traces of the myth, which in other places played a great part in the shape of long epic poems, and which in Hellenistic-Roman times were widely performed and interpreted. Although it appears that the movement which produced the Bible did not make use of many otherwise current forms of literature or their setting in life, in other fields it evolved entirely new ones. *Historical writing* such as that in the Old Testament is not to be found elsewhere in the literature of the Ancient Orient.[18] The *Gospels*, with their kerygmatic message built around the figure of Jesus, are unparalleled in contemporary literature. The same applies to the literary type of *prophetic speech*, and of

---

[16] See also above. The only other motive clauses are those in instructions for temple officials, ANET, 207 ff.

[17] English translations in G. R. Driver, *Canaanite Myths and Legends*, 1956 (Edinburgh, R. & R. Clark; New York, Scribner) and in C. Gordon, *Ugarit and Minoan Crete*, 1966 (New York, Norton.) Material for comparison in J. B. Pritchard *Ancient Near Eastern Texts relating to the Old Testament*, [2]1955 (Oxford University Press; Princeton University Press). And for the New Testament C. K. Barrett, *The New Testament Background*, 1957 (London, S.P.C.K.; New York, Seabury Press).

[18] But see Malamat: Doctrines of Causality in Hittite and Bibliography, VT 5, 1955, pp. 1–12.

course even more so the *apostolic letters* with which there is nothing comparable.

Anyone who is investigating Israel's particular mission will find that the study of the history of literary types provides the easiest and the most reliable method of doing so. Despite all cultural and linguistic relationship with the rest of the Ancient Orient, over the centuries the literature of Israel became more and more distinct from that of her neighbours. The analysis of literary types alone is enough to bring out Israel's highly distinctive acknowledgement of the one God, and of his influence upon her history. It is also just as interesting to compare the New Testament literary types with Hellenistic speech and writing. It shows that the way from the Old to the New Testament, the development of a closed nationalistic society into a free association of religious communities, was indeed the general pattern in Hellenistic-Roman times. But the message of the Israelite Jesus, as the kyrios and Son of God, and the implications of his eschatological message, led to the formation of completely new literary forms.

D. *Complex Literary Types and Component Literary Types*

Literary types are not static. They are constantly changing. Some are forgotten and fall into disuse and others take their place. The changes not only affect their actual existence, their basic construction, linguistic forms, introductions and conclusions, but the extent of their self-sufficiency also. One literary type can be united with another, or can be taken up into another.

At this point we must return to the definition of the term *literary type*. Hitherto it has been used as if it always referred to a completely independent linguistic unit. But in fact language does not merely consist of an innumerable series of literary types with a clear division between each. On the contrary, the relation of one literary form to another can change enormously.

But this is not always the case. An advertising circular, for instance, is rarely attached to any other literary type. A lyric is also usually independent, unless it is part of a loose collection of poems in an anthology. There are exceptions, of course; for instance, when the poem is written into a novel. Then it is only a small part of a wider context: the novel is the greater unit, with the lyric a mere part within the whole. But from the point of view of the lyric as a literary type, this association is purely coincidental. It has nothing to do with the nature of the lyric or of the novel. However, the situation is very different when a chorale is linked to a prayer and a sermon and becomes part of the greater literary type of the *liturgy*. The individual piece, the chorale, is to a certain extent a unit in itself. It has also probably been composed quite separately from the other pieces, but from the start it has a fundamental relation to them; for the chorale, by its nature, has a bearing on the service, and vice versa (at least in Protestant liturgy).

Therefore, whether in speech or in writing, there are *component literary types*, which build up into *complex literary types*. Formulas in particular, which are the smallest units of speech, are nearly always linked to or are part of greater literary types. The relation between a component type and a complex type may change over a period of time. Types can become merged, only later to divide again. For instance, fifty years ago there was a tendency to take the German Protestant chorale out of its place in the service, and thereby out of the complex type of the liturgy, and to consider it as a religious lyric. Today, on the other hand, the tendency is to revert to the old association, perhaps binding it even closer.

It is even simpler to determine the relationship between types in the Bible. The psalms, in so far as they are of cultic origin, have always been part of a wider context than their mere recitation, and are therefore associated with other cultic affairs, such as utterances by the priests. They are therefore as much involved in a liturgy as is the Christian chorale, and thus constitute a part of a complex literary type. When the Jerusalem cult suddenly came to an end in 587 many psalms were probably forgotten. Those that were remembered found a fresh place in collections. Thus they became part of another complex literary type. In other places it is evident that such a relationship arose only later. For instance, previously independent narrative units from the early Israelite period gradually built up into series of sagas, and then finally became mere sections of a larger written work, such as those found in the first part of the Old Testament. The Jahwistic narratives or the priestly narratives are complex types of this kind in which, with varying degrees of skilfulness, a number of units originally independent have been brought together. It was in a work of this kind that the Decalogue of Exod. xx was incorporated, whereas that of Deut. v. became part of a collection of laws. The New Testament blessings quoted above were merged with other logia of Jesus into an (early) form of the Sermon on the Mount, thereby becoming a component literary type. Then these were written down in the source Q, and finally taken up into the complex literary type of the *Gospel*. Indeed, component types can be so radically adapted when taken up into a written work that their previous formal characteristics have almost disappeared and are only distinguishable from their surroundings as a particular series of images or as a tradition-complex, such as the creation narratives in certain psalms (lxxiv. 12–17, cxxxix. 13–16), or allusions to these in the New Testament epistles (Rom. iv. 17; Col. i. 16).[19] *Each exegesis must therefore not only define the literary type, but also discover whether this literary type is associated with other, perhaps complex, literary types.*

The problem presented by component and complex literary types has been neglected hitherto in form-critical work. Gunkel dealt with it only in connection with cultic liturgies and collections of sagas. In both cases he asserted that the development of more complex types was a very late

[19] Component literary types are sharply distinct from the sub-varieties of one literary type, as for instance the different forms of the individual song of lament: Penitential songs of lament, songs of trust, etc. (Also the changeover by a sub-variety into a literary type in its own right is gradual and the distinction is largely a question of terminology. Are national songs of lament, or royal songs of lament literary types, or are they merely sub-varieties of the general literary type of the song of lament? But these questions are irrelevant to this discussion.)

occurrence[20]: 'A considerable period of time went in to the making of liturgy
. . . Liturgy is a marvellous art form, which with absolute sureness of touch
brings to expression the entire range of feelings of a sophisticated generation.'
Hence to Gunkel the simple, original literary type is the basic unit, and in his
opinion it is indivisible. But is this view compatible with the complexity of
the human way of living and of linguistic forms? The idea of an absolute
literary type led Dibelius (referring to the New Testament) to remark: 'It is a
recognised fact that form criticism is not concerned with complete works of
literature as such but with the small units which are handed down orally or in
writing, though of course we derive our knowledge of these from the books
into which they have been absorbed. Form criticism in the strict sense can
therefore only be applied to those works consisting of such small units, or to
texts which contain these units.'[21] Gunkel did not take such a narrow view.
He included books themselves in a form-critical analysis, in so far as they
represented an entity which provided something at least relatively new, and
were not simply a compilation of old material. Meanwhile in New Testament
form criticism it is now a matter of course to consider for instance the gospel
itself as a type, and thereby to include complex types in form-critical
studies. The problem which arises out of this more complicated theory of
literary types has not yet been thoroughly studied. As far as I know, only von
Rabenau has put it into words, in his study of prophetic sayings: 'If by the
term *literary type* we mean the overall structure in which statements forming
a unity of sense are expressed, then there will be times when we must call the
same form of the prophetic saying, for instance, both *type* and *section of a
type*, because the same passages are partly independent and partly used in
association with others.' He suggests that the word literary type should only
be used for the small, usually independent units. For the larger units which
we have referred to above as complex literary types he suggests the term
combinations.[22]

E. *Attempts at a Survey of Old and New Testament Literary Types*

What relationship do the many Old and New Testament types have with
each other? At the moment the problem is more evident with regard to the
Old Testament than with the New, because no systematic presentation of all
the New Testament types has yet appeared.[23] But with the Old Testament
Gunkel himself attempted a classification. He classified Israelite literature in
the following manner:

> I. National literature up to the great writers.
> II. The great writers.
> III. The epigones.

Gunkel's classification is therefore a historical one. His thesis (expressed
elsewhere) is: 'A classification will be compelled to give prominence to literary
types and to the different periods in the national and cultural history of a
people. A history of literature can naturally only exist when it is able to show
how a literature has come out of the history of a nation and is the expression
of the intellectual life of that nation.'[24] Later scholars have found this
historical classification unfortunate, for the literary type *historical writing*, for
instance, must appear in three different places very far apart from each other
Therefore in the form-critical section of Eissfeldt's *The Old Testament. An*

[20] GuB 28 f.
[21] ThR N.S. 1, 1929, p. 187.
[22] WZ der Martin-Luther-Universität Halle-Wittenberg, Gesellschafts- und
Sprachwissenschaftliche Reihe V, 1955/6, p. 673.
[23] The only exception is the slim volume by M. Dibelius, *Literaturgeschichte des
Urchristentums* I and II, Sammlung Göschen 934/5, 1926.
[24] RuA 37.

Introduction the writer has used a purely systematic classification which consists basically of two parts, poetry and prose. The same system was followed by Weiser (1939, 1957) and Sellin-Rost (1959),[25] for example. As a third section Eissfeldt has added 'Sayings'; Bentzen (1948, 1953) however has a section called 'From the Smallest Literary Units to the Great Literary Complexes'. Also within the sections the sub-division is purely systematic. Eissfeldt, for example divides his prose section into: (1) Speeches, Sermons, Prayers; (2) Records; (3) Narratives. In this way the material for a whole century is placed together. This system has the advantage of avoiding the often meaningless attempts at dating many of the Old Testament books or passages. Moreover, it is in keeping with the general conviction in modern German literary scholarship 'that the forces which shape the linguistic structure of literature and its form are the same almost everywhere.'[26] It is because of this that Jolles uses the term 'simple forms' to express something fundamental to all peoples and all periods. Here the literary types are arranged like beads on a string, freed from all shackles of time, and this makes it possible to make an assessment of each type in its own right.

The price paid by such a systematic appraisal is that it is impossible to assess the types historically. It is no longer a matter of interest that there are literary types in the Bible which emerged at a particular time, flourished, and then died away. Yet there is hardly a type which was in general use for the whole of the period between early Israel and Hellenistic Christianity, except perhaps the common formulas of greeting and farewell, and personal forms of writing such as the letter (but of course even this has changed).[27] The great upheavals in the literary history of Israel, such as those of the pre-Christian period, are passed over. Even here it is unavoidable to split types which properly belong to each other. A type which can be both poetry and prose is classed under two completely different sections, such as the (poetic) prayer for intercession of a psalmist and the (prose) intercession of a king (e.g. I Kings viii). Any method presenting a comprehensive classification of Old and New Testament literary types has its disadvantages, although those of a systematic classification seem to be heavier. But whatever the system of classification it is essential that the history of each individual type and the period in which it prevailed is made absolutely clear. And this is necessary even in a systematic presentation. Otherwise there is no foundation to form-critical exegesis.

3. SETTING IN LIFE

A. *Literature and Life*

How is it that all literature falls into groups with fixed characteristics of form? How did such a diversity of forms arise? The reason lies in the diversity of existence itself. A man writing a letter addresses it to a person known to him, or to a group of people which is more or less fixed. A speaker addresses a particular audience. The historical position of both

[25] The tenth edition 1965, revised by Fohrer, lists Historical Books, Song Books, Wisdom Books, and Prophetic Books. E.T. *Introduction to the Old Testament*, 1968 (Nashville, Abingdon Press).

[26] W. Kayser, p. 6 and elsewhere.

[27] It is the same in other languages. The Greek literary type of the tragedy, for instance, perished together with the theatre in late antiquity. When in the modern period it was used again, it was in imitation of the old literary type, and had been radically changed. There is therefore no such thing as a timeless form of the 'tragedy', common to all races.

men is therefore reflected in the kind of language they use. Whether their relationship to those they address is public or personal determines the form of their speech. Each literary type corresponds to a *setting in life* (*Sitz im Leben*), as Gunkel termed it. The regulations and needs of a particular sphere of existence determine and form the respective manners of speech and writing, just as in reverse the customary linguistic forms help to determine the face of a particular way of life. Therefore it is no indication of an excessive phantasy in the mind of a nation if its literature consists of innumerable types and formulas intermingled with one another, but it is merely an expression of the complexity of human accomplishment. Analysis of literary types, or the form-critical method, 'rests on the assumption that each individual literary type, as long as it preserves its own vitality, has a particular content and particular forms of expression, and that these two are closely connected. This is not the result of any arbitrary linking up on the part of the writers, but the two were linked right from the start. That is to say that even in primitive times material was shaped and handed down orally by the people generally, so that these forms correspond with the regularly recurring events and needs of a particular way of life, out of which the literary types arose naturally.'[1]

The advertising circular, with which I started, belongs therefore to the realm of commerce in our present-day civilisation. Such a form is an essential part of the Western economic structure, with the give and take of supply and demand. Through it a company seeks to establish a market. The publicity of a commercial enterprise is therefore the setting in life of an advertising circular. It serves a quite particular purpose, and its manner of expression and lay-out conform to this purpose.

The setting in life of the *sermon* is quite different. It belongs in the pulpit, i.e. in Christian worship, and for centuries it has remained within this tradition. Similar examples abound. Wherever there are literary forms they will be seen to correspond to a particular way of life. There is no 'neutral' speech or writing, which does not fall into literary types, and this is because each person, as soon as he speaks or writes, is adapting himself, usually unconsciously, to a particular situation. He assumes a certain part, as it is termed sociologically. Therefore it is not sufficient for a commentator to study the literary forms and their history: he must also inquire into their setting in life. Each type presents 'sociological data', and form-critical work is therefore closely associated with both the study of literature and sociology.[2] This is something which must be fully recognised, for

---

[1] ALT I, 284 f. E.T. in *Essays on Old Testament History and Religion*, 1968 (Oxford, Blackwell; New York, Doubleday).

[2] Cf. Dibelius, *From Tradition to Gospel*, p. 4 and Bultmann: *Tradition*, p. 4; similarly Mowinckel, *Prophecy*, pp. 42 f.: 'Every typical situation in life had its definite things that should be done and said.' Gressmann lists under those who provided the stimulus for form criticism Taine, Riehl, Naumann, Lamprecht and Wundt (*A. Eichhorn und die religionsgeschichtliche Schule*, 1914).

Gunkel wanted to speak of settings in life only in connection with *oral* literary types. It was his opinion that literary types to some extent lost their link with their parent soil, for as 'in the course of time they developed and writing won a dominating position in intellectual life, they gave up their original setting in life in favour of that of the written book.' (ZAW N.S. 1, 1924, p. 183). When he contested whether

otherwise a too simplified division is made between the history of ideas and politico-economic history.

Usually it is not a simple matter of associating a certain literary type with one particular setting in life. Commercial advertising is displayed on posters in shop windows, or even on hoardings; or it approaches business associates and private persons orally through representatives. And Sunday worship does not merely consist of a sermon. The connection with the setting in life will also help to define the relationship between component and complex literary types. Liturgy, for example, with worship as its setting in life, necessarily consists of a number of component types: song, prayer, blessing, sermon, and others, because the attitude of the congregation to worship changes. At one time the congregation will face God openheartedly, and another time it will meditate quietly to a reading of his Word. Hence *a setting in life comprehends a number of literary types, in near or distant relationship to each other*, each fulfilling a particular function.

A *setting in life* is a *social occurrence*, the result of customs prevailing in one particular culture at one particular time, and *which has granted such an important role to the speaker and his hearers, or the writer and his readers, that particular linguistic forms are found necessary as a vehicle for expression.*

B. *Background to the Blessing*

This applied just as much to early Christianity. The correspondence by letter between an apostle and his community was the setting in life which brought into existence the literary type of the *community letter*. Missionary preaching to the Gentiles resulted in the literary type of the *mission sermon*. The more complex the setting in life, the more literary types are evolved to give it expression. When Christians commemorate the Last Supper they use ceremonial forms to perform the sacrament: prayer and song. Sometimes, then, a single type suffices, such as the community letter. But at other times an intricate structure of component and complex types is needed, such as in the liturgy of the Lord's Supper. The *Beatitudes* also are certain to have had their own setting. This is first to be found in the Christian community after Easter, for it was from this community that the Matthew Evangelist (or his predecessor, the author of the logia sources) took this series of sayings. Unfortunately it is not possible to know the exact occasion in the early Christian community when the Beatitudes were uttered, though it was certainly at some ceremony celebrating the Kingdom of God close at hand. Was this part of a service with sermon, or was it the start to a proclamation to the community? The Old Testament custom of putting blessings at the beginning of a wisdom speech and the present position of the Beatitudes, in Matthew at the beginning of the Sermon on the Mount, and in Luke (ch. vi) at the beginning of the Sermon on the Plain, makes

---

the book itself had a setting in life he had in mind the modern book market, with its different sorts and conditions of literature, and not the ancient oriental writing customs, which were so very much bound by tradition. But even in connection with our present way of life it is only a cursory study of the problem which could produce such a view of things.

this seem probable, but it cannot be proved.[3] Unfortunately we know nothing further about the use of the eschatological blessing in apocalyptic circles before Christ. Was the speaker a man of particular authority, as was the case when the blessing was a wisdom saying? Did this man face a flock of eager students who learnt sayings of this kind by heart, and should we assume the same for the Christian community? On which occasion and to whom did Jesus himself, from whom the community adopted the literary type, proclaim these blessings?[4] The setting in life does not refer to the particular occasion upon which Jesus proclaimed the Beatitudes, but to the *typical* relationship between him and his followers which made a formal utterance of this kind possible. For the Beatitudes are not, as might be assumed by modern hearers, a spontaneous discourse, but they are carefully formulated *doctrine*, the result of the long history of the literary type. It presupposes pupils, disciples.[5] When Matt. v. 3 ff. is seen against a form-critical background, we are provided with important evidence for the controversy now current among New Testament scholars as to whether Jesus was merely a popular preacher inspired by the approaching *eschaton*, with no thought of an organised group of disciples, or whether he consciously tried to gather a circle of pupils around him.

C. *Background to Apodictic Series of Prohibitions*

We are frequently told that Moses engraved the Decalogue (and other similar prohibitions) on tables of stone, or, in another version, that God engraved the words himself and handed both tables over to Moses (Exod. xxiv. 4, xxxi. 18, xxxii. 15 f., xxxiv. 1, 4, etc.). This gives us an indication of its setting in life. If the historicity of this tradition is assessed according to the conventions of Israelite stories, the frequency with which this fact is mentioned could only mean that stones of that kind actually existed at the time of the narrator. According to Deut. xxvii. 1–4, Jos. viii. 32, xxiv. 25–27[6] such stones could be seen at the ancient sanctuary at Shechem. Later passages report that the tables found their way into the ark (Deut. x. 1–5). This also points to the cult as being responsible for their preservation.

It is certainly not sufficient to assert, as is usual today, that 'the cult' is the setting in life of the apodictic commandment. The word 'cult' signifies an

[3] Arvedson, *Das Mysterium Christi*, Arbeiten und Mitteilungen aus dem Neu-testamentlichen Seminar zu Uppsala, 1937, pp. 95 f. considers a connection between the cultic blessing and the Hellenistic mysteries cult. G. Braumann, Zum traditionsgeschichtlichen Problem der Seligpreisungen Mt V, 3–12, *Novum Testamentum* IV, 1960, 253–60, links it with baptism.

[4] The formal character of the blessing formula (*Seligpreisung*) has some relation to that of the act of blessing (*Segen*), and this prompts one to ask whether they were originally composed in the Aramaic national language, as is usually assumed, or in the Hebrew sacral language (as in the Qumran examples in Starcky, RB 1956, p. 67).

[5] It is in keeping with the literary type that the blessings of Matt. xiii. 16, xvi. 17; Luke x. 23 f., 42 are associated with the special instruction of the disciples.

[6] According to Deut. xxvii the entire book of Deuteronomy was inscribed on the tablets, which is however hardly feasible. Doubtless the custom was not restricted only to the *debarim*. In Jos. xxiv. 26–28 Joshua writes 'the words' in a *book* of the law, but at the same time a stone is mentioned in a rather unmotivated fashion which 'hath heard all the words of the Lord' and 'which shall be a witness'. Presumably in the course of time the book took the place of the stone inscription in Shechem.

aspect of life in Israel which cannot be rigidly distinguished from other aspects, but which for its own part can reflect widely disparate and sharply contrasting settings in life. The term 'cult' can therefore be only a very provisional definition.

Other references to such stones reveal that the commandments were not only engraved and set up in sacred places but that they were also uttered in the cultic community. Where and when did this happen? Only once, or often?

Mowinckel, the first to see the problem,[7] points to Ps. xv (also Ps. xxiv) where kindred passages are to be found:

> He that slandereth not with his tongue,
> Nor doeth evil to his friend,
> Nor taketh up a reproach against his neighbour (verses 3 f.).

This is obviously an echo of the apodictic commandment. The setting in life of the psalms is quite evident. It lies in the custom by which pilgrims coming to Jerusalem for a festival ceremonially mounted the temple hill. Before reaching the sanctuary they were halted by a priest (chorus) and asked to account for their presence. This they did by means of a temple admission liturgy, or, as it is sometimes termed, an Entrance Torah. This took place before the actual religious celebration, which then began within the temple itself. But this preliminary was a necessary part of the ceremony. Mowinckel maintains that this is the setting in life of the Decalogue. But there is much against this hypothesis. To begin with, there is a small but formidable anomaly: while the apodictic commandment is in the form of the direct address and is in the imperfect tense, the admission liturgy is impersonal and is in the perfect. (Closer examination reveals that the admission liturgies are based on series of apodictic commandments, but on those of a literary type apparently originated elsewhere.[8])

Von Rad[9] has quoted other passages from the psalms to determine the setting of the apodictic commandment. He refers to Psalm l, where, after a description of Jahweh coming with fire and storm to the cultic community, it runs:

> Gather my saints together unto me;
> Those that have made a covenant with me by sacrifice.

> Hear, O my people, and I will speak;
> O Israel, and I will testify unto thee:
> I am God (Jahweh), even thy God. (verses 5, 7)

The last sentence is obviously a quotation from the beginning of the Decalogue. Presumably the psalmist is using it as a liturgical catchword, playing upon its familiarity (in any case this is the only way to explain the conspicuous absence of parallelismus membrorum). This is followed in the psalm by a long exhortation. The whole concerns an occasion in the temple of Jerusalem, obviously to do with the celebration of the covenant (of

---

[7] *Le Décalogue. Etudes d'historie de philosophie religieuses* 16, 1927.
[8] K. Koch, Tempeleinlassliturgien und Dekaloge, in Studien zur Theologie der alttestamentlichen Überlieferungen 1961, 45, 60.
[9] Das formgeschichtliche Problem des Hexateuch BWANT IV, 26, 1938, GS 9 ff. E.T. *The Growth of the Hexateuch and other Essays* (New York, McGraw-Hill), pp. ff9.

Sinai). Indications of a similar cultic occasion can be seen in Psalm lxxxi, where again, after a mention of his saving acts, God's voice rings out:

> Hear, my people, and I will testify unto thee:
> O Israel, if thou wouldest hearken unto me!
> I am the Lord thy God
> Which brought thee out of the land of Egypt
> There shall no strange God be in thee;
> Neither shalt thou worship any strange God. (vv. 8, 10, 9).

The allusion to the Decalogue is unmistakeable. An exhortation follows here also.

The psalms lead us to suppose that the Decalogue was regularly proclaimed at a cultic occasion when all the people were present. Is it possible to know more about the exact nature of the occasion? (1) Ps. l refers to a *theophany* of Jahweh at the place of the cult, describing it as both magnificent and awe-inspiring. Exod. xix and Deut. v. 5, 22 f. also make a theophany precede the proclamation of the Decalogue. This explains the formula which introduces it and by which God announces himself: 'I am the Lord thy God.'[10] The apodictic series of prohibitions in Exod. xxxiv is also associated with a similar event (verses 5 f.). Thus the literary type is always linked to a theophany. (2) Ps. l makes the Decalogue follow a *covenant festival*, at which it appears that the covenant made at Sinai between God and Israel was renewed. (Cf. II Kings xvii. 35; Jer. xxii. 9; Deut. ix. 9, 11, 15). It is with this covenant that Exod. xx (with xxiv) and Deut. v (v. 3) link the first proclamation of the Decalogue. Also at points where it is not the Decalogue itself which is referred to but other *debarim*, the covenant is mentioned either shortly before or shortly afterwards (Exod. xxxiv. 10, 27 (xxiv. 8); Deut. xxvii. 8; Jos. xxiv. 25). At one time there must have been festivals of this kind for the renewal of the covenant at the sanctuaries at Shechem and Jerusalem.[11] There is no indication at all that the literary type was used other than at a covenant festival.[12, 13] Of course certainly

[10] Exactly how the theophany took place, which according to much evidence was witnessed by the cultic community in Jerusalem at great festivals, has not yet been explained.

[11] At a later date whole collections of Torah were read at festivals in celebration of the Covenant, II Kings xxiii. 1–3; Deut. xxxi. 9–11; Neh. viii.

[12] The one exception is the five rules which Jonadab the son of Rechab laid down for the founding of the sect in Jer. xxxv. 6 f., and which Gerstenberger sees as proof that apodictic prohibitions originated in tribal ethos. But this passage is in the plural and is more recent. The series of prohibitions on the relationship between the sexes in Lev. xviii. 6–17 points to the fact that the entire tribal family of several generations lived together. K. Elliger, ZAW 67, 1953, 1–25 asks whether this tribal habit of living together was not a custom dating from the nomadic period. But it is not in a nomadic tent that so many people live together, but in cramped houses in ancient Israelite cities. Therefore the importance attached to the tribe did not detract during the post-exilic period but rather increased (cf. P and the Chronicler) and remained of the greatest importance for the relationship between God and the people.

[13] A point often made against a connection between the Ten Commandments of Exod. xx and the cult is that these sentences contain nothing which specifies the cult. But God's name, the making of images, and the sabbath are quite clearly sacral matters. There is nothing about sacrifice and festivals in it merely because there were other series dealing with those. Moreover it is also to be borne in mind that 'The people addressed by the Decalogue were of course, the laity; and they were addressed with

not all apodictic series of prohibitions were used at the same sanctuary and on the same occasion. Thus it appears that the Decalogue itself was not always known in Jerusalem; the Jerusalem priest Ezekiel (Ch. xviii) and the admission liturgies of the psalms (as well as the Jerusalem Holiness Code Lev. xviii f.) only quote prohibitions from other series. The Decalogue itself—and also the 'Jacob and Joseph' psalm lxxxi—could well have come from *northern Israel*. It is the northern Israelite prophet Hosea who first refers to it (iv. 2). Perhaps the series was introduced in Jerusalem at the time of Josiah's reform of the cult in 622-1, which was inspired by Deuteronomic principles. (3) The speaker at the festival is a *cultic official*,[14] who proclaims the prohibitions as God's own word. The direct correspondence between cultic and divine speech will certainly have come into being over a period of time. The old wording of Ps. xxiv. 4 which uses the divine 'I' (Thou shalt not use my Power (נַפְשִׁי) deceitfully) becomes (under Deuteronomic influence) 'Thou shalt not take the name of the Lord thy God (third person) in vain' in Exod. xx. 7. Also the motive clause (Exod. xx. 5) 'For I the Lord thy God am a jealous God' becomes at a later date (Exod. xxxiv. 14) 'for the Lord . . . is a jealous God'. (4) Those addressed are the freehold *Israelite* farmers who have reached adulthood (apodictic series of prohibitions were not originally intended for the instruction of children!), who alone are privileged in cultic affairs.[15]

What we can glean in the way of information about the setting in life of apodictic series of prohibitions has much that is akin to what we know of the setting in life of Hittite covenants (Hittite state treaties cf. section 2). For these also are inscribed on stone tables kept at a sanctuary. Moreover they also were intended to be proclaimed ceremonially in public. The vassal had also to appear before the king personally once or more times a year, just as the Israelites were instructed to do (Exod. xxiii. 17, xxxiv. 23). However, there are differences which cannot be discounted. The kingly aspect of Jahweh's nature plays no decisive part in the covenant. And the commandments and prohibitions laid down for the Israelites were not enforced by oaths, as were those binding the Hittite vassal. This setting in life is naturally of the greatest significance for a theological interpretation of the Decalogue. Such series of prohibitions are not intended as an unchanging set of laws, by which the hearer is confronted with the absolute divine will and which will enable him to avoid sin. In fact, the cultic proclamation of these series implies that God's saving act, the covenant,

---

reference to their everyday affairs, their secular intercourse with one another in their communal life far and wide in the country, i.e. with reference to the life they had to live once the covenant was made and they had gone back to their homes' (von Rad, *Theology*, I, 1962, p. 193).

[14] Alt thinks it will have been a priest, Noth the 'judge of Israel' (*Festschrift*, A. Bertholet, 1950, 404 ff.); H. J. Kraus (*Gottesdienst in Israel* ²1962, pp. 128-33, *Worship in Israel*, 1965, Oxford, Blackwell; U.S.A., John Knox Press) a cultic prophet and bearer of the 'Mosaic' office.

[15] The public announcement of apodictic series could (right from the beginning?) have been followed by more detailed legal regulations (Exod. xxi f.; Lev. xx ff.?) or by exhortations (Ps. l, lxxxi; Deut. vi ff.). The festival appears to have ended with the proclamation of blessing and curse, cf. Exod. xxiii. 20 ff.; Deut. xxvii f.; Lev. xxvi; Ps. lxxxi. 14 ff.

was far more important than regulations about how a man should behave. The negative sentences mark only the limits beyond which community life is no longer possible. At the same time the *debarim*, the words proclaimed by the cult which gave the hearer the power[16] to act accordingly, provide him with the means of keeping within these limits.[17] Thus these words ensure that order within the community is maintained and safeguarded by the constant loyalty of the individual members of that community.

Form criticism is only a few decades old, but already it has made its impact: *no biblical text can be adequately understood without a consideration of the setting in life of its literary type.* And vice versa: *no way of life in ancient Israel and in the early Christian community can be exhaustively detailed without a thorough study of all literary types relating to it.* To establish the setting in life of a text the following questions must be posed: 'Who is speaking? Who is listening? What is the prevailing mood? What effect is sought?'[18] Although the period of time which has elapsed and the scarcity of material which has survived does not always make it possible to determine the actual origins of biblical literary forms, this does not detract from the necessity of such a study.

Where a way of life is particularly complex and has developed along its own line, a particular terminology comes into existence which then pervades all its literary types. For instance, the cult of the temple of Jerusalem has a style of expression quite different from the language used, say, in legal circles. One and the same word—*ṣedeq*, for instance (which means loyalty to the community)—can have very different meanings in different situations. In any study of Hebrew terminology it is therefore important to consider the literary type and with it the setting in life where the word under study belongs. This is a task that has hardly yet been touched upon. It is just as important in connection with the New Testament, for both the Palestinian and Hellenistic communities developed their own terminology which is quite distinct from that used in other walks of life. When Paul uses the word *dikaiosyne* in his dealings with Roman provincial authorities, he will mean something quite different to his use of the word at a Christian gathering.

D. *Relationship to the Ancient Oriental and Hellenistic Cultic and Social History*

Form critics are continually astonished to see how the way of living in pre-Christian Israel and the early Christian period differs from that of the present century. Modern science and economy would be as irrelevant then as the comings and goings of an Ancient Oriental court or the Hellenistic

---

[16] The function of the apodictic commandment is to testify (עוּד) to the covenant (Ps. l. 7, lxxxi. 8; Jos. xxiv. 27, cf. Exod. xxxi. 18, xxxii. 15 f.). What the Israelite understood by this needs further examination, which will be possible now that a form-critical study has revealed the setting in life. Cf. the Akkadian *adē* as the term for state treaties.

[17] The oldest traditions of the covenant between God and Israel (Gen. xv and the original source of Exod. xxiv) show no sign of detailed obligations imposed on the people. It appears that this connection between covenant and prohibition arose only gradually—under the influence of the Canaanite *el berit* of Shechem?

[18] Gunkel RuA 33; the word 'mood' (*Stimmung*) was usually used in the first decades of this century to mean only the 'mood of the situation', rather than a psychological condition in the narrow sense.

mystery cults would be today. The cultivation of wisdom, which found
expression in the book of Proverbs, has now disappeared. The Jerusalem
Temple no longer exists, and its institutional life and the types of literature
associated with it can hardly be compared to those of the modern church.
The role of the apostle ceased to exist with the end of the first generation
of Christians. The difference in the way of life then and now is reflected
in the difference in the linguistic forms used. Forms of literature which come
naturally to us were unknown then, and many types in the Bible seem very
inaccessible to us now. It is easier to understand those passages where
types, although much modified, have been maintained until the present.
This applies particularly to certain legal texts, or to the New Testament
passages which have the sermon as their setting in life. The psalms, too,
are easy to understand for the Christian churches, because there are comparable pieces in Christian song books. These literary types remain alive
because the institutions which support them are maintained. But such
cases are relatively rare. With most of the Old Testament literary types it is
essential to make a thorough historical study of the significance of a type
before attempting to understand it. But the very act of identifying a type
and naming it brings hazards of its own, for it is unavoidably conducted
with a modern vocabulary and this alone can lead to misunderstanding.
Mention of a prophetic saying, spoken in Jahweh's name, as a 'lawsuit',
brings a flood of associations to the modern reader. Or to say that certain
New Testament traditions have their setting in life in the sermon might
suggest all kinds of implications—particularly to a Protestant.

The ancient Israelite and early Christian ways of life, so foreign to us
today, are of course more closely connected with the institutions of the
ancient world. Court and temple determined the daily life of the Egyptians,
Babylonians and Assyrians as much as it did for the Israelites. There were
itinerant preachers like Paul—and Jesus—in the late missionary phase of
Judaism as well as in the popular philosophy of stoicism. It is not surprising, therefore, that many of the Old Testament literary types can also
be found in the literature of these neighbouring cultures. If the language
of the Bible brings us reliable information about the revelation of the one
God and about the ultimate determination of human existence, the form
it takes has not only been greatly influenced by the *languages* of the ancient
world but also by the cultic and *social conditions* of the nations who were
the neighbours of Israel and the early Christian church. *It is not enough to
show how Israel and early Christianity differed from the neighbouring nations
and cultures; it is just as essential to determine exactly how they were connected, intellectually as well as institutionally. Only then will the form-critical
recognition of the link between literary type and setting in life, between language
and external history, have serious theological meaning.*

E. *The Persistence of Literary Types and their Transition to Other Settings in Life*

Because of the close connection between speech and life any change in a
setting in life, and therefore in national, economic, religious and cultural

history, will result in changes in the literary types. Gunkel brought out this link very strongly with regard to the folk-sagas of Genesis: 'When a new race arrives and changes the outward conditions of life, or displaces the customary lines of thought, whether on religious or moral ideals or the conception of beauty, then in the long run the national saga must also change. Slowly and hesitantly, and always after a period of time has elapsed, the saga will to one extent or another follow the general pattern of change. It therefore constitutes extraordinarily important material for the study of such changes in a nation. Genesis provides us with a whole history of the religious, moral and aesthetic views of ancient Israel.'[19] This does not only apply to the sagas, but in fact to all literature. The connection between literary and non-literary changes is to be seen everywhere. The history of a type reflects the history of its setting in life.

In the above quotation Gunkel draws attention to the fact that there is always a delay before any changes in the ordering of life bring about changes in speech and writing. This is especially evident when a particular setting in life or even a whole way of living comes to an end and the literary types are severed from their place of origin. This occurred several times in the history of Israel. During the period of David and Solomon, when the old organisation of the tribal confederacy had to give way to the establishment of a monarchy, a considerable number of linguistic forms were torn from their roots, namely those associated with the amphictyonic constitution. At the same time the new royalty brought a large number of fresh types with it. The Old Testament shows that in spite of this the old stories based on the cult continued to be passed down. They contained no reference to the new constitutional order or to the freshly established religious centre on Mount Zion, just as if the tribal confederacy were still a fact. A more radical change was brought about by the destruction of Samaria in 721 and Jerusalem in 587 and the end of political independence. With the coming of kings and officials, the temple and the cult disappeared; prophets were dumb and sages rare. But the prophetic words about the Israelite and Jewish kings, and the songs sung about the sanctuary on Zion, were preserved in memory and passed on. They were even rewritten, although their content and also their form had in fact become irrelevant. Covenant festivals ceased, but the Decalogue lived on. Similarly, the direct preaching of Jesus came to an end with his death. But although the call to discipleship lost its concrete setting in life, because the earthly Jesus had disappeared, the traditions belonging to it remained alive. Indeed, the early Christian prophets probably added to the collection of sayings by virtue of divine inspiration. Thus the direct teaching of the disciples came to an end, but the Beatitudes continued to exist. The same applies to Paul's letters to his communities. After his death they continued to be read and passed on, although the particular circumstances which Paul wrote about were then past. Even fresh letters were written in Paul's name, or at any rate modified, such as the pastoral letters. The *persistence of written and oral types*, their tendency to remain even when their original setting in life has gone, is a fact that should not be forgotten. A literary

[19] *Genesis*, p. lxv.

type can continue in existence when its original setting in life has disappeared. The inference is only that it must have existed sometime. But no literary type remains in existence for long after it has been entirely severed from its point of origin. At some stage it fades from human memory, and the tradition dies out.

Individual elements of any literary type can at the most be preserved if they are taken up into another type to continue their existence in a modified form. The transition of a type to a second setting in life is very frequent indeed. It is most easily seen where a type which was of oral origin is inserted into a written work. Crudely stated, it goes straight from the street to the writing desk. This happened to our previous examples, the Decalogue and the Beatitudes. To begin with, both types survived their first setting in life (celebration of the covenant, or the eschatological proclamation in early Christianity), i.e. the oral tradition. (The transition into writing is accompanied by special problems, which are discussed in the sections on redaction history and the oral tradition.) Quite apart from their special association with a written work, both the Decalogue and the Beatitudes have ranged further afield and have found other settings in life. The Decalogue loses its cultic point of origin in 587 at the latest, with the destruction of the temple. It appeared in post-exilic times on synagogue stones, and will therefore have had some part in synagogue worship. Later it became, and still is, a catechism for the instruction of Christians. The Beatitudes can be found inscribed over the entrance or on the walls of Christian churches, or on house walls, and even on postcards. It has therefore found its way into many aspects of church life, with a multiplicity of settings.

The transition of a literary unit can be the result of the particularly striking character of the language which is used. Its charms make it tempting to use in other contexts. In such cases it is usually just a part of the type which is appropriated; but it can also happen that a setting in life develops to such an extent that new forms are needed and are appropriated from other settings. Then complete literary types are transferred, and the result is that a type is imitated. For instance, if some diligent society were to draw up 'Ten commandments for drivers on the roads' in an attempt to reduce the number of road accidents, then this would be an imitation of the Old Testament type. In a more serious context, the same happens when the Beatitudes are imitated in the Christian hymn:

Happy are they, they that love God.[20]

The same happens in the Bible: 'Just as present day Christianity, realising that the traditional types of the sermon and the catechism are not assertive enough to attract attention, has appropriated other types which were not basically religious and has produced Christian calendars, discourses, journals, and even newspapers and novels, indeed has established whole "Christian bookshops", so the prophecy, when its original manner of expression proved no longer effective, appropriated other types in the hope

[20] English Hymnal no. 398.

that they would be better received.'[21] The appropriation of types from other sources, and the transition from one to another setting in life which this brings about, is therefore an absolutely normal process that can by no means be disparaged but accepted as part of the nature of human existence.[22] The transition of individual parts of a type to another setting in life often produces a *mixed type*, which has not quite adjusted itself to its new setting and still contains evidence of the original one. This can be seen from formal inconsistencies which arise. There are psalms, for instance, which still belong to the literary type of song of the lament, but they were no longer sung on the proper occasion but were used by the sages who inserted wisdom sayings (e.g. Ps. cxix). *The relationship of a literary type or a formula to its setting in life* is so close that it is rarely capable of expression in simple terms, for it *is subjected to extremely various and far-reaching changes.*

For the theologian it is a matter of some importance that the various literary types which are found in the Bible are inseparably linked with actual situations in the life of Israel and of the early Christian church. For he realises that the elements which go to make up the sacred writings are not suspended between heaven and earth but are part and parcel of a history which is indeed 'sacred', but which is by no means confined to a limited and rarified area. On the contrary, it is a history which takes place within the ordinary everyday life of the ancient world. The recognition that the biblical message is rooted in actual historical situations is a standing reminder to the Christian church—which takes its bearings on the Bible as the supreme witness of divine revelation—that it is joined by the bond of history to the people of ancient Israel and equally to early Palestinian and Hellenistic Christianity.

It was Gunkel who had the genius to perceive that one cannot usefully study a particular literary type without at the same time taking account of its proper setting in life. Apparently this realisation came to him solely as the result of his study of the biblical material, and quite independent of general literary criticism. So it is not surprising that the *complete* involvement of a type with a setting in life became clear to him only gradually, and that the term 'setting in life' (*Sitz im Leben*) was a relatively late creation.[23]

Up till now the connection between literary types and sociological conditions has not usually been seen as a matter for philological study. P. Bockmann appears to be an exception. His thesis is that an analysis of Baroque literature, for example, will only be fruitful if its position in relation to the whole structure of the community is investigated: 'Only a consideration of the place of literature in the entire structure of the prevailing society can provide a true foundation for the study of the style of the period.'[24] Even scholars like Jolles, who do more than see the subject as a purely timeless consideration of the form of words, and who study literary types in their

[21] Gunkel, GrPro XLVI.

[22] It is another case if it is a matter of quite conscious falsification!

[23] The term 'setting in the life of the people' (*Sitz im Volksleben*) occurs first in 1906, and 'setting in life' (*Sitz im Leben*) apparently only in 1917. In Bultmann and Dibelius the phrase is used as a matter of course for the New Testament, but only in reference to general terms, such as the Sermon, or Apologetics. K. Stendahl speaks rightly of a 'lack of interest in a concrete understanding of the Sitz im Leben' (The School of St Matthew, Acta Seminarii N.T. Upsaliensis XX, 1954, p. 14.

[24] Von den Aufgaben einer geisteswissenschaftlichen Literaturbetrachtung, DVfLG IX, 1931, 465.

historical context, have attached little importance to sociological considerations. B. K. Viëtor, for example, (in a programme of research into literary types, concerning the transition of the tragedy from a court to a common institution[25]): 'I think it is possible to say that such things have no direct influence on the particular characteristics of the literary type of the tragedy. The heroic stand of men against fate and the disastrous clash of values are phenomena bound up with the tragic structure of life, and it is only an illusion on the part of the prevailing society that these things are unconditionally connected with their social system.' But at least an outsider, a historian interested in the history of ideas, has complained, albeit casually, 'that there is not yet a history of medieval Latin literature seen from a sociological standpoint'.[26] French scholars appear to be more discerning: 'Each romantic predilection, each social or religious need is the source of a different literary type, which can flourish or die away.'[27] In English-speaking philosophy the relationship between the literary type and setting in life corresponds to that between language-game and life-style of the late Wittgenstein. In German literature such questions have only been considered in the study of folk-lore, which of course is concerned only with the simpler literary types.

The connection between a literary type and a setting in life is another indication of the fact that form criticism is by no means only concerned with the formal aspects of literature, where the content is studied from a neutral point of view. Determining the forms of a text is a good part of the way to grasping its content. Gunkel rightly emphasised 'that a historical study of literature is not only concerned with form but just as much with content'.[28] A technical use of the expression 'form' should be avoided, as it is much too indefinite.[29]

4. THE HISTORY OF THE TRANSMISSION OF TRADITION

A. *The Different Stages in the Development of Single Units*

So far we have covered the first steps of form-critical exegesis: (*a*) the determination of the literary type, (*b*) its history and (*c*) its setting in life. These three steps have not included an actual exegesis of the text but have only studied its linguistic background, the general literary form which the passage takes. What has so far been said about series of apodictic prohibitions and their connection with the covenant celebration, or about the blessing as a formal eschatological proclamation, applies just as much to other series of prohibitions in the Old Testament, and to other blessings in the New. However, a form-critical study does not merely look into the

[25] Probleme der literarischen Gattungsgeschichte DVfLG IX, 1931, 436.

[26] K. Hauck in *Geschichtsdenken und -bild im Mittelalter*, ed. W. Lammers, Wege der Forschung XXI, 1961, p. 166.

[27] v. Tieghem (see above p. 13), p. 97. He goes on to say that in choosing a literary type a writer follows some internal impulse. On p. 99 he adds: 'But we must not forget that a work of art is in general the result of the collaboration of the writer and his milieu in which, and very often for which, he works. The public is the second element essential to an explanation of the distinction of types.'

[28] GuB 23, cf. Mowinckel, *Prophecy*, pp. 42, 44.

[29] It is amazing how much has been interpreted as constituting literary form. Jolles uses the term as one synonymous with literary types. Kayser uses it to refer to the separate elements of a literary type, starting with grammatical constructions; whereas Kees uses it to denote the manner of writing and writing material (HdO I, 2, 1 ff.).

background of a fragment of material. After the literary type and the setting in life have been ascertained, the study continues with a look at the text itself, at the history of its transmission,[1] known sometimes as 'tradition history'.

Transmission history analyses the isolated unity of a type (known briefly as a 'tradition'), its specific history and its own particular setting in life. Such an examination, which follows the changes the tradition has undergone, is needed because many biblical passages have been passed down either orally or in writing over a long period of time and have therefore been much modified before reaching their final shape. It is true that the changes take place mainly within the bounds of the history of the literary type, and they therefore correspond with the changes of the type itself and its setting in life; but it often happens—and this is a point which must never be overlooked—that a talented thinker or poet presents the piece in such an individual light that it no longer follows the usual course taken by the literary type. Or that the tradition in question once, or even frequently changes its type or its setting in life. Then the history of the tradition breaks the bounds of the one type and its changes. A familiar example from German literature is Goethe's Faust. As is well known this had its dramatic prototype in the Urfaust, and thus so far the transmission history of the Faust legend remains within the history of the literary type of the drama of that period. But at an even earlier stage the material originated in a popular book about Dr Faustus, which itself was dependent upon popular tales and sagas, and ultimately upon hearsay. Hence over the centuries the same fragment of material has changed its type, and thereby its setting in life, several times. However, Goethe's version ranges far beyond the contemporary bounds of the literary type of the drama.

How can the transmission history of a tradition be traced? This is easy when the same material has been used twice at different periods (i.e. popular book—Goethe's drama). A form-critical comparison is usually not only able to trace the path a tradition has taken from stage 1 to stage 2, but can also point to an even earlier form which existed before stage 1. The transmission history can also be traced where two independent versions have developed out of a primary version which has been lost. By comparing stages 2a and 2b it is possible to reconstruct stage 1. To illustrate this we can use the two examples already quoted from the Bible. Luckily both the Decalogue and the Beatitudes have been transmitted twice. And further parallels exist to individual verses.

B. *The Beatitudes* [2]

Matthew x. 3–10	*Luke vi. 20 f.*
3 Blessed are the poor in spirit: for theirs is the kingdom of heaven	20 Blessed are ye poor: for yours is the kingdom of God.

---

[1] The term *Überlieferungsgeschichte* was already used by Gunkel in *Schöpfung*, p. 209. But in his time it was more usual to talk of *Stoffgeschichte*, or *Traditionsgeschichte*.

[2] See literature given under heading of chapter 1, section B.

Matthew x. 3–10   *Luke vi. 20 f.*

5 Blessed are the meek: for they shall
  inherit the earth.[3]
4 Blessed are they that mourn: for they
  shall be comforted.
6 Blessed are they that hunger and thirst   21 Blessed are ye that hun-
  after righteousness: for they shall   ger now: for ye shall
  be filled.   be filled
7 Blessed are the merciful: for they shall
  obtain mercy.
8 Blessed are the pure in heart: for they   Blessed are ye that weep
  shall see God.   now: for ye shall laugh.
9 Blessed are the peacemakers: for they
  shall be called the sons of God.
10 Blessed are they that have been persecu-   I Peter iii. 14:
   ted for righteousness' sake: for theirs   But and if ye should
   is the kingdom of heaven.   suffer for righteous-
                                                       ness' sake, blessed are
                                                       ye.

The affinity as well as the disparity between the two versions[4] is very
apparent. The reason for this is not simply that one Evangelist took his
material from the other. On the contrary, both clearly worked quite
independently of each other from an earlier source, which could already
have developed along different lines before being taken up by the two
Evangelists. What can we discover about this earlier source? A very obvious
difference between the Matthean and Lucan versions is that Luke uses the
direct address (the 'thou') form and Matthew the impersonal third person.
Which is the older? Dibelius decided in favour of the direct address form,
as these sentences are 'addressed to believers'.[5] But the blessing as a type
has been shown to use the third person as a matter of custom, as we have
seen in the Old Testament examples, and it is much easier to imagine it
changed into the direct form than the other way round. Moreover, the
Lucan version could well have been changed to adjust it to the section
following it. It seems therefore that in this regard the Matthean version is
certainly the older of the two.[6]

It is a much more difficult problem to determine which sentences
originally belonged to the series. Matthew reproduces eight blessings, and
Luke only three. The third in Luke corresponds to the one in Matthew on
those that mourn, which Luke expresses more strongly and more generally
and therefore has given it another position. Matthew has added interpretations to single sentences. For instance, in the first Beatitude he adds, 'in

[3] According to old manuscripts verse 5 should be placed before verse 4. The
semitic parallels עָנָו-עָנִי were no longer understood by the Greeks. Dupont,
pp. 252–3.

[4] There is a third version in the Kerygmata Petri, and a fourth in the recently
discovered Gospel of Thomas. Saying 54.68 f. (7, 19, 49, 58, 103); K. Aland,
Synopsis Quattor Evangeliorum, 1964.

[5] *Botschaft und Geschichte* I, 92, 104 = Engl. *The Sermon on the Mount*, 1940
(New York, Scribner).

[6] Bultmann, *Tradition*, p. 109, Dupont, pp. 272–82.

spirit' to 'the poor' by way of explanation. Similarly in the fourth, 'thirst after righteousness' has been added to 'hunger'.[7] The fifth Beatitude will have been his own invention.[8] Again Matthew, but not Luke, will have found in his original source[9] a number of additions based on quotations from the Scripture. For instance, verse 5 could well be based on Ps. xxxvii. 11, verse 8 has echoes of Ps. xxiv. 4, 6, and verse 9 has a near parallel in II Enoch lxx. 11. However according to I Peter iii verse 10 was once an independent blessing. This will have been added later—though before Matthew—to the series, so that it began and ended symmetrically with promise of the kingdom of heaven.

Hence it can be seen that only three Beatitudes can be said with certainty to have been derived from the common source:

Blessed are the poor, for theirs is the kingdom of (?)God.
Blessed are they that mourn, for they shall be comforted.
Blessed are they that hunger, for they shall be filled.

These three sentences, which certainly go back to Jesus himself, might have some connection with Isa. lxi. 1–7:

1 The spirit of the Lord God is upon me . . .
  the Lord hath anointed me to preach good tidings unto the meek.
2 . . . to comfort all that mourn.
6 But ye shall be named the priests of the Lord: men shall
                              call you ministers of our God:
  ye shall eat the wealth of the nations . . .
7 For your shame ye shall have double:
  and for confusion they shall rejoice their portion:
  there in their land they shall possess double.

Despite the link with these Old Testament words of prophecy, the Beatitudes imply a correction. References have been dropped to the predominance of Israel over other nations and the usufruct of their property. Instead emphasis has been laid on the future unbroken communion with God himself.

This confirms what was shown earlier in our general interpretation of types that the Beatitudes were not originally intended to indicate virtues which must be practised. For it is precisely these three sentences which have less to do with the call for moral conduct than with consolation: for the promise of future compensation for the sorrows experienced in a world whose end was at hand. These three sentences must certainly go back to Jesus himself as part of his proclamation. Their paradoxical character: those who are poor will there reign themselves, those that mourn will there be comforted, those now enhungered will there be filled, is in keeping with the basic tenor of Jesus' eschatology.

During the process of transmission from this original unit to that which

[7] None of these additions are in the Gospel of Thomas.
[8] Matthew lays much stress on mercy (cf. xv. 22, xvii. 15, xviii. 33 with their synoptic parallels). The use of the same verb in the first and second halves of the sentence is unusual.
[9] Dupont rates the contribution of the Matthew Evangelist higher.

led up to the version given in the Gospel of St Matthew the Beatitudes will have been expanded to form three parallel sentences, with external parallelism[10]:

I Blessed are the poor,[11] for theirs is the kingdom of *heaven*.
II Blessed are the meek,[12] for they shall inherit the *earth*.
III Blessed are they that mourn, for they shall be *comforted*.
IV Blessed are they that hunger, for they shall be *filled*.
V Blessed are the pure in heart, for they shall *see God*.
VI Blessed are the peacemakers, for they shall be called the *sons of God*.

There is a strict correspondence between both the first and second halves of these sentences in the two related sentences. The poetic form that they take could well indicate that they were used liturgically. Not only is there further reference in II and VI to Isa. lxi., but also to passages from psalms which had been interpreted in an eschatological sense: Ps. xxxvii. 11 to II, Ps. xxiv. 4–6 to V. It is difficult to decide whether this version was still the work of the Aramaic-speaking Palestinian communities or already that of the Greek-speaking 'heathen' Christian communities. On the one hand the familiar Old Testament parallels, poor—meek, are still used, but on the other hand 'seeing God' is not an Old Testament concept.

In the course of time the pressure of persecution caused a further blessing to be added onto the end. It could have been uttered by Jesus on another occasion. Because it is placed at the end it marks the climax to the series:

VII Blessed are they that have been persecuted, for theirs is the kingdom of heaven.

Thus the three parallel sentences became a series of seven, in which the second half of the last cleverly echoes that of the first.

After this provisional end to the transmission history there is the Matthew redaction. The unit, which up to this point had been part of the flow of living language, was written down. With this it became frozen into an unalterable form.[13] Nevertheless at other levels the tradition developed along different lines. Later church practice led again (in Polycarp) to a shortened version:

Blessed are the poor, and those persecuted for righteousness' sake, for theirs is the kingdom of heaven.

And it was reformulated by the gnostics in the gospel of Thomas 69:

Blessed are they which are persecuted in their hearts.
It is they who have truly known the Father.

[10] See above section 8B.
[11] Hebrew עֲנִיִּים, Aramaic עֲנִייָא.

[12] Hebrew, עֲנָוִים, Aramaic עֲנְוְתָנִיָא.

[13] Matthew and Luke have a predecessor in Q, from which both took the three original blessings. It is possible that Matthew found the same wording as Luke; the expanded form may have come to him from the oral tradition, from the liturgical practice of his church.

Here, as for many other parts of the Bible, the history of the origin and development of the unit is continued in the history of its interpretation.

The second unit in the Beatitudes, originally independent, looks different:

Matthew v. 11 f.	*Luke vi. 22 f.*
Blessed are ye when men shall reproach you, and persecute you, and say all manner of evil against you falsely, for my sake.	Blessed are ye, when men shall hate you, and when they shall separate you from their company, and reproach you, and cast out your name as evil, for the Son of man's sake.
Rejoice, and be exceeding glad: for great is your reward in heaven: for so persecuted they the prophets which were before you.	Rejoice, in that day, and leap for joy: for behold, your reward is great in heaven: for in the same manner did their fathers unto the prophets.

The conformity here is substantially greater, but the Evangelists' own interpretation can be seen quite clearly.[14] In Luke 'men' are inserted as the oppressors (cf. Luke v. 18, 20 etc.), the Semitic expression 'cast out an evil name' becomes the Greek 'cast out your name as evil'. The Evangelist adds, 'Rejoice in that day' (compare the insertion of 'now' in v. 21) to emphasise the coming of joy at the moment of oppression. The final passages show greatest disparity. The indefinite construction, 'for so persecuted they the prophets' is inconsistent with Luke's Greek sensitivity to language; and 'which were before you' puts Jesus' disciples and the prophets to some extent on an equal footing, which is not in keeping with the general Lucan concept. So he constructs it afresh and leaves only 'the prophets'. Matthew makes less use of the original wording. The bitter experience of early Christianity causes him to contract and intensify 'hate' and 'separate' into 'persecute'; his characteristic caution leads him to append 'falsely' to the phrase 'all manner of evil against you'. Where the source said, 'for the son of man's sake' he makes Jesus say unequivocally 'for my sake' (also Matt. x. 32, cf. Luke xii. 8).

What information does this yield us about the primary source? Q depicted the increasing persecution of Jesus' followers: from hate, to exclusion from the synagogue, and thereafter to the outlawing of their name. The harsher the persecution, the greater the reward in heaven for those who, by such a fate, can be compared with the prophets. When it reads, 'for so persecuted they the prophets, which were *before you*', it is assumed that new prophets have arisen: that there were new prophets among the Christian readers who were being similarly persecuted. The prophecy does not describe a period long past. Of course the Rabbis will have considered this an outrageous assertion.

This expanded form of the Beatitudes cannot be traced back to Jesus with certainty. The use of the direct address, which appears to be part of the original tradition, was not usual with the historical Jesus,[15] even when he was speaking directly to his audience (Matt. xi. 6; Luke xvi. 23). Also

[14] See Dupont, pp. 227 ff.
[15] Matt. xvi. 17; Luke xiv. 14 are not the words of the historical Jesus.

Jesus does not elsewhere talk of exclusion (from the synagogue society) for his sake. They are likely to have been more the result of pressures put upon the early Christian community by its Jewish adversaries and accounted for as words of the risen Lord in the post-Easter situation. Thus we could be dealing with a *community saying*, a term used by form critics to denote those sayings which do not go back to the historical Jesus. (This expression is liable to misinterpretation. Better would be 'Gloss transmitted by early Christian teachers'.)[16] But we cannot completely exclude the possibility that these sayings originated with Jesus, for they are given great prominence in early Christian literature,[17] and are quoted in I Peter iv. 14 in a shortened form. The Beatitudes reveal very clearly how a biblical passage which at first seems lacking in life can achieve a new depth of feeling through knowledge of its transmission history. The stylised wording in the Gospels proves to be a late version of the sayings, but earlier stages can be made out quite clearly by a comparison through their transmission history of the sayings which appear in both Gospels.[18]

C. *The Decalogue*

The transmission history of the Decalogue is similarly informative:

Exodus xx. 2–17   *Deuteronomy v. 6–21*

I am the Lord thy God, which brought thee out of the land of Egypt, out of the house of bondage.

1. Thou shalt have none other Gods before me.

2. Thou shalt not make unto thee a graven image, (nor) the likeness of any form that is in heaven above, or that is in the earth beneath, or that is in the water under the earth:
    Thou shalt not bow down thyself unto them, nor serve them: *for* I the Lord thy God am a jealous God, visiting the iniquity of the fathers upon the children, (and) upon the third and fourth generation of them that hate me; and showing mercy unto thousands of them that love me and keep my commandments.

3. Thou shalt not take the name of the Lord thy God in vain; *for* the Lord will not hold him guiltless that taketh his name in vain.

4. Remember the sabbath day, to keep it holy.   Observe the sabbath day, to keep it holy, as the Lord thy God commanded thee.

Six days shalt thou labour, and do all thy work: but the seventh day is a sabbath unto the Lord thy God: in it thou shalt not do any work, thou,

---

[16] The expression 'community saying' (*Gemeindebildung*) to which Bultmann and Dibelius have given vogue, has been much criticised. Indeed it is questionable whether it is a happy phrase. It is of course quite possible that in the early Christian community as also in the ancient Israelite language certain narratives will have arisen and will have been much changed. But can something as formal as the blessing formula arise anonymously 'in the community'? Surely it calls for a professional speaker and thus a more restricted setting in life.

[17] W. Nanck, Freude im Leiden. Zum Problem einer urchristlichen Verfolgungstradition, ZNW 46, 1955, 68–80. It is disputed whether Jesus will have called himself the present Son of Man.

[18] J. D. W. Watts, Infinitive Absolute as Imperative and the Interpretation of Exodus 20, 8, ZAW lxxiv, 1962, 141–5.

nor thy son, nor thy daughter, (nor) thy manservant, nor thy maidservant, nor thy cattle (thine ox, nor thine ass, nor any of thy cattle), nor thy stranger that is within thy gates:

that thy manservant and thy maidservant may rest as well as thou.

For in six days the Lord made heaven and earth, the sea, and all that in them is, and rested the seventh day: wherefore the Lord blessed the sabbath day, and hallowed it.

And thou shalt remember that thou wast a servant in the land of Egypt, and the Lord thy God brought thee out thence by a mighty hand and by a stretched out arm: therefore the Lord thy God commanded thee to keep the sabbath day.

5. Honour thy father and thy mother:
as the Lord thy God commanded thee: that thy days may be long (and that it might go well with thee) upon the land which the Lord thy God giveth thee.

6. Thou shalt do no murder.

7. Thou shalt not (Neither shalt thou) commit adultery.

8. Thou shalt not (Neither shalt thou) steal.

9. Thou shalt not (Neither shalt thou) bear false-witness against thy neighbour.

10. Thou shalt not covet thy neighbour's house, thou shalt not covet thy neighbour's wife, nor his manservant, nor his maidservant, nor his ox, nor his ass, nor anything that is thy neighbour's.

Neither shalt thou covet thy neighbour's wife; neither shalt thou desire thy neighbour's house, his field, or his manservant, or his maidservant, his ox, or his ass, or anything that is thy neighbour's.

There are more than twenty differences between the two versions. Only the most important are detailed below:

1. The fourth commandment reads 'remember' in the first, and 'observe' in the second version. Obviously the second is stronger and of later origin.

2. Also in the fourth commandment Deuteronomy explicitly mentions the ox and the ass and has added the sentence, 'that thy manservant and thy maidservant may rest as well as thou'. The last sentence in particular is in keeping with the humanitarian tendency in the Book of Deuteronomy, and will have been added when the Decalogue was inserted into it.

3. The motive for the fourth commandment is given in Exodus as the creation, in Deuteronomy as the exodus from Egypt. This shows that they must both have been created independently of each other from an older source which at this point gave no comment at all. In that way the two commentaries will have arisen quite independently of each other. Here also the Deuteronomy comment is in keeping with a humanitarian viewpoint.

4. The comment in the fourth and fifth commandments, 'as the Lord thy God commanded thee' occurs only in Deuteronomy and is clearly a figure of speech peculiar to the linguistic usage of the book (i. 19, iv. 5, v. 32, x. 5), emphasising as it does the *obedience* due to the law.[19]

[19] Reference to Jahweh in the third person implies a late stage in the development of the literary type (see above pp. 19, 63)

5. To the fifth commandment Deuteronomy adds: 'that it might go well with thee.' This is another typically Deuteronomic expression (Deut. v. 29, vi. 18, xii. 25).

6. The ninth commandment in Exodus uses the common Hebrew expression 'false witness' (Ps. xxvii. 12, Prov. vi. 19, etc.). In the Hebrew text of the Bible this is made stronger in Deuteronomy: 'idle, worthless witness' *'ed shāw*: echoing, with *shāw*', the 'in vain' of the third commandment).

7. In the tenth commandment the first version puts the neighbour's house first, and then expands the theme in terms befitting the way of life of that period, with wife, manservant, maidservant, and cattle. In Deuteronomy, on the other hand, the wife is taken out of that context and is placed in front alone. Hence lust is separated here from covetousness.

It follows therefore that the Deuteronomy additions have many linguistic characteristics peculiar to that book, and which will therefore have originated with the Deuteronomist himself. Exodus xx shows signs of an older version in many places, but is not without additions; and one of these additions, the one in the fourth commandment, could well be younger than Deuteronomy, for the motive given in Exodus for this commandment has something of the creation story which was written down in the Priestly Code only in the sixth century.[20] The additions to both versions do not affect the number and scarcely the content of the commandments, but as a rule add motives for them. Apparently at the time when both versions were written down Israel considered it necessary to add explanations to Jahweh's commandments to make them intelligible to hearers. The laws ordained by him should not be obeyed blindly but should be interpreted rationally. Did this tendency already exist when the Decalogue was proclaimed at early festivals in commemoration of the renewal of the covenant, or did it first arise when priestly (Levitical) comment was added to the proclamation?[21] We still do not know the answers to these questions about the setting in life of these additions.

The two versions we have of the Decalogue are two quite independent elaborations (stages 2a and 2b) of a primary source (stage 1) which has been lost. It is relatively easy to trace their transmission history. But is stage 1 really the first version? The text common to both Exod. xx and Deut. v also contains many expressions which are specifically Deuteronomic or Deuteronomistic.[22] These are easy to determine.

---

[20] Gen. ii. 1–3.

[21] A Levitic interpretation of the law before the cultic community is inferred by G. von Rad = Deuteronomium-Studien, FRLANT 58, 1957. Engl. *Studies in Deuteronomy* 1953 from the history of the origins of Deut. and from Neh. viii. 7 f.

[22] The expressions which are against the old conception of collective responsibility: 'who love me and keep my commandments', 'who hate me', are also Deuteronomistic. Scharbert B 38, 1957, 130–50. 'Deuteronomic' and 'Deuteronomistic' are two sharply distinct terms. Deuteronomic denotes the linguistic usage of the Deuteronomic law. Deuteronomistic however denotes the manner of speech and thought which arose in so-called Deuteronomistic circles in the period of exile in connection with the book of Deuteronomy, but which was enriched by many other traditions, notably from Jerusalem. It is to be found mostly in the book of Judges and the books of the Kings. Hence Deut. v is Deuteronomic, whereas Exod. xx, and also Deut. i–iv. 43 (and Deut. v at a later stage of development?) are Deuteronomistic.

1. In the formula by which Jahweh announces himself he has delivered the people 'from Egypt, out of the house of bondage' (Exod. xiii. 3, 14; Deut. vi. 12, vii. 8 etc.). However the quotation from the Decalogue in Ps. lxxxi. 10 (cf. II Kings xvii. 35 f.) is worded slightly differently: 'which brought thee out of the land of Egypt'. This shorter version is most certainly the older.[23]

2. The expression 'other Gods' crops up frequently in Deuteronomy (13 times) but rarely elsewhere. Here also Ps. lxxxi. 9 gives us the pre-Deuteronomic wording: 'There shall no strange god (אֵל זָר) be in thee.'

3. The words 'any form which is in heaven above . . .' have near parallels in Deut. iv. 19, 23. The second commandment appears without these additional words (in Exod. xxxiv. 17, cf. xx. 23; Lev. xix. 4), referring only to the graven image (אֱלֹהֵי מַסֵּכָה), which is certainly the older wording. Once it was an image of Jahweh himself which was prohibited; but the versions of (Exod. xx and ?) Deut. v no longer see any temptation to make an image of the God of Israel, but only to make images of foreign gods. Thus the second commandment came to be linked to the first. Originally the second will have come later on in the series.

4. 'Thou shalt not bow down to them nor serve them' refers now to the likenesses of other gods (similarly Deut. iv. 19). But the sentence—and particularly its imposing motive clause—has more relevance to the first commandment, to which it is connected in Ps. lxxxi. 9: 'Neither shalt thou worship any strange god' (אֵל נֵכָר as in Gen. xxxv. 2, 4; Jos. xxiv. 20, 23). Linked to the first commandment the words make sense: if it is a god other than Jahweh which arises *within* the Israelite nation, then it would be a god of *foreign* nations, whom the Israelites were to worship. The two temptations have a close connection, and share a motive clause pointing to Jahweh's jealous nature.

5. In the motive clause the comments 'them that hate me' and 'them that love me', and also 'who keep my commandments', are also Deuteronomic in character, and are therefore later additions (see Exod. xxxiv. 6 f.; Num. xiv. 18).

6. The *name* of Jahweh is a Deuteronomic concept: God himself lives in heaven, but his name on earth, in the cult (Deut. xii. 11, etc.). Again the Psalter gives us an older wording in which Jahweh is still in the first person, in Ps. xxiv. 4: Thou shalt not use my Power (נֶפֶשׁ) deceitfully.

The motive clause following this will have run: 'For the Lord thy God (see LXX), will by no means clear the guilty' (נַקֵּה לֹא יְנַקֶּה Exod. xxxiv. 7; Num. xiv. 18).

7. In the fourth commandment the particulars which are given, 'thou, nor thy son, nor thy daughter, nor thy manservant, nor thy maidservant, nor thy cattle, nor any stranger' are Deuteronomic details (Deut. xii. 12, 18, xvi. 11, 14).

Another point of interest is that this commandment seems to have both a positive and a negative form: 'Six days thou shalt work, but on the

---

[23] עלה Hf is more liturgical. J. Wijngaard, VT XV, 1965, 91–102.

seventh day thou shalt rest' (Exod. xxxiv. 21, cf. xxxi. 15a), and also: 'thou shalt do no work on the sabbath' (cf. xxxi. 15b).[24]

8. In the fifth commandment the motive given is firstly 'that thy days may be long', and then, 'upon the land which the Lord thy God giveth thee'. This is Deuteronomic language (Deut. iv. 26, 40, etc.).

These typically Deuteronomic expressions will certainly have been later additions also. Thus a study of the transmission history reveals a source of even earlier origin than the source upon which Exod. xx and Deut. v are founded, whose form was very simple, easy to memorise and most certainly intended to be learned by heart.

In the last decades there were numerous attempts to reconstruct the primary version, if possible in the negative and metrically balanced throughout. Today it is usual to look at it differently. In accordance with Mowinckel's thesis, that the single apodictic commandment is the oldest discernible version of the literary type, the tendency is to assume that a variety of single, differently constructed commandments, or groups of commandments, constituted the primary source of the Decalogue.

At this point we must bring in another document, the *ritual Decalogue*, which is also called the 'ten commandments' (Exod. xxxiv. 28). We have two versions of this also, in Exod. xxiii. 10 ff. and xxxiv. 10 ff. In the first sentences its original form has much in common with the original form of the classical Decalogue.[25]

Ritual Decalogue (*Primary source*)	Classical Decalogue (*Primary source*)
xxxiv. 6f. And the Lord passed by before him (Moses), and proclaimed,	
The Lord, the Lord, a God full of compassion and gracious, slow to anger, and plenteous in mercy for thousands, forgiving iniquity and transgression and sin: and that will by no means clear the guilty; visiting the iniquity of the fathers upon the children, and upon the children's children, upon the third and upon the fourth generation . . .	I am the Lord thy God, which brought thee out of the land of Egypt.

[24] The great importance attached to the Sabbath in the (post)-exilic period meant that the fourth commandment was lengthened and given greater prominence. Thus the emphasis which had previously been laid on the commandments at the beginning of the Decalogue came to be laid on the central part of the series, so that in construction the series was no longer 'top-heavy'.

[25] The problem of the Decalogue cannot be dismissed by saying that Exod. xxxiv is a 'secondary collection of elements from many different sources' (ALT I, 317, note A), for this immediately raises the question of where they came from, and when. And another thesis, that the classical Decalogue naturally once had a place in the Jahwistic Exod. xxxiv but that later on it was superseded by the ritual Decalogue, is also unsatisfactory. What on earth could have caused this displacement? According to verse 28, Exod. xxxiv consists of 'ten commandments', but the present text contains a good many more, so that the exegete is absolutely forced to make a study of its transmission history. Indeed, this has often been done, with very varying results. In my opinion it is only possible to reach a conclusion if Exod. xxiii is placed alongside as an independent variant. The above exposition gives the text which is common to both. This makes it easy to make out the ten sayings. The sequence of xxiii. 10 f. has been rearranged in order to facilitate the link with the book of the covenant in xxi. 1–xxiii. 9. I therefore follow the xxxiv sequence.

xxxiv. 10. Behold, I make a covenant: before all thy people I will do marvels.[26]

xxxiv. 11b, xxii. 23, 28. Behold, I[27] drive out before thee the Amorite, and Canaanite, and the Hittite, and the Perizzite, and the Hivite, and the Jebusite.

I xxxiv. 12, xxiii. 32 f. Take heed to thyself, lest thou make a covenant with the inhabitants of the land whither thou goest, lest it be for a snare in the midst of thee.[28]

Ia There shall no strange god be in thee

II xxxiv. 13 f.; xxiii. 24. Thou shalt worship no other god, but ye shall break down their pillars (for the Lord . . . is a jealous God).

Ib Thou shalt not worship any strange god: for I the Lord thy God am a jealous God (visiting the iniquity of the fathers upon the children, upon the third and fourth generation, and showing mercy to thousands).

III xxxiv. 17.[29] Thou shalt make thee no molten gods.

II Thou shalt not make unto thee a graven image.

IV xxxiv. 18, xxiii. 15. The feast of unleavened bread shalt thou keep. Seven days thou shalt eat unleavened bread, as I commanded thee, at the time appointed in the month Abib: for in the month Abib thou camest out from Egypt.

III Thou shalt not use my Power in vain, for the Lord thy God will by no means clear the guilty.

V xxxiv. 20, xxiii. 15. None shall appear before me empty.

IV Six days shalt thou labour and the seventh day shalt thou rest. Thou shalt do no work on the sabbath.

VI xxxiv. 21, xxiii. 12. Six days thou shalt work, but on the seventh day shalt thou rest.

---

[26] The prologue (xxxiv. 6–10) was left out of xxiii when it was inserted into the Sinai theophany of chapters xix–xxiv.

[27] Or 'mine angel', 'the hornet', respectively.

[28] As the covenant prohibition also occurs in Deut. vii. 2 it is mostly Deuteronomistic. But it is not clear why such a prohibition will have arisen at so late a period. Therefore Deut. vii will probably be based on a more ancient tradition.

[29] Exod. xxiii is missing here because there is an earlier commandment which is similar in xx. 23.

5

Ritual Decalogue (Primary source)	*Classical Decalogue* (*Primary source*)
VII xxxiv. 22 f., xxiii. 16 f. And thou shalt observe the feast of weeks, even of the first fruits of wheat harvest, and the feast of ingathering at the year's end.[30] Three times in the year shall all thy males appear before the Lord God, the God of Israel.[31]	V Honour thy father and thy mother
VIII xxxiv. 25, xxiii. 18. Thou shalt not offer the blood of my sacrifice with leavened bread.	VI Thou shalt do no murder.
IX xxxiv. 25 f., xxiii. 18 f. Neither shall the sacrifice of the feast of the passover be left unto the morning (?) (The first of the firstfruits of thy ground thou shalt bring unto the house of the Lord thy God.[33]	VII Thou shalt not commit adultery. VIII Thou shalt not steal (a man[32]). IX Thou shalt not bear false witness against thy neighbour.
X xxxiv. 26, xxiii. 10. Thou shalt not seethe a kid in his mother's milk.	X Thou shalt not covet thy neighbour's house.

The similarity of the first commandments are obvious, but there is no similarity at all in the second halves. This leads us to the conclusion that the basis of both was a source consisting of only three or four prohibitions governing the special relationship of Israel to her God, rounded off with a positive commandment about the sabbath. This source probably also included motive clauses for every or for every other commandment. Later elaborations took two different directions: on the one hand as the result of ritual needs, and on the other the result of ethical considerations. Each time a series of ten arose.[34] Thus the transmission history can be seen in the following terms:

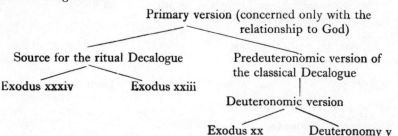

Primary version (concerned only with the relationship to God)

Source for the ritual Decalogue

Exodus xxxiv   Exodus xxiii

Predeuteronomic version of the classical Decalogue

Deuteronomic version

Exodus xx   Deuteronomy v

[30] The sabbath is followed by the feast of weeks, which is a sabbath of particular importance (7×7, like the sabbath year in xxiii. 10 f.) but which the writer of xxiii no longer understands.

[31] Taken out of another context, for the direct address form, the 'thou shalt', is missing. Superfluous when in conjunction with IV and VII.

[32] ALT I, 333–40: *Das Verbot des Diebstahls im Dekalog.*

[33] This positive construction is not in keeping with the prohibitions to be observed for sacrifices with which it is surrounded. Moreover, 'the house of the Lord' is a later addition.

[34] When the classical Decalogue was expanded the first two commandments were made one.

The primary version will most certainly date back to the pre-monarch-ical period (before 1000 B.C.). It is not impossible, although very improb-able, that it goes back to the period in the wilderness and to Moses. Indeed the prohibition against graven images must have originated in a time when the Israelites were already established at one place. But it is another question whether the idea of Jahweh demanding exclusive regard, with a cult that had no images, had already established itself during the wilderness period. If so, its incorporation into a series of prohibitions will be connected with the time when the covenant formular was accepted in the sanctuary at Shechem. Thus, unlike the Beatitudes, the transmission history here does not lead us back to a fixed point, to the time when the words were first formulated by a historically verifiable person, such as Jesus.

However, just as with the Beatitudes, the transmission history of the classical Decalogue was also not completely at an end when it was taken up into the books of Exodus and Deuteronomy. On the contrary, very soon —in fact, even in the period before Christianity—attempts were made to harmonise the two versions. The most important evidence of this is the Nash papyrus.[35] With the Decalogue also, then, the history of its trans-mission is taken further by the history of its interpretation. Against this background the Decalogue is seen as the expression of centuries of human striving to put in words once and for all how God's will rules his chosen people.

By following the evolution of such traditions (i.e. the units which make up a literary type), as we have done with the Decalogue and the Beatitudes, we have traced the history of the transmission of tradition, or transmission (tradition) history. A study of the transmission history of any detail begins with a look at the final form of a literary unit and aims then to expose first the different written, and afterwards the oral forms it has taken.

Therefore whereas the history of literary types discovers as many units as possible which make up a literary form, but does not study the units themselves, concerning itself more with the rise and fall of the type as a whole, transmission history starts with a single, isolated literary unit, and is only interested in the history of the type in so far as the tradition took shape within it.

D. *The First Steps in an Investigation into the Background of a Text*

We are only occasionally lucky enough to have two versions of a biblical passage.[36] What can be done with the mass of material of which there is only one version, but which obviously has a long history of transmission behind it. Is it possible to trace this history? Of course, it is possible although the greatest care needs to be taken. To begin with, a study of material with a double transmission will provide the experience necessary to deal with the more difficult passages. Moreover, it is essential to be familiar with the

---

[35] S. A. Cook: A Pre-Massoretic Biblical Papyrus, PSBA 25, 1903, 34–56.
[36] Many Old Testament narratives have parallels in other Ancient Oriental writings. The study of their transmission history has opened the way for a com-parison. Gen. i has parallels in Egyptian versions of the creation; and Gen. vi–ix parallels in Mesopotamian flood narratives.

history of all literary types in question. Only then is the study productive. The investigation should best begin with the reflection 'that certain features which once, in an earlier connection, will have made sense, have been retained in the new tradition although the original link has been lost. These features provide the form critic with a clue to the existence and also to the individual characteristics of an earlier form.'[37] Therefore where a long history of transmission can be assumed, the final result which the text under study offers usually contains many irregularities. It is these irregularities which are the starting point for the reconstruction of the different forms the tradition has taken. Evidence is also provided by the history of the literary type, for it can usually be assumed that the course a tradition has taken corresponds with that of its literary type. The potential of such an investigation can be illustrated by an accidental discovery in recent times. In the story of Nebuchadnezzar's madness in Daniel iv, it had been concluded for many reasons that it was not Nebuchadnezzar who was the original subject of the story but the last New-Babylonian king, Nabunid. Through the discovery of a prayer of Nabunid's in the Qumran texts, where a Jewish seer is described in detail who helped the king regain happiness and honour, the early stage arrived at through a study of the transmission history is brilliantly confirmed.[38]

The changes which a tradition undergoes in the process of its development must not be underestimated. An example of a case where the material has come to mean exactly the opposite to what was originally intended is the song of Lamech in Gen. iv. 23:

> Adah and Zillah, hear my voice,
> Ye wives of Lamech, hearken unto my speech:
> For I have slain a man for wounding me,
> And a young man for bruising me:
> If Cain shall be avenged sevenfold,
> Truly Lamech seventy and sevenfold.

This was once the triumph song of an Arab tribe, which was much given to boasting of its deeds of vengeance. Now it forms part of the Israelite Cain saga and has become a rather hateful example of human arrogance, wantonly disregarding the godly and human order.

How far back should the transmission history of a unit be traced? As far as possible, for the further back the development can be traced the greater will be our understanding of its final form. In Gunkel's time it was optimistically maintained that form criticism could trace material right back to its original form, but it is fair to doubt whether it is always, or even in the majority of instances, possible to do so. However, where the transmission history of a tradition does not stretch over too long a period its origin can often be discovered.[39] In spite of the revisions made to the

[37] Gunkel, *Schöpfung*, p. 6.
[38] R. Meyer, *Das Gebet des Nabunid*, Sitzungsberichte der Sächsischen Akademie der Wissenschaften zu Leipzig, Philol.-hist. Klasse 107, 3, 1962.
[39] The statement by Gressmann, that 'there is no material in the world which does not have its prehistory' (*A. Eichhorn und die religionsgeschichtliche Schule*, 1914, p. 35) must not be taken to mean that there was never any starting-point or any personal authorship.

original material in the books of the prophets it is usually still possible to discern the oldest form of a prophetic saying.[40] Similarly in the synoptic gospels it is often possible to discover the original form of the logia of Jesus.

Even the few indications given here will provide some idea of the fascination of tracing the course of a tradition back to its earliest stages. To achieve a real understanding of a biblical text it is essential to look deeper into it than merely study its present form. Consideration must also be given to its transmission history, i.e. to its earlier forms.

The most critical moment with all traditions which were originally oral is without doubt the point at which they were written down, for then the wording becomes fixed and is no longer readily alterable. At this stage it usually happens that they not only lose their self-sufficiency but nearly always change their literary type as a result of losing previous characteristics of form. But this will be discussed in the section on oral and written tradition.

In German biblical scholarship, and particularly in connection with the Old Testament, the present tendency is to bring out the term 'transmission history' and to reduce the extent of that of 'form criticism', which is then understood merely in the sense of a study of literary types. However, transmission history is used here in the sense in which Gunkel used it: as a branch of form-critical work. This is because form criticism, with its emphasis on the *historical* aspect of biblical writing, necessarily includes an investigation into the origin of a piece of literature, and not only of its type, but also of the details it contains. Without a consideration of the transmission history the study of literary types and their setting in life would easily become a timeless abstraction. The dangers are even greater if the process is reversed and the transmission history is considered apart from the study of the literary type and setting in life. Such a conception of transmission history will lead to arbitrary speculation. Only the history of the literary type and the setting in life provide it with a secure framework.

E. *Changes in the Units which make up Complex Literary Types*

The study of the transmission history of a unit is needed when the unit has a long period of development behind it; where the text as it stands does not go back directly to the creative inspiration of one writer but has been transformed once or even several times in the process of oral or written transmission. For instance, the extracts from the annals of the Jerusalem Court which found their way later into the books of the Kings, or the parting words at the end of the Pauline epistles, would not necessarily need a study of the history of their transmission because they were the creations of a particular moment. But with the great complexes of which these details are part it is very different. The material which comprises the books of the Kings only gradually came together, and while these books contain a great assortment of other kinds of writing as well as the court annals, the mere fact that they are juxtaposed lends even the annals a fresh emphasis. Even Paul's Epistle to the Galatians, which we have in its original form (this is disputed with regard to the Epistles to the Romans and to the Corinthians),

[40] Although it is no longer possible with many prophetic passages to discover whether and how far they go back to the *ipsissima verba* of a particular prophet, Birkeland takes the point much too far with his remark that 'it is never possible to determine with certainty what has come from the prophets and what has come from the tradition' (*Vom hebräischen Traditionswesen*, 1938, p. 18).

contains in some places pre-Pauline kerygmatic formulas, or material from the Hellenistic-Christian mission preaching, and both these provoke a study of their transmission history.

The larger the unit the more necessary it is to study the history of its transmission, particularly those parts which were originally independent traditions and which came together to form component literary types of a complex literary type. The most important instances of this are the great narrative writings of the Old and New Testament, and also the books of the prophets and the Revelation of St John. The greater the unit, therefore, the more profitable the study will be, because it will trace the developments of all the parts of the literary type which were originally independent. Hence it is not only a matter of the transmission history of the Jahwistic or priestly writings in the Old Testament, but also the transmission history of the composition into which both these were later incorporated, i.e. first the Tetrateuch, and then the Pentateuch which, as the Torah, developed into the fixed literary type of *sacred writing*.[41] In the New Testament the gospels did not reach the stage of becoming a similar great complex, for the harmonies of the gospels, although they were already evident at the time of the ancient Church, did not achieve a fixed final form. This position was filled by the individual gospels. Nevertheless a transmission history of the gospel of St Matthew not only involves the history of the origin and development of the single traditions but also of the gospel of St Mark, as well as the Logia source which is a second source of the gospel of St Matthew.

F. *The Question of the Historicity of Narratives*

What is the purpose of a study of the transmission of a tradition? In each case it brings out the background of the text under consideration, its literary type and the setting in life, and gives it the historical outline necessary for an interpretation. However it is particularly important for the narrative passages of the Old and New Testament, which can give us information of the religious and national history of Israel and the early Christian community. Here it is a matter of relating the material to events which we are to a greater or lesser degree able to date. By exposing the earliest forms of single, previously orally transmitted passages of the Old Testament historical books, the New Testament gospels, or the Acts of the Apostles, it is possible to discover information on periods for which there are no other contemporary records available.

This is of particular significance for the early history of Israel, i.e. before 1000 B.C. It was naive of the literary critics, and in the light of our present knowledge indeed impossible, to translate as they did the accounts of the early history of Israel, as presented in the earliest texts, directly into events. First of all it is essential to make a form-critical assessment of the changes which the pre-literary traditions will have undergone. It is only

---

[41] This aspect of form-critical work and in particular of transmission history was unknown to the first generation of form-critics. M. Noth and G. von Rad in particular have done much to establish it as part of form-critical work.

the tradition which has been preserved, not the fact; but by reconstructing their world we can approach the facts. What happened during the exodus of Israel's forefathers from Egypt on the Red Sea, or how did the conquest of Canaan come about? Such questions can only be investigated when the earliest sources of the traditions have been revealed. 'In the era (of literary critical research) now past, the main question for the critical examination of the Old Testament, and especially of the origins of Israel, was, in spite of its recognition of the legendary character of the older and oldest traditions, the question as to the content (the 'what') of the record, the question as to the historical course of events. It was a right and proper question, but . . . it was put to the text too soon, since with every single unit of tradition the first questions which should occupy us are these: Who is reporting it? What is the standpoint of the report, and what is the reporter's probable historical and theological position? What led him to report as he did? With what viewpoint and tradition is he aligning himself?'[42] Occasionally early sources also reveal puzzling connections with archeological finds in the Palestinian excavations, but a too hasty comparison of archeological dates with the text as it now stands is often unsatisfactory and can result in a questionable harmonisation of data. Transmission history is the only means by which the gap between archeological discoveries and the Old Testament narratives can be bridged. It is hardly necessary to stress the importance of investigating this early period in Israel, for it is then that the Israelite religion came into existence and the national characteristics took shape. But to do this transmission history is essential.

Only an approach of this kind can give us any certain information about the period of David, or later, for instance about Ezra's reform. There is no other way of making a reliable historical study of Israel, no other way of ascertaining dateable events. Martin Noth has given exemplary proof of this in the field of the political history of Israel. In his two works, *Überlieferungsgeschichtliche Studien I*, 1943 and *Überlieferungsgeschichte des Pentateuch* 1948 he traced the texts right back to their earliest level of tradition, and later he followed this with a complete presentation in his *Geschichte Israels*, 1950, The History of Israel, [2]1960 (London, A. & C. Black; New York, Harper & Row). It is in the search for the historical Jesus that transmission history is the most vital. We have no record of anything Jesus wrote himself. The history of Jesus outlined in the Gospels, which at the time of literary criticism was unhesitatingly made the basis for research into the life of Jesus, has now been shown to have been devised by the evangelists several decades after the actual events had taken place. Only the study of transmission history can give us access to the historical Jesus, throw some light on the course of his life and determine the content of his doctrines and teaching. Surprisingly, some New Testament form critics have tended to treat the question of the historicity of an event in the gospels as quite irrelevant, and even to dismiss it as illegitimate.[43] It is

[42] Von Rad, *Theology* I, E.T. 1962, p. 4.
[43] This is Dibelius' opinion, which Bultmann contests with some justification in *Tradition*, p. 5. But even Bultmann's idea of research into the historicity of material only goes so far as to query whether or not the logia come from Jesus, and if not whether they originated in Palestinian or Hellenistic early Christianity.

indeed possible to question whether the historicity of an event has any direct connection with a form-critical study; but in any case it has bearing on the discovery of the earliest forms of a tradition and its setting in life.[44]

It would be disastrous to interpret transmission history purely as a medium for obtaining 'facts'. Important though the earliest stages of a tradition may be, what became of it during the course of time in Israel or early Christianity is of even greater significance. The later the stage of transmission the more definite an interpretation of it can be. The essential merit of a study of transmission history lies in what it reveals about the tendencies in belief, thought, and teaching of those people who have handed the Bible down to us. As Gunkel said in his study of Genesis: 'If we want to grasp what is essentially Israelite, we shall have to consider not only the sagas themselves but also what Israel made of them, or the history they have undergone in Israel.'[45] The same applies to the New Testament texts. The history of their transmission helps to reveal the development of early Christian doctrine and liturgy.

Wherever possible the term 'transmission history', closely associated with the literary type and its setting in life, should replace the term 'tradition' in a historical study, for the latter has become confused. Transmission history sheds light on the connection between the divine action, the divine revelation, and the speech and writing of God's people, both old and new.

G. *The History of Motifs*

Here we must define what is known as the history of motifs (*Motivgeschichte*). Sometimes the term is used simply as an alternative to transmission history[46]; but more accurately the motif should be seen as 'an elementary and distinct part of a poetic work',[47] with the emphasis on 'part'. The motif is, so to speak, the smallest element which goes into the construction of a tradition; it can only appear as part of a literary unit and never alone. Understood in this way, the motif is roughly the same as the characteristics of a form. But as well as motifs which belong more or less to one particular literary type, there are also those which are found in many linguistic units, which crystallise sometimes in one, and sometimes in another literary type. We can consider them independent of a literary type, and term them unattached (*gattungsfreie*), or free ranging (*frei schweifende*) motifs. For instance numbers with a particular significance belong in this category, such as 3, 4, 7, 21. In the Old Testament these conceal a profound meaning (also frequently in the New Testament, e.g. in Revelation), and they crop up in the most disparate connections. To investigate the origins and development of such symbolism conveyed by numbers is really to engage in the study of the history of motifs, although in this particular case there is only a loose connection with form criticism and a closer relationship to popular psychology. But to take another kind of example: it is a recurring conception in the Bible that God singles out the man who in human terms would be judged unsuitable, and chooses him as his instrument, disregarding others who on the face of it are better equipped

---

[44] J. Dupont's remark is very much to the point: 'Before asking exactly what Jesus said or did it is necessary to study the conditions under which his words and deeds were transmitted by the primitive tradition and under which they were then written up by the Evangelists' (*Les Béatitudes*, [2]1958, p. 10).

[45] *Genesis* LXVIII.

[46] Mowinckel, *Prophecy*, p. 25

[47] Gunkel, *Genesis*, p. XX, note 1.

(Judges vi. 15; I Sam. ix. 21). It could be said that a motif such as this belongs to sagas describing the divine summons. But if we do so, we must bear in mind that it will not necessarily be a feature of every statement in which God calls men into his service. On the other hand it will not appear in a totally alien context, such as legal proceedings. Other motifs are found to be even more strongly bound to a literary type. For instance, it is a feature of certain types of sagas that they include descriptions of the typical daily affairs in the house and family, such as the relationship of the husband to the loved or unloved wife (I Sam. 1), or the relationship between father and sons (the Joseph romance), or between master and servant (Gen. xxiv). But when a motif of this kind crops up in a prophetic saying (Isa. i. 2 f.) it must then be considered unattached. There is an iridescence in the use of the term 'motif', for what it describes may sometimes come up for consideration when we are examining the history of a type, and at other times when we are examining the transmission of smaller units. Or again, the study of motifs may form part of a study of the ideas which underlie particular words at particular times. (Number symbolism is an instance of this.) The line of distinction between motifs which are dependent on a particular type and those which are unattached is difficult to draw with precision.[48]

5. REDACTION HISTORY

A. *Return to the Final Stages of a Tradition*

The history of the transmission of traditions, as we have just shown, takes the final form of a unit and investigates the various stages it has been through (from the standpoint of the literary type and the setting in life) in order to get back to the oldest ascertainable versions of it. But when this has been done the commentator returns to the text in its final form, and with his new understanding is able to see it in a fresh light. Enriched by the knowledge of the history of its transmission, he is better able to grasp and to interpret the significance of the fact that it came to be written down. This, the last, form-critical process is called *redaction history*: a written text is interpreted against the background of its literary type, setting in life, and its transmission history.

A *redactor* is one who revises a particular piece of writing. His work is different from that of an author or writer, who creates something new. Fifty years ago the term redactor was used in biblical scholarship in a depreciatory sense. Redactors, it was said, had made additions to the great works of the historical writers, prophets and evangelists of the Bible, and had inserted their own—usually irrelevant and very dull—comments, thus distorting the text. Form criticism has brought with it a thorough revaluation of the relationship between writers and redactors. The transmission history of most biblical texts reveals that the oral tradition went through a long process of development before it actually came to be

---

[48] This uncertainty has arisen because motifs are differently interpreted by different form critics. Gunkel saw them as necessary constituents of a form (*Genesis* XX, note 1; GuB 25), whereas Noth would like to exclude them entirely from the study of transmission history (ÜGP 67–69). The distinction given above is intended as a middle course between the two. Cf. the attempt by Bultmann to differentiate between constitutive and ornamental motifs in the logia in the gospels in *Tradition*, p. 69.

written down. Therefore the first writer, whether historical writer or evangelist, did not create anything of literary originality, but he collected and assembled into some sort of order traditions which had already existed and which he found in general circulation. The material which he put into writing had taken shape long ago. He merely took it out of the linguistic flow of oral tradition, and by writing it down he froze it into a fixed form. He banished it to a piece of papyrus. Of course the first writers did not merely record the oral unit as a tape recorder does today. They did in fact compose. From the material they appropriated they took out what in their opinion was no longer topical or what was misleading, and worded the piece in the language of their own times. They added explanatory details, perhaps chronological, or geographical. They provided the text with a central theme, thus giving it unity. This was what the first writers accomplished. But, other than a few New Testament letters, *no book in the Bible still retains the form it was given when it was first written down.* Subsequent generations of redactors took over the work of the first writer and brought it up to date, just as the first writer had done with the oral tradition. Of course the work done by the man who collects and writes down traditions which have hitherto been circulating only orally is greater and more difficult than the work done by those who later revise it. However, the basic approach is similar.[1] Redaction history therefore follows the work of both the first writer and the subsequent redactors. *It traces the path the unit has taken from the time it was first written down until the time it achieved its final literary form.* Therefore whenever the written transmission of a unit is reckoned to have been long, the study of its redaction history is essential. In fact, any text which calls for a study of its transmission inevitably requires a study of its redaction also. However, here the process is now reversed, for with redaction history the inquiry starts with the early versions and works up to the final one.

As redaction history is concerned with a fixed text the interpretation takes quite another line to that of transmission history, where usually only the outlines of the earliest versions can be ascertained. Redaction history can be expressed in far more definite terms than any other stage in a form-critical study. It becomes a running paraphrase, i.e. an exegesis of all the elements in the passage under consideration. Usually the work is evident of not only one, but a series of redactors: hence it is a *history* of redaction. Most biblical texts are not the work of individuals, but have originated from teaching institutions: from schools, whether of prophets, priests or evangelists.[2] The works were repeatedly rewritten, and were modified and

---

[1] The problem of differentiating between the first writer and redactor can be illustrated by the Tetrateuch. Was the Jahwist (J) really the one who first put things down in writing, or did he base what he wrote on an earlier written source? The same problem concerns the gospels of Matthew and Luke. Did Q, which the evangelists used as a source for the sayings of Jesus, circulate orally or in writing? Hence in the passages concerned with Jesus' sayings were Matthew and Luke first writers or were they redactors?

[2] Even Gunkel had some idea of the part that these schools had played in the J and E sources of the Tetrateuch (*Genesis* LXXXVI). In New Testament discussion the term was principally established by K. Stendahl, *The School of St. Matthew*, Acta Seminarii Neotestamentici Upsaliensis XX, 1954.

enriched with new ideas each time. But this does not mean that the men involved were insignificant. The setting in life remains the same at all stages of redaction, although of course it differs from that of the oral tradition. In the spoken parts in the Synoptic Gospels, for example, a threefold setting in life can be determined: the first lies in the proclamation of the historical Jesus, the second in (oral) worship or didactic recitation by the early community, and the third where the Evangelist himself, or his school is at work. (These conditions are analogous to those in the Old Testament prophetic books and the historical works.)

This form-critical process is facilitated in the Bible by the fact that most writers approached the material with the greatest reverence. What they have added of their own is usually only concerned with the framework of a piece, within which they have assembled the wide range of material taken from oral tradition. This is why the transition passages between the originally independent units are usually so brief. They consist of simple expressions such as: 'After this it happened that . . .', and so on. Or they link people and places out of different traditions. But chiefly they give the whole a structure which close analysis reveals to consist of clearly defined parts. The introductions and conclusions of the books and of the principal sub-sections are important in this respect. The redactors also often express their opinions in speeches which, some skilful, some not, they put into the mouth of the hero. This applies to the Jahwist and also to the compilers of Isaiah and the Gospel of St Matthew. Hence a study of redaction history first considers the beginning and end of the book, and its principles of construction and classification, and with this as a basis turns to an interpretation of the individual passage.

B. *The Position of the Beatitudes in the Gospels*

If we consider the Beatitudes in this way, we can start with the fact that the general opinion in New Testament scholarship today is that they were first recorded in the source of sayings or the logia source Q (a written source?), presumably in Aramaic. The literary type of this series is similar to that of the wisdom book of Ecclesiasticus, the Talmudic Pirke Aboth and the gnostic Gospel of Thomas, where the sayings of an authoritative teacher have been loosely joined together. As Q does not exist as such, but has only been inferred from an analysis of the material common to both Matthew and Luke, and moreover was itself apparently the subject of continual revisions and additions, it is not possible to make a redaction-historical interpretation of the Beatitudes in the light of their connection to Q. On the other hand we have a stage of redaction in both Matthew and Luke. Here the Beatitudes have become part of a new complex literary type, the gospel, which is an original Christian creation. It has only survived in a few individual pieces[3] from the first post-Apostolic generation, and presumably originated in the Greek-speaking early Christian world. It features the sayings and deeds of Jesus, and also his suffering: in short,

---

[3] However, the literary type is not only to be found in the four canonical Gospels, but also in the apocryphal gospel literature of the second and third centuries.

his whole career, understood as a joyful message from God, a revelation of God for the salvation of mankind. Jesus was so distinctive a figure that he could not be assessed in conventional terms. In order to write about him, it was necessary to invent a new literary form.[4] This was first evolved in Mark, and the taken up in Matthew and Luke. 'The earthly deeds of Jesus are used to present the message of Christ.'[5] To put it cautiously, the setting in life of the Gospels is to be found where the roots of Christian theology lie.[6] The second generation of Christianity was looking back on the inspired and inspiring proclamation of Jesus and his Apostles; the leading minds of this period began to consider the disparities and affinities between the old nation of God (Israel) and the new (Christianity), and also the relation between the story of Christ and the imminent end of the world.

Each Evangelist has his own characteristic point of view. The *Matthew* Evangelist is at pains to present Jesus as the promised saviour of the Old Testament, with his messianic proclamation of the kingdom of God, from which the old nation is puzzlingly excluded. This is why there are repeated references to the Old Testament wisdom sayings. The rejection of Jesus by Israel leads to the establishing of the church, whose creation is of particular interest to the Evangelist. Matthew sees it his duty to bring out the association between the Messiah, ecclesiology and the eschatological hope.[7] This he states both at the beginning and end of his book. He begins: 'The book of the generation of Jesus Christ, the son of David, the son of Abraham', and appends a genealogical tree. He is the only evangelist who links the story of Jesus with that of Israel in his introduction, following the style of the Old Testament historical books (Gen. v. 1, etc.; I Chron. i–ix). And he ends his gospel with Jesus' charge to the disciples to win the nations and to baptise, i.e. to extend the sway of the Church: 'And lo, I am with you alway, even unto the end of the world.' Thus the eschatological limit is revealed. As for the construction of the gospel, the fact that the two previous examples, St Mark's Gospel and the logia source, are mixed up together makes it difficult to analyse. Do the five similarly constructed conclusions to speeches, 'And it came to pass, as Jesus ended these words . . .' (vii. 28, xi. 1, xiii. 53, xix. 1, xxvi. 1) mark the caesuras between separate sections of the book?

But it is, however, clear that the Beatitudes came to Matthew as already part of a longer discourse by Jesus, as the parallels in Luke prove. But Matthew turned this speech into the Sermon on the Mount (ch. v–vii) by incorporating other logia, and made the Beatitudes the start of the first fundamental proclamation of Jesus. By previously reporting that Jesus had announced the coming of the kingdom of heaven (iv. 7), and had proved his

[4] Though of course the word *euangelion* was not originally a term intended to denote a literary type. Only gradually—in the second century—did it become so.
[5] G. Bornkamm, RGG [3]II, 749.
[6] K. Stendahl, *The School of St. Matthew*, 1954, talks of schools of Christian 'teachers', comparable to the system used by the Rabbis, as the transmitters of the Gospel material.
[7] G. Bornkamm, *Überlieferung und Auslegung im Matthäusevangelium*, 1960, [2]1961; *Tradition and Interpretation in Matthew*, 1963 (London, S.C.M. Press; Philadelphia, Westminster Press).

power by working the first miracle (iv. 24), he presents the Beatitudes as 'the proclamation of the terms laid down by God for entry into his kingdom'.[8] This gives the sayings, originally derived from Jesus, a new emphasis. Whereas at the oral stage—in accordance with the literary type of the apocalyptic blessing—it was the promises which were emphasised (i.e. the 'blessed' and the second half of the sentence), here it is the manner of conduct: being poor in spirit, meek, persecuted. (It was for this reason that the Evangelist attached the two following logia (verses 13–16) on salt and light, and on the light which belongs on the stand.) The followers of Christ should demonstrate their greater 'righteousness' (verse 20) to the world. Hence a reference to righteousness was inserted into the Beatitudes (verses 6, 10). Perhaps this also called for a particular beatitude on mercy.[9]

Matthew indicates the significance of the Beatitudes through a simple introductory sentence to the Sermon on the Mount. In Q the Beatitudes were probably said to have been directed only at the disciples (Luke vi. 20). Matthew links this statement with a passage found in Mark in which the multitude around Jesus is mentioned and it finally says, 'And he goeth up into the mountain'. Matthew combined all these together: 'And seeing the multitude, he went up into the mountain: And when he had sat down, his disciples came unto him: and he opened his mouth and taught them, saying. . . .' Matthew frequently stresses the multitude around Jesus (iv. 25 f., vii. 28, etc.). In this passage, however, he also emphasises the special position of the disciples, standing around Jesus, just as the Levites stood around Ezra when he proclaimed the law (Neh. viii. 4). For Matthew the disciples are the heart of the Church and eschatological humanity. However, the mountain shows that Jesus is intended as a counterfigure to Moses; a new set of God's commandments (Torah) are proclaimed, as once they were on Mount Sinai. But the Beatitudes show how much stronger the promise in God's message has become, now that the Messiah has arrived and the eschatological kingdom of heaven is near at hand.[10]

Luke also adopted the Beatitudes. But he does not restrict himself, as do the other Evangelists, to relating the story of Christ. He presents this period as the middle of time,[11] which is followed after Easter by the time of the church, described in Acts, the second half of his work. It is significant that the literary type of the gospel had already become so fixed in his time that when reading his work we accept the first part as complete in itself, although this was not the intention of the author. We do not feel that a sequel is needed after Luke xxiv.

---

[8] Bornkamm, p. 14 after Windisch, *Der Sinn der Bergpredigt*, [2]1937; though here the expression is used for the whole of the Sermon on the Mount.

[9] The nine blessings could be intended to present a series of 3×3. Matthew loves symbolic numbers (seven in chapters xiii, xxiii).

[10] The replacement of the expression 'kingdom of God' by 'kingdom of heaven' in Matt. v. 3 (and 10) accords with the Rabbinic unwillingness to utter God's name. It is therefore likely that the Evangelist—if he was indeed an individual—had been a Jewish scribe; or had the expression already changed in the tradition of the community?

[11] Hence the title of the book by H. Conzelmann, *Die Mitte der Zeit*, BHTh 17, 1954, [2]1960; *The Theology of St. Luke*, 1960 (London, Faber & Faber; New York, Harper & Row), which has opened the way for the redaction history of St Luke.

Luke thinks in historial epochs: the time of the old nation of God, the middle of time, the time of the church, the end of the world. This influences even such brief passages as the Beatitudes. Twice in the first half of the sentences he inserts the word 'now', thus separating sharply the present feeling of urgency from the future hope of salvation. Whereas in the source the last blessing ran: 'for so persecuted they the prophets' (Matt. v. 12 after Q), Luke expands the wording to run, 'in the same manner did their fathers unto the prophets' (vi. 23). The addition of 'their fathers' shows a sharp differentiation between generations. The time of the prophets is past. The present adversaries are not the same, although a pernicious continuity does exist.

In the first section Luke uses only those blessings concerned with the poor, hungry and weeping. It could be that only these three blessings were to be found in the source, but it also happens that they exactly fit his theology of poverty. Luke shows Jesus taking up the cause of the despised and the proscribed, the tax collectors and sinners (vii. 36 ff., viii. 1 ff., xii. 13 ff.). Another characteristic of Luke's version is that the blessings are not directed to a multitude but purely to the disciples, and are in the direct address (the 'thou') form. Is this a reflection of the Greek blessing, which was chiefly concerned with prominent people, or does the Evangelist mean that it is the disciples and future leaders of the church themselves who must live in poverty and need, hated by those around them? The redaction history also shows that the evangelists gave some thought to their work. In their desire to show their contemporaries the full significance of the story of Jesus they did not hesitate to extend or even to change sayings by him. Knowing themselves to be filled with the spirit of the living *kyrios* they not only felt it their duty to do this, but in fact an obligation. This has quite a considerable bearing on the subject of the inspiration of the biblical writings.

C. *The Decalogue's Position in the Historical Writings and Books of the Law*

The redaction history of the Decalogue is similarly informative. The Decalogue appears twice: Exod. xx and Deut. v. In the first it is possible to make out only a very rough outline of its redaction history. In its present form the series has an unmistakeably Deuteronomistic flavour: expressions such as Egypt as the 'house of bondage', 'other gods', 'bow down to them nor serve them', 'the name of the Lord thy God' are strikingly Deuteronomistic. Hence Exod. xx. 1–17 is one of the very few Deuteronomistic passages in the first four books of Moses (others are Gen. xxv. 1–6, 13 f., Exod. xiii. 3–10). However, where and when these Deuteronomistic additions arose is still unknown. They make the Decalogue part of *Israel's saving history*. This is a complex literary type which arose only in Israel, and is just as much a characteristic of the faith of Israel as the gospels are of early Christianity. If the Decalogue had belonged in a literary context to the Sinai pericope before these Deuteronomistic revisions, then supposedly this would have only been in the Tetrateuch source of the *Elohist*, which is of old prophetic origin, and of which only fragments remain. This supposition is substantiated by the name given to God in the introduction: 'God (אֱלֹהִים) spake all these words.' Moreover the passage on the commandments does not fit at this point in the Jahwistic, or priestly, thread of the Sinai-story, but very well in the Elohistic.[12] It could have been placed after xix. 19:

The voice of the trumpet waxed louder and louder,
Moses spake, and God answered him by a voice.

or, under the supposition that the Elohist sequence was disturbed by later redaction and xx. 18–21 belongs before xx. 1, as a sequel to xx. 21:

The people stood afar off, and Moses drew near unto the thick darkness where God was.

What purpose the Decalogue had in the Sinai pericope, what relationship the writer considered to exist between command and covenant, and what light the Elohoistic work as a whole can bring to the single commandment are questions which have yet to be answered by a study of the redaction history.

The position of the Decalogue in Deuteronomy is clearer. Deuteronomy is by nature a book of the law of a special kind, intended for cultic utterance (cf. xxxi. 10 f.), with its construction based on the covenant formular (see section 2): exhortatory interpretation of the saving history (iv. 44, vi. 4–11, 30), the law (xii. 1–xxvi. 15), the making of the covenant (xxvii. 16–19), blessing and curse (xxvii f.).[13] The earlier Deuteronomist, conforming to cultic usage, addressed Israel in the singular, as 'thou'. However, the Decalogue of chapter v does not belong to this period. Although the 'thou', used by ancient custom in apodictic series of prohibitions, is retained here, nevertheless the Decalogue is inseparably bound to material which otherwise favours the plural,[14] and is therefore directed at the individual within the nation rather than at the nation as a whole (iv. 46–vi. 3). Thus it is the work of the later Deuteronomist, writing probably in the sixth century B.C., who drastically revised and extended the book of the law and turned it into the literary type of the *farewell speech*: just before his death, on the border of the Promised Land, Moses again feels himself inspired and gives a condensed account to his fellow Israelites of God's historical guidance and his will. (The book of Jubilees belongs to the same literary type.) The Decalogue is built into the older Deuteronomy, which uses the singular form of the verb, by means of two transitional passages (iv. 44–v. 5, v. 23–vi. 3) giving the contemporary and local situation. It is dependent upon Exod. xix–xxiv and refers to the covenant made on Mount Horeb, 'today' completed. On that occasion the people received the Decalogue direct from the mouth of God. This had so terrified them that they asked Moses

[12] Though it is true that otherwise in the Tetrateuch the Deuteronomistic passages are built into the work of the Jahwist.
[13] Von Rad has pursued this subject several times in his books.
[14] Minette de Tillesse maintains very attractively in VT XII, 1962, 29–87 that the later Deuteronomist, writing in the plural, and the writer of the Deuteronomistic historical writers (Jos.–II Kings) are one and the same.

to receive any further divine injunctions alone. Only now, when he faces death and his people stand within sight of the Promised Land, is Moses empowered to repeat what he had heard on Sinai as single statements, as the basic law of the ten commandments. Redaction has altered the effect and content of the sayings. The Decalogue here becomes the will of God, terrifying the people and making them aware of their weakness; it is no longer the direct, saving word of God, conveying the faculty to do good. It has a prominent position, before the exhortatory section, chapters vi–xi, and the actual body of the law, chapters xii–xxvi. In this position the Ten Commandments hold a vital place in the book as a whole. The chief intention is to present the whole Deuteronomic law as an interpretation of the Decalogue as it was proclaimed on Horeb. For the redactor, therefore, the Decalogue is the essence of God's message to Israel, linked directly to the formation of the covenant on Sinai. Thus this series of apodictic commandments, originally one of many of a similar nature, acquires a new meaning and a tremendous significance for the relation between God and Israel. It becomes quite simply God's Word. But this is only a result of the work of the (second) writer of Deuteronomy.

These few observations on the Beatitudes and the Decalogue by no means exhaust the possibilities of a study of their redaction history. But they will have been enough to show how decisive this method is for an interpretation of biblical texts. *By tracing the redaction history of a linguistic unit we follow the changes that take place within it when it was written down, its subsequent redaction, until it reaches its final form.* This ends the form-critical analysis.

D. *The History of Research*

The programmes for research which were conceived in the early days of form-critical study reveal that the need for a history of redaction was acknowledged right from the start. Gressmann, for instance, remarks that in the search for the earliest versions 'the later developments should never be forgotten'.[15] In *Genesis* Gunkel says, 'If we wish to grasp what is essentially Israelite, we shall have to consider not only the sagas themselves but also what Israel made of them, or the history they have undergone in Israel.'[16] Bousset, on the Revelation of St. John, is even more definite: 'The fact is far too often overlooked that it is much more important to ascertain what the Apocalyptist himself made out of this (his source) than to grope uncertainly after the apocalyptic tradition which lies behind him. However, this also must be investigated, for an accurate study of the sources and of the tradition on which the Apocalypse is based will indirectly provide a better insight into the essential characteristics of the piece.'[17] Thus right from the beginning redaction history has been taken as part of the form-critical theory, though in practice Gunkel and Gressmann gave it little consideration. They limited themselves to a study of the changes undergone by a narrative from its earliest ascertainable stage until its final oral form, just before it was written down. This final oral form, before the tradition is absorbed into a written collection, is what Gunkel called the 'Hebrew narrator', and is the actual

---

[15] *A. Eichhorn und die religionsgeschichtliche Schule*, 1914, p. 35.
[16] *Genesis* LXVIII, p. 60. See above p. 56.
[17] *Die Offenbarung Johannis*, 1896, p. 164 (MeyerK).

objective of his interpretation. What follows, the work of the Jahwist and the later redactors, he considered the work of mere compilers.[18] The material was taken over into the Tetrateuch in essentials just as they found it: 'They have not impressed it with the mark of their intellect.'[19] Only a certain 'spiritualisation' (*Vergeistlichung*) of the story comes from them, and it is questionable whether their modifications are not to be regretted. The men who compiled the prophetic books in their present form are allowed even less significance. At the most (in the book of Ezekiel the prophet did it himself) they brought the material into a chronological order, with no regard for content. This antiliterary conception is obviously the result of the influence of the German Romantics, with their emphasis on folk-lore.[20] (Perhaps also the contemporary life-philosophy (*Lebensphilosophie*), with its high regard for the actual living flow of life, for what has not yet been conceptualised.)

These views were also held in connection with the New Testament. Where the history of the synoptic tradition was studied from a form-critical viewpoint the Evangelists' activity as compilers was indeed mentioned, but such little value was attached to it that Bultmann, for instance, as late as 1953, is not inclined to make any separate appreciation of the concept of the individual Evangelists—apart from John—in his formidable *Theology of the New Testament*. 'The Message of Jesus', 'The Kerygma of the Earliest Church' and of the 'Hellenistic Church', 'The Theology of Paul and John' are discussed at length, but not that of the Synoptic Evangelists.[21] Dibelius expressly restricts form criticism to the period of oral transmission.[22] The Evangelists are compilers [23]: they bring nothing new in principle [24]: therefore they are not writers on their own merits. Similarly Schniewind: 'The reconstruction of trains of thought, which in Paul is a matter for deep study, would be a methodological error in connection with the Synoptic Evangelists.'[25]

In the Old Testament field, redaction history was already touched upon by Mowinckel in his studies of the prophetic books and their construction.[26] In doing so Mowinckel admitted that his interest was entirely the result of Gunkel's influence.[27] But his attempts remained sketchy, and are too bound up with literary criticism to be effective. In his later work, *Prophecy and Tradition*, 1946, he did go deeper into the subject, but by that time this method of investigation of the Old Testament had developed along other lines. The turning point came with Gerhard von Rad in his book, *Das Formgeschichtliche Problem des Hexateuch*.[28] Perceiving the potential of the

---

[18] His estimation of this stage can be seen from remarks such as: 'Once the tradition has been fixed in writing . . . all other fragments of material remaining in the oral tradition will die out, just as the written law brought an end to the institution of the priestly Torah, or the New Testament canon an end to the early Christian transmitters of the oral tradition' (*Genesis* LXXX.)

[19] *Genesis*, p. LXXXII f.

[20] L. Uhland, *Vorlesung über die Geschichte der deutschen Poesie im Mittelalter*, p. 112: 'In studying a written work as such, or the individual poem as an artistic entity, the writer or arrangers of it is not of essential interest to the reader; they concern us only in so far as a closer acquaintance with their particular characteristics provide us with the means for a critical appraisal of the written saga as an authentic expression of the people generally.'

[21] The synoptic writers are only briefly covered in the section 'Paradosis and Historical Tradition', E.T. Vol. II, 1955, pp. 119–27.

[22] *From Tradition to Gospel*, p. 3.

[23] *Ibid.* p. 1.

[24] Bultmann, *Tradition*, p. 321.

[25] ThR 1930, p. 164.

[26] *Zur Komposition des Buches Jeremiah*, Skrifter utgiv av det Norske Videnskaps Akademi i Kristiania 1913, 5; *Die Komposition des Jesajabuches*, chapters 1–39, AcOr 11, 1933, 267–92.

[27] *Buch Jeremia*, p. 67.

[28] BWANT IV, 26, 1938 = GS 9 ff. cf. p. 30 for E.T.

tradition history of most of the Hexateuch material, von Rad wheels sharply
round and asks how it was that a uniform final composition such as the work
of the Jahwist could actually have come about. Here form criticism has at last
reached its highest point. The structure of the Jahwistic work, which links
such a variety of disparate material, so von Rad discovers, is not merely a
literary compromise: it is the result of the very ancient cultic custom of
reciting the salvation history (from the patriarchs or from the Exodus from
Egypt up till the conquest) ceremonially at festivals, and to express joyous
acknowledgement of it. The traditional confession of faith became the framework for the first Tetrateuch source, the Jahwist. The conception of an
overall framework lends particular weight to the individual parts, and the
previously independent traditions gain fresh points of emphasis. Von Rad's
work on the first books of the Bible is paralleled by Martin Noth's work on
the Deuteronomistic and Chroniclers' histories in *Überlieferungsgeschichtliche
Studien* 1943, and later in *Überlieferungsgeschichte des Pentateuch* 1948. What
Noth treats under the title of transmission history is basically only that part
of the form-critical method which is concerned with the development of the
written material, i.e. redaction history.

This term has of course only arisen since the Second World War, and was
first adopted by W. Marxsen in his research into the Synoptics.[29] Marxsen,
and also Conzelmann[30] in his parallel work on the formation of St Luke,
have taken over for the field of New Testament studies the methods evolved
by von Rad and Noth for the Old Testament.

Redaction history is still a relative newcomer to the field of form criticism.
By no means all biblical works are investigated in this manner. However, if
form criticism is to be thorough redaction history must play a part. Only a
redaction-historical analysis will provide the basis for a truly historical
exegesis of individual passages.

A summary of the different aspects which are the necessary parts of a
form-critical analysis: study of the literary type and of the setting in life,
investigation into the history of the type and into its transmission and
redaction history, shows how wide is the front on which form-critical
research operates, and how great is its importance for interpreting all
biblical writings. 'The study of literary types therefore . . . is no mere
trifle, to be undertaken for amusement or else ignored, but it is the ground-
work without which nothing can be maintained with certainty.'[31] Just as
any serious interpreter studies the grammatical and syntactical forms as a
matter of course, the literary forms—or more accurately, oral and written
types—must be studied also. Form criticism is thus essentially a kind of
'higher grammar'. 'The ancients were as familiar from infancy with the
laws of literary forms as they were with the rules of Hebrew grammar.'[32]

---

[29] Der Evangelist Markus, FRLANT N.S. 49, 1956,
[30] See note 11.
[31] GuB 88.
[32] Gunkel RuA 32. The traditional standpoint grammatically is that the *sentence*
is the fundamental unit and the essential means of expression of thought. But the
organic units of language are formulas and types, not sentences. The sentence is a
logical abstraction and not a primary form: it is comparable rather to molecules in
the field of physics than to the physical body. 'But on the other hand we do not
speak in sentences, neatly formed one after another, but in "speech". An exact
analysis of a passage is not merely a study of the manner in which sentences are
connected but of the images which make up the relatively isolated unit of speech'
(W. Kayser, *Das sprachliche Kunstwerk*, p. 150).

This applies no less to the New Testament than to the Old. A knowledge of the principles of form criticism is therefore essential in any accurate exegesis.[33]

[33] Although the Israelites and the early Christians were completely and utterly involved with the laws which govern literary types—as is the case in any linguistic community—this does not mean of course that we can make an exhaustive study of these literary types from the Old Testament. Form criticism does in fact have its 'limits', just as a study of Hebrew grammar or of Koine-Greek does also. This occurs when a literary type only rarely occurs and there are no parallels outside the Bible for comparison, or where the setting in life can no longer be determined.

Section Two: A Wider View

6. LITERARY CRITICISM AND FORM CRITICISM

A. *The Determination of Sources*

H. Gressmann : *Albert Eichhorn und die Religionsgeschichtliche Schule*,
1914. By the same author: Die Aufgaben der alttestamentlichen
Forschung, ZAW N.S. 1, 1924, 1–33. W. Baumgartner: Wellhausen
und der heutige Stand der alttestamentlichen Wissenschaft, ThR
N.S. 2, 1930, 287–307. By the same author: Zum 100. Geburtstag von
Hermann Gunkel, VTS IX, 1963, 1–18. J. Schniewind : Zur Synopti-
ker-Exegese, ThR N.S. 2, 1930, 129–89. H.-J. Kraus : *Geschichte der
historisch-kritischen Erforschung des A. T.* 1956, 74–78, 80, 83 f., 89–
92. W. G. Kümmel : Das Neue Testament. Geschichte der Erfor-
schung seiner Probleme, Orbis Academicus III, 3, 1958, 177–230,
310–93, 417–38. R. H. Lightfoot : Form Criticism and the Study of the
Gospels, in : *The Gospel Message of St Mark*, 1950, 98–105. J. Bright:
Modern Study of Old Testament Literature, in : *The Bible and the
Ancient Near East*, 1961, 13–31 (London, Routledge; New York,
Doubleday).

A student approaching the exegesis of a biblical passage for the first time
is often astonished to find that in the older commentaries little or nothing
has been printed about the literary type and setting in life. On the other
hand he finds a vast amount on sources and redaction, and glosses. In short,
it is literary criticism which holds the field. What relation does this older
method have to the newer form criticism? Even today form criticism is
sometimes subordinated to it, and is considered purely the handmaid to
this exalted discipline. And then on the other hand there are attempts to
reject literary criticism altogether and to admit only of form criticism. And
in the midst of all this are many desperate students who cannot make out
the differences and the relationships between the two methods of approach.
It is only possible to make this clear by a glance at the history of research.

The form-critical method, analysed in the first part of this book, is now
quite generally recognised in biblical scholarship.[1] Even at those institutions where it is not practised it is quietly tolerated. It is seldom challenged
outright. Where, in the case of the Gospels, its 'limits' are emphasised and
certain of its conclusions are dismissed, this is not a rejection of form

---

[1] The Catholic viewpoint from the encyclical '*Divino afflante spiritu*', Sept. 30,
1943: anyone with a right understanding of the biblical inspiration will not be
surprised to find that 'the biblical writers as well as the other writers of antiquity
employ definite forms of presentation and description. This is a characteristic
particularly typical of the Semitic languages.' It refers expressly to the fact that
this viewpoint has achieved full recognition in the last few decades. J. Dupont
comments: 'The Pope views the study of literary types and forms as the primary
task facing Catholic exegetes at the present moment' *Les Béatitudes*, ²p. 25. Latin
text by H. Denzinger, *Enchiridion Symbolorum*, ³²1963, no. 3830. Cf. the instruction
of the Papal Bible Commission of 21.4.1964 on the historical truth of the Gospels
(cf. F. J. Helewa de la Croix, Ephemerides Carmeliticae 16, 1965, 371–83).

criticism as such, but of ways in which it is used.[2] It is extraordinary how this line of research has established itself, for it is only fifty years ago that it came into existence, and in its early days it experienced fierce attacks from the dominant scholarship of the day, whether 'liberal' or 'conservative'.

At the close of the last century the generally established method of research was *literary criticism*. In the Old Testament field (and beyond) the most prominent representative was J. Wellhausen. There was no one figure of comparable standing working on the New Testament, though the nearest to him who can be mentioned was H. J. Holtzmann. What is the difference between literary criticism and this relatively new discipline, form criticism? Literary criticism begins with the recognition that the period of origin of a biblical writing presents enormous difficulties, and that the situations of the writers have also become greatly obscured through a many levelled process of redaction. Formerly independent sources were linked together, even merged, or torn apart and made up into different and separate units.[3] The literary critic therefore attempts to discover the original writings, to determine exactly their date of origin, and to grasp the personality of the writer as much as is possible. This means that he approaches the text with, so to say, a dissecting knife in his hand, looks out particularly for breaks in continuity, or missing links in the train of thought, and also for disturbing duplications and factual inconsistencies, and for variations in the use of language which will have originated in another set of circumstances or at a period of different religious concepts. The literary-critical method leads to a determination of sources. The original written sources are reconstructed more or less hypothetically in their original wording, and all later explanatory comment or re-interpretation is dismissed as the inessential work of later redactors. This method, since its rise in the eighteenth century and its widespread acceptance toward the end of the nineteenth, has doubtless yielded impressive results, which, chiefly in connection with the Old Testament historical books (the Tetrateuch particularly) and the prophetic books (the discovery of Deutero-Isaiah, etc.) and with the New Testament gospels (Mark the oldest Evangelist; also the sayings source Q) have attained general recognition in the field of biblical research. The problems and achievements of this line of enquiry are to be found collected together in the 'Introductions' to the Old and New Testament.

[2] Cf. H. Riesenfeld, *The Gospel Tradition and its Beginnings*, with the sub-title, 'A Study in the Limits of "Formgeschichte" ', 1957 (London, Mowbray). Indeed I have to admit that I do not understand the sub-title. For when R. looks into the setting in life of the Gospel tradition he applies good form-critical arguments; as he does also when rejecting Dibelius' opinion that the origin of the Tradition is to be found in the sermon. His argument on this point is that this view is too Protestant in outlook and does not accord with the character of the early Christian kerygma and the instruction of the people, which was very much fixed in form. However it is quite contradictory to the form-critical method of approach that R. should completely pass over the question of differences between literary types, as he does from three points of view: in connection with (1) the Gospel material (2) the contemporary Israelite literature, and (3) the assessment of the Old Testament at that time (Was the Torah on a level with the prophets and even with the Hagiographa?).

[3] The lack of order in many of the biblical writings had long been noticed by theologians; cf. Luther's remark note 19, p. 11.

In their attempt to be quite free of prejudice, literary critics maintain that basically the Bible contains the same sort of writings as that on the modern book market. Israelite and early Christian writers are therefore to be appraised in the same terms as modern writers. The fixed and logically constructed order maintained in any relatively talented modern writer is expected of a Tetrateuch source, a prophet, a gospel, or an apostle's letter. Naturally it could not be ignored that the biblical writings used the language of their day and were therefore to some extent influenced by it, and that also large blocks of already existing tradition had been appropriated; but this was considered irrelevant. Thus, on the stories about the Egyptian plague, for instance, it was said that "The oldest form of this tradition is no longer possible to determine, and can therefore be of no interest to us.'[4] Wellhausen, speaking of the Revelation of St John, remarks in the same vein that in places material has actually been taken over 'which is not always fully imbued with the concept of the author; but where this material comes from is methodologically irrelevant.'[5]

Our grandfathers' generation threw themselves into the analysis of the biblical texts with an amazing zeal, discovering each break in continuity and each inconsistency with meticulous accuracy, in an attempt to dissect the work into original sources and later redaction. Anyone who had not been carried away in the process of such an intricate single analysis should not properly be called an exegete. Literary criticism is the analysis of biblical books from the standpoint of lack of continuity, duplications, inconsistencies and different linguistic usage, *with the object of discovering what the individual writers and redactors contributed to a text, and also its time and place of origin.*

B. *Modern Literary Criticism's Concept of History*

Wellhausen did not invent literary critical methods; he merely applied them very skilfully. His own particular contribution was to link together the results of literary criticism with an entirely fresh conception of the history of Israel (and of early Christianity), completely rejecting the church's traditional view of biblical history. His method was to turn directly from the chronological or geographical placing of a written source or a redactor to the outward events of that particular period, for the biblical writers were much influenced by the national or religious political life of their day, and did not consider the old traditions merely as such. They intended their work to have some effect upon contemporary conditions. This *direct connection between determining sources and historical events* is the main characteristic of Wellhausen's treatment of the different historical fields.

(a) *The History of Literature.* The Old Testament legal corpora only came to be written down after the time of the prophets. This means, so the advocates of pure literary criticism maintain, that the concept of Israelite divine law did not exist before this time. And in the New Testament it is the Paulinic

---

[4] Baentsch, Exodus (HKAT I/2), 1903, p. 57. And even today similar opinions prevail among American Old Testament scholars of the Albright school: '. . . Nor is there any objective method by which the history of the traditions may be traced' (J. Bright, *The History of Israel*, 1960, p. 69, London, S.C.M. Press; Philadelphia, Westminster Press).
[5] *Skizzen und Vorarbeiten* 6, 1899, pp. 233 ff.

writings which first contain dogmatic statements about Christ, which means that the earliest Christian church was without a christology and that in particular Jesus himself was entirely 'undogmatic'. According to this view of history, which stems purely from literary criticism, each biblical writer bases his work on that of earlier generations of writers, without intermediary links. With the Old Testament books of the law the results are roughly as follows: The oldest element was the Book of the Covenant (Exod. xxi-xxiii); in the seventh century this was taken up by Deuteronomy, or even replaced by it; then in post-exilic times the Priestly writing rejected Deuteronomy and replaced it with a new work. And with the New Testament the following conclusions are reached: Jesus founded his proclamation on the Old Testament works and developed his doctrine out of them. St Mark's Gospel and Q are based on the doctrine of Jesus, and Matthew and Luke for their part on these. The one writer could be said to pass his work into the hands of the next. (Only when the attempt was made to fit Paul's work into this rigid system did misgivings arise; he appears increasingly as the second founder of Christianity.)

The determination of sources had an even more restrictive effect on the conception of the (b) general and (c) religious history of Israel and the early Christian community. Wellhausen—and in the New Testament field F. C. Baur could be said in some ways to have anticipated him—perpetually impressed upon his students the fact that each biblical writing was determined by the 'tendency' or 'bias' (*Tendenz*) of its author, and was therefore to be viewed mainly as a source for the history of the time of its composition. What Paul writes about Jesus is firstly a document on the christology of this apostle and his life. What the Priestly writings tell us about Moses reflects the experiences with the cult and the law which the writer had at the time of exile or in post-exilic times.[6] What is left in the way of historical details after the tendency of the author has been allowed for, and all possible improbabilities have been deducted, can then be regarded as documentary evidence relating to the period which the source is said to represent. For example, the description of the founding of the Covenant and the proclamation of the law on Sinai is governed by the tendency of those who wrote the Pentateuchal sources. It can therefore tell us only about the history of the time when these sources were written. On the other hand, there is no reason for thinking that a writer should have a particular interest in telling us that Jahweh should have appeared to Moses on Sinai in a thorn bush, and that thereafter Moses should have travelled to Egypt; therefore this is reliable information on the time of Moses. In ascertaining the age of a text, the simple eighteenth-century scheme of evolution was used, by which religion had developed in the following stages: Fetishism (later: Animism)—Polytheism—Monotheism. Wellhausen's *Israelitische und jüdische Geschichte*[7] is based on this unsophisticated, easily assimilable system, and is a model for a great many similar writings on the Israelite and early Christian period. It was only in the case of the synoptic evangelists that most literary critics were inconsistent in their use of this system. In Wellhausen's view the greater part of what Mark wrote of Jesus' doctrine was really the doctrine of Mark himself, most particularly the eschatological and christological statements. To him the historical gospel of Jesus was 'unmessianic' and 'uneschatological'. Most of his professional colleagues were in agreement with his rejection of the eschatological, but that Jesus' messianic claims should fall to the historian was too much for the representatives of the liberal quest for the historical Jesus. However it was

[6] Also the events of the day have a direct bearing upon the origin of a text, e.g. in Deuteronomy, for 'in all circles where appreciation of scientific results can be looked for at all, it is recognised that it was composed in the same age as that in which it was discovered, and that it was made the rule of Josiah's reformation.' J. Wellhausen, *Prolegomena zur Geschichte Israels,* [6]1927, E.T. *Prolegomena to the History of Ancient Israel* (1885) reprinted 1957, p. 9. (London, Mayflower Books; New York, Meridian Books)

[7] [1]1894, [8]1958.

generally allowed that everything which was not the result of the tendency of the evangelist must have come directly from the apostle or from Jesus.

The methods used in literary criticism and the *direct transition* it made *from the study of literary sources to the study of the passage of history* was so clearly and convincingly developed, and was so substantiated by the abundance of material, that it seems that only dogmatic prejudice could protest. The desire for accuracy in the biblical scholarship of this period is comparable with that of classical physics, which about this time was also at the height of its prestige. It is understandable that there are still Old and New Testament scholars who hold that literary-critical methods are the only truly valid and objective ones.[8]

C. *A Wider Range through Form Criticism*

The exponents of literary criticism did not lack confidence in their method; but what if many of its supposedly objective assumptions should turn out to be not so objective after all, but too modern in conception? One of Gunkel's most important insights, which his friends and students adopted from him,[9] was that the idea of literary originality, which has such importance today and which is one of the primary considerations in modern literary criticism, is quite foreign to the Old and New Testament writings. The creative personality was of far less importance at that time. So it can be objected that literary criticism is 'too exclusively concerned with great personalities', and, 'misled by lack of knowledge, sets them up too much as originals, without due consideration of the historical link with the

---

[8] But it was and still is accepted that progressive literary-critical methods lead to an increasing atomisation of the material. Again and again new anomalies and new breaks in the continuity were disclosed and demanded yet further dissection. More and more half and quarter verses were divided up and apportioned to different sources and redactors. In Jos. v, for instance, an eminent representative of literary criticism, H. Holzinger (KHCAT), attributed verses 4–8 to no less than five different writers, with only verse 8 belonging to a real source. Of the remaining verses he says, 'It seems most natural that v.5Rje, v. 6aJEs . . . v. 6bDs, v. 4, 7 are the work of a glossator of the P school'. (The letters denote modifications to the text at different periods.) Breaking down a text so minutely lays literary criticism open to the suspicion of hair-splitting.

[9] Gunkel's circle consisted for the most part of those working with him on the exegetical work *Die Schriften des AT in Auswahl übersetzt und für die Gegenwart erklärt* (Selected biblical writings analysed and interpreted for the modern reader), and the monograph series *Forschungen zur Religion und Literatur des A und NT*, and the RGG[1]. First among the OT scholars was Hugo Gressmann, resourceful and knowledgeable if a little uncritical, then Willy Staerk, Paul Volz, Hans Schmidt and Max Haller. To the second generation belonged Sigmund Mowinckel, a spirit kindred to Gunkel, and also Joachim Begrich, Kurt Galling, Emil Balla, Walter Baumgartner, Otto Eissfeldt, Johannes Hempel, Friedrich Horst, Curt Kuhl, and Christian Johannes Lindblom. In the N.T. field only Wilhelm Bousset supported form-critical theories to begin with, and then only in connection with the Apocalypse (he was uncertain about their application to the Gospels). The breakthrough came only with the second generation, in particular through Martin Dibelius and Rudolf Bultmann; also worth naming are Martin Albertz, Georg Bertram, Lyder Brun, Paul Fiebig, Ernst Lohmeyer, Karl Ludwig Schmidt and Julius Schniewind, while in England, Robert Henry Lightfoot showed the way to the understanding of form criticism. After Gunkel's death there was a period of relative inactivity in the field of form criticism. In the O.T. it was restricted almost entirely to the circle around Albrecht Alt, to which Gerhard von Rad and Martin Noth belonged, both of whom have done much to elucidate the fundamental problems. There was also stagnation in the field of the N.T. But after the second World War form-critical work suddenly flourished. To name all those involved, in Germany and in Scandinavia, and to some extent also in America, would be impossible.

past and their involvement in contemporary surroundings'.[10] The historical books of the Old and New Testaments are not the original work of 'authors' but are a compilation of a large number of traditions which have a long process of evolution behind them. Without analysing this adopted material, it is quite impossible to attain a just understanding of, say, the gospels. The origins of the material and its structure in oral form are therefore by no means 'methodologically irrelevant', despite the assertion to the contrary of the scholarship of that period. 'If the significance of a personality is to be correctly estimated, it must first be discovered to what extent his thoughts are bound up with those of past generations and with his surroundings.'[11] It is not enough to assume that a biblical writer hands over his work directly to the next writer as a basis for stimulation, and for recasting. It is more the case that the biblical writers are all part of a highly complicated movement of religious thought and language, in which it is by no means the written word which is the most important. To follow this up it is necessary to consider the productivity of anonymous groups, of religious communities, and of folk-lore. One of the first discoveries of this kind was that as a rule only short traditions were transmitted *orally*. Therefore the framework of a piece such as one of the Gospels, or the Tetrateuch, must be the work of the writer, but individual passages with a meaning in themselves are part of the oral tradition. The determination of the older, smaller units which these books contain became the starting point of the form-critical method.

Although these considerations could still be brought within the established method of distinguishing sources, a further consideration arose which compelled the literary critics to question some of their own assumptions: did the writers derive all their material from a single tradition? This is scarcely possible in view of the very apparent variety of literary types in the biblical writings. There was reason to think that the writers of the historical books appropriated traditions from many people and places and then linked them together in writing. But where pieces of a different nature and origin were linked, it was very possible that barely sealed gaps in the continuity of story should be apparent, and that duplications and contradictions would occur. A firmly logical construction, which we expect from a modern novel or an academic treatise today, was therefore impossible. By no means every break in the continuity of the story justifies a separate attempt to determine its source; the faults in the coherence of the work are often merely an indication that different types of tradition have come together when still at the oral stage. Duplications are intentional in oral transmission: they impress certain points more firmly upon the memory.

A further point in Gunkel's programme was to make a comparison between the vast quantity of *Ancient Oriental and Hellenistic material* and the biblical texts. This had only become possible after the history of literary types and transmission history of the texts had been considered.

---

[10] Gressmann, *A. Eichhorn*, p. 38. Schniewind, ThR N.S. 2, p. 152 maintains 'that even Papias' and Justin's views of the Gospels are tarnished by an analogical misunderstanding'.
[11] Gressmann, *ibid.* pp. 32 f.

It was no mere coincidence that Gunkel was a leading member of the school which advocated the study of religions in their historical context. Literary criticism was almost helpless in face of the growing number of non-Israelite texts which were being brought to light by archeological excavations, and was utterly helpless when these were played off by opposing circles against theology, as happened in the so-called Bible-Babel controversy. A methodologically reliable way of comparing biblical texts with Ancient Oriental and Hellenistic texts was only developed under the auspices of form criticism.[12] Many previously obscure issues could now be cleared up, thus distinguishing Israel's exceptional destiny against the background of neighbouring cultures, and also the unique quality of Jesus' person. At the same time these documents, often centuries older than those in the Bible, proved what a long period of existence many Old and New Testament traditions had behind them before they were taken up into the sources. All this meant that the commentator had to change his attitude to the text completely. He must also now attend to its setting in life, and must continually consider sociological factors. The flat division into sources and redaction was more and more superseded by the three-dimensional concept of a long history of language.

D. *A Change in the Concept of History*

The picture of (*a*) a *literary history* was rapidly becoming complicated. The exegete could no longer base his work on the idea of a closed chain, where one writing automatically follows the preceding one without pause. Today he has to reckon on a crowd of oral (or even written?) traditions between, say, Mark's Gospel and Q and St Matthew's Gospel, which bring with them the concepts and conditions of a quite other circle of people. It is therefore not enough to deduct the tendency of the later writers (i.e. what is considered to be the result of their own interests, or their 'bias') to find the original wording. This is what happens if we try to get back directly from Mark or from Q to the teaching of Jesus himself. If I remove the tendencies of the two, I only arrive at the Palestinian or Hellenistic early Christian community and their oral traditions of Jesus, and by no means at the original teaching of Jesus.

It was also suddenly discovered that (*b*) the *religious history* of Israel and early Christianity was far more complicated than had been thought. It could no longer be seen in terms of the two fixed points, source and redaction. To the literary critic early Israel's religion was a primitive one which then developed quickly and quite independently. However, form critics recognise that, 'In reality even in the earliest times it (the religion) was the product of a history; it had taken over determinative motifs from the Canaanite religion; thus even at the earliest period of which we have knowledge it was already a complicated phenomenon.'[13] The earlier view of biblical religious history therefore proves to have been much too naive: 'When it had been determined when and by whom an idea cropped up for the first time, it was usual to conclude mistakenly that this idea arose first then, and from just that writer in whose work it was first discovered. It very seldom occurred to the investigator that a concept or a topic could also have a prehistory, with the result that conclusions were reached which seem very strange to us now: Zephaniah first conceived the notion of a world catastrophe, Amos evolved the

---

[12] It began with Gunkel's *Schöpfung*, 1895.
[13] Gunkel, *Schöpfung*, p. 157.

predicate 'Jahweh Sabaoth', and Zechariah invented the devil. It was no better in the New Testament field: the kingdom of God was an idea obviously devised by Jesus, the quest for union with God was a sign of specifically Paulinist mysticism, and the opposites of truth and falsehood, light and dark originated in John.[14] But there is now a new principle for the study of historical writing; 'The idea that a religious concept does not date from the time of its codification is now becoming established in the field of the Old Testament, and must also be applied to the history of early Christianity.'[15] The customary simple evolutionary system was shattered, for it allowed Israel to succeed to the heights of monotheism from primitive fetishistic beginnings in not much more than a thousand years.[16] But it does not only happen that innumerable biblical passages suddenly appear much older to the form critic than was assumed by the literary critic, because a study of the transmission history pushes the date of origin right back to the original history. Just as often it happens the other way round. For in passages describing (c) *historical events* the true literary critic could find no way of deducting the tendency of the writer, and therefore took for genuine historical facts all that remained after the removal of improbable and incredible aspects of the story. But the form-critical approach is first to study the history of the literary type and of the individual passage and to compare these with the setting in life, so that all that had been added in the course of oral transmission could be ascertained. This process proves many details in a story to be much more recent than was previously assumed. Much that the strict literary critic had taken for the reporting of actual events turns out to be merely interpretative. Thus the accepted chronological framework of the Tetrateuch (or the Hexateuch) as well as that provided by the evangelists, proves to be only the 'theological' calendar of later generations.[17] In analysing the historicity of a story of, say, Moses, there is very often found to be little left. This critical view of the course of oral traditions has led to a revolutionary transformation in the general concept of history, particularly with the Jesus narratives, and has in fact brought about the end of the quest of the historical Jesus, which flourished in the nineteenth century. For not only is there a sudden mass of the different stages in the development of a tradition, usually difficult to date, crowding in on the historical picture instead of the few relatively easily dateable sources; as well as this congestion in the vertical, there is also an accumulation in the horizontal, for instead of moving in a purely literary realm a quantity of settings in life suddenly crop up, all of which must be considered. Behind the transmission of biblical material there lie previously unsuspected spheres of life, such as cultic festivals of ancient Israel, and the worship of the early Christians, the administration of the law, and the use of folk-lore. These are realms of which we have no direct information, but which can only be inferred by indications in the text, which in their turn shed light on other aspects of the text. The smooth course of Wellhausen's study of history is suddenly strewn with obstacles which the historian must first laboriously tackle before he is able to get down to an actual commentary. It is not surprising that the first generation of form critics did not succeed in producing any general overall scheme, either of literary, political or religious history.

Anyone who grew up in the strict school of literary criticism, whose ideal

---

[14] Gressmann: *A. Eichhorn* p. 31.

[15] Dibelius 1919, quoted by Kümmel p. 334.

[16] Wellhausen based his assumptions on the naive idea of a 'popular belief' which was common to both the Israelites and (sic!) the 'Gentiles'. *Skizzen und Vorarbeiten* 6, 1899, pp. 232 f.

[17] Von Rad remarks of the literary critical school: 'Although previously the legendary character of many of the individual traditions was fully recognised, it was still believed that the great framework (the period of the patriarchs—the oppression in Egypt—the Exodus—the Revelation at Sinai—the Wandering in the Wilderness—the Conquest) yielded a fairly reliable indication of the course of the history', von Rad: *Theology* I, p. 5.

is that of positivist objectivity, and who is accustomed to have these methods at his fingertips as a surgeon his operating knife, will shrink back in horror at these conclusions. The literary-critical school were so certain of their methods that they regarded Gunkel and his friends with the utmost scorn. When Wellhausen read Gunkel's first work on transmission history, *Schöpfung und Chaos in Urzeit und Endzeit*, his impression was 'that all one can do is protest'.[18] The second great name in Old Testament literary criticism, B. Duhm, countered: 'The idea that it is more critical and historical to explain world-shattering ideas in terms of a half unconsciously ensuing accumulation of views and reflections, that greatness is not the achievement of great men, but is to be thought contrived by the nameless mass or through the effervescence of the material itself, is one that has arisen from the envy of the lowest elements of the intellectual world'.[19] The New Testament scholar B. Weiss did what he could to keep Gunkel away from Berlin University so that his audacious theories could not confuse the students. But this formal rejection was far less embittering for Gunkel than the fact that most exegetes tacitly ignored his ideas.[20] At most, a complaint against his lack of objectivity was once raised.[21] Doubtless the view of Old and New Testament literature, and also that of Israelite and early Christian history, was more straightforward in the age of pure literary criticism than it is today, when form-critical concepts have slowly won acceptance. This is not because of any diffuseness in form-critical theories, but because of the complex character of historical reality.

E. *The Discovery of the Kerygmatic Nature of Certain Writings*

Form critics consider many Old and New Testament narratives to be of an interpretative character, and are wary about the historicity of what has been written about Moses, and even about Jesus. Much of the reason for this is the recognition that such narratives and narrative complexes have long been of a *kerygmatic* nature. Kerygma means the announcement of a divine action exhorting the hearer to faith. This kerygmatic quality was first recognised in the gospels. 'The first understanding afforded by the standpoint of Formgeschichte is that there never was a "purely" historical witness to Jesus. Whatever was told of Jesus' words and deeds was always a testimony of faith as formulated for preaching and exhortation in order to convert unbelievers and confirm the faithful.'[22]

It was later discovered that the Old Testament historical writings also possess a kerygmatic quality. Von Rad has shown that the Jahwist and the

---

[18] He later moderated his judgment (*Skizzen und Vorarbeiten* 6, 1899, pp. 225 f.).
[19] *Jesaja*[2] (HKAT), p. 99 on xiv. 26.
[20] GuB 21.
[21] 'A concept of history from a literary-critical point of view, interested only in a particular phenomenon at the point at which it became literature, could bring forth the criticism that it is too slavishly devoted to the literary tradition and does not take into account the fact that this is very much subject to chance. But in its defence it must be admitted that it is able to apply a very high degree of objectivity. But the more a view based on tradition-historical (*stoffkritisch*, see note 1, chapter 4) considerations hopes to reject the results of literary criticism the more it loses sight of objectivity.' O. Eissfeldt, Preussische Monatshefte 23, 1919, p. 175, Kleine Schriften I, 1962, p. 35. I quote this passage as it is symptomatic of the opinions prevailing at that time. Eissfeldt presumably holds different views today. Against this the tradition-historical point of view: 'There are people who really believe that the oldest recognisable tradition must be identified with the actual historical event.' (Eichhorn, quoted in Kümmel 320).
[22] Dibelius, *From Tradition to Gospel*, p. 295.

Elohist follow the scheme of an ancient creed with its roots in the cult, and have no intention but to interpret this as vividly as possible (cf. also section 12 below). Accordingly therefore the biblical traditions were formed by faith and confession, and are very far from being 'objective' presentations in the modern historical sense. We are deluded if we suppose that this complex of amassed tradition can simply be by-passed and the historical 'facts' freely discovered. The exegete or historian must first subject himself to the process of real understanding, and to a certain extent must identify himself with the Israelite or early Christian faith and confession before he can deduce any possible facts.[23]

F. *The Abiding Significance of Literary Criticism*

Is literary criticism exhausted, now that the need for form criticism has been proved? Only a few radical outsiders have drawn this conclusion. With some biblical writings, such as the books of the Kings, the work of the Chroniclers or St Luke's Gospel, it is still necessary to distinguish sources, for they refer directly to them.[24] For such convinced form critics as Bultmann or Dibelius the two sources theory in the Synoptic Gospels is the natural assumption, and Gunkel was very anxious not be behind any of Wellhausen's pupils in the accuracy of his literary-critical analyses.[25] And research into the showpiece of the literary-critical school, the Tetrateuch, has been advanced quite considerably by one of the foremost modern advocates of form-criticism, Martin Noth.

But it is true that the scope of literary criticism has contracted considerably since former times. Properly understood, literary criticism can now only be considered as a branch, along with many others, of form criticism. It is that aspect of form criticism which is concerned with the transmission of books, tracing their development right back to their many written sources.[26] This period of written transmission until its final, canonical form is sometimes quite short in comparison with the previous long span of oral tradition. Understood in this way, literary criticism is a part of redaction history, or at least a preliminary stage to it. It should never be forgotten in literary-critical work that the written transmission of a unit has usually been preceded by an oral one. Also, literary-critical work is only conclusive when it is directly linked to other branches of form criticism, to the determination of the literary type and the setting in life, and to the study of the pre-literary tradition history.

In the exegesis of a passage it is usually best for practical reasons to start

[23] The form-critical discovery of the Kerygma had a tremendous influence upon dogmatic theology in Germany after World War I. See RGG III³, 1251–1254.

[24] Mowinckel: *Prophecy*, pp. 20 f.

[25] It is proof of Gunkel's fine critical judgment that he never for one minute sympathised with his friend Eichhorn's indignation against the literary critics; for whereas Eichhorn's influence on Gunkel's theories of the history of religion was strong, on the other hand it was very limited on the latter's views on the form-critical method.

[26] 'Our assessment of literary criticism has already been influenced by what form criticism has shown us. Literary criticism, accurately defined, is the history of traditions.' *Schniewind*, p. 161.

with the present final form, and to work back, on the basis of the literary-critical method, to the first literary form. Only then is it possible to tackle the other aspects of form criticism. These are the lines taken by those commentaries today which approach their subject form-critically.[27] But this, it must be emphasised, is for practical reasons, and by no means implies that literary criticism takes precedence. On the contrary, each tentative literary-critical solution must be checked against the literary type, setting in life and the tradition history, to see whether a knowledge of the oral tradition does not make the literary-critical conclusions superfluous. Though the basic observations of the literary critic are usually correct, often his conclusions are invalidated by the wider, form-critical, picture.[28]

To explain this we can refer once again to the Decalogue. The usual literary-critical conclusion is that Exod. xx. 1 ff. has no relation to the work of the Elohist, and that there are no later indications of it in his work; but this argument will not hold water as soon as it is known that the Tetrateuch sources link together a great variety of previously independent traditions. On the other hand it is disquieting to see how many commentators, in the name of form criticism, pass over what literary criticism has incontestably shown to be Deuteronomistic influence in Exod. xx, and cheerfully assert Elohistic influence. Would it not be difficult to show, on purely literary-critical grounds, that there is evidence of Deuteronomistic influence also at other places in the Elohist material? Surely it would then be possible to indicate the period to which other Deuteronomistic elements in the Tetrateuch can be assigned, and the interests which motivated their inclusion.[29] An important example such as this shows that literary criticism still has an essential part to play. But it is also not possible to allow literary criticism to maintain that, for instance, the Elohist was the author of the Decalogue. A religious document of this kind would not have been 'composed' in ancient Israel by any one man.[30]

7. THE DEBATE ABOUT ORAL TRANSMISSION

Oral transmission is given precedence over written transmission in the formation of the OT by H. Birkeland: Zum hebräischen Traditionswesen, ANVO 1938: 1, and I. Engnell: Methodological Aspects of OT Study, VTS VII, 1960, 13–30; by the same author: Gamla Testamentet, en traditionshistorik inledning 1, 1945; and also by E. Nielsen: *Oral Tradition*, Studies in Biblical Theology (London: S.C.M. Press, 1954).

Critical of this point of view are R. P. J. v.d. Ploeg: Le rôle de la tradition orale dans la transmission du texte de l'AT. RB LIV, 1947, 5–41; G. Widengren: Literary and Psychological Aspects of the

---

[27] This was so even in Gunkel's early commentary on Genesis. Today particularly in the Biblische Kommentar series (Neukirchen).

[28] 'The modern tendency in literary criticism must not be allowed to predominate. We must make an end to this sort of dissection of every bit of the text, and the dismemberment of sources. It is more important to gain a better knowledge of what binds the material *together*, before actual criticism can begin' (Bousset, *Der Antichrist*, 1895, p. 5).

[29] According to Noth, ÜGP 32, note 106, the Deuteronomistic passages are 'chiefly connected to J elements', and not to E.

[30] But G. Fohrer, *Kerygma und Dogma* II, 1965, p. 66, thinks otherwise: 'We must then assume that it was E who put together the Exod. xx Decalogue, just as J had done that of Exod. xxxiv.'

Hebrew Prophets, UUÅ, 1948: 10; the same author: Oral Tradition and Written Literature among the Hebrews in the Light of Arabic Evidence, with Special Regard to Prose Narratives, AcOr (H) XXIII, 1959, 201–62. A. H. J. Gunneweg: Mündliche und schrift-liche Tradition der vorexilischen Prophetenbücher als Problem der neueren Prophetenforschung, FRLANT 73, 1959.

Occupying a middle position are S. Mowinckel: Prophecy and Tradition, ANVAO 1946: 3; H. Ringgren: Oral and Written Trans-mission in the OT, StTh III, 1950/1, 34–59; R. C. Culley: An Approach to the Problem of Oral Tradition, VT XIII, 1963, 113–25.

The importance of oral tradition in the formation of the NT was first demonstrated by H. Riesenfeld: *The Gospel Tradition and its Beginnings* (Oxford, Mowbray, 1957), and then later more compre-hensively by B. Gerhardsson: Memory and Manuscript, Acta Seminarii Neotestamentici Upsaliensis XXII, 1961, and: Tradition and Transmission in Early Christianity, Coniectanea Neotesta-mentica XX, 1964. Uncommitted: W. D. Davies: Reflections on a Scandinavian Approach to 'The Gospel Tradition', in *Neotesta-mentica et Patristica*, Festschrift for O. Cullmann 1962, 14–34; critical *ibid.* A. N. Wilder, 3–13, and M. Smith, JBL 82, 1963, 169–76.

Gunkel himself recognised that 'nearly all Old Testament literary types were not originally written but spoken'.[1] He was the first to conclude from this that an exegesis should not only be concerned with the written stages of the text, but also with their oral pre-history. His great Genesis commentary (HKAT) sets us a brilliant example of what can be deduced about the early oral stages from the written word. But it is only rarely that Gunkel differentiates at all sharply between the oral and written traditions or the written literary types and those of speech[2]; he hardly ever makes a special study of it. Quite early on in New Testament form criticism Schniewind attempted to differentiate between the use of sources in the Synoptics as against the use of the particular kind of oral tradition which had circulated earlier.[3]

Oral types are usually termed *pre-literary* by exegetes. But this term, whether recognised or not, reflects a certain judgment on their value. The con-viction appears to be that, whatever has become literature has achieved so to say a higher 'manner of being' ('*Seinsweise*') than has the material which circulates orally. The definition pre-literary is therefore not only understood in chronological terms as the stages of oral transmission which precede the written texts, but also 'in a sub-literary sense': material 'from the sub-stratum of popular life and cultic activity' moves for ever upwards 'into the literary sphere',[4] as if it is the highest achievement of any thought to be written down. But why should not the spoken word exist in its own right on a level with and not merely as a preliminary to the spoken word? The earlier literary types in the Hebrew language and those used by the New Testament evangelists are nearly all pre-literary, as far as we know. We can only gain some knowledge of those earlier oral traditions from the text before us; but though for reasons of method we have to begin with the written word, it should not happen as a matter of principle. Perhaps it is advisable to avoid the term pre-literary wherever possible.

[1] RuA 33.
[2] 'Speech' (*Rede*) is used here comprehensively, to include not only public speech before a particular group of people but also informal everyday speech.
[3] ThR 1930, 141 ff.
[4] Eissfeldt, *Introduction*, p. 9 (italics by the present author).

A. *The Tradition History School*

The slight estimation in which the oral transmission of tradition is at present often held has resulted in a controversy in biblical scholarship about the status of literary types and units which are transmitted in this way. The controversy was not stirred up by form-critical considerations, but rather by ones of textual criticism. In his *Studien zum Hoseabuch*[5] the Swedish Semitist, H. S. Nyberg, tried to prove the absolute reliability of the Masoretic text, and to reject quite categorically all previous textual criticism. His assumption was that in pre-Masoretic times the Old Testament was chiefly orally transmitted, and that even after it had been written down (to him the written Old Testament is a creation of post-exilic Jewry, p. 8) it still circulated orally. But it is no longer possible to make out a history of the oral transmission, though it can be assumed with certainty that under Ancient Oriental conditions it was subject to much less change than was the written transmission which followed.

The flag unfurled by Nyberg for an assault on current opinion was hoisted higher by Birkeland,[6] who compares the Arabic-Mohammedan practices of transmission with those which prevailed in Israel. Even today no learned Muslim deigns to turn up a passage in his Koran: he knows it all by heart. In the medieval controversy over different methods of reading in the Koran and Hadiths (legendary traditions from the early Islamic period) what was known by heart by the learned men was considered conclusive. The following admonition by an Arab historian of the thirteenth century is indicative of the mistrust of the written word at that time[7]:

> 'My friend! Never stop striving zealously (after traditions).
> Do not acquire them from written sources, otherwise you may be struck by the disease of textual corruption.'[8]

Birkeland concluded from this Mohammedan example that there would have been authorised bearers of tradition, or 'tradition groups', also in Israel, whose job it would have been to transmit the authoritative religious traditions from generation to generation. When, and as far as, written copies existed, these were repeatedly verified and perfected from what was known by heart.

His thesis was adopted by the tradition history school, formed in Scandinavia after the second World War (in the main by Engnell in Uppsala; but Norwegians, such as A. Kapelrud, and Danes such as Nielsen, also belong). The conviction that in pre-Masoretic times oral transmission alone was the rule, and that it is pointless to look further into the different stages of oral tradition, means the rejection not only of traditional textual criticism, but also—and this with particular severity—of the literary criticism of the Wellhausen school; and finally—just as much, although it has not been stated in so many words—of the research into the transmission history of biblical units as instituted by Gunkel. For instance, to query

[5] UUÅ 1935, 6.
[6] H. Birkeland, *Zum hebräischen Traditionswesen* ANVO, 1938, 1.
[7] Abu-l-Qasim ibn 'Asakir (Birkeland, p. 11).
[8] Translated from the German.

which words in a book of the prophets go back to Isaiah or Jeremiah them-selves, i.e. the search for what is called the *ipsissima vox*, is a mere fancy. The consequences of this line of approach have also been felt recently in the New Testament field, particularly in connection with the narratives and speeches of the Gospels. Can this theory be correct that oral transmission played a pre-eminent role in Israel and early Christianity, and that there were authoritative groups acting as bearers of these traditions?

The basic structures of Arab culture, which was Birkeland's starting point, were subjected to a thorough examination by Widengren, who arrived at a quite opposite conclusion. Even in Mohammed's time writing was already widely established. Attempts to give oral tradition a higher rank than the written occur first later, and were by no means always conceded. Arab poets admonished their audience to write down their poems forthwith:

> 'A book does not forget or alter words or phrases which have taken the poet a long time to compose.'[9]

The tradition historians have since abstained from making comparisons with Islamic conditions. But the problem has by no means been settled for the Old and New Testaments, as will be shown.

B. *Oral Tradition in Old Testament Texts*

Birkeland and his followers were in fact quite right in pointing out that Orientals, both ancient and modern, have a different capacity for remember-ing from the Western man. Even today in many Mohammedan schools the entire Koran is still learnt by heart. An Old Testament example: the prophet Jeremiah still retained the prophecies of his early days in his memory after twenty years.[10] Also writing played a far smaller part in Israelite culture than is usual in modern civilisations since the invention of printing. Today most of which is written and printed is never spoken. But nearly all the Old Testament, whether the Tetrateuch stories, the psalms, or prophetic speeches, had been passed down orally for a long period before they came to be written down[11]; and they were only written down with the intention of repeating the words aloud at the next occasion, whether to a prophet's group of disciples, or at the Jerusalem Temple (Jer. xxxvi. 6) or later in the synagogue. Regard for oral delivery was incomparably greater than it is now. When a professor holds a lecture today, what he reads is indeed his learned opinion, but he would rather not be held to it as he would to anything he allowed to be printed in his name. Anything 'in black and white' is considered more reliable, and of greater worth. Oral transmission still exists in a restricted form. When a rumour is abroad, the typical question is, 'Have you heard it already?' But such transmission brings with it a hint of inaccuracy, and of suspicion. For the Israelite quite another attitude is to be presumed. The ancients

---

[9] Dhu-l-Rummah (Ummayad period) Widengren 1948, p. 24.

[10] Jer. xxxvi. 4. Though it appears that Jeremiah's follower Baruch did not know the sayings by heart and had to be dictated to again.

[11] The proverbs of Solomon which the men of Hezekiah collected had obviously circulated orally up to that point (Prov. xxv. 1).

7

reckoned on a firmly moulded unchangeable oral tradition. Such passages as Exod. xii. 24–27, xiii. 7 f. 14 f.; Num. xxi. 27; Deut. iv. 9 f., vi. 6 f. 20–25, xi. 19, xxxii. 7; Jos. iv. 7–22, xxii. 24–28; Judges vi. 13; Ps. xliv. 1, lxxviii. 1–5; Isa. xxxviii. 19 show that rigid standards were laid down in the family for the transmission of religious formulas and traditions, for whose accuracy the father of the house was responsible. People used to such a discipline from their youth always take great care in anything they deliver orally, just as children today will demand a story read to them which they already know by heart, and will listen with the utmost attention to hear the familiar words in their appointed places.[12]

The persistence of oral tradition can be emphasised by an example: in Amos iv. 11 the prophet threatens his people with ruin, which would take a similar form to 'when God overthrew Sodom and Gomorrah'. The use of the term God (Elohim) is exceedingly striking here, for at all other points the prophet uses the term Lord (Jahweh). But it is obviously part of the Sodom-Gomorrah tradition as it prevailed in his time, and even the prophet cannot free himself from such usage. Perhaps without noticing it himself, he is bound by the force of oral tradition. Also the word 'overthrew' is a fixed part of that tradition, which is the only reason for its retention in this particular passage (see also Gen. xix. 21, 25, 29; Deut. xxix. 23).

In view of such information to be discovered in the Old Testament itself, it is easy to see why members of the tradition history school persist in their opinion that only a fraction of the present canon had been written down before the exile, and that also even after it had been written down, right up to the time of Christ, oral transmission persisted alongside the written, and was even decisive in points of controversy.

C. *The Importance of Written Records in the Old Testament*

However, as well as references to the value of oral transmission there are also indications that writing too was considered important. First of all it is an incontestable fact that the Ancient Orient, of which Israel was a part, had known the use of writing since the second millenium and had used it in many spheres of life, as the existence of thousands of inscriptions and clay tablets prove. There are less references to oral transmission in Egypt or Mesopotamia than in the Old Testament.[13] Also pre-Israelite Palestine was remarkable for a particularly wide use of writing, which can be seen from the diplomatic correspondence between the small Palestinian princes and Pharaoh, which are in the archives of El-Amarna and the numerous clay tablets of political, religious or commercial import which were recovered from the excavations at Ugarit, where a proper school of writing was discovered near the temple. And the name of the Canaanite town Kiriath-sepher, 'book town', speaks for itself. It was not only the language native

---

[12] A similar attitude by adults to the oral narration of fairy-tales and jokes was observed only a few decades ago in a remote corner of Germany (Westeifel).

[13] The few examples of oral tradition from Mesopotamia which Nielsen produces are insufficient to prove the point. *Learning* a written text *by heart*, with which these writings are mostly concerned, is not necessarily the same as oral transmission. This technique is still much used in school-teaching.

to the area which was written down, but there also appear to have been written exchanges between nations. 'In each of the small domains in the land of Palestine . . . the king had at least one official who was able to read and write Babylonian.'[14]

There is a radical change in the manner of writing and the materials used between the second millenium, to which Ugarit and El-Amarna belong, and the first, i.e. Israel. The use of clay tablets and cuneiform writing, or hieroglyphics, which were laborious to acquire and complicated to apply, was superseded by the use of the easily acquired alphabet writing on papyrus or ostrakon. Thus it was possible for a wide measure of the populace to use it. That Israel did so is shown by the ostraka from Samaria, and the letters from Lachish,[15] which were written by civil or military officials. This difference speaks for a greater, rather than a lesser, significance of the written tradition in the Israelite period, although the literary inheritance of the (pre-Israelite) second millenium is much better preserved because of the comparative permanence of the material which was used to write on.[16]

Hence it is not surprising that there is direct evidence that certain individual passages of the Old Testament were written down. Series of commandments, such as the Decalogue, were either written down or engraved in stone (Exod. xxiv. 4, xxxii. 15; Jos. xxiv. 26; Isa. x. 1; Jer. viii. 8; Hos. viii. 12), and at least since Deuteronomy, i.e. since the seventh century, there have been books of the law (Deut. xvii. 18, xxxi. 24; Jos. viii. 31 f.).[17] There are also written documents of legal transactions (Deut. xxiv. 1; I Sam. x. 25; Jer. xxxii. 10, cf. Judges viii. 14), as well as a cultic catalogue of curses (Num. v. 23). Important historical events were inscribed (Exod. xvii. 14), or were recorded in ancient works such as the Book of the Wars of the Lord (Num. xxi. 14), or the Book of the Upright (Jos. x. 13), which have unfortunately been lost. After the time of Isaiah prophets wrote down short oracles, to give them more widespread effect (Isa. viii. 1 f., xxx. 7 f.; Jer. li. 60; Hab. ii. 2). Soon afterwards we hear of a great prophetic book which, though in Jeremiah xxxvi (and xxx. 2) owes its existence to particular circumstances, is referred to in Ezek. ii. 9 f. as a familiar literary type (cf. Ezek. xliii. 11 f.). Naturally enough there were annals of the northern Israelite and Judean courts, and wisdom sayings were written down in the Egyptian fashion. On important occasions letters were sent (II Sam. xi. 14 ff.; I Kings xxi. 8 ff.; II Kings x. 1 f.). Later more ambitious chronicles arose, such as the Books of the Days of the Kings, which the books of the Kings refer to several times in what appears to be an established quotation formula (I Kings xi. 41, xiv. 19, etc.). Thus in certain spheres of life a great desire was felt to express things in writing.

[14] Hempel: *Literatur* p. 12. In the old kingdom in Egypt there were already priests in the cult whose special duty was to read aloud. They stepped forward with a roll of papyrus. [15] ANET 321. f

[16] Engnell's argument, that despite intensive archeological exploration of Palestine, as good as no texts have been found compared with those discovered of other oriental cultures, is not therefore enough to prove that oral transmission alone was effective (*The Call of Isaiah* UUÅ, 1949, 4).

[17] And not only textual but also archeological evidence: in Qumran many fragments from Genesis to Deuteronomy were found in pre-exilic script.

At least in pre-exilic times one of the chief reasons for writing something down was that the written word was considered to be endowed with a particular power. Although letters were not considered to have quite the magical effect of the old pyramid writings, where it was thought possible for a particularly dangerous hieroglyphic, such as that depicting a snake, to harm the reader, yet in Israel also the writing down of a text was also considered to have some consequence. If a divine judgment, or an oracle, were put into writing, it was endowed with additional power (Num. v. 11 ff.; Isa. viii. 1; xxx. 8 f.). This is also evident in Jeremiah xxxvi: King Jehoiakim destroys the roll containing the prophetic words of disaster in an attempt to check, if not destroy, their effect. But Jeremiah re-writes the roll so that the power of the word is restored.

D. *The Relation between Oral and Written Transmission in the Old Testament*

In face of such contradictory intelligence, how was it that the biblical writings came into existence, and were transmitted from generation to generation? Obviously there can be no straightforward answer. Oral and written transmission existed alongside each other and intermingled right from the earliest times. 'The Israelite literature . . . grew out of two elements: from the living tradition of the invaders, of which at least the greater part was oral, and the Canaanite literature in which the Israelites became to a certain extent involved.'[18] It is in keeping with the special character of Israel that, even after the Israelites had established themselves in Canaan, both the oral and written methods of transmission existed side by side for quite some time. What was decisive was the literary type and its situation in life. Certain groups of divine commandments were written down very early and preserved at the sanctuaries. Perhaps the 'sacred narratives' in the Temple which were used on cultic occasions had also been written down[19]; but of all literature liturgical material is the most likely to have been delivered from memory (Deut. xxxi. 28). This by no means precludes the possibility that written transmission had been customary for some time, for learning by heart is not the same as oral transmission.[20] Writing will certainly have been more widely used in court circles. Anything which originated there is likely to have been written down. Collections of prophetic sayings were also written down, at least since Jeremiah. About the same time narratives about the lives of the prophets began to be put into writing, although this did not happen to all stories of this kind.[21] But popular

[18] Hempel, *Literatur* 11.

[19] A. H. J. Gunneweg, *Mündliche und schriftliche Tradition der vorexilischen Profetenbücher als Problem der neueren Profetenforschung*, FRLANT 73, 1959, takes this idea too far when he assumes that all Israelite traditions from the sanctuaries were written. To prove conclusively that even before the conquest collections of legal texts and reports on the most important events were in writing (p. 28) would only be possible through a study of the transmission history.

[20] Widengren, 1959, p. 214.

[21] When Jeremiah (xxvi. 18) had to answer for his prophecy of disaster before a gathering of the people, the elders not only quote a prophetic saying by the prophet Micah, which is actually to be found in the book of Micah (iii. 12), but they also know of accompanying circumstances which are not reported, despite the fact that

stories, such as those in the early books of the Old Testament, from Genesis to Samuel, were written down relatively late,[22] and even when this had been done the living oral tradition by no means came to an end. The same will have happened to the psalms. Cultic regulations, such as on sacrifice, or similar matters, seem to have circulated only orally up till the time of the Priestly writings, i.e. at least into the sixth century. Many literary types, such as legal and prophetic texts, were circulated both orally and in writing. Thus it can be seen that the findings turn out to be extraordinarily complex, at least until the time of the Babylonian exile. For each kind of literature the method and period of transmission must be determined anew, indeed for each literary unit. Moreover, the manner of oral tradition itself can vary very much according to the literary type and setting in life. All 'oral literature' (Culley), particularly poetry, is transmitted with great care, and with little modification, by means of a fixed group of persons. But it is quite the opposite with sagas and proverbs created by the people themselves, who cheerfully modify them over and over again.

The period of exile in the mid-sixth century drove a deep cleft in the literary history of Israel. In the post-exilic period most of the religious traditions were naturally in written form. Before the exile this applied only in part, as has been shown. Therefore it is a matter of great interest that other texts managed to survive the exile. How was this? When the Judean state was destroyed in 587, to what extent was the literature destroyed with it? Did conditions differ from place to place? Are most of the pre-exilic writings only preserved because they were known by heart and were written down afresh as soon as the situation allowed? The Deuteronomist, who wrote the books from Joshua to II Kings, probably in Palestine during the period of exile, had some sources at his disposal, but apparently only some.[23] Were the Judeans who were deported to Babylon allowed to take rolls with them, or did they manage with the store of religious traditions which they retained in their memories? How and where the pre-exilic writings remained alive is a vital point in the present discussion.[24] At any

---

the incident occurred a century previously. Here we are probably faced with the oral tradition. The introductory sentences of the book of Jeremiah (i. 1–3) probably composed some little time after the death of the prophet, state that Jeremiah was himself the son of a priest, a fact which is not mentioned elsewhere in the book and which the writer will have picked up from hearsay (similarly Ezek. i. 3).

[22] The evidence supplied by such passages as Ps. lxxviii. 3 should hardly be brushed aside, as Gunkel did: 'In his ceremonial introduction the writer calls upon oral tradition for his knowledge of the past . . .; but in reality the psalmist's knowledge has been derived from the ancient historical reports in the written sources which have also come down to us' (*Psalmen* HKAT, p. 341). But on the other hand it must be asked whether *narratives* were transmitted by means of isolated circles of tradition. 'Where do we find in the O.T. a passage mentioning a circle of traditionists faithfully preserving by means of oral traditions some prose narratives of the character found in the pentateuch?' Widengren, 1958, p. 229.

[23] The Deuteronomistic writings often describe a prophet coming forward to deliver what he has to say; therefore these traditions were known, but never (as in the reports on kings) is there mention of a source. Therefore it appears that the Deuteronomist had no written prophetic texts at his disposal.

[24] Reference to Qumran, where numerous rolls were hidden (Gunneweg, p. 50) is not enough, as the Qumran sects lived in perpetual fear of persecution and their precautionary measures were therefore taken in an entirely different spirit.

rate, as far as we know, there was an intensive and methodical attempt during the exile and also shortly after it to put religious traditions down in writing. This is indicated not only by the Deuteronomistic revisions and the Priestly writings, but also by the compilation of the Pentateuch material, and that of the Psalter, which could well have followed it. This supports Engnell's thesis,[25] which is that the changeover to written transmission is often the result of some crisis in public confidence, and arises in face of the threat that transmission will cease. The same happened with the (original) Deuteronomy, if, as is usually assumed, it was composed and written immediately after the end of the northern kingdom. (And also in Meso-potamia, where there was a great movement to write down the Sumerian language, which was dying out.[26] And in the nineteenth century after Christ there was a similar movement to write down European folk-lore.[27])

E. *Oral and Written Tradition in the Early Christian Environment*

The Hellenistic age, in which the early church began, was an age of tremendous literary production. Nevertheless, in the immediate surround-ings of the early Christian community a fashion for oral transmission also prevailed. This was the work of the Rabbis, the spiritual fathers of the Talmud, by whom oral transmission was methodically cultivated, and regulated more rigidly than had even before been customary. Although the Old Testament sacred writings were constantly copied down there was nevertheless a surprising importance attached to their oral transmission. This is the only way to account for the editing done by the Masorites, whom we have to thank among other things for the vowel signs of the Old Testament texts. As well as retaining the sacred writings in their memories, the Rabbis also retained their interpretation of them, as well as sections which they added to them, such as the Haggadah (narrative material), and the Halakah (legal precepts). The oral Torah, the Mishnah, was trans-mitted with particular care, for it is ordained that this must never be written down at all.[28] A legend associated with the actual founder of the Rabbinic schools tradition, Jochanan ben Zakkai, relates that when he was imprisoned in Vespasian's camp he could always tell the time of day purely by knowing how long it took to recite a particular passage of the Mishnah.[29] Even outside the Rabbinic-Pharisaic circle it was natural for any pious Israelite to learn passages of the Bible by heart. At synagogue services it was usual to recite the Torah from memory, not to read it.[30] Perhaps it should also

---

[25] *Gamla Testamentet*, p. 42

[26] Falkenstein/von Soden = *Sumerische und Akkadische Hymnen und Gebete* 1953, p. 12 f.

[27] 'As the art of oral narrative disappeared in Europe in the nineteenth century the brothers Grimm and their followers rescued the fairy-tale and the saga by writing them into a book. Of course their action accelerated the decay of the oral tradition. But despite this it is still possible to speak of "rescue", for it was inevitable that the old communities narrating these tales, and hence the oral tradition, would perish' (M. Luthi, *Volksmärchen und Volkssaga*, 1961, pp. 7 f.).

[28] The age of this regulation is a point of controversy; it could even be later dogmatic theory.

[29] Midrash Echa I, 31 (in G. Dalman, *Aramäische Dialektproben*, [2]1927, pp. 19 f.).

[30] Mowinckel, *Prophecy*, p. 17.

be asked whether each small community in the Diaspora could financially afford a roll of the Torah, not to speak of the whole Old Testament.

There are also indications of a widespread religious literature outside Pharisaic circles at that time. The small community sect of Qumran, with an estimated two hundred inhabitants, possessed its own scriptorium, and has left us over a thousand hand-written texts (Bible manuscripts, community regulations, and songs). The apocalyptic movement which was so widespread at that period produced a large number[31] of ample works, though most of these have unfortunately been lost; and these cannot be explained except by some zealous writing activity on the part of the wise in Israel. Certainly books such as Daniel and I Enoch, both apocalyptic, were to a great extent fashioned out of oral tradition; but their transmission, both orally and in writing, was of a very different kind to the painstakingly fostered traditions of the Rabbis. Every inspired teacher obviously made his own contribution to the material, and on his own authority changed whatever he felt inclined.[32] How it was with other groups in Israel at the time can only be conjectured. Perhaps the Sadducees only admitted the authority of written traditions alongside the Torah.[33]

F. *Oral Tradition in the New Testament*

Ever since form criticism has been applied to the Gospels it has been clear that great significance was attached to the oral tradition of Jesus' words and deeds. It is well known that the single pieces were transmitted for decades before they were written down. It can even be questioned whether Q circulated in a written form, or whether it was not perhaps an oral collection of sayings.[34] But even if it was written, oral traditions would have existed with the same authority. But what was the setting in life of these oral traditions, and how strictly was the wording preserved? Dibelius maintains that the sermon, with its two-fold activity as mission and community sermon, was the setting of most of the Jesus traditions, and therefore the charismatic adaptation of tradition was given freer reign right from the start. Bultmann discriminated to a greater extent and saw not only the sermon but also the instruction of followers and the disputes with Jewish antagonists as the setting in life of the synoptic tradition. And of Jesus himself he observed: 'In face of the entire content of the Tradition

---

[31] II Esdras xiv. 44–66 mentions seventy secret books.

[32] Though Gerhardsson, 1961, p. 30 denies that in these groups a 'technique of transmission substantially different from that of the Pharisees was applied', he does add that his conclusion was the result of only 'a superficial check'. But then how can he explain the origin and development of the highly complex apocalyptic writings? His verdict on p. 20, note 1 is just as audacious: 'The thesis put forward by D. Rössler, *Gesetz und Geschichte* (1960), that the Apocalyptic groups had a quite different conception of the Torah than the Pharisaic Rabbis is exaggerated.'

[33] Gerhardsson, 1961, p. 24.

[34] And from that point it is even easier to think that the differences between the two series of blessings in Matt. v and Luke vi are not the result of the different concepts of the two writers, but in part because the two Evangelists know different versions of Q. But it is just possible that the Matthew Evangelist knew an *orally* transmitted (liturgical?) series of blessings as well as Q; for the six (or seven) sentences which Matthew inserted from another source (see above p. 41) are so brief and easy to remember that they are well suited to oral transmission.

it can hardly be doubted that Jesus did teach as Rabbi, gather disciples, and engage in disputations.'[35] But he does not discuss the consequences of this teaching activity on Jesus' part, or whether in some circumstances it was continued by his followers. Both Bultmann and Dibelius make no reference to the theory that there were special bearers of tradition. They speak more generally of the theology of the community, by which the Jesus traditions were handed down from generation to generation.

This generalisation has brought forward protest in recent years, particularly from Swedish scholars. Next to the sermon, which was by no means as unfettered and as Protestant as Dibelius supposed,[36] there were other and at least as important tokens of community life, such as prayer, sacred meals, exorcism, church order: all aspects of life which cannot be overlooked in any exegesis. But the most important aspects of all was the traditional method of teaching. From the reference to Jesus as teacher, *didaskalos*, and his activity as teacher, *didaskein*, Riesenfeld and Gerhardsson have concluded that a strong chain of tradition was passed on by Jesus to the Twelve as 'teaching authorities',[37] on the lines of the Rabbinic schools. Later Paul joined the Twelve, and then the tradition passed on to the early fathers of the church, where Irenaeus attached much importance to the fact that he had received his schooling orally from Papias, who himself had been the student of an apostle. The established expressions for receiving the tradition, *paralambanein*, and for the transmission of it, *paradidonai*, which are used in the letters of Paul (I Cor. xi. 23 ff., xv. 1 ff.) to introduce the kerygmatic formulas, go back to this teaching of the apostles, which was carefully fostered in Jerusalem. Occasional references in later New Testament writings to Jesus and his disciples as untaught men (John vii. 15; Acts iv.13) appear to be a later dogmatic invention.[38] If the Rabbinic pattern was followed and there were recognised bearers of tradition, it is to be assumed that the wording of the sayings and stories was meticulously preserved. Charismatic revision, on which Dibelius and Bultmann base their ideas, would then have played a far lesser role. From this view of things the entire Synoptic material is probably to be traced back to Jesus himself, including the descriptions of his own work.

What is there to say about this theory put forward by the tradition history school? It is certainly right in regarding the idea of a 'community theology' (*Gemeindetheologie*) as weak and too general. In fact it seems that there must have been some sort of tradition of teaching after Jesus.[39] The *paradosis* conception of the early Christian community needs some explanation. But there are two problems which are all too quickly overlooked by tradition historians. Firstly, is it right to consider the whole of the Synoptic material to have been subject to such a rigid system of transmission? Surely this theory calls for a particularly careful analysis of the

[35] *Tradition*, p. 50.
[36] The odd scattered reference in the New Testament to the early Christian sermon proves that 'Of anything which recalls the material from which our Gospels were constructed we have, alas! not the least trace' (Riesenfeld, p. 12).
[37] 'The word of God' was entrusted to the Apostles, i.e. interpretation of the Old Testament and transmission of the Jesus traditions, c.f. Acts ii. 42, vi. 2, 4.
[38] 'Distinctly dogmatic', Gerhardsson, 1961, pp. 13 f.
[39] See above paragraph.

differences in literary types and settings in life. The position held by such passages as the Beatitudes and the Lord's Prayer is very easy to determine (although the deviations between the Matthean and Lucan version show how radical such differences can nevertheless be). But with other literary types the conditions are less certain, and to interpret all Synoptic stories of healing in the light of such a fixed method of transmission is extremely hazardous. And secondly, is it really possible that the Rabbinic system of transmission was quite simply taken over by the early Christian community? Is it mere chance that no chain of tradition exists from the early Christians? Surely it is more relevant to compare the apocalyptic style of the transmission of tradition,[40] with its strong charismatic quality.[41] These are questions which form criticism has yet to resolve.

G. *General Exegetical Consequences*

It is a phenomenon of everyday existence that people express themselves differently in writing than in speech. It happens involuntarily. A quick observation of one's own habits will show that other and more deliberate expressions are used in a letter than when talking face to face to a person. It is only natural that these different styles of expression must also be . present in the biblical writings. The points raised by the tradition history school should lead to a completely fresh approach to the differences in style which become evident through a study of the history of the literary type and of the transmission history of an Old or New Testament unit; for these are differences which have arisen out of the different methods of transmission.

First of all the importance of the transition from oral to written transmission must never be forgotten. As a rule the actual process of being written down produces a fundamental change in the previously oral tradition. Usually the single unit is incorporated into a greater whole, and the introduction and conclusion is adapted to fit in with the more complicated process of thought of the greater work. For instance, we have reason to assume that a prophetic saying originally delivered orally was always introduced by the *messenger formula*, 'Thus saith the Lord'. However, the expression is frequently missing in the books of the prophets, because the title of the book rendered it superfluous and the previously independent units made up a continuous line of thought. Here the repeated use of formulas would have been a distraction. When pieces constructed in a form distinctive enough to be learnt by heart came to be written, they were encumbered with prosaic explanations, and thus lost their original form. The unvarying style and the frequent repetition of expressions of the

---

[40] Gerhardsson 1961, himself refers to the great freedom with which the Jesus tradition was quoted by the Apostolic Fathers, p. 198.

[41] We pass over the fundamental question as to how far the Talmudic material about the Rabbinic system of tradition for the period before A.D. 70, i.e. for the period before Jochanan ben Zakkai, is of use. Without the sociological and economic deterioration brought about by the decline of the Israelite state in the two revolts, which ended in 70 and 135 B.C. with the dissolution of the united ethnic federation, it is quite probable that the Rabbinic system would have been a good deal less rigid. Smith, JBL 1963.

oral tradition would have been considered too monotonous and were therefore modified. New, more extensive literary types arose, whose characteristics of form are more obscure than those of the oral tradition.[42] To unearth
the shorter forms of the earlier oral stage of the tradition is very difficult.
It is not always easy to distinguish the bounds of the original unit from
the later written version. This is particularly true of the Synoptic Gospels.

Once the unit has been written down the history of its transmission also
develops along other lines. Between the bearer and the recipient there is now
an 'impersonal material medium', which can be reproduced quite independently of the creator and the original recipient.[43] Here the problem of interpretation arises, because with a written passage there is time for reflection,
which is not the case when the words are merely heard. Also the written
words become outmoded in the course of time, whereas when the material is
transmitted orally the words are constantly adapted to fit in with contemporary linguistic usage. Where in oral transmission changes occur quickly and
easily and quite unintentionally, with the written text even the smallest
addition is the result of conscious reflection. This does not mean that changes
in written texts occur only rarely. On the contrary, as the idea of literary
originality was quite unknown in Israel and in early Christianity, written
texts were revised again and again, and were brought into keeping with the
contemporary attitude. But on the whole a revised written text still retains the
material in its original wording; it is only modified, or arranged differently,
or comment is added. It is thus quite easy to discern the earlier sources
behind the later revisions to some extent or other. In other words, literary
criticism is made possible. However, in oral transmission the extent of change
is considerably greater. Each generation acts as a 'melting pot'; indeed, every
single bearer of the tradition changes it just a little. Moreover, constant selection occurs. Anything which is not understood, or which no longer concerns
the particular circle fostering the tradition, or is perhaps no longer enter-
taining, is excluded and forgotten.[44] (An example of this is that many of the
prophetic proclamations, and still more of the accounts of the lives of the
prophets, have been lost. Only those sayings were retained which turned out
to be right, or those which, perhaps the subject of later reinterpretation,
remained of topical interest). Individual units gradually came together, and
their association became formal through the process of being written down.
These compilations might well prompt the exegete to investigate their
sources. Such grouping took place just as frequently orally, but without
formal links.[45] Hence in the history of the oral tradition the content of the
earlier stages of a biblical unit can be only roughly determined, and it is only
very rarely, and then usually in the case of poetry, that the exact wording can
be determined.[46] Ringgren investigated passages which occurred twice in the

[42] However, this change is denied by tradition historians. The crucial parts of the
Old Testament were 'definitely modelled and fixed already at the oral stage, the
taking down in writing itself meaning nothing absolutely new or revolutionary',
Engnell, *The Call of Isaiah*, p. 57.
[43] Nielsen, p. 34.
[44] Birkeland speaks of a 'socio-historical struggle for existence' and a 'survival of
the fittest' (p. 16). 'Oral literature depends for its existence upon its acceptance.
Unless at least one person is willing to receive and pass on the work, the tradition
will end', Culley, pp. 121 f.
[45] A European example: An English researcher has collected roughly 300 versions
of Cinderella. Many of these turn out to be mixed up with other fairy-tales, such
as Allerleirauh, Snow-White, Rapunzel, etc. Thus oral traditions easily become
linked to each other. van der Leyen, *Das Märchen*, [2]1917, p. 32.
[46] The fact that more far-reaching changes occur in oral transmission is not only
contested by Islamic scholars but also by Engnell and his friends, who consider this
means of transmission to be on the contrary much more reliable. But although

Bible (II Sam. xxii—Ps. xviii; Ps. xiv–liii; Isa. ii. 2–4—Mic. iv. 1–3, etc.) and discovered that although there were a number of simple copy errors in the two previously identical texts, the great number of differences occurred as a result of oral transmission.[47] If Mowinckel is right in asserting [48] that the prose parts of the book of Jeremiah have a longer oral tradition behind them than the poetic parts, then those sections are particularly striking proof of the more radical recasting of tradition conveyed by word of mouth.

But even within the bounds of oral transmission the traditions vary enormously. Psalms and prophetic sayings were much more carefully transmitted than were narratives or love songs, not only because of their poetic form but also because of their sacred quality. In the New Testament the Beatitudes, the Lord's Prayer, and the logia of Jesus as a whole retained a much more fixed form than the descriptions of what Jesus did, or of the apostles' experiences.

To what extent a biblical text is moulded by the oral tradition and to what extent by the written will depend on the literary type and the setting in life. This is something which must be borne in mind in the study of the history of any literary type, or of the history of its transmission.

8. CHARACTERISTICS OF HEBREW POETRY

J. Begrich: Zur Hebräischen Metrik, ThR N.S. 4, 1932, 67–89, and F. Horst: Die Kennzeichen der hebräischen Poesie, ThR N.S. 21, 1953, 97–121, give good surveys of the present position, and comprehensive bibliographies. The most recent full treatment of this subject is by Mowinckel: *The Psalms in Israel's Worship*, II, 159–175, 1962 (Oxford, Blackwell; Nashville, Abingdon Press).

Before we come to the final section of the book it would be as well to touch briefly on a subject which, although not so much a matter of controversy in modern biblical scholarship as is the relative importance of oral and written transmission, is of scarcely less consequence in a study of the Old

---

modern travellers are quoted as having discovered an extraordinary power of memory in the Near East, this does not disprove the fact that even in the Orient oral transmission is more unreliable than written. Nielsen, p. 24, describes a blind Veda student who could quote with accuracy any passage in the printed Vada editions. Nyberg, pp. 57 f., knows of a Parsee priest who could recite the Yasna although (or perhaps because!) he did not understand it. But even weak-memoried Europe can produce instances of such acrobatics; and they are hardly to be considered as the usual vehicles of established traditions. For these it is more likely that the lines of the Arabian poet quoted on p. 81 will apply. An inviolable 'faith in the reliability' of oral transmission (Nielsen, pp. 39 f.) is needed before the standpoint of the tradition historian can be accepted.

[47] The origins of the divergences between the texts can be determined because the sources of the mistakes in oral or written transmission are different. Characteristic of *written* errors are confusion between similar letters, the omission or duplication of the same or similar words. Whereas in *oral* transmission it is the sound of the word which produces the error. Words are replaced by those similar in sound, or an obsolete word is changed, or the position of parts of sentences or verses (though such mistakes can also occur through dictation of the written word and is not absolute proof of oral transmission, Widengren, 1958, p. 213). Additions which occur in oral transmission adapt themselves organically to the context and do not strike the hearer as comment disturbing the flow of the narrative.

[48] *Prophecy* 21.

and New Testament. This is the realm of poetry, which is characterised by an elevated and rhythmical language, and which belongs to quite particular literary types and settings in life.

Ever since the ancient Greeks began to reflect upon what we call literature, the difference between poetry and prose, between a rhythmical composition and common day-to-day talk, has been one of the fundamental aspects of all literary scholarship. Anyone who has looked at the Hebrew Old Testament knows that in Kittel's *Biblia Hebraica* the poetic sections are typographically quite distinct from the rest. The use of different styles of writing, though often inconsistent, can already be seen in the old handwritten versions of the Bible.[1] In the New Testament, however, the poetic passages are more difficult to determine. Nevertheless, in Nestles *Novum Testamentum Graece* the songs in the prelude to St Luke's Gospel and in the Revelation of St John are quite distinct from the descriptive parts. But at other points, such as in the christological hymn in Phil. ii. 5–11, the ordinary reader does not notice the poetic construction. It is difficult to determine the rules of form for any New Testament poetry. This can be explained firstly by the fact that in early Christianity there was no pronounced art of writing as there was at the Jerusalem Court and at the sanctuaries; and secondly, because the New Testament writings are partly translated, so that the structure of the Jesus logia, for example, has been very much obscured.[2] Thirdly, where a New Testament composition was originally composed in Greek, the Semitic and psalmodic style of the Greek translation of the Old Testament (the Septuagint) has been used as the model, so that the laws governing Greek poetry have only been followed to a very limited extent. Hence an understanding of early Christian poetry is only made possible through a knowledge of the laws of Old Testament poetry.

A. *Parallelismus Membrorum*

J. Begrich: Der Satzstil im Fünfer, Zeitschrift für Semitistik 9,1933/4, 169–209. For the closely related Ugaritic poetry see UT I Section 13, 107–170, and C. I. K. Story: The Book of Proverbs and Northwest Semitic Literature, JBL 64, 1945, 321–324.

The most prominent characteristic of European poetry, the rhyme, occurs only rarely in biblical writings (e.g. Jer. i. 5). Thus the fundamental poetic unit is not obliged to consist of at least two lines intended to harmonise with each other. A poem can also consist of a single line comprising a single unit of meaning, divided by a caesura. This is called *long verse*.

In Hebrew verse the stylistic device of alliteration, much loved in

---

[1] As well as the Bible there is the inscription of poetic lines on Aramaic grave stones and clay tablets, B. Meissner, *Die babylonisch-assyrische Literatur*, 1930, pp. 25–27.

[2] The attempt by C. F. Burney, *The Poetry of Our Lord, An Examination of the Formal Elements of Hebrew Poetry in the Discourses of Jesus Christ*, 1925 (London and New York, Oxford University Press) is unsatisfactory in that he dispenses with any transmission-historical analysis. The significance of the problem is not diminished by an inadequate handling of it.

Germanic poetry, is occasionally used. It crops up in parallel bars (feet), as in Prov. xiii. 14:

תּוֹרַת חָכָם מְקוֹר חַיִּים

or the parallelism can be chiastic, i.e. a crosswise arrangement, as in Prov. xiii. 3:

נֹצֵר פִּיו שֹׁמֵר נַפְשׁוֹ

But the primary characteristic of the poetic passages in the Bible, observed by Lowth[3] over two hundred years ago, is *parallelismus membrorum*, i.e. a duplication of the poetic statement, which for a European is highly strange. It has been called a 'thought rhyme'.

1. Its simplest form can be illustrated by Num. xxi. 28:

> For a fire has gone out of Heshbon,
> a flame from the city of Sihon.

The word 'fire' in the first half has the word 'flame' in the second as its parallel, and the name Heshbon is reflected in the city of Sihon. Also the sense of the two half-verses (also known as line, half-line, row, stichos, colon) is the same. The poetic verse (also period, distichon, bicolon) is comprised here of variations on the same thoughts. This simple form is usually called *synonymous parallelism*.[4]

A closer study reveals two sub-species. In the above example only two parts of the sentences are varied, while a third, the verb, appears only once (as well as the verb there is frequently an adverb which applies to both rows: Prov. vi. 21). This is Begrich's 'Form 3' (a–b–c/a'–$c1'c2'$).[5] However, all members can be repeated, i.e. two similarly constructed sentences can make up the verse (a–b–c/a'–b'–b' cf. Ps. xxvii. 5). This is Begrich's 'Form 4'.

2. An ancient form is the *stair-like*, or climactic, tautological, or repetitive *parallelism*, such as in Ps. xxix. 1:

> Give unto the Lord, O ye sons of the mighty,
> Give unto the Lord glory and strength.

Here similar expressions are not juxtaposed, as with double parallel verse members, but two members are repeated word for word, with the line of thought taken further by exchanging the third member (a-b-c/a-b-d). It is seldom found in the Old Testament (Judges v; Exod. xv; Hab. iii; Ps. xxix, lxviii), but very frequently in Ugarit.[6]

---

[3] *Praelectiones de sacra poesi Hebraeorum* 1753. E.T. *Lectures on the Sacred Poetry of the Hebrews*, 1839 (London, T. Tegg).

[4] In the New Testament Matt. x. 16: 'Be ye therefore wise as serpents, and harmless as doves.' In the Psalms there are fixed pairs of words which are frequently used as parallel members. It is the word which is first used which is the decisive one; R. G. Boling, Journal of Semitic Studies V, 1960, 221–55.

[5] J. Begrich, *Der Satzstil im Fünfer*, Zeitschrift für Semitistik 9, 1933/4, 169–209 = Ges. Studien 1964, 132–67. In such cases a member is frequently twice as long in the second half-verse as in the corresponding part of the first: c comprises $c1'$ together with $c2'$. (In UT chapter 13, 116, the longer parallel member is called the 'ballast variant'.)

[6] UT chapter 13, 111.

3. It often happens that the second line intensifies the thought by means of a contradictory expression, such as in Prov. x. 1:

A wise son maketh a glad father:
But a foolish son is the heaviness of his mother.

Such cases are spoken of as *antithetic parallelism.*

4. More complicated is the relation between the two stichoi in examples such as that in Ps. xxx. 6:

As for me, I said in my prosperity,
I shall never be moved.

Here the thought is not repeated, and neither is it carried further: it is elucidated. The reference to carefree meditation in the first two is interpreted more concretely in the second. Also, the poem does not progress, it marks time, not through variation, but through a continuation of the sense. This is *synthetic parallelism.*[7] It can also happen that the saying in the second half-section continues the line of thought, and that the caesura has no logical significance, but purely rhythmical (enjambement).[8] A familar form of the blessing from the later period (Ps. cxxvii. 5):

Happy is the man that hath his quiver full of them (of children).

The last example is Begrich's 'Form 1', and the previous example 'Form 2'. (The association of different sayings not logically connected.)

5. A variation of the synthetic is the *parabolic parallelism,* which makes a comparison in such a way that the image presented in the first row is taken up as the point of the second:

For as the heaven is high above the earth,
So great (high) is his mercy toward them that fear him.
(Ps. ciii. 11)

Not only Israelite, but also Canaanite, Egyptian and Akkadian poetry employ this device of parallelism. Hence it is a characteristic of all Ancient Oriental poetry. To our ears the duplication of expression checks the progress of what is being said, deadens it, and also impairs its clarity and straightforwardness, for no two words are completely synonymous. The fact that this manner of composition prevailed for thousands of years can only be explained by a way of thinking which is not ours today. Underlying it is the unspoken conviction that final truths about human existence can never be expressed by one line of thought, but only by a number of varied statements.[9]

These few observations will suffice. To look further into this aspect of biblical scholarship would be to go beyond the proper limits of form-critical research. For a knowledge of literary types and their histories it

---

[7] In the New Testament for instance, Matt. vi. 34: 'Be not therefore anxious for the morrow: for the morrow will be anxious for itself.'

[8] This is disputed by Robinson, ZAW N.S. 13, 1936, p. 30: 'Where there is a break in the sense, there must also be a break in the metre.'

[9] For this way of thinking, cf. the description of the 'multiplicity of approaches' in H. Frankfort and others, *The Intellectual Adventure of Ancient Man,* 1946, repr. as *Before Philosophy* 1949 (Penguin). Also *Ancient Egyptian Religion,* 1948, p. 4. It was so foreign to the Greek language that the Septuagint had to make radical changes; see G. Gerleman, Studies in the Septuagint, LUÅ N.S. Avd. 1, Vol. 52: 3, 1956, p. 18.

would be useful to know more about the origin and particularly about the development of parallelismus membrorum. But research into this has hardly begun.

B. *The Structure of Poems and Songs*

A long verse is often a complete unit. This is the form taken by most wisdom sayings (see above Prov. x. 1), and it is also used in the apodictic decree of the death penalty in the divine law in Exod. xxxi. 15b:

Whosoever doeth any work in the Sabbath day, he shall surely be put to death (מוֹת יוּמָת)[10]

This also applies to many of Jesus' sayings. Sometimes the verse is extended by a third row, and becomes a tricolon:

As vinegar is to the teeth, and as smoke to the eyes,
So is the sluggard to them that send him (Prov. x. 26).[11]

Two verses linked to a double period can be found quite early on, in the wisdom literature. This happens particularly frequently in synthetic parallelism (which is thereby parallelism in the strictest sense):

Let all those that seek thee rejoice and be glad in thee:
Let such as love thy salvation say continually: The Lord be magnified (Ps. xl. 16).

Many of the wisdom sayings in Proverbs xxv–xxvii are in the form of double periods. This results in an 'external' parallelism, or parallelismus versuum, which involves two or more consecutive lines.[12]

In greater poetic units the use of parallelism is not sufficient in itself. The poem is then arranged in accordance with the literary type, as can be seen from the psalms which are used as examples in the second section; the grouping of the lines is decided by the sense of the poem.

In larger formations there are a few characteristics which do not appear to be restricted to one particular type. There is the heavy, or weighted ending (*schwere Schluss*), where at the end of a poem or a section a long period[13] or tricolon appears. Or a half-line, without parallelism, can also serve as a conclusion (Ps. ii. 12b). Another peculiarity of Hebrew poetry is the use of *anacrusis*, when introductory formulas and terms of address are inserted without regard to parallelism.[14] As in a prayer (Ps. xiii. 1):

How long, *O Lord*, wilt thou forget me for ever?
How long wilt thou hide thy face from me?

---

[10] ALT I, 307 ff. (cf. p. 27 for E.T.) assumes that these and other participial legal sayings in the Book of the Covenant and Holiness Code make up an ancient series of 'crimes worthy of death'. But it is very hazardous indeed to link sentences into an original unit which, although they are of the same literary type, belong to very different works of literature (as is also the linking of participial sentences with apodictic commandments, cf. below, p. 121).

[11] Mowinckel, Real and Apparent Tricola in Hebrew Psalm Poetry, ANVAO, 1957, 2.

[12] Th. H. Robinson, Some Principles of Hebrew Metrics, ZAW 54, 1936, 28–43. This kind is to be found in a certain stage of the Beatitudes. See p. 42 above.

[13] Cf. UT chapter 13, 110.

[14] T. H. Robinson in Werden und Wesen des AT, BZAW 66, 1936, 37–40.

Or in a prophetic proclamation (Jer. ii. 9):

Wherefore I will yet plead with you, *saith the Lord*,
and with your children's children I will plead.

Finally there is the *acrostic* device used in certain literary types of songs, i.e. each line starts with a letter following the alphabetic sequence. For instance, in Ps. ix f., the first two lines begin with *Aleph*, the next two with *Beth*, and so on. In the same way each three lines of Lam. i–iii form a group, and in Ps. cxix even eight. The same stylistic device is to be found in Babylonian hymns.[15] In some places there is a *refrain*, which is clearly intended to end a section (Ps. xlii. 5, 11 and xliii. 5, xlvi. 7, 11, lxxx. 3, 7, 19). As the number and the rhythms of the periods within such sections can vary, it is better not to refer to them as 'strophes'.[16]

C. *Short Verse Series*

G. Fohrer: Über den Kurzvers, ZAW 66, 1954, 199–236. S. Mowinckel: Marginalien zur hebräischen Metrik, ZAW 68, 1956, 97–123.

Recently the question has arisen whether, as well as long verse (the existence of which has long been recognised), there is also *short verse* in Hebrew poetry without a caesura or parallelismus membrorum which does not exist alone but as a group of short verses. This was vigorously asserted by Fohrer,[17] and just as vigorously denied by Mowinckel.[18] The second half of the Decalogue gives us a clear example:

Thou shalt not kill.
Thou shalt not commit adultery.
Thou shalt not steal.
Thou shalt not make false witness . . .

At one time these commandments will certainly have been delivered formally at covenant festivals (see above), although the text as we now have it is much altered, particularly at the beginning. This series undoubtedly proves Fohrer to be right. In Israel apodictic commandments were frequently composed in the form of a series and proclaimed *ceremonially* without having any relation to the art of parallelismus membrorum. Mowinckel's objection is founded on the belief that the series has been devised out of many separate sayings. This idea cannot be ruled out, but it establishes nothing; for here it is a question of the stylistic means which brought about the formation of the series, at whatever time that may have been, and whether there was any value attached to their ceremonial delivery to the cultic community, i.e. whether the language was felt to be metrical. This is undoubtedly so. These series have an affinity to parallelismus membrorum in that sentences juxtapose related thoughts 'synthetically', but with no regard for parallelism.

[15] It is often asserted that these acrostic songs are intended more for the eye of the educated reader than for the ear of the hearer. But this takes no account of the fact that the Semitic has a quite different awareness of consonants than the European. He takes much less notice of vowel sounds.
[16] Those parts of a poem which are divided by a refrain are called 'groups' (*Wenden*) by Eissfeldt, *Introduction*, pp. 63 f.
[17] G. Fohrer, Über den Kurzvers, ZAW 66, 1954, 199–236.
[18] S. Mowinckel, Marginalien zur hebräischen Metrik ZAW 68, 1956, 97–123.

Fohrer's enthusiasm for his discovery[19] ran away with him. He discovered short verses in every conceivable prophetic text, without producing completely conclusive evidence for them. However, the existence of short verses cannot be denied. For the New Testament this is of very great significance, for it proves that the blessings in Matt. v and Luke vi are of a poetic nature, notwithstanding their lack of parallelismus membrorum.

D. *The Role of Poetry in Israel*

Metrical language doubtless had a far greater significance in Israel than it does in our present, prosaic times. Poetry was not only read privately, and recited to circles of enthusiasts. It was not art for amusement's sake, and therefore dispensable. It occupied a necessary, even vital place in the life of the people. There is reason to suppose that a priestly saying at a sanctuary, or a prophetic speech to the community, and indeed even political slogans, were composed rhythmically and had to be so. Today public speaking and poetry are very different things; modern Western society formulates its final truths in prose, whether in philosophical treatises or in church proclamations, and poems are in our opinion only the symbolic expression of these. But the ancient orientals were only able to express the profound questions about human existence in poetry. Moreover, poetry is not intended to follow certain aesthetic rules, but is the result of a particular sensitivity to language (as are also the use of grammatically correct forms in common speech).[20] Probably poetic language was considered to be endowed with a greater effective force than common speech.

A further point is that in Hebrew it is common to switch over to poetry from prose very quickly. A traveller crossing the desert in Southern Arabia over twenty years ago reported of the Bedouins: 'When moved, Arabs break easily into poetry. I have heard a lad spontaneously describe in verse some grazing which he had just found: he was giving natural expression to his feelings.'[21] It will have been the same with the Israelites. And from the Old Testament it is easy to see that the switch could occur the other way round, particularly when poetry was written down. In the prophetic books comments in prose are quite blatantly inserted into rhythmical language. It seems therefore inadvisable to ascribe certain comments in predominantly poetic books of the Old Testament simply to a 'poetic language', for this would be to presuppose that poetry and poets had special status in Israel. In fact this was not the case. Words and turns of phrase of a particular style which are found in the psalms, for instance, are better ascribed to cultic professional language, and similar peculiarities in the book of Proverbs to the language used by the wise.

At this point we must glance at the general Old Testament form-critical commentaries. Even though, as in Gunkel's outline of Israelite literary history,[22] it is usually approached historically rather than systematically,[23]

[19] To be more accurate the idea originated from Fohrer's tutor Balla.
[20] Robinson, ZAW, 1936, p. 29.
[21] W. Thesiger, *Arabian Sands*, 1964 (Penguin), p. 87.
[22] In KdG.
[23] See above, pp. 25 f.

8

the contrast between poetry and prose is used as a general division.[24] This has the disadvantage, already referred to, that the interpretation of a literary type which in the Hebrew is part prose and part poetry, such as a prayer of intercession, is split between the two sections. This presents a particular problem with the old narrative stories, which are prose in the first instance, but switch to poetry at the climax, as at the end of the paradise story in Genesis ii. 23:

> This is now bone of my bone, flesh of my flesh,
> She shall be called Woman, because she was taken out of Man.

Similarly in Gen. xvi. 11 f.; Lev. x. 3, etc. This is a device much used in Arabian narrative stories also. How shall such types be classified? Do they belong to prose, under which they are usually placed, or to poetry, because the core of the piece is poetic? These few comments will show how questionable it is to apply the classification of prose and poetry, taken from our own cultural background, to the Hebrew language. Besides, it makes it difficult to show the connection of poetic literary types to *different* settings in life.

E. *Metrics*

Survey and bibliography in Eissfeldt: *The Old Testament: An Introduction*, Ch. 6, 1965 (Oxford, Blackwell; New York, Harper & Row). Important new evaluation by S. Segert: Problems of HebrewProsody, VTS VII, 1960, 283–91.

Poetic language differs from common speech in that it has a marked rhythm. The psalm headings indicate that many of the Old Testament compositions which employ the device of parallelismus membrorum were meant to be sung to the accompaniment of instruments. They therefore possessed a fixed melody. Hence there must have been metrical laws for Hebrew poetry. Is it possible to reconstruct them? Though so much energy has been expended on this in the last hundred years, the fact that we have no direct evidence means that no solution has yet been arrived at which has attained general recognition.

However, two things can be asserted with certainty, which will provide us at least with a rough notion of Hebrew metrics. Firstly, for the last fifty years it has been recognised that in certain literary types an asymmetrical verse formation is used, in which one member is longer in the first half-line than in the second ('limping verse' (*hinkender Vers*)): this is *Qinah metre*, so called because it is always used in funeral laments (קִינוֹת).

But it is also found in other poems, such as in Lamentations. In Amos v. 2 the prophet imitates the literary type of the funeral lament:

נָפְלָה לֹא־תוֹסִיף קוּם   בְּתוּלַת יִשְׂרָאֵל

Besides this there is the *Mashal metre*, so called by Mowinckel because this is the form taken by the wisdom sayings (מְשָׁלִים). In this case both half-verses are symmetrical, at least in length. Prov. ii. 1:

בְּנִי אִם־תִּקַּח אֲמָרִי   וּמִצְוֺתַי תִּצְפֹּן אִתָּךְ׃

The period (the verse) of this metre has a relatively wide scope. There

---

[24] See the introductions mentioned on p. 25–26.

were certainly metres other than these, but they are not as easy to determine or to classify under literary types.

What else is there to add about the basic structure of the metre? Is it possible to determine the verse feet (bars) which make up the half-line? At present there are two opposing views. The one advocates an *accentuating* system, in which the verse foot is composed of a stressed syllable together with one or more unstressed syllables. Only the stressed syllables are counted in the period; their accentuation corresponds with the word stress. The example from Amos v. 2 would therefore be scanned thus:

naf^elā lo' tôsîf qûm b^etûlat yiśra'el

+ +=| + = |+ = / ++ =| + + =|

The virgin of Israel is fallen; she will no more rise.

As only the stressed syllables (marked =) are counted, the result is a metre of $3+2$ stresses, i.e. a 'five'. (The corresponding Mashal metre would be $3+3$, or a 'double-three'.) This interpretation (following that by Ley) has been brought general recognition by the Germanist E. Sievers.[25]

A minority, however, which includes Hölscher,[26] Mowinckel[27] and Horst,[28] advocates an *alternating* metre. In conformity with the simple dance rhythm and the Masoretic placing of accents they assume that in Hebrew poetry each stressed syllable was as a rule followed by one unstressed syllable, which make up the verse foot. However, it is possible for the unstressed syllable to be absorbed into the stressed syllable preceding it, so that the verse foot can consist of one syllable. Amos v. 2 would then look like this:

naf^elā lo' tôsîf qûm b^etûlat yiśra'el

+ =| = | + = | = / + =|+ = | + =|

Here the Qinah metre consists of $4+3$ verse feet. (The corresponding Mashal metre $4+4$.)

This is not the place to go into the two theories.[29] Their weakness lies in the fact that we have very little certain knowledge about the pronunciation of Hebrew when it was in common use. Both theories correspond with the ultimate stress laid down by the Tiberian Masoretes. But there are indications that the earlier pronunciation stressed the penultimate syllable of a word.[30]

A noteworthy attempt to tackle the problem of metrics from the historical angle for the first time was made by Segert. He distinguished three stages in

[25] *Metrische Studien* I–III, 1901–7.

[26] Elemente arabischer, syrischer und hebräischer Metrik, BZAW 34, 1920 (Festschrift for K. Budde), 93–101.

[27] *Zum Problem der hebräischen Metrik*, Festschrift for A. Bertholet, 1950, 379–94. *Zur hebräischen Metrik* II, StTh VII, 1953, 54–85.

[28] F. Horst, Die Kennzeichen der hebräischen Poesie, ThR N.S. 21, 1953, 97–121.

[29] The vocal signs in Babylonian epics suggest an accentuating system (Falkenstein/von Soden, pp. 39 f.) whereas the Syriac and Arabic metres support Hölscher's theory.

[30] On the basis of new knowledge of the history of the Hebrew language see D. N. Freemann, Archaic Forms in Early Hebrew Poetry, ZAW 72, 1960, 101–7, who attempts a clearer exposition of the accenuating theory.

the use of the Hebrew language: 1. In the earliest times every Hebrew word was a poetic unit (as in Ugarit and a branch of Akkadian).[31] 2. In the monarchical period an accentuating system prevailed. 3. In the later period an alternating system, owing to Aramaic influence.

This sketch will show that all theories of metre in Hebrew poetry are theories only and can be only cautiously applied. However, they have been referred to briefly here for the sake of completeness.

9. THE CANON, AND A LITERARY AND LINGUISTIC HISTORY OF THE BIBLE

The following section differs from the previous ones. Up to this point my task has been to enquire into the principles of form-critical research, but now I shall try to tackle paths which have been so far little frequented. It concerns what we might call the keystone to the construction of form-critical exegesis, the theological consequences. Most Old and New Testament scholars working from a form-critical standpoint do not consider the points which I now put forward, and as a rule no one appears to be interested in them. However, the longer I work with form criticism, the more I feel that these additional, and perhaps final, problems can no longer be evaded, even though few people other than Gunkel have touched upon them.

A. *The Relevance of Transmission History for the Church*

The form-critical considerations presented in the last chapters, general though they were, will have been enough to show the complexity of the language phenomenon which underlies the genesis of the Bible. The student meets a diversity of literary types, all strongly bound up with a setting in life, but with a history abounding in changes. Poetry proves to be distinct from prose, not only in form but also in meaning. Moreover, behind nearly every biblical passage there lies a long history of transmission, revealing the vicissitudes of its oral transmission, its writing down, its redaction or its incorporation into other books. This is the picture presented by any form-critical study of the origin of the biblical writings. Whereas fifty years ago in biblical scholarship the number of 'authors' of the Old and New Testament writings could be counted on one's fingers, now form criticism has revealed that the number of persons and circles of tradition who had a part in the formation of the Old and New Testament constitutes an incalculable choir. The biblical word has proved to be not truth in a fossilised, unchanging sense, but truth which is constantly adapting itself to the circumstances of the time.

Anyone active in the church today is faced with a peculiar problem concerning the interpretation of biblical texts in sermons or teaching. Whereas earlier he could start with the inspiration of the psalmists, apostles, and so on, and could concentrate on what they were saying, now the inspiration does not appear to have been a unique quality held by a few,

---

[31] This also applies to the time up to the exile. H. Kosmala, VT XIV, 1964, 423–45.

46066

but the development over centuries of moulding and remoulding of linguistic traditions into established literary types and sharply defined settings
in life. Prophets and evangelists do indeed play an important part, but they
are only a few among many. If the preacher or catechist wishes to translate
a text with a long tradition into modern terms he is faced with the decision
as to which stage of transmission must be considered the binding, and
therefore the canonical one. For it is the church's lot to use the Bible as
canon, as a model for life and teaching. Which parable of Jesus, for example,
is canonical: what he himself said, or what the early community thought
he said, or what Matthew thought he said? The first answer which suggests
itself is that what Jesus himself wanted to say, i.e. the primary form, is the
essential one. But apart from the fact that the parable of Jesus must be translated back out of the Greek into Aramaic to restore the original meaning
quite clearly (and how little theologians are in a position to do this), does
this not imply that the influence of the Holy Ghost on the post-Easter
community is to be ignored? Surely the change in interpretation was
determined to a great extent by the experience of the community under
the leadership of the post-Easter kyrios? So it seems more fitting to
consider the final form of the transmitted material as the decisive one.
However, even then there are problems. In the Pentateuch—to take an
Old Testament example—the final redaction can be ascertained only very
occasionally, and there is little that is definite to be grasped of their interpretation, whereas we can distinguish the attitude of the earlier stages,
such as the Jahwistic or Priestly writings, relatively easily. Surely it is
more logical to use this stage. In my opinion there can be no binding
principles. It must be left to the judgment of the individual as to which
version of the tradition should supply the main thought of a sermon or
other treatise. The choice not only depends on the level of exegetical
clarity required, but on what would most profit those listening. The main
thing is to acknowledge that not only the biblical text as it stands but also
the earlier stages in the history of its transmission are imbued with the
spirit of God, and are therefore also canonical.

Of course the ideal is to trace the entire transmission history of a tradition
in a sermon or bible class, and thereby bring out the vitality of the text.
Naturally a certain intellectual and spiritual level is required of those
taking part. Then the interpretation can be very lively and productive.

But this is not enough. Is it right that biblical statements are dependent
on their transmission history and their respective setting in life, and that
they can only be truly grasped with a knowledge of these? The preacher
will have to discuss this point also. He will show his congregation the significance which the cultic happenings in the temple of Zion, or the love
feast of early Hellenistic Christianity have for them, i.e. how far our
present way of life has been influenced by its origins in these Old and New
Testament institutions. But does such a connection between the modern
church and the 'external' history of Israel and the early Christian community exist at all? Must it, or rather, may it, go beyond the mere wording
of the text and be expressed in the proclamation? These are contro-
versial and as yet unsolved questions in modern theology. But they crop

up inevitably in connection with the relevance of form-critical methods in church practice.

B. *The Scheme for a Literary History of the Bible*

Gunkel: see bibliography to Section 1. Bultmann-Gunkel: Literatur-geschichte, Biblische in: RGG III² 1675–82. Horst-Marxsen= Literaturgeschichte, Evang. Kirchenlexicon II, 1958, 1124–28.

If the canon is analysed from the aspect of its transmission history does not its unity collapse? Gunkel attempted to meet this danger by calling for a synthesising literary history of the Old and New Testaments. Such a history would not be based on individual creative personalities but on the history of the literary types and the individual units (traditions). Certainly the author should have his place, but only within the context of the literary types and traditions which the language has evolved and kept alive. Literary history would then not be understood in the current sense of literary criticism, nor as a sympathetic exploration of the outstanding writings, but as a running historical narrative, in which literature in its widest sense, including material orally transmitted, would be understood as the natural expression of a human society. For the Old Testament this would be 'penetrating through to the great and coherent picture of the history of the whole literature of Israel.'[1] The history of Israelite literature is therefore so strongly bound up with what is generally called Old Testament kerygma, or the Old Testament proclamation, that 'one cannot enter successfully into the world of religious ideas without a knowledge of the material and of the form it takes. Hence both the religious and literary history have no other aim than to make the actual religious content of the sacred writings accessible'.[2] This is precisely how the practical work of the church is accomplished. As indeed literature and religion are inseparable from all other spheres of life in Israel, 'the final expression of Old Testament biblical scholarship will be a history of life in Israel in all its manifestations'.[3]

Gunkel was not able to develop his scheme, or to go further into the connection between 'literature' and 'religion', so to him it remained an open matter what the history of both in Israel would lead to. If the history of literature were to become a running historical narrative, then the whole must indeed have a certain direction. He did once express the following aim: 'The Hebrew language died out as a spoken language. But the history of the collection of collections had already begun: the canon was born.'[4] The history of literature thus ends in the formation of the Old Testament canon, which Gunkel links up with the end of Hebrew as a spoken language, and therefore with the end of the particular language types associated with it. But his statements are not consistent. On one side he dismisses the late period as the time

[1] RGG III, 1677. As early as 1856 E. Meier, *Geschichte der poetischen National-literatur der Hebräer*, wrote on similar lines: 'In place of the unclear and undefined "Introduction" there must be the idea of a history of Old Testament literature. It is this that will show us where our real duty lies, and it is this that will determine the necessary bounds of our study and the only correct genetical method.'
[2] RuA VII.
[3] RGG I², 1073.
[4] RuA 36.

of the epigones,[5] and on the other he emphasises the theological importance of the post-biblical writings of the Apocrypha and Pseudepigrapha.[6] But his weakest point is that, despite the heading of his project, 'A Literary History of the Bible', and the assertion that the Israelite literary history continued *without a break* into early Christian times and the Talmud, the connection between the Old and New Testament remains obscure. These obscurities doubtless helped to precipitate the demise of his idea of a literary history after he himself had died. At present it is entirely forgotten.

As well as the problem of its goal, the project itself came up against strong opposition. Eissfeldt[7] has scruples on two grounds: firstly, he thinks that a literary history undertaken on a form-critical basis would concentrate too much on the small units and would neglect the great compositions and the books as we have them; and secondly, that the object of Old Testament research 'is not simply the literature of a nation, or the remains of such a literature. The Old Testament is rather an entity which has come into being within the development of a particular political and religious history, and which has to be understood and evaluated as such and not simply as the remains of a richer mass of written material.' His first objection is undoubtedly right in connection with the form criticism of Gunkel's generation, but not with the present day principles and practice of it, which would now include a survey of redaction history. As for the second objection, Gunkel's intention was precisely to avoid a view of the (Old Testament) canon as a mere remnant of a richer pre-history, but rather as the final achievement of a highly complex movement. A study of the literary history of Israel and early Christianity as a whole should point to the fundamental motive underlying the genesis of the Bible, and to how it became 'the instructor of humanity.'[8] Gunkel had never lost sight of the fact that the Old Testament was not simply a compendium of Israelite national literature. Nevertheless, from this collection of religious writings he maintained it was possible to deduce a literary history, basing his deduction on two characteristics of the Israelite nation: firstly, that religion in Israel was always so closely bound up with the people and the state that an enormous amount of national literature could and must have been recorded in the writings compiled for the edification of the Jewish nation; and secondly, it is very apparent that 'sacred' literature always dominated 'profane' literature. To him this made it conceivable that a literary history, though fragmentary, could be gleaned from the canon, and that this would for its own part give the canon backing. Eissfeldt's scruples are therefore not serious enough to refute Gunkel's ideas completely.

The problem is even greater with a literary history of the New Testament. This was already apparent in Dibelius' sketch published in 1926 entitled *Geschichte der urchristlichen Literatur.*[9] This is how, in introducing it, he outlined the task: 'In writing the history of primitive Christian literature, or in seeking to become clear as to its origins, our first task is to show how

---

[5] Shortly before the quotation given above he says: 'Finally the tragedy of Israelite literature: inspiration declined, literary types became exhausted, numerous imitations appeared, and original creations were replaced by adaptations of old material.'

[6] In RGG I[2], 1090 he writes: 'Apocrypha and Pseudepigrapha, which have previously been left out of biblical theology, must now be drawn into the discussion; for in the real course of the history of religion there was no division sharp enough to justify the exclusion of these later writings.'

[7] *Introduction*, p. 5.

[8] 'For what can we do but to understand in all its urgency the judgment of history, which has made the Bible the guide of humanity, banishing all other Ancient Oriental religions to the lumber-room', RuA VII.

[9] A fuller study incorporating the material in this book was published in English in 1936 under the title *A Fresh Approach to the New Testament and Early Christian Literature*, 1936 (London, Nicholson & Watson; New York, Scribner).

it came about that the earliest Christians ever entered the field of literature at all. . . . In as far as the historian is describing the forms in which this literary output was cast, he is writing the history of primitive Christian literature.'[10] This is good form criticism. Bultmann, however, remarked rightly that even in this presentation 'the character of the old "Introductions" still predominates', i.e. it is an analytical treatment of the individual writings, and gives little more consideration to the setting in life and the cross-influencing of the Aramaic and Greek languages within early Christianity than did the old 'Introductions'.[11] Here the difficulties mount up all the more, for the Christian communities came together from many different branches of a variety of nations and cultures. The Jewish Christian in Palestine speaking Aramaic belongs within the context of the Israelite-Jewish literary history, from which also the literary types of exegesis, study of history, liturgy and apocalyptic were derived (see the blessings). On the other hand, the Greek-speaking Christians follow the language forms of the Hellenitic Israelite diaspora, which for its own part is closely connected to Hellenistic minor literature generally. Literary types such as the New Testament epistles and their parenetical passages, and also the virtue and vice lists, originated there, as well as the monotheistic mission sermon. The influence of both spheres is evident in the new wealth of language available to the Christian world, such as in the literary types of kerygmatic formulas, the community sermon, christological hymns, and the gospels themselves. Anyone attempting a New Testament literary history from a form-critical point of view must therefore know the literary history of Israel, and also the variety of different paths it took in the later period when Hebrew had become a sacred language. He must also know something about the Aramaic language at the time of Jesus, and the extensive material of Hellenistic minor literature, including that of Hellenistic Judaism. And even this is not enough. Also important is a knowledge of post-biblical Christian writing, where many New Testament literary types crop up again and have been developed. All this is more than an individual could hope to accomplish. It is not surprising that since Gunkel's death as little has been heard of research in this quarter as in that of an Old Testament literary history.

Nor is this all. As this book is concerned with the methods and the range of form criticism, we must put the difficult question anew: Do the many single solutions reached through form criticism fit into any general framework? Such a framework has not yet been evolved, but this is no reflection on the task itself. We must ask not only the reason for such an exhaustive investigation of individual units but quite simply the motive behind any interpretation of the sacred writings. Is an interpreter's work finished with his study of the individual text? Is it enough, as is often said today, to extract the kerygma from biblical pericopes? Or must the interpreter seek further for a relation between the individual passages and the books, between the Old and New Testaments and the Bible as a whole? It

---

[10] p. 16.
[11] RGG III[2], 1682. This deficiency is just one aspect of the general unsatisfactory state of research.

is no longer possible to connect them up into a 'system', in which state-ments from very different biblical writings are more or less forcibly assembled into a Christian dogmatics. Only a historical presentation of the biblical writings will provide us with a clear guide line running right through from the earliest writings to the latest.[12] Surely then a literary history along the lines of the one planned by Gunkel is urgently needed, if form criticism is to have any point at all.

It is therefore nothing less than astounding to discern similar endeavours in present-day Old Testament scholarship, although without any express connection with Gunkel's project. On the Evangelical side R. Rendtorff,[13] and on the Catholic N. Lohfink[14] have put forward the idea that the con-tinuity of Old Testament literary history (or transmission history, the term used in a wider sense than the one outlined above) should be traced right up until it merges into that of the New Testament. In this way the gap between the historical and the Christian interpretation of the Bible would at last be bridged. Just as Gunkel urged that Old Testament liter-ature should be constantly seen in relation to other manifestations of Israelite life, Rendtorff recognises the necessity of linking transmission history (as he understands it) with the political history of Israel. Martin Noth had already expressed this idea in his book on the Pentateuch: 'Transmission history . . . is itself a part of the history of Israel.'[15]

Is it enough to link up all the literary types and the numerous biblical traditions which these comprise with the other spheres of life in Israel and in the early Christian church? There is one province as yet unconsidered, but which has gained some prominence in biblical scholarship in the last decades: the investigation into the exact meaning of single words and their verbal roots, i.e. the so-called *history of concepts (Begriffsgeschichte)*, as it is presented in Kittel's great *Theologisches Wörterbuch zum Neuen Testament*. Would it not be logical to combine this with form criticism? It would surely be helpful to discover in which literary types and to which setting in life the respective word is used and receives its particular meaning. In this way the history of concepts would be freed from the straitjacket of etymological-semasiological constructions, which restrict it considerably.[16] A history of literature on a form-critical basis could then become a true *history of language (Sprachgeschichte)*; not in an external grammatical-lexicographical sense, as in philology, but one that would involve a history of thought and speech. Thought and speech arise out of the complexity of the human way of life, and they in their turn influence this manner of living by reacting back upon it.

In fact it is not only possible but also necessary to compile a list of all literary types and settings in life belonging to each epoch of Israelite and

---

[12] To a certain extent G. von Rad has followed this line in his *Theologie des Alten Testament*; *Old Testament Theology*, vol. I, 1962; vol. II, 1966 (Edinburgh, Oliver & Boyd; New York, Harper & Row), although of course without the basis of a literary history.

[13] *Hermeneutik des AT als Frage nach der Geschichte*, ZThK 57, 1960, 27–40.

[14] *Die historische und die christliche Anslegung des AT*, Stimmen der Zeit 978, 1966, 98–112.

[15] UGP 272. Lohfink puts the fundamental theological question: 'Is belief in Christ based on grounds which are dependent upon historical considerations or does this belief arise . . . out of association with history itself? The second theory is the more likely one.' p. 111.

[16] Strong criticism by J. Barr, *The Semantics of Biblical Language*, 1961.

Christian history. It should also be asked what is meant by what literary scholarship calls the *epochal style*,[17] or von Rad the *spirit*, or *intellectual attitudes* (*Geistigkeit*) of an age, i.e. the linguistic background which is responsible for the form which a type takes, and which endows each sphere of life with its own distinctive qualities. Von Rad has established the attitudes of a 'solomonic humanism'[18] as the source of a whole series of literary types, such as the salvation history written in the Jahwistic style, the early historical writing (the history of the succession to the throne of David in II Sam. (*Thronnachfolgeschichte*)), and the oldest wisdom sayings. It would also be helpful to discover the attitudes governing the late monarchical period, the post-exilic period, and the time of Jesus, and also to show what motivated the changes which led from one to the other.

C. *The History of Biblical Interpretation and the History of Language*

The tremendous power of the biblical writings is demonstrated by the steady stream of interpretative additions and elaborations which they brought forth. The conclusion of the gospel of St Mark (xxvi. 9 ff.) is a later addition, the so-called Western text of the gospel of St Luke adds fresh comment, and Paul's letters were later revised, quite apart from the glosses on and the redactions of the Old Testament writings. A literary history as eventful as this speaks much for the vigour of the biblical faith. Divine truth was never considered to possess a fixed form, but was expressed by the continual relinking of what had been written with the present reality of life. However, the *canonisation* of the biblical writings brought with it a new attitude. It is well known that the Bible was canonised only gradually. The first stage of it was the books of Moses (the Pentateuch) which were canonised as law in post-exilic Israel, and the last certain of the New Testament writings such as the Acts of the Apostles and the Revelation of St John. As long as any part of the Bible had not been raised to canonical status, comment was added to the text itself to bring it up to date, and it was not clear what was part of the original and what was later interpretation. The authors and hence the setting in life of these pre-canonical additions are the disciples or followers of the original writer, rather than agents of an official religious institution. As soon as a text was made part of the canon it became fixed and unalterable. However, it was constantly found necessary to adapt the text to the new situation and to add fresh comment, and professional teachers and scribes were officially instituted by the church or synagogue to provide interpretation. Their work was no longer to adapt the text itself but—as far as their work took written form—to provide independent commentaries. Hence canonisation makes a deep divide in the transmission history of a biblical book. The text became finally fixed. It was then in this form, as a complete canon, that the Bible had such incomparable influence on the belief and the way of life of two millenia.

However, the transmission history of the Bible did not end completely

[17] See above, p. 16.
[18] *Theology* I, 48–56.

with its canonisation. The practice of providing written interpretations took it further in a new form. This custom produced its own literary types: commentaries, anthologies, dictionaries. The fact that the historical development of the biblical language has been a constant process means that the Bible still interests us today. It still provokes dogmatic and ethical discussion, and it is still the basis of the beliefs of countless people. The theologian must not forget that the history of biblical interpretation is a very necessary intermediary discipline. The history of the biblical language has not yet come to an end.[19]

But the canonised Bible did not only have the effect of bringing forth independent interpretations. A form-critical study of it must also consider the position of this unique collection of books within the general history of the literature and language of mankind. The Bible is not only the most universally known book, with the greatest number of editions; nor is it only the most translated written work. It has had a unique influence upon the culture, the law, the economic and political life—in fact, upon the language of whole nations and communities of nations. A translation of the Bible gives on the one hand a new resonance to the old written text (the concepts behind Luther's German Bible differ from those of the original Hebrew Text, see Ps. xlvi as an example), and on the other it quite transforms a language by making it accommodate the biblical message. Its profundity is increased, as is its vocabulary. A translation can also sometimes mean that heathen customs and linguistic traditions die out (as in the Germanic culture pre-Christian traditions have almost completely disappeared). It can also raise a dialect to the level of a written language. Schools are founded, and a national literature (and also a national consciousness) arises. Any literary history of the Bible would necessarily include a study of its position within the history of languge as a whole. A study of this kind would confer upon the exegete a deeper understanding of his own form-critical and linguistic position, as well as of his Church and of the society he inhabits.

These observations are primarily starting points for investigation. The future will show whether they will be of any help to form-critical research. At the moment, however, there is a new awareness and fresh reflection about the nature of language in both philosophy and theology, and it seems to be very much to the point to see how the findings of form criticism relate to the notion that 'being is speaking' (*Sprachlichkeit des Daseins*). This is the more urgent because, surprisingly, the advocates of modern linguistic theology, even those schooled in the form criticism of Bultmann, are not looking for such a connection themselves.

A last word. The Old and New Testament claim to be the revelation of a god whose word and deed are fundamental to true human existence. For two millenia Christian theology has repeatedly reinterpreted this claim, checked it, and found it to be right. Form criticism provides the means for a more accurate interpretation and examination than has been possible before. If the thesis is right that form criticism culminates in a language

[19] This brings fresh light to the theological controversy between Protestants and Roman Catholics over scripture and tradition.

history (literary history, transmission history) involving all manifestations of life then that claim cannot be justified by appealing merely to isolated texts, but to *a complete history of all the biblical writings,* to which each Old and New Testament book would contribute, and in which each would gain the recognition due to them, and this history would be carried further by church history. Within an overall historical framework of this kind it is possible to see why the early Christians (and Christians even now) recognise in Jesus the Christ. I do not believe that such a large historical enquiry will lead to our being less convinced than our fathers in the church were that Scripture is of God's making and prompting. On the contrary, we have clearer grounds for sharing their conviction, for careful historical analysis enables us to see each stage of the biblical compilation as a living response to God.

PART II

Selected Examples

Section One: From the Narrative Books

10. THE ANCESTRESS OF ISRAEL IN DANGER

The books Genesis to II Kings, which in the Hebrew canon are known collectively as the Torah and the Former Prophets, are the oldest of all transmitted material, and are predominately of a descriptive nature. The influence of these stories has been tremendous, and not only upon Jewish, Christian and Mohammedan thinking. This is because of their astounding directness which, even after all this time, still has the power to stir the hearts of hearers, scholars and simple people alike. This plainness is by no means awkward or ungainly. Indeed it is profoundly and unwaveringly directed upon the essential problems of human existence.

These narratives have been arranged in the form of a continuous account of the period from the creation until the Babylonian exile. However, a close look will quickly reveal that most passages were originally independent short stories complete in themselves, which on the whole are only loosely linked to each other. The fact that they were previously separate narratives is evident from the way in which individual stories about Abraham, Moses or Joshua are taken out of their context and are used quite independently of each other in church-service pericopes, or in the instruction of young people in the Christian church, or even in Western art. This would by no means occur as a matter of course. Where a written work is all of a piece such as St Luke's Acts (or, outside the Bible, the Greek tragedies), it is much more difficult to select individual passages.

Form-critical research is not only concerned with an accurate definition of the outline of ancient narrative units but it also attempts to achieve a better understanding of them by looking into their setting in life and the changes they undergo over a period of time. Therefore to provide the reader with a firm basis to start from it is best to begin by looking at narratives which crop up twice or even three times. There are a few examples of this in the Old Testament, although not as many as in the Jesus narratives.

The story of the ancestress of Israel in danger occurs three times in Genesis (xii. 10–xiii. 1, xx. 1 f., xxvi. 1 ff.) and is also found in late Israelite literature. It is therefore very suitable material for a first form-critical study.

A. *Defining the Unit*

The following with reference to Gunkel: Genesis esp. pp. 255 ff. For the redaction history von Rad, ATD, is instructive, E.T. *Genesis*, 1961 (London, S.C.M. Press; Philadelphia, Westminster Press). For later developments: O. Osswald, ZAW 72, 1960, pp. 7–25, and Wacholder, HUCA 35, 1964, pp. 43–56.

| A | B | C |

A

xii. 9 (And Abram journeyed . . . the South).

10 And there was (וַיְהִי) a famine in the land:

and Abram went down into Egypt

to sojourn there; for the famine was sore in the land.

11 And it came to pass (וַיְהִי), when he was come near to enter into Egypt, that he said unto Sarai his wife, Behold now, I know that thou art a fair woman to look upon:
12 and it shall come to pass, when the Egyptians shall see thee, that they shall say, This is his

B

xx. 1 (And Abraham journeyed from thence toward the land of the South,

and dwelt between Kadesh and Shur;

and *he sojourned in Gerar*.

2 *And Abraham said of Sarah his wife, She is my sister:*

C

xxvi. 1 And there was (וַיְהִי) a famine in the land, beside the first famine that was in the days of Abraham. And Isaac went unto Abimelech king of the Philistines unto Gerar.
2 And the Lord appeared unto him, and said, Go not down into Egypt; dwell in the land which I shall tell thee of:
3 *sojourn in this land*, and I will be with thee, and will bless thee; for unto thee, and unto thy seed, I will give all these lands, and I will establish the oath which I sware unto Abraham thy father;
4 and I will multiply thy seed as the stars of heaven, and will give unto thy seed all these lands; and in thy seed shall all the nations of the earth be blessed;
5 because that Abraham obeyed my voice, and kept my charge, my commandments, my statutes, and my laws.
6 And Isaac dwelt in Gerar.
7 and the men of the place asked him of his wife; *and he said, She is my sister*: for he feared to say, My wife; *lest, said he, the men of the place should kill me for Rebekah: because she was fair to look upon.*

xii	xx	xxvi

wife: and they will kill me, but they will save thee alive.

13 *Say, I pray thee, thou art my sister: that it may be well with me for thy sake*, and that my soul may live because of thee.

14 And it came to pass (ויהי), that, when Abram was come into Egypt, the Egyptians beheld the woman that *she was very fair*.

15 And the princes of Pharaoh saw her, and praised her to Pharaoh: *and the woman was taken* into Pharaoh's house.

16 And he entreated Abram well for her sake: and he had sheep, and oxen, and he-asses, and menservants, and maidservants, and she-asses, and camels.

17 And *the Lord plagued Pharaoh* and his house with great plagues because of Sarai Abram's wife.

and Abimelech king of Gerar sent, and *took Sarah.*

3 But *God came to Abimelech* in a dream of the night, and said to him, Behold, thou art but a dead man, because of the woman which thou hast taken; for she is a man's wife.

4 Now Abimelech had not come near her: and he said, Lord, wilt thou slay even a righteous nation?

5 Said he not himself unto me, She is my sister? and she, even she herself said, He is my brother: in the integrity of my heart and the innocence of my hands I have done this.

6 And God said unto him in the dream, Yea, I know that in the integrity of thy heart thou

8 And it came to pass (ויהי), when he had been there a long time, that Abimelech king of the Philistines looked out at a window, and saw, and behold, Isaac was sporting with Rebekah his wife.

A	B	C
xii	xx	xxvi

B:

hast done this, and I also withheld thee from sinning against me: therefore suffered I thee not to touch her.

7 Now therefore restore the man's wife; for he is a prophet, and he shall pray for thee, and thou shalt live: and if thou restore her not, know thou that thou shalt surely die, thou, and all that are thine.

8 And Abimelech rose early in the morning, and called all his servants, and told all these things in their ears: and the men were sore afraid.

A:

18 *And Pharaoh called Abram, and said, What is this that thou hast done unto me? why didst thou not tell me that she was thy wife?*

19 *Why saidst thou, She is my sister?* so that I took her to be my wife:

B:

9 *Then Abimelech called Abraham, and said unto him, What hast thou done unto us?* and wherein have I sinned against thee, that thou hast brought on me and on my kingdom a great sin? thou has done deeds unto me that ought not to be done.

10 And Abimelech said unto Abraham, What sawest thou, that thou hast done this thing?

11 And Abraham said, Because I thought, Surely the fear of God is not in this place; and *they will slay me for my wife's sake.*

12 And moreover she is indeed my sister, and daughter of my father, but not the daughter of my mother; and she became my wife:

13 and it came to pass (ויהי), when God caused me to wander

C:

9 *And Abimelech called Isaac, and said, Behold, of a surety she is your wife: and how saidst thou, She is my sister?* And Isaac said unto him, Because I said, *Lest I die for her.*

10 And Abimelech said, *What is this thou hast done unto us?* one of the people might lightly have lien with thy wife, and thou shouldest have brought guiltiness upon us.

xii   xx   xxvi

from my father's house,
that I said unto her,
This is thy kindness
which thou shall show
unto me; at every place
whither we shall come,
say of me, He is my
brother.

14 And Abimelech took
sheep and oxen, and
menservants and wo-
menservants, and gave
now therefore *behold thy*   them to Abraham, and
wife, take her, and go thy   *restored him Sarah his*
way.   *wife.*

20 And Pharaoh gave   15 And Abimelech said,   11 And   Abimelech
men charge concerning   Behold, my land is be-   charged all the people,
him: and they brought   fore thee: *dwell where it* saying, He that toucheth
him on the way, and his *pleaseth thee.*   this man or his wife
wife, and all that he had. 16 And unto Sarah he   shall surely be put to
                        said, Behold, I have   death.
                        given thy brother a   12 And Isaac sowed in
                        thousand pieces of sil-   that land, and found in
                        ver: behold, it is for   the same year an hun-
                        thee a covering of the   dredfold: and the Lord
                        eyes to all that are with   blessed him.
                        thee; and *in respect of all*
                        thou art righted.

                        17   And   Abraham   13 And the man waxed
                        prayed unto God: and   great, and grew more
                        God healed Abimelech,   and   more   until   he
                        and his wife, and his   became very great.
                        maidservants; and they
                        bare children.
(xiii. 1 And Abram went (18 For the Lord had
up out of Egypt . . . into fast closed up all the
the South)   wombs of the house of
                        Abimelech, because of
                        Sarah Abraham's wife.)

The first task in any form-critical investigation is to define the exact
extent of the literary unit. Only a piece which was self-sufficient at least at
one stage in its development would prove to have any significance in such
an investigation. Do the narratives printed above give any indication of
self-sufficiency? Even as they stand there is some affinity in subject matter.
This impression can be examined more closely by first looking at the
introduction and conclusion of the stories. Do they begin and end a
complete narrative unit?

Narrative A begins: 'And there was a famine in the land; and Abram
went down into Egypt to sojourn there; for the famine was sore in the land.'
To the modern reader this is an unsatisfactory beginning to an independent

narrative. Which land is referred to? Who is Abraham, the central figure? But the Hebrews do not like full expositions; they prefer to go directly to the heart of the matter, as in the book of Job, or Ruth. Moreover Abraham was naturally a familiar figure to them. And then form criticism cannot be applied to a translation: when the translation says, 'the land' we ask 'Which land?' But when it is הָאָרֶץ, without any closer definition, it is quite clear to any Israelite that the land referred to is Palestine. And to him it is very natural for a Palestinian to journey to Egypt at a time of famine, for Egypt has the Nile for its water supply and is not dependent upon rain. It therefore has means of sustenance when, as frequently happened, those in Palestine were starving though lack of rain.[1] But the most important fact that a study of the introduction in the Hebrew text reveals is that the introductory clause 'And there was . . .' or 'It came to pass' (וַיְהִי) is a much-used method of starting off a narrative (cf. xxvi. 1, 14; but also vi. 1; xi. 2; I Sam. i. 1, etc.). The phrase is then repeated with a time-indication at the start of a new scene (verses 11, 14; I Sam. xviii. 6,10, etc.). So for an Israelite verse 10 is a completely satisfactory beginning to a story. It tells all. The well-known figure of the patriarch has to journey to a foreign, hostile country, where he has only the limited rights of a sojourner. This provides the basis for the story as it immediately develops. And the conclusion? Pharaoh bids Abraham, 'Now therefore behold thy wife, take her, and go thy way', and the narrator concludes, 'And Pharaoh gave men charge concerning him: and they brought him on the way, and his wife, and all he had.' This ends the narrative very satisfactorily. The Hebrew often ends a tale with a speech which is intended to abate the suspense, and a subsequent short narrative remark on the further fate of the hero (Gen. ii. 23 f., iv. 15 f., xi. 7–9, etc.).

The context in which A stands also indicates that it was once a complete unit. Chapter xii. 1–9, which immediately precedes it, describes Abraham leaving his home at the command of God, and with his promise, to go into an unknown land. He arrives *in Palestine*, and there he founds two sanctuaries, in Shechem and Bethel. At this point A begins. This is odd. For now Abraham wanders *out of* Palestine, just after God had said to him in Bethel, 'Unto thy seed will I give this land' (verse 7). So Abraham unhesitatingly leaves the land which according to the text has just been given him. Why it is that the author inserted this story at this point is a matter which will concern us later; here it is sufficient to say that the link between the two tales is loose. A look at what happens in chapter xiii, which follows the tale, will show even more clearly that the author has squeezed in the story in its present position:

> And Abraham went up out of Egypt, he, and his wife, and all that he had, and Lot with him, into the south. And Abram was very rich in cattle, in silver, and in gold. And he went on his journeys from the south even to Beth-el, unto the place where his test had been at the beginning, between Beth-el, and Ai; unto the place of the altar, which he had made there at the first.

[1] See the Joseph narrative and ANET 259; also the well-known picture of Beni Hassan ANEP 3.

So the narrative of Abram's journey through the Promised Land, which was in the process of being narrated before the story of the ancestress of Israel, (xii. 5–9), is now resumed. Only a few intermediary sentences have been inserted to provide a link with our story. In fact, A could quite simply be taken out of the context. Indeed, if this were done, the description of Abram's journey through the Promised Land in chapters xii and xiii would flow more easily. This can only be explained by assuming A to be an independent narrative which was in general circulation, of course in oral form. So long as it continued to be retold by word of mouth the story remained a brief one. It impressed itself easily upon the mind, so that everyone could easily remember it.

Narrative B begins: 'And Abram journeyed from thence toward the land of the South, and dwelt between Kadesh and Shur; and he sojourned in Gerar.' This looks even less like a proper introduction than that of A. Abram journeyed 'from thence'. This presupposes a previous indication of place and also a previous piece of narration. But this link proves to be the writer's later insertion, for the setting out 'from thence'[2] is as little motivated as the stay in Gerar. This happens often in other places in the narratives about Abraham's travels and elsewhere in the Genesis stories. In A famine was the straightforward reason; as there is none given here it is possible that the author inserted the journey 'from thence' to the south merely to provide a link between the two passages. Also there is no reason given for the second journey from the south to Gerar. It seems probable that famine was once also mentioned at this point, but because of its mention in chapter xii (A) and later in xxvi (C) the author left it out for he did not want to mention it too often. The introduction to the independent oral version which we assume also existed here, could well have begun: 'And there was famine . . . Abraham sojourned in Gerar.'

The conclusion in verse 15 provides a completely satisfactory ending. After all that has been said and done things return to normal. Abraham is given permission to stay, and what is more he will no longer be troubled by others; Sarah is compensated, and Abimelech's house recovers. Here too the tale is ended after two conclusive statements (verses 15 f.).

A look at the overall context shows that B can be taken out of its present position just as easily as A. Before it is the story of Sodom and Gomorrah, which certainly has nothing to do with the ancestress of Israel. (Originally chapter xx must in any case have had a different context, for it appears to have been written by the Elohist. Chapter xix is by the Jahwist—but we will look into this later. In general it is supposed that as with chapter xii narrative B was also preceded by the promise of great issue to Abraham[3]; but this is most certainly a later connection.) But the connection is closer with the chapter which follows, which was originally by the same writer, the Elohist, and which is about Abraham's sons, Ishmael and Isaac. But even here this can scarcely be the original link, for it is assumed in the story

---

[2] Von Rad ATD reflects whether the Sodom catastrophe was the cause of this departure; this would have been a weak motive, which will clearly have been added later, by the first writer of the story at the earliest.

[3] Were traces preserved in chapter xv?

that they do not yet have children. Chapter xx (B) could just as easily be taken out of its present context without affecting the progress of the story.

With *narrative C* things are a little more complicated. However, the beginning is clearly the start of a previously independent unit: 'And there was famine in the land . . . And Isaac went unto Abimelech king of the Philistines unto Gerar.' As with A, the narrative is characterised by the clause 'And there was' (It came to pass) . . . , which is a traditional beginning to a narrative unit. But the supplementary clause, 'beside the first famine that was in the days of Abraham' has a clumsy ring to it in the Hebrew, and is likely to have been inserted by a later writer to make C compatible with A. The writer therefore knows chapter xii. Otherwise to the Hebrew mind the beginning is thoroughly satisfactory; all that is presupposed is a familiarity with the person of Isaac, and with Palestine as 'the land'.

But the conclusion to the narrative is not so straightforward. It is true that verse 11 contains a conclusive statement which dissolves the tension created by the tale, and that verse 12 provides a correct ending. From now on Isaac and his wife enjoy the protection of both God and the king. But the passage describing Isaac's wealth in verses 12 f. stands out, and seems to have been expanded by the writer to prepare his audience for the next story about the envy of the Philistines.

The overall context of this narrative also reveals that it was preceded, as was A and B, by the description of a divine promise. But here the connection is not merely external: the two stories are in fact merged. Yet the transmission history will show that they were merged relatively late. It will also show that the close link with the second half of the chapter is not an essential one. Yet even in the oral tradition narrative C had become part of a series of sagas about Isaac, telling of the favour he enjoyed in Gerar and Beersheba and the envy that this aroused among his neighbours there. However, looking at the wider context there seems to be no particular reason why this section should have been inserted at this point in the book as a whole. In the previous chapter, chapter xxv, Jacob and Esau are born, but here their parents, Isaac and Rebecca, do not appear to have any children, thus contradicting not only the previous chapter but also the following one. If they had already had children no one in Gerar would have believed the story that they were brother and sister. The collection of narratives in chapter xxvi could well have grown up in oral form, and could have been taken over by the writer just as they stand. Nevertheless there is still reason to assume that at an earlier stage they were individual units. The promise of favour at the beginning, which has been squeezed in between the command, 'Sojourn in this land', and its performance, 'And Isaac dwelt in Gerar', is almost distracting. The second half of the chapter is even more loosely connected. Not only does it begin with the customary introduction to an independent unit, 'And it came to pass . . .', but it also presupposes a place other than the city of Gerar. Thus C, even more than A and B, is only intelligible as a component literary type in a complex unit; though in spite of this there is indication enough that it was once an independent unit. Therefore all three tales about the ancestress of Israel once circulated as independent narratives.

B. *Determination of the Literary Type*

As the tales were once independent their literary type must be determined, irrespective of their present, written context. What type of story are they? Obviously all three are of the same type. Past centuries of Christian and Jewish thought believed them to be historical, but a closer study of them has made this seem very unlikely. A fundamental condition for any historical report is that the narrator of the tale is quite sure of the path the material has taken between him and the original eye witness. Here this alone is enough to present difficulties. How can the narrator know what happened in the harem of a foreign potentate? Indeed, what can he know of a dream giving divine injunctions? Further, is it possible to imagine the patriarchs describing this kind of delicate event in detail for the benefit of their descendants? And Abraham did the same thing twice! Usually this kind of experience is not one which would be bandied around. And the Israelites were particularly sensitive about such matters. These considerations need not be conclusive; what is more important is that the story contains nothing that could positively indicate a historical report. There is no indication at all of when the events took place, and dates are vital to any history. It is significant that later, when the story was built into a historical narrative, a date was added (Jub. xiii. 10 f.). The story is not concerned with a constitutional or national crisis, but rather with family matters. Narrator and audience obviously believe themselves to be descendants of this Abraham and this Isaac; the fortunes of the patriarchs are theirs also, and the beauty of the patriarch's wife is a matter for pride. And what is important is that God so ordered the world as to show favour to their own ancestors (at least in A and B). Against this figures of any political importance have only a secondary position in the story. We are not even given the name of the king of Egypt. The presentation of a world event of this kind in terms of the family will later be more exactly shown to be characteristic of the *saga*.

It is hoped that the use of the term saga in connection with biblical narratives, which are regarded by the church as the word of God, will not shock some theologians, or horrify the more devout. But the reader must not make the crude mistake of dismissing the saga as a fantastical, primitive, and therefore 'untrue' phenomenon. The next but one paragraph will show that on the contrary biblical sagas conceal much that is true, and are of vital importance for the preaching of Christianity.

But to the details of the literary type. Apart from the characteristics of the saga which have already been mentioned, the introduction also, 'And there was *or* It came to pass . . .', is not of a type which is concerned with the narration of historical events. Also, the speeches near the end are more the climax to a personal dispute. And the presentation of simple scenes[4] (introduced by 'And it came to pass . . .') is also typical of the abrupt manner of story-telling: Abraham bids his wife pose as his sister; it is assumed as a matter of course that she will do this. A gives no details of what happens between Sarah and Pharaoh at the palace, but it is made

---

[4] Gunkel, *Genesis* XXXIV sees the scene as a narrative unit, which is distinguished from the preceding or following one by a shift in either characters, scene of action, or in the action itself.

obvious from the tale itself. In A also no details are given of what Abraham says in answer to Pharaoh's admonitions. And we are not told at the end whether Pharaoh's house recovered health. On the other hand there are embellishments which are very characteristic of the saga: a long list of sheep, oxen, asses, she-asses, camels, manservants and maidservants (obviously of great interest to the writer and his original audience), and the humorous feature when Abimelech looks out of a window and sees how things really lie. This is the state of affairs in A and C. But B, with its long speeches, reveals other characteristics which need some investigation.

But the term saga is not enough to provide an accurate designation of the literary type. It is too indefinite. It includes a whole group of literary types, each of which must be more closely defined. With material as limited as our three narratives this need only be a preliminary. But one prominent feature of these narratives is that although there are no indications of when the events actually happened there are quite definite indications of place. Great importance is attached to the rights which the patriarchs are allowed in a foreign country; in C the position of a sojourner is even emphasised by a command from God. The official escort in A, after the happy ending, is also emphasised, as is the compensatory gift in B, and the king's ruling (verse 11) in C. Abraham, the ancestor, is pictured as a stranger in a foreign society: as a nomad he and his people are of inferior status and have few rights as soon as they enter the bounds of a 'state'. It is not a matter of Abraham's relation to individuals but to strange nations established in a particular area. It is true that in B and C Abimelech the king appears as interlocutor for the other side, but he is only representing the conditions in the land of the Philistines, in 'this place' or 'that land'. And when Pharaoh in A is given no name this is because he is merely a typical representative of Egypt. In such sagas, therefore, the position of the nomadic Abraham and Isaac, including their strikingly beautiful women and their people, is contrasted with the soft lascivious people of an established land. Gunkel therefore termed this literary type the *ethnological saga*. In such sagas the predominant fact for the Israelite is that his God, the God of Israel, has influence on what happens between nations, and reveals himself as a divine leader. Because of the emphasis on ethnological relations other races also appear, and it is made quite clear that the power of God is by no means restricted to his own nation. The God of a small, nomadic people, not yet become a nation, can guide the Egyptian Pharaoh as well as the king of the Philistines. Stories of this type are of particular importance in assessing what later became the universal Israelite concept of God. (Gen. xxxiv is also of the same kind, showing the relations between the Jacob group and the established peoples of Shechem, as is the saga of the curse of Canaan in Gen. ix. 20 ff.).

The ethnological saga is a complex literary type comprising a host of smaller component types. One of these is the form in which God's commandments appear. C starts with a simple command from God, with the imperative usual in such cases (verses 2, 3a), and then a longer benediction which has at least some resemblance to poetic language and *parallelismus membrorum*:

'And I will be with thee, and will bless thee:
For unto thee, and unto thy seed, I will give all these lands.
And I will establish the oath: / which I sware unto Abraham thy father.
And I will multiply thy seed as the stars in heaven: / and will give unto thy
   seed all these lands.
And in thy seed shall all the nations of the earth be blessed.
(All this) Because Abraham obeyed my voice, / and kept my charge, my
   commandments, my statutes and my laws.'

This style of such divine benedictions can also be seen in xii. 1–3 (also with
an introductory command); xii. 7, xiii. 14–17, xv. 15, etc. However a divine
communication which is revealed in a dream has a different ring to it, as in
B, verses 3, 6 f., where we have a lament by the king. But there are also
literary types used in communication between people. The king's language
is very distinctive when he calls a subordinate to account. It often begins
with a blunt question (xii. 18, xx. 9 f., 15 f., cf. xxvi. 9): 'Why hast thou
done this to me?' (see also iii. 13, xxix. 25; Num. xxiii. 11, etc.[5]). The
apologetic answer given by a subordinate begins with 'Because I thought'
in xx. 11, xxvi. 9. When the king dismisses a man from his presence it is
usually with a command: xii. 19, xx. 15. And in xxvi. 11 the king commands
his people:

'He that toucheth this man or his wife shall surely be put to death'

הַנֹּגֵעַ בָּאִישׁ הַזֶּה וּבְאִשְׁתּוֹ מוֹת יוּמָת:

This command is of particular interest, because this is also the way in which
an Israelite king ended an obligatory command to meet a critical situation;
it is also the style in which the gathering of the people expressed itself in
I. Sam. xiv. 39; Judges xxi. 5, etc. But examples of this form are chiefly
to be found in the Old Testament collections of laws, e.g. Exod. xxi. 12:

'He that smiteth a man, so that he die, shall surely be put to death'

מַכֵּה אִישׁ וָמֵת מוֹת יוּמָת:

A. Alt has brought all such 'enumerations of crimes worthy of death',
which begin with a participial clause and an object belonging to it, and
which end with a paronomasia (מוֹת יוּמַת) under the heading of apodictic
divine law,[6] thereby including the literary type of the divine commandments
(the Decalogue), although these take a slightly different form. Whether
this classification is right is open to question; but in any case it is a point
to be borne in mind that the words which the saga has put into the mouth of

---

[5] Called 'formula of reproach' (*Formel des Vorwurfs*) by I. Lande, *Formelhafte
Wendungen der Umgangssprache im AT*, 1949, pp. 99 f; or 'accusation formula'
(*Beschuldigungsformel*) by H. J. Boecker, Redeformen des Rechtslebens im A.T.
WMANT 14, 1964, 26–31, who thus sees it associated with legal proceedings.
Better would be 'Reproach for an action against the common good' (*Vorwurf der
gemeinschaftswidrigen Tat*). Narrative 3 refers to an 'protestation of innocence'
(*Sundenbestreifung*) in verse 9: 'Wherein have I sinned against thee that . . . which
is customarily used before holy persons (Abraham as prophet) and before kings
(I Kings xxviii. 9; Jer. xxxvii. 18).
[6] *Die Ursprünge der israelitischen Rechts*, ALT I, 307–13 (cf. p. 27 for E.T.). See
above p. 95, n. 10.

the foreign king are those of a customary legal form in Israel. The manner in which a man speaks to his wife is less distinctive. xii. 11–13, xx. 13 show how he addresses her while they are travelling.

A look at these component literary types reveals that the most disparate psychological, religious and legal aspects of life have gone into the making of this tale. (But this does not mean—as Keller maintains[7]—that the story was written for the sake of embodying such motives.)

C. *Transmission History*

When we defined the extent of the unit we came to the conclusion that the three sagas probably existed for a long time previously in oral form. However, material transmitted orally changes its form only imperceptibly. Are there obscure sentences which are survivals of an earlier stage? In the first place we must investigate the relationship the three narratives have to each other. Are they all based on one original story? It is only a question of dialect which makes them appear in A as Abram and Sarai, and in B as Abraham and Sarah. Such a custom still prevailed in Germany as late as the eighteenth century.[8] It is unlikely that a couple should fall twice into the same strange predicament, or that he should practice the same deceit or mental reservation twice, having already once got into difficulties because of it.[9] In C it is true that the couple is different, but the foreign opponents are the same, and so is the city. Isaac must surely have known of his father's experience: is he likely to have made the same mistake himself? Abimelech knows the people he is up against, and how they behave: is he likely to allow himself to be hoodwinked again? (It is just as unlikely—if we take the story as a saga and not as a historical report—that such embarrassing circumstances should be twice ascribed to the fore-fathers.) It therefore seems probable that all three versions come from a common source. This is further indicated by synonymous wording at the decisive points: each time the patriarch is in a foreign country as a 'so-journer'. Each time he fears death. Each time he is reduced to passing his wife off as his sister. Each time the foreign potentate discovers the ruse and calls the patriarch to him, greeting him with the reproof: 'What hast thou done unto me (us)?' The divergences in the three narratives do not seem to have arisen intentionally, but rather through the course of oral transmission which will probably have taken place in different regions, and perhaps at different times. Is it possible to resurrect the original story? For a start it must be made clear that it is never possible to reconstitute the actual wording of the original story through a study of the oral tradition, at best only its content. But with three parallel texts at our disposal, it should be possible to gain some idea of what preceded the present versions.

[7] C. A. Keller, Die Gefährdung der Ahnfrau, ZAW 66, 1954, 181–91.

[8] Though in its present context in Genesis the difference in pronunciation of the names was developed by a later writer into a particular theory: xcii. 5.

[9] Speiser (Anchor Bible 1964) sees in xii. 10 ff. the survival of a Hurrite legal principle by which the marriage tie was stronger if the woman (possibly by adoption) was also the man's sister. This might have played some part in the saga originally. The Israelite narrators no longer knew of it. Cf. xxvi. 10.

(*a*) The first task is to discover if there are any parts of the three tales which could have been added later. Chapter xii is brief and fluent. There are no inessentials, only external events. Psychological considerations, such as Sarah's feelings, or how Abram felt after leaving Egypt, are lacking completely. Yet the narrative shows a sophisticated perception of what should be left unsaid. What happens to Sarai in the harem is only vaguely hinted at. All this gives the narrative an archaic quality. The delicacy of the situation has been least noticed by the writer of this version of the story. In fact he sometimes describes it with his tongue in his cheek as if it were a comic episode. It is not considered a bad thing that Abram should induce his wife to lie. Pharaoh does indeed call him to account, but notwithstanding he lets him depart loaded with gifts. The narrator seems to glory in the cunning of his ancestors. But the narrative has one obscurity. Although it is reported that Pharaoh and his house were stricken with plague, it is not explained how it was that Pharaoh knew that it was because of Abram's wife. This is the actual peripeteia of the narrative, which is always strongly brought out in any good Israelite story (cf. the more elaborate version in B). Here it seems that something has been lost. Perhaps it was offensive to a later generation. How can a Pharaoh determine the reason for his misfortune? Only through his gods, through the medium of a soothsayer; but that heathen gods could have told Pharaoh the truth was considered suspect by the writer and he has left it out. This has created a gap in the story. Other than this, however, the original material has been retained intact. There are no later additions.

Chapter xx differs from A chiefly in its long conversations. The characters' speeches give some indication of their psychological state. The king of the Philistines is timid, but absolutely honest: and the 'prophet' Abraham asks wherever he goes whether the people there are god-fearing. This version of the story is more artistically constructed. It does not merely follow the simple course of events, but in many places doubles back on the story by adding details at a later stage, only indicating for instance the real relationship between Abraham and Sarah quite late in Abraham's speech to the king. The malady which has affected Abimelech's house is only mentioned at the end; the fact that Sarah was not touched is also reported relatively late (verse 4), as is the fact that it was God who prevented the crime (verse 6). Abraham has been clever but is not pleased by his cleverness. At the end he does indeed go away with gifts, but also slightly shamefacedly. There is nothing humorous about the story. Instead, serious words are used, such as *saddiq*, 'faultless in social relationships' (verse 4), 'integrity of heart and innocence of hands' (verse 6), 'great sin' (verse 9), 'fear of God' (verse 11). Whereas in A Abram was a simple Bedouin, here he is a chosen man of God, a Nabi (prophet), who is capable of interceding effectively on behalf of foreign kings. These are all views of a later period. In no other place in Genesis is Abraham seen as a Nabi. Here also he does not lie: although he has suppressed the fact that Sarah is not his wife, according to this narrative it is quite true that she is his sister (verse 12). Hence this is a much later stage of the story than A. The most important development is that he no longer acts unseen on behalf of his people. The story now has religious overtones. God first warns the man who is about to commit an offence even though he is a heathen, and only later takes positive action. However there are still indications of an earlier version of the story. No motive is given for Abraham's journey to Gerar in verse 1, although it involves leaving the Promised Land, which is no small matter for an Israelite. In an earlier version the famine would have been given as the cause, just as in A. So here something has dropped out. Then verse 9, 'Thou hast brought on me and on my kingdom a great sin' assumes that Abimelech has actually committed adultery; it is true the writer has extenuated it in verse 6, where he says that Abimelech had not touched Sarah, but this sentence is clumsy and was therefore added later. Hence over the course of time the story became more sensitive in sexual matters. Also when Abraham justifies himself in verse 12 by saying that Sarah really was his sister, this not only doubles back on the story, but is obviously a later insertion. The narrative does not expressly say that Sarah was a very beautiful woman, for its present position in Genesis would make Sarah well past an age when this could have been so. So this sentence will also have been dropped. Therefore what can be discovered of an earlier version from this text is nearer in content to narrative A than to its wording here.

Narrative C is so broken up by speeches that it is scarcely a story any more. The king of Gerar becomes the king of the Philistines, which itself is an anachronism, for at the time of the patriarchs there were as yet no Philistines in Palestine. At the beginning there is the great blessing given by God, which is a repetition of that given to Abraham merely transferred to the person of Isaac. This is followed by the dialogue between Abimelech and Isaac in verses 9–11, which does not begin, as in A and B, with a blunt statement in reproof, but with an astonished assertion. Nothing dangerous happens in the whole of the story, other than when Abimelech looks through a window and sees Isaac sporting with Rebekah. The delicate situation has become a mere eventuality; there is no longer a threat from a foreign king, but at the most one from his people. Therefore there is no need for any direct intervention by God: the protective words of the king suffice. The blessing at the end does not come from the Philistines, but from Jahweh, and has little to do with the actual story. Everything points to a later stage in the development of the saga, where the story has lost its original form.

The long speech by God at the beginning shows signs of having been much elaborated. The passage 'Go down into Egypt . . .' was only inserted when the saga was written into its present context. And the blessing in verses 3[10]–5 is also of a later date. It can be found almost word for word in other passages attributed to the same writer. 'For unto thee, and unto thy seed, I will give all these lands' suggests xii. 7, xiii. 15. 'I will multiply thy seed as the stars of heaven' is a promise already stated in xv. 5. 'In thy seed shall all the nations of the earth be blessed' is similarly expressed in xii. 3, xviii. 14. And the speech, 'And I will establish the oath which I sware unto Abraham thy father' appears to be an even later insertion, for it is first found again in Jer. xi. 5, as is the reference to the keeping of 'my

[10] From: 'and I will be with thee.'

charge, my commandments, my statutes, and my laws' (Deut. v. 29–31; x. 13, xi. 1, etc.). A benediction which promises land is particularly unsuitable in Gerar, for this is a Philistine city far down in the south on the Palestinian coast and did not belong to ancient Israel, the Promised Land. The whole passage incorporating the blessing is therefore a later addition.

Crudely stated A is the most ancient, B the middle version and C the most recent version of the story. Yet this does not mean that A is the oral tradition or even the written source for the two other versions. The situation is more complicated than that.

(b) This is shown by comparing the three versions, in an attempt to discover the original form of the story.

1. According to A the patriarch travels to Egypt, to the land of Pharaoh, and according to B and C only to Gerar, the city of Abimelech. Pharaoh and Abimelech are the counter-heroes. Abimelech and Gerar have the advantage over Pharaoh in that they appear twice. However it is much easier to imagine a story being transferred from a relatively small and insignificant king and country to one that is generally known, such as Egypt and its ruler, than it would be the other way round.

2. In chapter xii it is not stated whether Pharaoh touched Sarai; in chapter xx he had not done so, but this is a point which has clearly been added later. In chapter xxvi it had not even reached the stage when Rebekah entered the king's harem. The oldest narrative is the one with least scruples: it will have described an actual, although unwittingly committed, case of adultery.

3. The discovery of the mistake in C, where it is only a matter of the possibility of a crime, occurs by chance. In B it is the God of Israel who reveals the situation, through the medium of a dream; and in A, the earlier version, it is revealed through a foreign god, or soothsayer. This last fits in least well with the later attitude in the Old Testament, so this will be the original version.

4. In chapter xii the patriarch has to leave the country; in xx and xxvi he is allowed to remain. It is not possible to determine which will have been the older version.[11]

5. In A Abraham receives gifts when Pharaoh takes Sarah, in B only later, after they are reconciled and honour is satisfied. In C, however, the blessing comes after the event, and from God, not from men. Each succeeding narrative reveals an increasingly refined moral attitude.[12]

6. The story as a whole is told almost entirely in dialogue; but the speeches have been inserted in different places in the narrative, and have therefore arisen quite independently of each other. A dialogue between the patriarch and his wife crops up in A and B, but at different points: in A following the run of events, but in B only later in the conversation with Abimelech. When the patriarch is summoned before the king in B and C a dialogue ensues. In C there is also a dialogue between Isaac and God,

[11] Though later in chapter xxvi Isaac is asked by the Philistines to leave the land.
[12] The difference is easy to explain along tradition-historical lines, and one cannot agree with Keller (see note 7) who sees the end of the incident reported quite differently in each of the three sagas.

and a ruling announced by Abimelech to his people. B contains the most conversation; other than those speeches already mentioned, there is a dialogue between God and the king, and Abimelech talks to Sarah. Also a talk between the king and his servants is indicated, as well as a prayer of intercession by Abraham to God.

7. The style of A is exceedingly concise. The listener must assume many of the essentials himself. In C all the important points are elaborately laid out. Narrative B on the other hand does not just follow the course of events. The writer doubles back on his tracks very sophisticatedly. Here A is most definitely the earliest version. It is written in the style of the old saga, which Gunkel terms the *concise style*, while the style of B and C corresponds to the *elaborated style* of a later period.

8. The biggest difference is in the name of the hero. Was Abraham or Isaac the original subject of the story? The general rule in the transmission of the saga is that the least known figure is the original (compare the change from the king of the city of Gerar to the Pharaoh of Egypt). Accordingly Isaac was originally the subject; he was later replaced by Abraham, who for the Israelites represented their ideal of the god-fearing Israelite. Here narrative C, the latest version, contains the original matter.

The original version will thus have run: Because of famine Isaac travelled from the desert in southern Palestine to the nearby Canaanite city of Gerar, to live there as 'sojourner', i.e. to keep within the pasturage rights on the ground belonging to the city. He told everyone that his wife was his sister so that his life would not be endangered by those who desired her. However, Rebekah's beauty could not pass unnoticed. The king of the city, Abimelech, took Rebekah into his harem, amply compensating Isaac. As a material sin was about to be committed, God[13] struck the people of the palace with a mysterious illness. Through the medium of his gods, or a soothsayer, Abimelech recognised what had happened. Abimelech called Isaac to account: 'What is this that you have done to me?' He then restored him his wife and sent him away, loaded with gifts.

All the variations have occurred in their own particular fashion, but when compared with what we know of the original version they reveal a general tendency which gives us some basis for a history of the literary type of the ethnological saga.

(*a*) The narratives become elaborated by speeches, which gradually achieve a status equal to the deeds of the hero. Through them the thoughts and impulses of the people are expressed. This method of expression is one that is used increasingly later on in the Bible (cf. the long speeches in the Genesis-Apocryphon).

(*b*) Moral sensitivity becomes gradually stronger. Sexual matters become treated with more and more restraint.

(*c*) God's intervention is less tangible in the later versions. Divine action is understood in a more universal way. Sometimes God even intervenes on behalf of the heathen king and his people. Thus when the patriarch

---

[13] The name Jahweh (in A and C), which first arose at the time of Moses, will not have been part of the original version of the story. We do not know what was the earlier designation for God.

of Israel associates with such people he is obliged to maintain his loyalty and faith for his God's sake.

(*d*) During the story's development there is a tendency to transfer the action of the story to more familiar people and powers.

D. *Setting in Life*

Where would such a story circulate? It is a robust kind of tale, and would be in keeping with the small nomadic tribes of pre-Israelite times living with their herds of cattle in the desert of southern Palestine. In fact, the hero of the story is one of them. It is significant that sheep are considered a man's greatest possession. Also it will concern people who were very familiar with the conditions in Gerar. In other words, this was a story narrated by the forefathers of Israel before the conquest; in fact, by that particular branch of the Israelites who would trace their descent back to Isaac, and who roamed about in the south of Palestine with their small herds of cattle. Such a story would perhaps have been related by men before the tents, when it was evening, after the herds had been settled and the children slept. When times were hard these people were compelled to go to a city in the civilised region and there to beg permission to graze their cattle on the city outskirts. On the one hand they were inferior to the city dweller, who possessed a quite different means of authority. Their position was one of men in need of protection. On the other hand they felt themselves superior to the men living in established cities. Their own ancestor had been cleverer than the townspeople. 'The narrator gloats over Abraham's astoundingly successful lie, which made a virtue out of necessity. He identifies himself joyfully with his forebear's sharp practice' (Gunkel). That is why they are so proudly conscious of the fact that their women are more beautiful than those living in the cities. Their own nomadic god is more powerful; when need is greatest he intervenes in favour of his flock. In moral considerations, too, they consider themselves superior: the city dwellers are weak and susceptible to feminine charm. (Even today our own country people have sometimes the same feeling of superiority over the townspeople in that respect.) A man of Isaac's people cannot be seduced quite so easily. There is one feature of the story missing which would be natural to us: there is no reluctance to surrender the woman's honour, 'that my soul may live because of thee'. However, it seems obvious that the Bedouin women are so devoted to their menfolk that to protect a husband's life they would willingly lose their honour. All this points to very early conditions. Moreover, at a later time exception would have been taken to the marriage between half-brother and sister in B (Lev. xviii, xix, etc.). The conception of objective guilt which calls down punishment even though the crime was committed unwittingly and unintentionally, is also an old one.

Now that we have come so far in investigating the transmission history and setting in life, it would be as well to look into the historicity of the story, and to look for a connection with archeological findings and with what we know of the geography of early Palestine. This will enable us to determine the setting in life more exactly. To begin with it must be recognised that the saga is wholly imbued with the atmosphere of the period it describes, and therefore must certainly belong to the period before the settlement of the later Israelite tribes. The saga's 'framework' is historical; its local colour, its moods and feelings, are undoubtedly those of Isaac's people in Palestine. Also historical is the position of 'sojourner' in the city of Gerar. Unfortunately we have not yet been able to place this city. Archeologists are still uncertain whether it was on *tell dshemme*, 14 km. south of Gaza (Fl. Petrie) or on *esh-shĕria*, 25 km. south-east of Gaza (Alt), or on *tell abu hurĕre*, which is 7 km. from there.[14] Only the first of these hills has been excavated, and this produced nothing which specifically applies to our story. But we cannot yet say that Abimelech never existed. Archeological evidence may yet show that he did. In any case the saga gives us a good picture of a Canaanite city king of the second millenium. However, Isaac's part in the story cannot be substantiated by archeological evidence; for it seems from the Genesis traditions that it was unlikely that Isaac and his people knew writing, and that therefore there will be no written evidence to excavate. And as they lived in tents it seems unlikely that other sorts of material evidence will be found. With this we have reached the point where we can prove nothing else in the story to have a historical basis. As Isaac is assumed in the saga to be an ancestor of the people relating it, he is likely once to have been leader of their group. It cannot entirely be ruled out that in his lifetime he did get into the delicate situation which the story presents, but it is highly unlikely. The origin of the story is more likely the result of the general disposition and situation of Isaac's people than of the personal experience of Isaac himself. Anyone looking for a historical 'core' in this saga will be looking in vain.

When the Isaac group settled and was united with the Abraham group to become the tribe of Judah, Isaac was then replaced in the story by the more familiar Abraham. The setting in life also changed. The nomads with their small herds became farmers, living together in established villages. Oxen also came to be mentioned as part of Pharaoh's gift (A). According to C Isaac lived in a proper house; and seed and harvest are the images used in the divine benediction. Later still the story is taken up by prophetic circles, or at least an earlier version of narrative B. These will have been people like those around Elijah and Elisha in about the ninth century; no later, for there is no sign of the melancholy outlook of the later writing prophets. In this setting in life Abraham is raised to the rank of a prophet; he is given the office of intercessor. It is now a question of sin and purity, lies and unwitting offence. The saga has now become a *legend about the prophets* (see under). Finally, however, the story of the ancestress of Israel becomes an episode in a greater written unit. With that we come to the last section.

E. *Redaction History*

What is the point of tracing back the tangled threads of this tradition? For a start it discloses important facts about the beliefs and the way of life of

---

[14] Gunkel, *Genesis*, pp. 225 ff.

the pre-Israelite period. Secondly, displayed on such a background the meaning of the story is quite startlingly revealed. Once the tradition history has been traced, it is then possible to discover the purpose behind the source of writings. It is no longer a question of the cunning Isaac, overcoming all enemies with the help of God, but of a stage in the great salvation history of God. The story is now no longer an isolated literary type, but an integral part of a greater whole.

The fact has long been established that Genesis is not the uniform work of one writer, but goes back to three of four sources running parallel to each other describing the same period of time, and which are continued here and there in the books of Exodus and Numbers. Chapter xx (B) is the work of the so-called Elohist, i.e. the source describing the period before Moses which only uses the general term Elohim (God) for God. Technically he is known as E. His authorship is indicated in Chapter xx by the word 'God' in verses 3, 6, 11, 13, 17. Verse 18 is an exception, for here the word 'Jahweh' (Lord) is used, but this verse is stilted and was added later by way of explanatory comment. It is not the work of the original author. The Elohist was also responsible for the Abraham narrative in chapter xxi, and perhaps for chapters xv and xxii. There is a particular linguistic usage common to these passages, for instance the word אָמָה[15] for maid, while other sources use שִׁפְחָה.[16] It is an open question whether the Elohist, of whose work only traces remain, wrote a complete history, or whether he merely collected individual narrative units. But in any case chapter xx is clearly the work of a different writer from that of chapters xii and xxvi. It seems unlikely that the latter author should have also taken up narrative B and inserted it along with his own pieces, for then he would have reported the story three times altogether, and twice of Abraham. Even if this were so, it is inconceivable that he should not have adapted the style of the story to fit in with his own. Typical of E is that striking tendency to double back on the story, and not merely to follow the course of events. Chapter xxi, also Elohistic, does the same. Moreover E has a weakness for long speeches (cf. the Elohistic chapter xxxi). As we only have fragments of the E source it is difficult to pinpoint the writer's general outlook. However, the many place indications[17] at the beginning and the reference in verse 13 to 'when God caused me to wander from my father's house' (lit. to go astray), infer that he saw Abraham as a wanderer, and a wanderer with the rank of a prophet. It is for this reason that he does not simply fear the foreign country, as he did in the original story, but establishes that the people there are not god-

---

[15] *Biblisch-Historisches Handwörterbuch* I, 1962, 547 f.; BRL 179 f.
[16] However in VT III, 1958, 293–7 A. Jepsen has brought forward a strong argument against crediting the two designations to different sources. For E it is also significant that God appears to men in *dreams*.
[17] The Elohist obviously had little idea of the geography of southern Palestine, otherwise he would not have placed Gerar, which is situated near Gaza, between Kadesh and Shur, which are two towns on the Sinai peninsula (cf. Speiser, who thinks differently). Perhaps he was thinking of a town with the same name on that peninsula, which could live on in the present Dsherur near 'en qdes (Kadesh). Indications such as this lead us to believe that the Elohist was a native of northern Israel and not of Judah.

fearing enough, which is of course to be presumed in a heathen community. Morally he is not at fault: he does not lie, for Sara is indeed his sister. Many of these 'theological' concepts will have come from the author, but it is difficult to extract his share of them from those which will have already been part of the oral tradition when he took it over from the prophetic circles.

Narrative A, on the other hand, is the work of the Jahwist. He is the writer who in Genesis, from the creation onwards, always uses the term 'Jahweh' (Lord) for God, and whom we refer to briefly as J.[18] We have considerably more information about him, because a large part of his work was taken up into the Tetrateuch. It ranges from the beginning of the world and mankind, over the time of the patriarchs, to the Exodus from Egypt and the wandering in the wilderness right up to Israel's conquest of Palestine. The time of the patriarchs is given particular emphasis because in it God's relationship to mankind, previously quite unrestricted in any way, became concentrated entirely on one clan and the nation which arose out of it. The selection of this particular clan was made known through the command given to Abraham to start on his travels, and particularly through the benediction which accompanied it, which extended to a promise to Abraham of great issue, possession of the Promised Land, and a blessing of all the families of the earth. This is first formulated in Gen. xii. 1–3, 7, which is the real core of the Jahwistic material, for everything that happened, right up until Isaac took over the land, is understood in the light of this divine benediction. The writer intends to show how this blessing is transformed from a promise into a fact. This does not happen quickly and straightforwardly, but in a thoroughly complicated fashion. Again and again the realisation of that promise seems endangered, either by the subject of the blessing himself, or by his human adversaries. This theme running through the book lends fresh meaning to the story of the ancestress of Israel[19]; for Sarah is Abraham's only legitimate wife, and only through her can the 'seed' be expected. If Sarah is taken into the harem of a foreign potentate then Abraham's hopes are shattered, and God's promise comes to nothing. To the Jahwist it is undoubtedly important that Abraham, 'when he was come near to enter into Egypt', had forgotten the divine blessing which accompanied him, otherwise he would not have feared death, or felt personal anxiety: 'that my soul may live because of thee'. But Jahweh is not as fickle as man. Although Abraham had forgotten him, he intervenes in Abraham's favour and plagues the house of Pharaoh 'because of Sarai Abram's wife', for the sake of the promise he must see

---

[18] This is substantiated by other particularities of linguistic usage. For instance, the word כבד used in connection with plagues—here with a famine—is a characteristic of the Jahwist xliii. 1; xlvii. 4, 13; Exod. ix. 3.

[19] This interpretation also applies even if the preceding verses xii. 1–8 are not the work of the writer of A, i.e. the Jahwist, but of an older lay source (L). This is Eissfeldt's opinion: Hexateuch-Synopse 1922 (following that of Gunkel). And in that case also an act of blessing will presumably have preceded it. Although surely the argument for dividing chapter xii into two sources, with verses 10 ff. as a distraction from the main story between the stay in Bethel xii. 8 and xiii. 2, does not take into consideration J's custom of gathering together and combining different material.

realised. It is clear that the humorous aspect of the story has been 'entirely banished' (von Rad[20]). The saga has become a historical narrative.

To link this previously independent saga with his other material on the Abraham period, the writer needed to add comment. The beginning of the chapter saw Abraham on the way from Mesopotamia to Shechem and Bethel, i.e. to mid-Palestine. However, the oral tradition of A gave the southern part of Palestine as the starting point of the story. The Jahwist therefore links up this distance with the sentence: 'And Abraham journeyed, going on still toward the South'. At the end of the narrative also comment had to be inserted to connect it with further Abraham traditions taking place back in central Palestine. So J adds: 'And Abram went up out of Egypt, he, and his wife, and all that he had, and Lot with him, into the South'. With this the starting point of the previous tradition (xiii. 7 ff.) is reached. And then, in xiii. 2–5, we are again told that Abram and Lot acquired large herds and one day came again to Bethel. Thus the path is prepared for the following dispute between Lot and Abram. This passage is a particularly good illustration of the Jahwist's aptitude for linking previously independent units by explanatory comments, and thereby divesting them of their self-sufficiency and making them components of a complex literary type.[21]

Chapter xxvi also gives the impression of having been written by the Jahwist, despite the use of the word God in verses, 2 and 12. It is difficult to know where this version of the story belongs, because J had already described the birth of Esau and Jacob, Isaac and Rebekah's children, but in here they appear to be still childless. This problem can be solved either by assuming, with Eissfeldt,[22] that there is a second Jahwistic source which he calls the Lay source, and that xxvi. 1 followed immediately after xxv. 11: 'And it came to pass that after the death of Abraham that God (?) blessed Isaac his son; and Isaac dwelt by Beer-lahai-roi.' Or it can be assumed that the original J sequence ran xxv. 11—xxvi—xxv. 22 ff.,[23] and that it was rearranged only later by the final redactor of the Genesis material, for an as yet unknown reason. In both cases it must be recognised that the writer had already found the saga of the Israelite ancestress Rebekah connected with other Isaac traditions (xxvi. 15 ff.), but the literary type of these traditions was not quite as fixed as that of others, so that it could therefore be more easily incorporated into a greater complex. Chapter xxvi does indeed give the impression of a mosaic. To bind the Isaac material more closely together, and to give it an overall theme, the

[20] Von Rad, ATD.
[21] Noth, ÜGP 40–44 has put forward the thesis that J as well as E goes back to a common element (G) which, whether written or oral, was very fixed in form. But then it would have to be assumed that G had developed along different lines in different places, and that E and J had different versions, with different wordings, at their command. In any case in our example it would be difficult to attribute the tremendous divergences between A and B entirely to the conscious intervention of the two writers.
[22] In the *Hexateuch-Synopse* mentioned above.
[23] Wellhausen, *Composition*³, p. 28 put forward this theory quite early, and recently C. A. Simpson, *The Early Traditions of Israel*, 1948 pp. 91 ff. (Oxford, Blackwell; New York, Macmillan Company).

writer has assumed and has therefore inserted a divine revelation at the start of chapter xxvi. He also repeats the promise of benediction which was earlier bestowed on Abraham. The oral stage of the tradition will simply have begun with Isaac departing to Gerar because of the famine, under the command of God. No reference to the blessing would have been necessary. With this new concept of the story the end is also modified with a reference to the realisation of the divine blessing (verses 12–14).

In A the writer obviously holds much by the idea that the recipient of the blessing was in fact his own greatest enemy, because no sooner had he received God's promise than he thoughtlessly jeopardised it. But this is not an idea which has much prominence in narrative C. Here it is more a question of the inheritance of the blessing. In J's (or L's) opinion the blessing is not naturally inherited by the next in succession, as was earlier assumed, but had to be reaffirmed to each new generation. Hence its strong representation in verses 12–14. The story of the ancestress of Israel, although it has lost much of its strength through retelling, is thus inserted into the Isaac material to bring out this point. Against this background we can see that it has been 'preserved for purposes of admonition' (von Rad[24]), and was intended for the ears of those people who were to become the Israelite nation.

Here also the writer's method of procedure is very involved. This is very evident from the reference at the beginning to the earlier famine in the days of Abraham, and to Abimelech as king of the Philistines, which is of course a reference to the history of a later period, when the Philistines became the arch-enemies of the Israelites. Indeed the blessing of verses 3–4 is complication enough.[25]

The redaction history does not end with the story's incorporation into the Jahwistic and Elohistic writing. There are later Deuteronomic revisions (xxvi. 5), and additions in the Samaritan recension of the Pentateuch (xxii. 20) and in the LXX. And in the book of Jubilees and the Genesis-Apocryphon the story has been even more clearly remodelled. Thus it is that the final versions of the story are the start of a long history of its interpretation.

11. SAUL AND DAVID IN THE WILDERNESS
(I Sam. xxiii and xxvi)

Up till now the second half of Samuel I has only been studied from a form-critical point of view in the commentaries by H. Gressmann: (SAT II, 1 [1]1910, [2]1921) and W. Caspari (KAT 1926).

We have two descriptions of a meeting between King Saul and his former army leader in the wilderness:

---

[24] von Rad ATD.
[25] The changes made by J and E would be clearer if we knew the setting in life of both.

<table>
<tr><td>

A

(I Sam. xxiii. 14 ff; xxiv)

</td><td>

B

(I Sam. xxvi)

</td></tr>
</table>

And David abode in the wilderness in the strong holds, and remained in the hill country in the wilderness of Ziph. And Saul sought him every day, but God delivered him not into his hand.

15 And David saw that Saul was come out to seek his life: and David was in the wilderness of Ziph in the wood.

16 And Jonathan Saul's son arose, and went to David into the wood, and strengthened his hand in God.

17 And he said unto him, Fear not: for the hand of Saul my father shall not find thee; and thou shalt be king over Israel, and I shall be next unto thee; and that also Saul my father knoweth.

18 And thy two made a covenant before the Lord: and David abode in the wood, and Jonathan went to his house.

19 *Then came up the Ziphites to Saul to Gibeah, saying, Doth not David hide himself with us in the strong holds in the wood, in the hill of Hachilah, which is on the south of the desert?*

| | 1 *And the Ziphites came unto Saul in Gibeah saying, Doth not David hide himself in the hill of Hachilah, which is before the desert?* |

20 Now therefore, O king, come down, according to all the desire of thy soul to come down; and our part shall be to deliver him up into the king's hand.

21 And Saul said, Blessed be ye of the Lord; for ye have had compassion on me.

22 Go, I pray you, make yet more sure, and know and see his place where his haunt is, and who hath seen him there: for it is told me that he dealeth very subtilly.

23 See therefore, and take knowledge of all the lurking places where he hideth himself, and come ye again to me of a certainty, and I will go with you: and it shall come to pass, if he be in the land, that I will search him out among all the thousands of Judah.

24 *And they arose, and went to Ziph before Saul:* but David and his men were in the wilderness of Maon, in the Arabah on the south of the desert.

| | 2 *Then Saul arose, and went down to the wilderness of Ziph,* |

25 And Saul and his men went to seek him. And they told David: wherefore he came down to the rock, and abode in the wilderness of Maon. And when Saul heard that, he pursued after David in the wilderness of Maon.

26 And Saul went on this side of the mountain and David and his men on that side of the mountain: and David made haste to get away for fear of Saul; for Saul and his men compassed David and his men round about to take them.

A

B

(I Sam. xxiii. 14 ff; xxiv)

(I Sam. xxvi)

27 But there came a messenger unto Saul, saying,
Haste thee, and come; for the Philistines have
made a raid upon the land.

28 So Saul returned from pursuing after David,
and went against the Philistines: therefore they
called the place Sela-ham-mahlekoth.

29 And David went up from thence, and dwelt in
the strong holds of En-gedi.

xxiv. 1 And it came to pass (וַיְהִי כַּאֲשֶׁר), when Saul

returned from following the Philistines, that it was
told him, saying, Behold, David is in the wilderness
of En-gedi.

2 *Then Saul took three thousand chosen men out of
all Israel, and went to seek David* and his men upon
the rocks of the wild goats.

*having three thousand
chosen men of Israel
with him, to seek David
in the wilderness of
Ziph.*

3 And he came to the
sheepcotes by the way,
where was a cave; and
Saul went in to cover
his feet. Now David
and his men were abid-
ing in the innermost
parts of the cave.

3 And Saul pitched in the hill of Hachilah, which
is before the desert, by the way. But David abode
in the wilderness, and he saw that Saul came after
him into the wilderness.

4 David therefore sent out spies, and understood
that Saul was come of a certainty.

5 And David arose, and came to the place where
Saul had pitched: and David beheld the place where
Saul lay, and Abner the son of Ner, the captain of
his host: and Saul lay within the place of the
wagons, and the people pitched round about him.

6 Then answered David and said to Ahimelech the
Hittite, and to Abishai the son of Zeruiah, brother
to Joab, saying, Who will go down with me to Saul
to the camp? And Abishai said, I will go down with
thee.

7 So David and Abishai came to the people by
night: and, behold, Saul lay sleeping within the
place of the wagons, with his spear stuck in the
ground at his head: and Abner and the people lay
round about him.

8 Then said Abishai to David, *God hath delivered
up thine enemy into thine hand* this day: now therefore
let me smite him, I pray thee, with the spear to the
earth at one stroke, and I will not smite him a

4 And the men of David
said unto him, Behold,
the day of which the
Lord said unto thee,
*Behold, I will deliver
thine enemy into thine
hand,* and thou shalt do
to him as it shall seem
good unto thee.

second time.

xxiv   xxvi

6 And he said unto his men, *The Lord forbid that I should do this thing unto my lord, the Lord's anointed, to put forth mine hand against him, seeing he is the Lord's anointed.*

7a So David checked his men with these words, and suffered them not to rise against Saul.

4b Then David arose, and cut off the skirt of Saul's robe privily.

5 And it came to pass afterward, that David's heart smote him, because he had cut of Saul's skirt.

7b And Saul rose up out of the cave, and went on his way.

8 David also arose afterward, and went out of the cave, and cried after Saul, saying,

9 And David said to Abishai, *Destroy him not: for who can put forth his hand against the Lord's anointed, and be guiltless?*

10 And David said, As the Lord liveth, the Lord shall smite him; or his day shall come to die; or he shall go down into battle and perish.

11 *The Lord forbid that I should put forth my hand against the Lord's anointed:* but now take, I pray thee, the spear that is at his head, and the cruse of water, and let us go.

12 So David took the spear and the cruse of water from Saul's head; and they gat them away, and no man saw it, nor knew it, neither did any awake: for they were all asleep; because a deep sleep from the Lord was fallen upon them.

13 Then David went over to the other side, and stood on the top of the mountain afar off; a great space being between them:

14 and David cried to the people, and to Abner the son of Ner, saying, Answerest thou not, Abner? Then Abner answered and said, Who art thou that criest to the king?

15 And David said to Abner, Art not thou a valiant man? and who is like to thee in Israel? wherefore then hast thou not kept watch over thy lord the king? for there came one of the people in to destroy the king thy lord.

16 This thing is not good that thou hast done. As the Lord liveth, ye are worthy to die, because ye have not kept watch over your lord, the Lord's anointed. And now, see, where the king's spear is, and the cruse of water that was at his head.

17 And Saul knew David's voice, and said, Is this thy voice, my son David? And David said It is my voice, *my lord, O king.*

My lord the king. And when Saul looked behind him, David bowed with his face to the earth, and did obeisance.

9 And David said to

18 And he said, *Wherefore doth my lord pursue after his servant? for what have I done? or what evil is in mine hand?*

19 Now therefore, I pray thee, let my lord the king

A   B

(I Sam. xxiii. 14 ff: xxiv)   (I Sam. xxvi)

Saul, *Wherefore heark-enest thou to men's words, saying, Behold, David seeketh thy hurt?*

hear the words of his servant. If it be the Lord that hath stirred thee up against me, let him accept an offering: but if it be the children of men, cursed be they before the Lord; for they have driven me out this day that I should not cleave unto the inheritance of the Lord, saying, Go, serve other gods.

20 Now therefore, let not my blood fall to the earth away from the presence of the Lord: for the king of Israel is come out to seek a flea, as when one doth hunt a partridge in the mountains.

21 Then said Saul, I have sinned: return, my son David: for I will no more do thee harm, because my life was precious in thine eyes this day: behold, I have played the fool, and have erred exceedingly:

10 Behold, this day thine eyes have seen how that *the Lord had delivered thee today into mine hand* in the cave: and some bade me kill thee: but mine eye spared thee; and I said, I will not put forth mine hand against my lord; for he is the Lord's anointed.

11 Moreover, my father, see, yea, *see the skirt of thy robe in my hand*: for in that I cut off the skirt of thy robe, and killed thee not, know thou and see that there is neither evil nor transgression in mine hand, and I have not sinned against thee, though thou huntest after my soul to take it.

12 The Lord judge between me and thee, and the Lord avenge me of thee; but *mine hand shall not be upon thee.*

13 As saith the proverb of the ancients, Out of the wicked cometh forth wickedness: but *mine hand shall not be upon thee.*

14 After whom is the king of Israel come out? after whom dost thou pursue? after a dead dog, after a flea.

15 The Lord therefore be judge, and give sentence between me and thee, and see, and plead my cause, and deliver me out of thine hand.

16 And when it came to pass, (וַיְהִי) when David

22 And David answered and said, *Behold the spear*, O king! let then one of the young men come over and fetch it.

23 And the Lord shall render to every man his righteousness and his faithfulness: forasmuch as *the Lord delivered thee into my hand today,* and *I would not put forth mine hand against the Lord's anointed.*

24 And, behold, as thy life was much set by this day in mine eyes, so let my life be much set by in the eyes of the Lord, and let him deliver me out of all tribulation.

had made an end to speaking these words unto Saul, that Saul said, Is this thy voice, my son David? And Saul lifted up his voice, and wept.

17 And he said to David, Thou art more righteous than I: for thou hast rendered unto me good, whereas I have rendered unto thee evil.

18 And thou hast declared this day how that thou hast dealt well with me; forasmuch as when the Lord had delivered me up into thine hand, thou killedst me not.

25 Then Saul said to David, Blessed be thou, my son David: thou shalt both do mightily, and *shalt surely prevail.*

xxiv   xxvi

19 For if a man find his enemy, will he let him go
well away? wherefore the Lord reward thee good
for that thou hast done unto me this day.
20 And now, behold, I know that *thou shalt surely
be king*, and that the kingdom of Israel shall be
established in thine hand.
21 Swear now therefore unto me by the Lord, that
thou wilt not cut off my seed after me, and that
thou wilt not destroy my name out of my father's
house.
22 And David sware unto Saul. And Saul went
home; but David and his men gat them up unto
the hold.   So David went his way,
                                                     and Saul returned to
                                                     his place.

A. *Defining the Literary Unit*

The passage preceding story A, which describes David's defence of Keilah,
does not prepare us at all for this narrative, and the narrative which follows
it, describing Nabal's folly (ch. xxv), also has nothing to do with it.
Hence if A were dropped from its context there would be no break in
the course of events. Is our narrative sufficient enough in itself to have
once been an independent unit? The beginning is not markedly typical of
the start to a Hebrew story. There is no definite introduction. But xxiii. 14
does provide an audience of the early monarchical period with all the
information it needs: detailed place indications, the figure of David, and
the situation he is in, i.e. that he is being pursued by Saul. The fact that
hostility reigns between the two is assumed to be already known.[1] Although
the introduction is not stylistically correct this may well be because the
(later) writer has plunged more quickly and deeply into the story than
would be normal in a Genesis narrative. The repetitions in the first verse:
'David abode in the wilderness', and 'remained in the hill country' seem
clumsy, and can best be explained by a desire on the part of the writer to
incorporate both the introduction to the unit in its independent form and
a link with its present context. But in any case the resounding end of the
narrative, its climax a speech which resolves the complexities of the situation, and the few closing sentences, provide us with a clear indication that
the narrative was previously independent. It is very similar in construction to that of all the sagas of the ancestress of Israel. The narrative as a
whole is clearly constructed and concise. The scenes begin either with a
verb of motion, followed by a speech, e.g. 'Then came up the Ziphites . . .
saying' (xxiii. 19, xxiv. 8). (There were similar beginnings in the ancestress

---

[1] Perhaps this enmity will originally have been thought to have arisen quite
differently from its presentation here; for when in xxiii. 22 Saul says that others
have told him David 'dealeth very subtilly' this does not allow for a lengthy stay by
David at Saul's court (as now in chapter xvi ff.); for then Saul would himself have
known what sort of man David was.

of Israel e.g. Gen. xx, l. 8); or there are a series of verbs of motion followed by a nominal clause, e.g. xxiii. 24, xxiv, 3.[2] Or the phrase 'And it came to pass' *or* 'And there was' (וַיְהִי), already familiar from Genesis, is also used as the start of a scene (xxiii. 26. xxiv. 1, 5, 16).

With B too the links both with the narrative preceding it—Nabal's folly —and the one following it—David fleeing to the Philistine king—are exceedingly loose. The beginning is even less satisfactory than that of A. But as the end is stylistically correct, with a speech and counter-speech which sorts everything out, and some concluding sentences, the inadequacy of the beginning will have occurred when the writer took out the original introduction so that the tale fitted into its present context. Originally it will have started similar to A, with an account of David's stay in the wilderness. The original unity of the story is quite evident from the straightforward flow of events. Although the scenes are longer than those in A, they are grouped in the same way; again we have as a beginning a verb of motion followed by a speech (in xxvi. 1) or a series of verbs of motion followed by a nominal sentence (xxvi. 2, 5, 13), which has the effect of momentarily staying the progress of events. From this it must be assumed that A and B once circulated independently of each other and of their present context, and doubtless in oral form.

B. *Determination of the Literary Type and Setting in Life*

There is no doubt that the two narratives belong to the same literary type. And similarities in form to the ancestress of Israel are so obvious that once again we must classify them as *sagas*, although in this case not ethnological ones. In any case, there is again no question of interpreting them as historical reports: chronological dates are lacking, and again the course of history is not vitally affected by the story. However, there is a certain affinity to history in that the main figures, Saul and David, are acknowledged to have some historical importance. However, their involvement in the political, social and intellectual life of their time, which for the most part makes up their historical status, has no bearing on the oral version of this story. Interest is focused entirely on the two men and their private war. Their characters are brought out in sharp relief: David, bold, generous, godfearing, and Saul, dogged by failure, grimly opposing his destiny. These are the characteristics of the *heroic saga* as it is also found in Germanic literature. A figure such as Saul would fit well into a saga of the period of the barbarian invasion of Europe.[3] In this literary type the characters are always sharply delineated, and not only the main characters. The Ziphites are arrant traitors; Saul's men are not very alert—in fact they are downright slow, for they sleep. Exaggerations, such as the figure of 3,000 men,

---

[2] Hempel, *Literatur* 84 sees these nominative clauses as statements of the situation before the start of a new development in the story.

[3] Even the brothers Grimm differentiated between the heroic saga and the usual national saga. An investigation into the literary type of the heroic saga in the European languages is difficult and a comparison with those in the Old Testament of little use, because we only know the Germanic heroic saga in its later, literary form, or in modern versions of it, and not in its original prose version.

are also a characteristic of the literary type of the saga. This is far too great a number either for an expedition in the wilderness or for Saul's circumstances. Another characteristic of the heroic saga is the emphasis laid upon accurate place indications.[4] A hero cannot perform anywhere: he needs to be set against a particular landscape. Here it is the wilderness. The identification of the saga with its locality is so strong that in xxiii. 28 there is even an explanation given of a name: the Hebrew expression סֶלַע הַמַּחְלְקוֹת could be translated 'rock of escape', thus preserving the great moment for ever; or even more exactly, 'rock of slipperiness', a reference to the unusually smooth surface of the rock. The story interprets it as 'slippery escape', thereby linking the landscape with the story, and at the same time indulging, as is characteristic of the saga, in a play on sounds and meaning. Such 'etymological' details are already to be found in the Genesis sagas (Gen. ii. 23; xi. 9, etc.). They do not usually withstand analysis.[5]

The ancestress of Israel in danger, an ethnological saga, saw the world reduced to terms of family affairs. Unfortunately there are as yet no detailed studies of the Samuel sagas, so here it is only possible to make a few marginal observations about the heroic saga. Indeed it is no accident which makes Abishai David's courageous companion, for as the son of Zeruiah he is also his cousin; but this is not stated in so many words. Rather the emphasis is on tribal connections and national feeling. Saul wants to search out David from 'among all the thousands of Judah' (xxiii. 23). But concord does not reign as a matter of course between the tribes of Judah, for the treacherous Ziphites also belong to Judah. What could well be more important is the link between a man and his home land. David looks for hiding places in the land of his own tribe; the only thing he could not bring himself to do in his dispute with Saul was to leave the Promised Land and his inheritance. And then came national considerations, the hostility between Judah and the Philistines in xxiii. 27 f. This needs no explanation. It also accounts for the high estimation of the Lord's Anointed, whom Jahweh has put over Israel, and who for this reason must be accorded unconditional respect. But the predominating theme is that of loyalty between men. Jonathan bound himself absolutely in a covenant with David, and David and the men who followed him constituted an absolute unit. The same applied to Saul's side: Abner would have quite freely given his life for Saul. Also the relationship between Saul and David is determined by these views of loyalty between men. Observe the form of address they use to each other: that of father and son.

The literary type of the heroic saga developed relatively late in comparison with the Genesis sagas. It first appears during the period of the judges (Judges iii. 14–26 is perhaps the oldest example). From the start it was written in the later *elaborated* style. Much of the material in this style which in the ancestress of Israel was clearly inserted later is part of the original in the heroic saga, such as the long speeches and the use of the flash-back which

---

[4] The involved indications of place given in xxvi. 3 and xxvi. 13 led Gressmann to suppose they are versions of the same thing, and he condensed them.

[5] A similar example from German sagas: Odenwald as 'o du Wald'.

in the previous story was only to be found in the version in chapter xx. With our present story, however, there is a flash-back in xxiv. 4 to a divine prophecy of victory to David; in xxvi. 1 Saul only learns of David's whereabouts through the agency of the Ziphites; in xxvi. 5 it is added that Saul's camp was pitched in the form of a circle, or laager. The style is so elaborated that the speeches occasionally repeat what the story has already told us (xxiii. 15, 19; xxiii. 29 f.; xxiv. 4, 6, 10 f.; xxvi. 11, 15 f.). Important speeches moreover are repeatedly interspersed with the phrase, 'And he said' (xxvi. 10. 18; xxiv. 8 f., 16 f., cf. Gen. xx. 10).

Why is it that the heroic saga only developed some time after the conquest and settlement? What is its setting in life? Obviously the literary type circulated amongst people accustomed to the conditions of war. In many of the David narratives the conditions of war were taken for granted, so that the literary type will have originated with the men used to fighting and battle, i.e. with the warriors in the king's service. These stories will have been recounted in the evenings by warriors around the camp fire or in their quarters when duties were over, in praise of their army leaders. Obviously they also concern people with a minute knowledge of the wilderness of Judah, who will themselves have travelled through it, and who will have strong associations with the places mentioned.[6]

However, the setting in life is in a period very much removed from the period when the action of the story took place. The atmosphere which prevails in A and B could only have arisen after David had consolidated his kingdom and had established himself with great oriental ceremony in Jerusalem. Even the fact that at the beginning the Ziphites came to Gibeah and had no difficulty in meeting up with Saul is hardly in keeping with the unsettled conditions of Saul's time, and the perpetual wars he had to wage. 'It would have been as easy to find the historical Saul as it is now to find a busy doctor at home' was Caspari's view,[7] comparing it with the practice of doctors of his day. The formality of the Ziphite's address to their king, in xxiii. 19 f., particularly, is definitely an imitation of the Jerusalem manner, and not in keeping with the simpler practice of Saul's day.

With this we come to the component literary types. One of the most used is the speech addressed to the king and its reply. In xxiv. 1 and xxvi. 1 it is given in a much shortened form (Caspari[7] will be right in assuming that the preceding לֵאמֹר presupposes and condenses many earlier sentences of the speech). It is significant that in xxvi. 1 the Ziphites do not make a straightforward statement, but in the Hebrew text form what they have to say into a question: 'Is not David hidden at our place?' They avoid a direct statement to the king, clothing it rather in the form of a rhetorical question, so that the king forms the conclusion himself (cf. xxvi. 18). A messenger addressing the king can only come straight to the point when it is a matter of dire necessity; and in fact in xxiii. 27 he goes so far as to use the imperative. The Ziphites speech in xxiii. 19 f. is more elaborate, showing something of the courtesy due to the king: 'Now therefore, O king . . . according to all the

[6] The three places which play a part in the story can be found on the map 1 : 100000 Palestine Sheet 12 Hebron. They lie south-east of Hebron. At a distance of about 4 km. from each other are, from north to south, Kh.Zif.=Sif, Kh. Khureisa=Choresha and Kh.Ma'in=Maon. They are situated on the watershed marking the divide between the cultivable land and the wilderness of Judah.

[7] W. Caspari, KAT 1926.

desire of thy soul, come down.' When David hazards a call across to the king he uses the address befitting that of a subordinate: 'My lord the king' (xxiv. 8, xxvi. 17) before getting to the point of his speech, though again he inserts the honourable title of 'my father' (xxiv. 11, cf. xxvi. 19). Where a speech turns from an explanation of the situation to the actual desire of the speaker the Hebrew shows the transition by means of 'Now therefore' (וְעַתָּה, cf. Gen. xx. 7).[8] For the king this is immediately followed by a small courtesy such as in xxiii. 20, or at least an extenuating particle נָא such as in xxvi. 19.

David intentionally avoids pointing out that it is the king himself who is responsible for his plight, although this is very obviously the case (xxvi. 19).[9] The king's replies are just as distinctive. If he wishes to be particularly gracious he answers with a blessing (xxiii. 21, xxvi. 25). Otherwise it is more fitting for a man in his office to operate by means of a series of imperatives (xxiii. 22 f., cf. xxiv. 21). It is a very particular circumstance[10] which will make him answer, 'Thou art more righteous than I' (xxiv. 17), or even 'I have sinned'[11] (xxvi. 21). This indicates the change in the relationship between the two, although by calling David 'my son' Saul maintains his superior rank. A comparison with the dialogue between the king and Abraham in the story of the ancestress of Israel reveals how much less formal it was at that earlier period. The lapse of time has brought great changes; even the setting in life is completely different. The high estimation of the royal office means that both A and B end with a speech by Saul, despite the fact that David is the chief character in the tale. Other speech types can only vaguely be determined, such as the *divine oracle*, which appears to have been given in a much shortened form in xxiv. 4 (xxvi. 8). The *oath*, with its typical introductory phrases, can be seen in David's words in xxvi. 10, 11, 16; xxiv. 6 (cf. xxiv. 21 f.). A *curse* is uttered in xxvi. 19. This combination of benediction, oath and curse is typical of the language of soldiers, and substantiates the belief that this is the setting in life.

C. *Transmission History*

The first detail in narrative A which appears out of keeping with the rest of the story and is therefore probably a later insertion is that of Jonathan's visit to David in xxiii. 16–18. Jonathan predicts quite definitely that 'Thou shalt be king', thus detracting from the suspense of the story. Also the words 'strengthened his hand in God' add a pious note to the tale which, though not unreligious, is essentially a straightforward, rugged heroic saga. Moreover the incident presupposes a link with events quite outside the saga itself. The passage therefore belongs to a time when A was already circulating in conjunction with other traditions; or it could even have been composed by the writer himself.

[8] A. Laurentin; *We 'attah-Kai nun*. B45, 1964, 168–97 sees the expression as a point of connection, p. 192.

[9] It is the same in the speech to David in xxvi. 8. The comparisons used: dog, flea, and partridge, fit the situation; cf. II Sam. xiv. 7, 14, xvi. 9, xvii. 8–13.

[10] An exception in that it approaches a legal contest. xxiv. 12, 15 is an appeal formula (*Appellationsformel*), xxiv. 17 a declaration of innocence (*Unschuldigerklärung*), and xxvi. 18 an appeasement formula (*Beschwichtigungsformel*) in H. J. Boecker's Redeformen des Rechtslebens im A.T., WMANT 14, 1964, pp. 48–50. The legal terminology is misleading. No group of people meet together to consider it, nor is any judgment expected. The 'judgment' of Jahweh implies a direct, *wordless* intervention in favour of the man loyal to the community.

[11] Formula for the admission of guilt, used only before God or the king (here it concerns a future king) II Sam. xix. 21; II Kings xviii. 14.

The same applies to xxiii. 26b–xxiv. 2, the Philistine *intermezzo*. This is also an inessential, and not part of the original unit. It disturbs the course of events. However, it is not as late an addition as Jonathan's visit. Saul's departure to fight the Philistines has been put in to accommodate the reference to the 'rock of slipperiness' (of escape), but at the same time it considerably heightens the tension of the story: Saul only succeeds in approaching David at his *second* attempt.

B also occasionally gives the impression that in its original form it was shorter. The speeches in the second part are surprisingly long compared with those at the beginning. The oath in verse 10 is unnecessary in face of the stronger one in verse 11, and is certainly of later origin. When David calls across to Abner to the effect that he is worthy of death because he has failed in his responsibilities, adding an oath for emphasis (verse 16), this goes far beyond the competence of David at that time, who was then a mere army leader in the desert. It is more the attitude of a king strongly established in Jerusalem. This could also be a later addition to the story. In xxvi. 11 f. David is reported to have taken a cruse of water as well as the spear. Verse 22 only mentions the spear, so the cruse of water is a later elaboration. Doubling items in this fashion heightens the event.

When these inessentials have been taken out, the two narratives have a greater similarity to each other than they have in their present written form. According to I Samuel they relate to two different events, but a closer analysis makes it appear likely that they are merely two versions of the same source; for

> (*a*) it is inconceivable that David should have fled to the land of the Ziphites a second time, once they had proved themselves traitors;
> (*b*) it is surprising that David's men should again suggest that God had played Saul into his hands and that he should kill him, when David had already categorically rejected the idea;
> (*c*) there is no mention at all in chapter xxvi that a similar episode had just occurred. Twice Saul is remorseful and promises peace, without mentioning or explaining the fact that he had once gone back on his word; and
> (*d*) xxiii. 19 runs almost word for word like xxvi. 1; and there are many other verbal parallels.[12]

These similarities are only explicable if the two narratives go back to the same source. The conformity between the two is in fact quite great. On both occasions David is in the wilderness of Judah fleeing from Saul. On both occasions he has the opportunity to kill the king. On both occasions there is the suggestion that it has been ordained by God, but though he is tempted to murder Saul, David strongly resists the impulse: he cannot violate the sanctity of the Lord's Anointed. But on both occasions he takes

---

[12] In the period of pure literary criticism—which includes Caspari—the points of similarity between the two narratives were put down to a great extent to later adjustment, and were therefore considered secondary. But the question is more one of whether it could have happened the other way round: later writers differentiated as much as possible between them and divided the two completely from each other. At any rate this is the practice in the LXX, in xxvi. 20 for instance.

some material evidence with him. In the conversation which follows Saul recognises David's superiority, and departs as he came. All this supports the assumption that it must be two versions of the same story, both of which developed in oral form quite independently of each other. How will the source of the story have looked?

Variations in detail between the two narratives include:

1. The characters in the story. In A, the Ziphites, Saul and David, are mentioned by name, and David's and Saul's men are present, though anonymous. In B the same people appear, but this time David's follower Abishai is given a secondary role, and the Hittite, as well as Abimelech and Abner the army leader are also mentioned. B's greater number of characters is certainly the result of later elaboration. In A only those characters are named who are essential to the story.

2. On both occasions David approaches the king unnoticed. But in A David is already in the cave when Saul comes up, so that each is put into a situation which has not been willed by himself. In B, however, David quite voluntarily steals into the enemy's camp. His heroism is therefore heightened in the eyes of the audience. This is no doubt intentional. During the course of the story's transmission the scene of events is therefore taken out of the cave in order to add emphasis to David's greatness.

3. In both narratives David takes a token with him. Yet in chapter xxiv he only removes the skirt of Saul's robe, whereas in chapter xxvi he also takes Saul's weapon. Here also B must be the later version. The story is lent a more soldierly aspect if the adversary is robbed of his weapon and not merely of a piece of his apparel.[13]

4. In A David's men refer to an earlier pronouncement by God. This was not known to the narrator of B, so he turns it into a pronouncement by Abishai to David. It seems that this narrative was written at a period more distant from that of David, and the narrator knows nothing of this divine pronouncement.

On the whole chapter xxvi (B) appears to be a later stage of the tale. A and B have been formed quite independently of each other from the source narrative, though A is closer to the original. But A also gives evidence of later insertions, such as Jonathan's visit at the beginning. The speeches of both narratives do not show the influence of their parallel versions. In A there is a reference to Jahweh as judge (xxiv. 12, 15), whereas B contains the primitive idea that Saul's animosity could only have been instigated by God (verse 19), as was also the deep sleep of his men (xxvi. 12). Over the course of the transmission history the tendency has been to bring out the background to the events more sharply: the thoughts of the men become evident in their speeches, and it is God who is considered essentially responsible for the direction of men's thoughts.

How far is the tale historical? Again, the structure of the story is historical, as are the formalities surrounding the Lord's Anointed at the court of

[13] H. Gressmann SAT II, 1, ¹1910, ²1921: chapter xxvi does not like to tell of the hem of Saul's robe being stolen as a robe is part of a person, so that Saul's person was wronged by David. Hence chapter xxvi is of later origin. But for an Israelite surely a weapon is as much a part of a person as is his robe.

Jerusalem, and the immense enthusiasm of David's warriors for their leader. Also the characterisation of David as bold and generous seems to be correct, a man who 'for an Oriental despot was surprisingly respectable' (Gressmann). Less reliable, but on the whole reasonably correct, is the characterisation of Saul. For the mere grasp of characters this tale is indeed a 'little masterpiece' (Gressmann). As the saga did not circulate orally for as long a period as a saga about the patriarchs, it is possible here to arrive at a historical core. There is no doubt that Saul the king pursued his successful army leader, David. The hiding place in the wilderness of Ziph is certainly also historical, though it is not absolutely certain whether Saul's pursuit was quite without result. The facts that they came into close touch with each other, and that David's generosity was proved before everyone, will have arisen as the material was gradually moulded till it found expression in the form of the saga.

D. *Redaction History*

Pure literary criticism had thought that A and B were derived from two individual written sources, as they had with the Genesis stories. It was even thought possible to see a continuation here of the Tetrateuch writings (L) J and L. But, unlike Genesis, it is not possible to distinguish any definite use of language which would indicate sources; even the use of the words God (Elohim xxiii. 16) and Lord (Jahweh xxvi. 9) seem to determine nothing. So there is just as much justification in the theory that the affinities between the two are to be traced back to one original source, with later revisions.[14] We have no clear solution yet about this.

Nevertheless it is easy to see that A and B could scarcely have been taken out of the oral tradition and written down by the same writer at the same time. This would have been possible if the two traditions had been built around different characters, as in the case of the ancestress of Israel (Gen. xii and xxvi), but it is inconceivable in the present context. A historical writer (see under) would hardly repeat in verse 1, for instance, almost word for word the facts he had already given in xxiii. 19. But the chief point is that chapter xxiv ends with such a formal, sworn, peace agreement, that if chapter xxvi came from the same source Saul's breaking the peace would have been at least briefly mentioned. The literary disparity between the two becomes clearer by looking at their different contexts. It has long been recognised that xxv. 1 is the correct sequel to chapter xxiv: David's protector Samuel dies, so David retreats to the south beyond the province of Judah. But in xxv. 2 David is suddenly and inexplicably back in his own province. This is the work of another hand, which had not yet described David's flight. However, xxv. 2 ff. is the logical introduction to chapter xxvi and also to chapter xxvii, where David again leaves Judah, this time over the western border. Thus two literary blocks can be distinguished, of which the first (xxiii. 14–xxv. 1) fits more easily into the context of the

[14] H. U. Nübel's thesis, that a later writer made the two stories out of one report from the original written version is hardly convincing (*David's Aufstieg in der Frühe israelitischer Geschichtsschreibung*, Diss. Bonn, 1959.

previous chapter on David's rise than does the second. For in xxiii. 14 David is back at the place he had arrived at in xxii. 5, and Jonathan's covenant with David in xxiii. 14–18 points back to chapter xx. We are twice assured that David will become king (xxiii. 17, xxiv. 20 f.), a mysterious reference to a tradition in chapter xvi or xvii, where David arrives at the court as secret pretender to the throne.[15] On the other hand in xxv. 2–17 it is not possible to discover similarly convincing references to previous material in the book.

It is therefore possible that the redaction history of A points back at least to a written work, which began at the latest with David's arrival at the court, with the general theme that, despite all obstacles, the divine ordinance was realised and he became king of Israel. This also gives us some idea of the sequel to A. The source will have described David's progress, at least as far as his enthronement in II Samuel v. His oath in xxiv. 21 not to destroy Saul's seed or his name is obviously linked with the story of Mephibosheth, the last direct descendant of Saul, in II Samuel ix (xvi. 1–4, xix. 24–30); and this chapter for its own part is closely linked to the story of David's succession to the throne in II Samuel vii; x ff. All this reveals A as part of a book intended to describe the rise of David's kingship (and its preservation through the succession of Solomon?). The complex literary type to which A belongs is therefore *historical writing*, for only a writer of history has as his theme the rise of a monarch's power over a particular nation and its persistence in face of external and internal danger. Thus the writer is proved by this example to have incorporated heroic sagas into his work. The modern reader will ask whether this is compatible with historical writing, for surely a saga is the result of a completely different mental outlook, which fundamentally precludes any link with history. But in antiquity historical writing had little to do with historical *science*. The conception of historical criticism as a philological investigation of sources has only existed for two and a half centuries. Herodotus and Thucydides incorporated many sagas into their work. Yet they, and perhaps the Old Testament historical writers even more so, are the forebears of modern historical research; for they had already established the fact that as well as a careful examination of sources there must also be a general theme which governs all the events, binding the material together, and in fact making it into a history. They also realised that it is not the description of the life of a man which makes history, be he ever so great, but his position in the community he lives in, which for its own part is perpetually changing. As there was scarcely any material other than sagas about the rise of David's dynasty the historical writers had no option but to use them.[16] But in doing so they gave them their own interpretation and thus a completely fresh meaning. This is very evident in A. All the points in this previously

[15] Eissfeldt, *Die Komposition der Samuelisbücher* 1931, pp. 16 f. and others take the double assurance that David will be king (together with the duplicated statement that David remained where he was in xxiii. 18 and xxiv. 22) as a sign that within xxiii. 14 and xxiv. 22 there was a third source from which xxiii. 14b–18 were taken. But probably these repetitions were intentionally inserted by the one writer to provide the emphasis he wished.

[16] Other than a few annals passages such as II Sam. x. 6–19, xii. 26–31, or lists as in II Sam. iii. 2–5, v. 13–16.

independent heroic saga which assume some relationship to the other Davidic and Saul material are open to the suspicion that they have been inserted later. And if these sentences can indeed be taken out of the story without damage to the structure of the saga then this will be proved.

Jonathan's speech in xxiii. 17: 'Fear not: for the hand of Saul my father shall not find thee; and thou shalt be king over Israel, and I shall be next to thee; and that also Saul my father knoweth' looks far beyond the saga itself to events which do not take place until the second book of Samuel. At the same time the writer's theme is very evident: the kingship of David. The sentence above can quite easily be taken out of its context, and was therefore inserted when the story was written down. In Saul's command to the Ziphites, at least xxiii. 23b[17] is strange: 'If he be in the land . . . I will search him out among all the thousands of Judah.' According to the Ziphites it is quite certain that David is in the land, and it is also certain that he has no connection at all with the thousands of Judah. But for the writer it is a question of the king's relation to his country. Moreover he is aware of the difficulties which Saul, a northener, had to face in southern Israel. He uses the opportunity to call this to mind, and adds the reference to the thousands of Judah. In Saul's final speech, also, there is a point worthy of notice. xxiv. 20 contains the same figure of speech 'now therefore' as verse 21 'Now, behold': 'Now, behold, I know that thou shalt surely be king, and that the kingdom of Israel shall be established in thine hand.' Hence at another place where the story has been obviously patched up there are again references to the kingship and to the relationship of the two men to the nation as a whole. It is not so much a matter of what happens between the two, but more a question of the community's stability which depends upon them. These are characteristics of historical writing.

The writer is not only responsible for the references to the greater whole of which the heroes are part but also probably for many of those references to God as the hidden pilot of the course of events. Indeed the mention by David's men in the cave of a promise which Jahweh had already given: 'Behold, I will deliver thine enemy into thine hand' (xxiv. 4, cf. xxvi. 8) will have come down through the oral tradition. But the theme crops up at other points, where it apparently had no place in the framework of the oral tradition. For instance, right at the beginning it is worded in the negative: 'But God delivered him not into his hand' (xxiii. 14). And also in xxiv. 10a, in David's speech to Saul: 'Behold this day thine eyes have seen how that the Lord had delivered thee today into mine hand.' At one time the beginning of the verse and the end of the second half of the verse were quite simply juxtaposed thus: 'Behold this day . . . some bade me kill thee'; for the double use of הַיּוֹם is conspicuous here. Then in xxiv. 18 Saul makes the same reference: 'When the Lord had delivered me up into thine hand, thou killedst me not'; this sentence also gives the impression of being too tightly packed.[18] It seems that the writer can only finally explain the

---

[17] The overloading of verses 22–24 had already been noticed by Budde (HKAT).
[18] The double use of אֵת אֲשֶׁר is much too unwieldy for oral transmission.

political upheaval by making the almighty God of Israel deliver up one ruler into the hands of another. The historical writer has thus given the saga religious as well as political overtones, because in his view history and the will of God are one and the same thing. Thus we must assume that the repeated wish that Jahweh should 'judge' שָׁפַט xxiv. 12a, 15, 19b was also only added when the story was written down, for after such a clash between two men a wish that has been emphasised to such an extent must surely be fulfilled. The reader expects an indication here that David will finally be victorious, which the saga itself could not provide, but which is later realised in the sequel in II Samuel. Also the sentences referred to have been so obviously squeezed into the flow of speech that they could hardly have been part of the straightforward, oral version of the story. They could only be written, not spoken. They are part of the writer's interpretation of the story as a judgment of God. What was added when the story was written down, and the saga transformed into history, was for the most part inserted into the already existing speech passages. This was a custom generally followed by the ancient historical writers.

However, not all references to a larger context can be considered the work of the writer of the narrative. Much is so woven into the run of events that it must be of earlier origin, although the parallel version in chapter xxvi proves that it was not part of the original narrative. An example of this is Saul's departure to fight the Philistines, which could conceivably have been a link to a report of a war against the Philistines. Or an even more obvious example is David's oath at the end of the story when he promises not to wipe out Saul's name. Although this alludes to David's relationship to Saul's children after the latter's death, it is very much part of the original story. Perhaps the Jonathan episode (xxiii. 14–18) is also linked to this. These details were obviously added while the story was still circulating orally, but after the parallel tradition B had taken another direction. They make it seem probable that even before the story had been written down there was a whole series of sagas circulating orally of which A, though originally independent, was a part.

It is more difficult to discover the present meaning of B as its wider context is unknown. The links with the material before and after are much less satisfactory than those of A. It is never once expressly stated that David will become king. Therefore it is difficult to determine what was already part of the story in its oral form, and what was added when it was written down. Whereas the second oath by David is a necessary, and therefore original, part of the story, the first oath in verse 10 could have been inserted by the writer to express his own opinion that there would somehow be an end to Saul. Also the repetition of the phrase 'Now therefore' in verses 19 and 20 could mean that the reference to Jahweh's 'incitement' of Saul against David was only added when the story was written down.[19] This may also explain the reflection in verse 23, to the effect that Jahweh renders 'to every man his righteousness'. This strikes

[19] The conception of God is much cruder here than in the equivalent passage in A. That Jahweh should stir men up against each other in this fickle fashion shows that the writer has no conception of him as the creator of a coherent history.

the reader as a duplication of the simpler and more concrete statement in the next verse. There is little therefore that can be discovered about B's redaction history. It is not even clear whether it was during the actual process of being written down that the heroic saga became part of the complex literary type of *historical writing*, or what the literary type of the written material could otherwise have been.

The setting in life of the complex literary types of which A and B are a part can only be determined reliably for the former of the two narratives. The court of Jerusalem is the only place where such historical writing is thinkable for such an early period.

12. SAGAS IN THE BIBLE?

A. *General Characteristics*

For many contemporary readers any interest they might have had in these narratives will be quenched by the use of the term 'saga'. It is an expression which has been spoiled by nineteenth- and twentieth-century positivism. But ever since the days of the brothers Grimm Germanists have repeatedly pointed out that sagas, to whatever sphere of language they might belong, contain fundamental truths which have often more point than any historical evaluation. However, this fact has had little effect on opinion generally. Important literature on this subject is A. Jolles: *Einfache Formen*, 2nd ed. Halle 1956, or Darmstadt-Tübingen 1958; a survey of the present position of research by L. Röhrich: Die deutsche Volkssage. Ein methodischer Abriss; Studium Generale 11, 1958, 664–91. Important for the characteristics of the saga is A. Olrik: Epische Gesetze der Volksdichtung; Zeitschrift für deutsches Altertum und deutsche Literatur, 51, 1909, 1–12. And in connection with the Bible Gunkel's great introduction to his Genesis commentary: *Die Sagen der Genesis*, E.T. *The Legends of Genesis*, 1964 (London, Bailey; New York, Schocken), presented in a shorter form in his article Sagen und Legenden, RGG ²V, 41–64. See also Eissfeldt, *The Old Testament: An Introduction*, 1965, pp. 38–42 (Oxford, Blackwell; New York, Harper & Row).

The narratives of the ancestress of Israel in danger and of the meeting between Saul and David in the wilderness have much in common, despite their disparity of content. Surprisingly enough these similarities in form are not only consistent with the results of form-critical studies of other material in the books Genesis to II Kings, but also to a great extent with what Olrik has described as the rules governing 'the composition of all European sagas'. Let us begin, paradoxically, with the end of the narratives. In the ancestress of Israel, or Saul and David in the wilderness, the reader is not suddenly deflated at the end of the story by a sudden end to the tension with the final speeches, but is gradually released by a few calm, conclusive sentences. Olrik terms this the law governing the conclusion (*Abschlussgesetz*) of all European sagas.[1] For instance, a tale does not end

---

[1] A. Schulz, Erzählkunst in den Samuel-Büchern, Bibl. Zeitfragen, XI 6/7, 1923, calls this the 'mitigating conclusion' (*beruhigender Schluss*).

with the death of the lovers, but with two roses sprouting from the graves, their branches interwining. Here also the previous course of events has been centred around a very few persons and objects. In fact, each time there are only three characters, or groups, before the eye of the hearer. In the Genesis saga, for instance, the patriarch, his wife, and the king, or in the Samuel saga, Saul, David, and his men. 'Nothing distinguishes folk-lore more clearly from modern writing and reality than the triad' (Olrik). Added to this there is the law of scenic duality: only two main characters (or groups) appear at one time. When a fresh one appears, another retreats. When David stands face to face with Saul there is nothing more said about the men who had just been talking to David. When the king talks to Abraham, or Isaac, the wife recedes into the background. (When in Gen. xx. 15 f. Abimelech speaks to both Abraham and Sarah this is one of the many indications that this version of the story is not a saga in its purest form.) Despite the number of characters there is a definite concentration upon the main character of the story: the saga about the meeting in the wilderness is recounted for David's sake, not Saul's; the patriarch, not the king, is the central character in the Genesis saga. All characters are polarised, i.e. set in sharp contrast to each other. The patriarch is represented as the homeless wanderer, in contrast to the all-powerful ruler, established in his own kingdom; or the noble David is contrasted to the paranoiac Saul. Such sharp delineation of character strikes the modern reader as exaggerated, but for the saga teller this represented reality, for his experience of life was one of stark contradictions, such as good and evil, courage and cowardice, beauty and ugliness.

As well as the grouping of characters and the particular points of emphasis, the straightforwardness of the story is also typical. The narrator recounts one event after another right through from the initial complications to the end. Rebekah/Sarah enters the harem, the king discovers the mistake, calls Isaac/Abraham to account, returns the woman. This is told absolutely straightforwardly, and all inessentials or matters of chance are left out (again Gen. xx is an exception in that it does double back on the story; this again is an indication of change taking place in the literary type). It is true that the narrator likes to repeat similar incidents two and even three times, but this is for the sake of suspense. In such cases it is always the last attempt which is successful. Saul sets out twice against David, but the first time he is forced to return because of the Philistines (I Sam. xxiii f.). When David is in the enemy's camp he first calls across to Abner, and then twice starts to address the king, and only the second time does he come to the point. Abimelech is twice spoken to by God in a dream: the first time the situation is represented as hopeless, the second suggests a remedy (Gen. xx). In these cases of repetition the progress of events is held back, and only finally is the hearer's suspense relieved and the situation resolved.

After such a comparison of European and Old Testament sagas it is not at all surprising to find that much Old Testament material not only greatly resembles Ancient Oriental sagas, but also bears a conspicuous resemblance to Greek sagas. Presumably many sagas recounted by travellers were taken up into the Old Testament, such as Jephthah's vow in Judges xi, or the three divine men's visit to Abraham in Genesis xviii. These tales will have passed through many lands, and will not have evolved along the same lines everywhere.

There are marked differences between European and Israelite sagas, as is shown by the significant variations which have occurred in what is basically the same material.[2] Not all the rules described by Olrik apply to the Old Testament saga. For instance there is no use of the device (*Gesetz der Plastik*) by which the story reaches its climax with the confrontation of the main opposing characters. Instead the climax is reached in speech, which usually takes the form of dialogue. The king presents the patriarch with a solution, or Saul recognises the fundamental superiority of David. It is true that there is an earlier dangerous point of contact, when David removes Saul's cloak, or his spear, but that is not the climax of the story. Also in the story of the ancestress of Israel the climax is not at the point when the woman is taken into the harem of the foreign king; here the contact between the main characters is not even directly stated. In each case it is a speech in which the climax of the story is reached. To the Israelite speech was of the utmost importance, capable of transforming history, and this is doubtless linked to the conception of the transforming power of the divine word. The initial complications of the story can also be set in action by a speech. This applies to a certain extent to Abram's speech in Gen. xii (and more clearly to Gen. ii. 18, vi. 7, xviii. 17 ff.; in such cases it is usually a monologue[3]). The importance attached to speech in Israel is made very evident by the custom of dividing long speeches by means of the expression, 'And he said', as in Gen. xx. 9 f.; I Sam. xxvi. 9 f. (Gen. xxi. 10 f.; I Sam. xvii. 10, 37, etc.).[4] Compared with the European, especially the Germanic sagas, the Israelite saga is conspicuously less warlike in nature, even where the two parties oppose each other fully armed. Saul and David do not actually fight. This is essentially Israelite, as is also the religious tone of the saga, which is always determined by the belief in the one God. There is hardly a story where God does not play a positive part, whether in a foreign country, as in the case of the ancestress of Israel, or in the internal conflicts in Israel, such as those between Saul and David. The divine word not only decisively influences the main course of events, but also the minor speeches, such as that of the men to David (referring to God's previous promise of victory over the enemy, Sam. xxiv and xxvi). With only the one God in Israel, there is not the colourful medley of the Greek pantheon, or the Germanic intermediate realm of giants, dwarfs, trolls and spirits. Mythical features are rare; and literary types such as sagas about devils or death could have no

---

[2] A notable parallel in this connection is the transformation in the German language of pre-Christian sagas into Christian sagas.

[3] N. Bratsiotis in Der Monolog im Alten Testament, ZAW 73, 1961, though very informative, is at fault in considering the monologue as an independent literary type.

[4] The most important person speaks the longest. Though Hebrew speeches are always brief.

relevance in connection with belief in Israel. Thus although the rules outlined by Olrik cannot be unqualifiedly applied to the Old Testament, yet there are similarities which very much justify the use of the term 'saga' here.

B. *Two Stages in the Development of the Saga in Israel*

Olrik points out that sagas do not only have common characteristics of form but also their own peculiar logic. Jolles attempted to discover the way of thinking (*Geistesbeschäftigung*) which leads to the conception of the saga, basing his study on Germanic, Greek and Israelite examples. His thesis was, as we have already seen, that the basis of saga-telling lay in a conception of the world in terms of the family. If tribes or nations are described, it is purely in the capacity of blood relations. Salvation history is converted into family history (and also in the world of the gods the family aspect is emphasised).[5] Genealogical trees are therefore a necessary accompaniment to the saga. These characteristics apply to a great extent to the sagas in the Old Testament. Genesis, for instance, does not describe kings and princes as such, but as members of particular families; it recounts 'narratives set around wells and drinking places, and in the bedroom'.[6] Collective powers are unknown: the victory of an army is the victory of the head of one family. But on the other hand the heroes are not entirely independent of their surroundings. Their characteristics, whether good or bad, are those of their clan. This way of thinking is particularly dominant among wandering tribes, but when states come into being it atrophies, and is only maintained in rural areas. The concept of the state drove the saga out of Israel, just as it did from ancient Iceland.

Jolles' conclusions have not passed uncontended. Petsch[7] maintained that German sagas, such as the Pied Piper of Hamelin, or the *Schildbürger-streichen*, by no means view the world in terms of the family, and that the actual background to the saga was the heroic, understood in its widest sense to include fighting courage as well as religious sanctity. It also took a horrific form, as in the Pied Piper. The saga is thus interpreted as 'particular instances of the heroic'. Whereas Jolles considered the heroic saga to be only one aspect of the family saga, with the hero as no individual but rather the heroic representative of a race, Petsch sees it the other way round, with the family saga as an offshoot of the heroic saga.[8]

From the point of view of the Old Testament, Petsch must certainly be considered right in so far as the sagas about David do not really present the world in terms of the family. True, it is probably no mere chance which

---

[5] To this extent there is a relationship to the myth, though often this has led to the idea of a dependence of the one upon the other. Even J. Grimm was of the opinion that 'the basis of all sagas is myth . . . without such a mythical background the saga cannot take shape'. Quoted in Jolles[2] Halle, p. 76, Darmstadt-Tübingen, p. 92.

[6] Gunkel, *Genesis*, p. IX

[7] *Die Lehre von den 'Einfachen Formen'*, DVfLG X, 1932, 335.

[8] Gressmann wrote similarly of the saga: 'All events are merely the pedestal to which personalities are affixed', SAT[1] II, 1, p. 263. (In the second edition the word 'pedestal' (*Postament*) is reduced to 'footstool' (*Schemel*)!)

makes Abishai David's companion when he hazards an excursion into the enemy's camp (I Sam. xxvi); but then a Hittite, whose tribe was completely foreign, is mentioned simultaneously. If family connections had been really strong Jonathan and Saul would have acted in unison, when exactly the opposite was the case. Therefore Jolles' explanation of the way of thinking behind the conception of the saga is unsatisfactory when applied to the Davidic sagas. But on the other hand it is an inescapable fact that the basis of the Genesis saga is not a general one of heroism, as Petsch maintained, so that here Jolles must be right. This means that the Israelite saga underwent quite considerable changes between the time of the nomadic patriarchs and their people and the start of the monarchical period, when the tribes were permanently settled. There is no consistent 'simple form' of the saga, arising from an unchanging attitude of mind, at least in Israel. As Gunkel has already established,[9] it is rather a case of two different stages in the development of the literary type. In the first place there are sagas of the early patriarchs. Then there are the sagas about national heroes, which are better described as *rural-national sagas* because they presuppose a settled existence and a national consciousness in Israel. The second stage of the saga is also by no means intended to be historical; political motives are again presented in personal terms. David comes to Saul's table as a famous warrior of an honourable race, and not because of any political development.[10]

Neither Gunkel nor Gressmann were yet in a position to study the particular way of thinking which lies at the basis of such sagas. They considered the origin of the literary type to be merely a mixture of memories of historical incidents and ancient poetry.[11] In the story of the ancestress of Israel Gunkel considered a journey by Abraham or Isaac into foreign parts to be the possible historical background, to which the motif of regaining the wife was taken from other sources, probably from a fairy tale.[12] Baumgartner objected to this interpretation on the grounds that it was too narrow, but without suggesting an alternative.[13]

The transformation of the saga of the nomadic patriarchs to the rural-national saga is indicated by the change in the use of language. The style changes from the *concise* to the *elaborated*. Whereas the oldest traditions only report essentials, pack the speeches with matter, and do not attempt to describe the inward struggles of the characters (Gen. xii. 10 ff. is a particularly striking example), in the second stage of the saga the characters express themselves at length. The story is fitted out with 'novelistic'

---

[9] KdG 71.

[10] The transition was completed in Mesopotamia several centuries earlier. Sumerian epics already anticipate the heroic saga.

[11] Today the material is considered 'mythical' rather than 'poetic'. For instance, v.d. Leeuw, *Phänomenologie der Religion*[2], p. 472 writes: 'The saga is a myth which in the course of its development has become connected to a particular place or a particular historical event.' E.T. *Religion in Essence and Manifestation* (London, Allen and Unwin).

[12] *Genesis* XXVI.

[13] RGG[2] V, p. 43. 'These accessory motifs which are to be found in all sagas . . . must not be underrated. They are more than merely fleeting elements haphazardly affixed to already existing material' (Kraus, see below, section C) p. 327.

details, and inner feelings are expressed by such comments as, 'And afterwards David's heart smote him' (I Sam. xxiv. 5; II Sam. xxiv. 10). Any of the older sagas originating from the time of the patriarchs which retained their vitality were carried over into the second stage, where to some extent they adapted themselves to the new style and the new outlook. The patriarchs no longer appear as forefathers or leaders of a tribe, but as representatives of Israel. This is particularly evident in the Moses and Joshua sagas, but also in the figure of Abraham in Genesis xx.[14]

The concise patriarchal saga and the elaborated rural-national saga can therefore only be called literary types in a very wide sense of the term. In fact they are more an attitude of mind (*Geistesbeschäftigung*) which when it takes concrete shape naturally assumes a minor form, and is thèrefore a literary type in its narrow sense. The patriarchal saga appears as an ethnological saga (the ancestress of Israel), or a saga giving the aetiology of a place (e.g. Sodom and Gomorrah); and the rural-national saga as the heroic (Saul and David in the wilderness), or as a saga of holy war (mainly in Judges). Of particular interest are the literary types which could arise at either the patriarchal or the rural-national level. For [example, there are sagas about the rise of the cult, describing the establishment of a sacred place with its venerable objects, both in the more ancient, concise style (such as Gen. xxxii. 22 ff.: Jacob in Penuel), or in the elaborated rural-national style (story of the ark in I Sam. iv–vi and II Sam. vi).

After the monarchy was established sagas were no longer composed in Israel. At any rate the later Old Testament books do not contain sagas, and this can hardly be explained by the unfortunate fact that only fragments of Israelite literature have been handed down to us. It seems rather to confirm Jolles' belief that the formation of a state is hostile to concept of the saga.[15]

C. *The Saga as the Expression of a Particular Way of Thinking*

In both stages of the Israelite saga individuals are depicted whose action and whose fate have more than a personal significance. What Isaac or Abraham experience in a strange country sums up by means of special 'linguistic devices' (*Sprachgebärde*: Jolles) the experience of their whole family or tribe. Just as David is generous and unfearing, the men who relate stories about him and who are under him feel themselves also. They want to be like their king. The manner in which God helps the patriarch or the king has a bearing on the relationship of God to those who tell the story. To the Israelite it was obvious to link up the two, for to him the relationship of the individual to his social group was extremely important. The individual is not a free or independent member of a community, from which he can in particular circumstances detach himself of his own free will. He is an essential part of the tribal group. The group—whether family, tribe or nation—is the only responsible and autonomous unit. It is a 'corporate personality',[16] in that it faces its God or other human institutions in the

---

[14] Or they become examples of fundamental human behaviour within the family, Eissfeldt, *Introduction*, p. 245.

[15] We have only *legends* from the later Israelite period. For these see below.

[16] Wheeler Robinson, The Hebrew Conception of Corporate Personality, BZAW 66, 1936, 49–62.

manner of a super-ego. Nowhere in the Old Testament do we have such a clear idea of 'corporate personality' as in the saga, where the fate of whole groups of people is described in terms essentially 'personal'. This applies to both stages in the development of the saga in Israel, with the only difference that in early sagas it was the clan (as in the ancestress of Israel), and in later ones the nation (as in Saul and David in the wilderness) which was the corporate personality.

A survey based on only two examples can only be sketchy. But it is sufficient to show that saga-telling is an activity of some significance, and should not be dismissed lightly, in Israel or elsewhere. A view of the world in terms of the family, or as a show-place for heroes, has as much to say for itself as has other ways of thinking, such as the chronicling of historical facts (*Historie*). Therefore it is wrong to take out the supernatural, and perhaps also the unlikely elements of a saga, thus reducing it to its historical core and making it part of a historical investigation as if it were nothing but an extravagant elaboration of historical events. The literary type of the saga evolved for quite other reasons. It is more concerned with the present than the past. It aims to give the hearer an unconscious awareness of his own place in the world, for he is inspired, moved, and warned by the events, and emboldened by the praises which are sung for the hero. He is swept off his feet, and taken up into the events as they are described. Every saga is the work of a definite social group, unconsciously expressing its desires and ideals. It is the voice of the people.[17] Thus as soon as it is written down it dies. The literary type only retains its vitality when it is transmitted by word of mouth; and because it is transmitted orally, it develops along a variety of different ways. Although from a historical point of view persons and events appear exaggerated, they are in fact true to a reality seen from the point of view of the literary type. Sagas can end, sometimes, inconclusively (as in Saul and David), or even in failure. A historian can always make use of them by discovering the historical framework in which the saga is embedded; but he should take them firstly as evidence for sociological, cultural and religious conditions. Only then is it sometimes possible to find a historical core to the story, i.e. an event to which it is more or less possible to affix a date.[18] But historical research of this kind can only be undertaken in the full awareness that this cuts right across the natural tendency of the material.

For the information which sagas provide is not so much objective fact, but poetry. The narrator expresses his own judgment as to what is good or

[17] 'Nevertheless there are two things essential to any genuine, properly developed national saga: it must have circulated by word of mouth, i.e. like the popular saga it must have played its part in a community; and secondly it must have originated out of the sheer joy of narration', M. Lüthi, *Volksmärchen und Volkssaga* 1961, p. 46. 'Most German death sagas are also sagas in the defence of right; they are the people's expression not only of their concepts of belief but also of their ethical-legal views', Röhrich, 669.

[18] 'Hence it is not only the core of the saga which is historical, but also the experience, which extends right up into the time of the narrator': von Rad, who differentiates between 'primary experience' and 'secondary experience' (ThLZ 88, 1963, p. 411). Of course the 'credibility' of the core of the narrative cannot be the criterion by which literary types of sagas can be classified; Bentzen, *Introduction*[2], 233.

bad, noble or mean. But these aspects of the saga are only discernible between the lines: they are not stated outright. The saga is therefore much more free of conscious evaluation than any historical writing.[19] Literature in this sense cannot be given the general definition of entertainment (as can the fairy tale), or of artistic performance (such as the epic).[20] It is only today that the saga is considered to be a pure poetic composition. For the original narrators it was pure reality, for they saw the world in mythical terms.[21] The saga-teller differs from the singers of Homeric epics in that he is convinced of the reality of what he says. 'The stories in the sacred writings do not, like those of Homer, court our favour; they do not flatter us out of a wish to please or enchant us: they want us to surrender, and if we refuse we are rebels.' These words of Auerbach's in fact apply to all original sagas.[22] They show that the saga is a phenomenon which must indeed be taken seriously. Naturally Old Testament sagas are of particular importance, and have been seen from a literary-historical viewpoint as 'the most beautiful, sublime and charming of all world literature'.[23]

D. *Theological Evaluation*

All we have said so far confirms the words which A. Stoeker wrote over sixty years ago: 'There is no doubt that the early biblical material contains sagas and legendary elements; this is a fact which cannot be denied, and it is time that it was brought to the attention of professing Christians.'[24] This touches on a serious omission on the part of the church, for no one as yet has gone to the trouble of pointing out the legendary elements in the Bible and what they signify. Instead people have preferred to swim with the tide of a most barren positivism which insists on the absolute truth of these sagas as though they were exact history. Such people labour under the delusion that by proceeding thus, without reservation or reflection, they are showing proper piety. So it is a fact of the greatest importance that

---

[19] 'Anyone who has recognised the peculiar poetic charm of these old sagas finds himself irritated by the barbarians—and there are also pious barbarians—who can only appreciate such a narrative by classifying it under prose or history. The fact that this narrative is judged to be a saga should not detract from it in any way; it should express the judge's appreciation of the poetic beauty of the narrative, and show that this is the way in which he has understood it', Gunkel, *Genesis* XII.

[20] This also applies even if Gunkel should be right in saying that there was a special profession of the narrator in Israel, who came forward on ceremonial occasions (Gen. XXXI).

[21] W. E. Peuckert, *Sagen* 1965, shows how German sagas can arise out of seriously intended narratives concerning the narrator himself (pp. 11 ff.).

[22] *Mimesis*[2], p. 17. It is a weakness of the otherwise splendid introductory chapter to this book that it compares a Greek epic with an Old Testament saga, which are two quite different literary types, and from this maintains that much is specifically characteristic of the Old Testament when in fact it is characteristic of the literary type of the saga as a whole. However, the continuation of the quotation given above is more satisfactory when it deals with characteristics which are particularly Israelite: 'Doctrine and promise are incarnate in them.' For this refers to a point which is in fact peculiar to Old Testament narratives and which plays a part in the heroic saga of I Sam. xxvi, where it concerns David's stay in the land which Jahweh has promised.

[23] Gunkel, RGG[2] V, 49.

[24] In Gunkel, *Genesis* XIII.

today no less a one than Karl Barth has made a thorough study of the theological significance of the saga. "That it does actually contain a good deal of saga (but also legends and anecdotes) is due to the nature and theme of the bible witness.'[25]

The knowledge that a biblical story is legendary does not detract from its significance. Sagas are reality poeticised. As everyone knows, some of the greatest Old Testament books are poetic, such as the Psalter, or the book of Job, for poetry can provide insights into the final truths of human existence which are inaccessible to science. Therefore poetry plays a necessary part in any attempt to approach these final truths, i.e. the search for God. Why then should not the poetry of the people themselves be a medium for divine revelation? Who would presume to dictate to the Almighty that his will can only be made known through historical protocol? The knowledge that much of the oldest parts of the Old Testament are legendary is a fact which must be more widely broadcast, for it is a matter of positive gain to both Christians and non-Christians alike.

It is incontestable that the Old Testament does in fact also contain historical writing. II Sam. vii–I Kings ii contains the world's first historical writing, written 400 years before Herodotus. Yet the theological content of this and other similar passages is small, and their usefulness for church sermons and church instruction even less.

For our present discussion this means firstly that the saga has a different effectiveness from that of historical writing, bridging the gap between the present and the past, and showing that what appears as past events contains a hidden relevance to the present. The narrator and his hearers identify themselves with the deeds and sufferings of their forebears. God's intervention in favour of their forebears is intervention in favour of themelves.[26] Those who learn about the danger which threatened the ancestress of Israel are made conscious of the inherent danger to themselves from the established peoples in Canaan by whom they are surrounded. They hope for divine protection also. The warriors who tell of David's courage identify him with their present leader, who will be granted Jahweh's favour as David and the other earlier leaders were. Thus it is natural that in the course of the transmission history the later narrators' experiences of God and the world affect the stories of earlier periods. The saga is a repository for the economic, intellectual and religious experiences of countless generations. It draws all periods together, and compresses the events into a language with highly symbolical overtones. A further merit of the saga is that it links the dimensions of divine guidance and protection directly with the historical,[27] and not only with the proceedings of various individuals (through the historical core), but also to a great extent with the highly inaccessible sociological, ethnological, intellectual and religious

[25] *Church Dogmatics*, III, I, p. 81, 1936–62 (Edinburgh, R. &. R Clark; U.S.A., Allenson).
[26] Hence the Israelite can relate his own life to that of the hero, because the conception of 'corporative personality' is natural to him. See H. Wheeler Robinson, The Hebrew Conception of Corporate Personality, BZAW 66 (1936), pp. 49–62.
[27] 'There is little cause for the concern that Israel could have lost contact with history in these descriptions of the earliest periods', von Rad, ThLZ 88, 1963, p. 413.

movements (through the historical framework). The saga can be quite uninhibited in its description of benediction and curse, sin and grace, promise and rejection.[28] The earliest forms had a far better grasp of the association between God and history than later Israelite and Christian historical writing. The sagas in the books from Genesis to Samuel have had a far greater inspirational effect than has the historical writing of, say, the books of the Kings. And their influence on the fine arts has been tremendous. Even today those concerned with the chronicling of historical facts have not yet been able to discover an intelligible link between the search for the motivation and aim of history generally, which is ultimately the search for God, and the individual projects of historical research. The Old Testament saga is therefore vital in any attempt to discover the fundamentals of human existence as a historical phenomenon, when not only the historical meaning of the individual (*die Geschichtlichkeit*) is sought but also the meaning of history as a whole. Moreover the field of history is such a wide one, that without the use of poetic material historical research alone is insufficient to provide real insight. Gunkel was right in emphasising that 'poetic narratives (sagas) are much more able than prose to be the vehicles of thought, even thoughts of a religious kind'.[29]

But have we the capacity today to grasp the true significance of the saga? It is difficult for us to see them as more than mere isolated fables. Perhaps Gunkel took these critical points too lightly when he repeatedly urged that the saga must be heard to be truly absorbed. This raises very obvious difficulties, for the saga has not been in current use as a literary type for centuries. It cannot simply be transposed into another literary type. It needs to be narrated aloud, and to be experienced only by hearing. All interpretation and comment can only be a preliminary to this. But for us comment is essential: for to start with the hearer or reader must know not so much about Isaac as about his people and the unenviable position they were in as they camped outside Gerar. Otherwise the full implication of the story of the ancestress of Israel is lost. And to grasp the full significance of the conflict between Saul and David when they met in the wilderness we must also know about such things as the relationship of David's men to their leader and David to his god. We also need some idea of the concept of the world as family, and also of the custom of the ancients to eulogise persons or relationships. Thus the hearer today is at a disadvantage in not being able to experience the saga directly, as the original hearers will have done. It comes to him now as a historical phenomenon, already analysed and broken down. But the most important thing is that he does still hear or read it. It has yet to be seen how far the church will promote this; for there is no doubt that a correct understanding of these Old Testament passages depends upon its doing so.

The reader should not now jump to the conclusion that the saga is the only legitimate way to talk of history in theological terms. It is not the only

[28] The wide use which was made of the saga in Israel is linked to the lack of abstract thought in Israel; this meant that all statements of thought were voiced in the form of the saga. Only through narratives such as these was the Israelite able to describe the omnipotence of God or the power of action of a leader.

[29] *Genesis* VIII.

kerygmatic form able to speak of divine intervention on earth. The fact that the saga was also an established form in other, non-Israelite cultures proves the point. Although the church can never promulgate its doctrines without making use of these poetic elements, there is no way by which this early literary type can be revived and fresh sagas composed. The path which the Old Testament took, from the early patriarchal sagas to the rural-national sagas, and thence to historical writing, cannot be retrodden. But it is most important that a fresh approach be made to the sagas which we already have in the Old Testament. Otherwise we lose track of much that went into the development of our present way of life, Christian or otherwise.

Section Two: From the Songs

As well as the narrative books the Old Testament contains an even larger complex of poetic and didactic writings. Of these the most important is the Psalter, not only from a theological but also from a form-critical point of view. The psalms provide the easiest means for analysing Israelite songs. The fundamentals for the determination of the literary types were laid down by Gunkel in his great commentary on the psalms (HKAT), 1926, and in the most informative compendium which he published with Begrich: *Einleitung in die Psalmen*, 1933. C. Westermann: *Das Loben Gottes in den Psalmen*, 1953, ²1961, comments on the formal structure of the literary types, E.T. *The Praise of God in the Psalms*, 1965 (London, Epworth Press; Richmond, John Knox Press). His attempt to change Gunkel's designations of literary types has found little support. The setting in life has been fully studied by W. Mowinckel in his six-volume *Psalmenstudien*, 1921–24. Mowinckel's work has been finally brought together in his new two-volume *The Psalms in Israel's Worship*, 1962. The Old Testament Introductions give short surveys of the literary types of the psalms, chiefly Eissfeldt. Indispensable for the history of the literary types is a comparison with the psalms of Mesopotamia; Falkenstein/von Soden: *Sumerische und akkadische Hymnen und Gebete* (Die Bibliothek der Alten Welt), 1953, is splendidly produced, with a good form-critical Introduction.

13. THE HYMN[1]

There is no point in trying to read straight through the Psalter. The uninitiated reader comes up on the one hand against a bewildering variety of statements, and on the other against a steady repetition of typical expressions which all appear to be very similar to one another. What do these songs mean? It is with them that form criticism has made its greatest impact, and has opened the way for an unexpectedly broad understanding of the conceptions which underlie the Old Testament. Close analysis has revealed that the Psalter contains a whole series of established literary types. To begin with there is the *hymn*. Here are three examples:

Psalm cxxxv

A   1. Praise ye the Lord (Halleluja)
      Praise ye the name of the Lord; / Praise him, O ye servants of the Lord:
    2. Ye that stand in the house of the Lord, / In the courts of the house our God.
    3. Praise ye the Lord; for the Lord is good: / Sing praises unto his name; for it is pleasant.

B   4. For the Lord hath chosen Jacob unto himself, / And Israel for his peculiar pleasure.

---

[1] As form criticism has become part of the general exegesis of the psalms (cf. the new commentaries) I can be brief in the next two sections.

5. For I know that the Lord is great, / And that our Lord is above all gods.

6. Whatsoever the Lord pleased, that he hath done, / In heaven and in earth, in the seas and in all deeps.

C 7. He causeth the vapours to ascend from the ends of the earth; / He maketh lightnings for the rain; / He bringeth forth the wind out of his treasuries.

8. Who smote the firstborn of Egypt, / Both of man and beast.

9. He sent signs and wonders / into the midst of thee, O Egypt, / Upon Pharaoh, and upon all his servants.

10. Who smote many nations, / And slew mighty kings;

11. Sihon king of the Amorites, / And Og king of Bashan, And all the kingdoms of Canaan:

12. And gave their land for an heritage, / An heritage unto Israel his people.

D 13. Thy name, O Lord, endureth for ever; / Thy memorial, O Lord, throughout all generations.

B₂ 14. For the Lord shall judge his people, / And repent himself concerning his servants.

E. 15. The idols of the nations are silver and gold, / The work of men's hands.

16. They have mouths, but they speak not; / Eyes have they, but they see not;

17. They have ears, but they hear not; / Neither is there any breath in their mouths.

18. They that make them shall be like unto them; / Yea, every one that trusteth in them.

D 19. O house of Israel, bless ye the Lord: / O house of Aaron, bless ye the Lord:

20. O house of Levi, bless ye the Lord: / Ye that fear the Lord, bless ye the Lord.

21. Blessed be the Lord out of Zion, / Who dwelleth at Jerusalem. Praise ye the Lord (Halleluja).

Psalm cxlvi

A 1. Praise ye the Lord (Halleluja [of Haggai and Zechariah]) Praise the Lord, O my soul.

2. While I live will I praise the Lord: / I will sing praises unto my God while I have any being.

3. Put not your trust in princes, / Nor in the son of man, in whom there is no help.

4. His breath goeth forth, he returneth to earth; / *In that very day* his thoughts perish.

B 5. Happy is he that hath the God of Jacob for his help, / Whose hope is in the Lord his God:

C 6. Which made heaven and earth, / The sea, and all that in them is; Which keepeth truth for ever: / Which executeth judgement for the oppressed;

7. Which giveth food to the hungry: / The Lord looseth the prisoners;

8. The Lord openeth the eyes of the blind; / The Lord raiseth up them
that are bowed down;
the Lord loveth the righteous; / The Lord preserveth the strangers;
9. He upholdeth the fatherless and widow; / But the way of the wicked
he turneth upside down.
10. The Lord shall reign for ever, / Thy God, O Zion, unto all generations.

D   Praise ye the Lord (Halleluja).

Psalm xlvii   For the Chief Musician; a Psalm of the sons of Korah.

A   1. O clap your hands, all ye peoples; / Shout unto God with the voice of
triumph.

B   2. For the Lord Most High is terrible; / He is a great King over all the
earth.

C   3. He shall subdue the peoples under us, / And the nations under our
feet.
4. He shall choose our inheritance for us, / The excellency of Jacob
whom he loved.
5. God is gone up with a shout, / The Lord with the sound of a trumpet.

A   6. Sing praises to God, sing praises: / Sing praises unto our King, sing
praises.

B   7. For God is the King of all the earth: / Sing ye praises with understanding.

C   8. God reigneth over the nations: / God sitteth upon his holy throne.
9. The princes of the peoples are gathered together / To be the people of
the God of Abraham:

D   For the shields of the earth belong to God; / He is greatly exalted.

A. *Characteristics of the Literary Type*

Each of these three psalms has its own individuality, and is evidently the
work of a different author. Nevertheless, there are considerable formal similarities. Each of them begins with a summons to praise the great god
Jahweh (A): *an invitation to song*, as it was earlier named, or a *hymnic
introduction*, as Gunkel termed it. As a rule there are a series of imperatives
in the plural at the beginning, as in the first and third example, directed
to those to whom the invitation is extended. They may be people who have
found themselves within the forecourt of the temple on some ceremonial
occasion (Ps. cxxxv), or the invitation may concern the peoples generally
(Ps. xlvii). But occasionally the hymn begins by the singer addressing
himself: 'Praise the Lord, O my soul' (Ps. cxlvi); but then as the song
develops a larger group of persons is called upon (verse 3), so that the
opening here belongs to a precentor, or chorister, whose praises precede
those of the group as a whole.

This is followed by section B, the shortest part of the hymn, which is
obviously intended to be as concise as possible. This is a transitional
passage introducing the theme of the hymn, or *thematic sentence* (B). It is

usually introduced by 'for', and gives the reasons for praising God. Jahweh is praiseworthy in his role of the Almighty, whose power is unrivalled by that of any other god (cxxxv. 5 f.), or in his role as king of the universe (xlvii. 3). Sometimes his might is referred to indirectly by calling those people lucky whom he has helped (cxlvi. 5). In this case there is a blessing in place of the introductory 'for'. Jahweh's uniqueness also lies in his special relationship with Israel. In Ps. cxxxv this is given as the reason for praise (verse 4).[2] The thematic sentence is so closely bound up with the invitation to song that in fact it has already been preluded in those first few sentences. There is therefore a close correspondence between the two. In Ps. cxlvi, for example, the introductory invitation warns against a trust in men, in whom there is 'no help'; this anticipates the thematic statement in verse 5 to the effect that only Jahweh can help. When the hymnic introduction in Ps. cxxxv rejoices in the *name* of Jahweh, which is *pleasant*, this is a prelude to the thematic sentence on the unapproachable majesty of Jahweh, and the special nature of his relationship with Israel; the two are linked by mention of God's *name*. In Ps. xlvii the invitation to praise 'our king' (verse 7) is intended to lead on to the thematic sentence in verse 8, in which God is represented as king of all the earth. The thematic sentence is of outstanding importance for the hymn. It is in fact the central point of the song. It reveals whether the psalmist is moved to more than lyricism, whether he is urged by 'theological' considerations. Hence this section is missing in only a very few hymns, and those appear to be particularly ancient (e.g. Ps. xxix, civ). Gunkel/Begrich can hardly be right in seeing the thematic sentence as a mere point of transition between the hymnic introduction and the main part of the hymn. In fact it is the point at which the thought underlying the hymn is concentrated.

Part C, the main part of the hymn, is the most extensive. The thematic sentence is developed into an enumeration of God's historical deeds. The word 'history' is used here in a wide sense, for it comprises not only the salvation history of Israel in a narrow meaning of the term (Ps. cxxxv), and Jahweh's power over nature and the fate of the individual (Ps. cxlvi), but also the primeval event of Jahweh's accession to the throne, by which he originally became king of the universe, and which, like other saving events, was also remembered in cultic celebrations in Israel. This main section is interesting in that it shows the Israelite way of speaking about God. The subject of the transitional thematic sentence, of divine uniqueness in face of human existence, is developed merely by describing events brought about by God. God's nature cannot be grasped or described in any other way.[3] Enumerating these historical deeds not only praises God but also helps towards the salvation of the people singing. The syntax of the main part of the song often takes the form of a series of participles, as in Ps. cxlvi. Or

[2] In ZAW 67, 1955, pp. 206–9 I discuss the relationship between the formula (or 'statement' would be better) of avowal of membership of the community (*Zugehörigkeitsformel*) and the avowal of individuality (*Einzigartigkeitsformel*) in references in the hymns to Israel as the chosen people.

[3] Instead of 'hymn' Westermann suggests that it is the literary type of a 'descriptive psalm of praise', which he sharply separates from a 'reporting psalm of praise'; but it is precisely in the hymn that a 'description' of God takes the form of a 'report' of his doings.

it starts with a participle at the beginning (Ps. cxxxv. 7), and is then followed by sentences in the perfect tense, a tense which is seldom used in the Hebrew, and which to Israelite ears would probably stress the character of the events which have been described.

These three sections, A, B and C, are essential parts of an Israelite hymn and their sequence is inalterable, although it can be repeated a second time for greater effect, as in Ps. xlvii. On the other hand, the conclusion varies considerably. As a rule the introductory invitation to song is repeated (cxxxv. 19), occasionally by means of one brief phrase (cxlvi. 10); or the hymn can just as well be ended by a thematic sentence (xlvii. 9b); or a thematic sentence can be placed before the conclusion to the song (cxlvi. 10a), sometimes including a reference to those who do not have this unique relationship to the one God (E cxxxv. 15–18).

The three psalms thus belong to a literary type of a very distinctive style, of which there are about 35 examples in the Psalter. Gunkel introduced the term 'hymn' as a translation of the Hebrew term *tehillah*, which in later headings was replaced by Halleluja, or Praise ye the Lord, which has the same meaning (e.g. cxlvi and cxxxv). The Hebrew term tells us much. *Tehillah* does not only mean a song in praise of Jahweh, but תְּהִלָּה is also Jahweh himself (e.g. cxlviii. 14), and his praiseworthy actions. Therefore it follows that any intervention by Jahweh immediately and inevitably brings forth human praise. In fact, any divine action is inseparably bound up with human praise. Hence Israel's praise of God is a reflection of divine action, and is not to be interpreted in entirely human terms. Therefore it can also mean that Jahweh's תְּהִלָּה is spread over the whole earth (Hab. iii. 3; Ps. xlviii. 10). But this general term תְּהִלָּה was used in a particular way in Israel, and, as the psalms show, in a distinctive form.

The hymn refers to Jahweh in the third person. It is rare for the singer to insert in his enthusiasm a direct address to his God (e.g. Ps. lxxxvi. 13). When this happens it is completely spontaneous, and does not alter the structure of the hymn. The hymn is not addressed to God, but to a wide public. It is therefore—and this may surprise the Bible reader—not a prayer. However, it is also not a sermon in rhyme, nor a proclamation addressed to a particular group of people, as the Christian theologian perhaps too rashly assumes. It is to the glory of God before all the world; and though a direct address to God is avoided it is in fact indirectly addressed to him and not merely to those listening. These songs are motivated by a tremendous enthusiasm on the part of the singer. This is very evident in Ps. xlvii, where the people are invited to clap their hands in joy for the deeds of Israel's God.

What position would these songs have held in life in Israel?

B. *Setting in Life*

A hymn cannot be sung anywhere. It needs some kind of ceremonial background. This is quite evident from the introduction and conclusion to the song. Here we are told that the song is to be accompanied by musical instruments (xlvii. 7, cxlvi. 2).[4] According to the heading therefore, the *Tehillah* belongs to the group of מִזְמֹר, songs which are sung to the accompaniment of music (xlvii. 1; but also xxix. 1, xlviii. 1, etc.). It also needs to be sung in a particular place, namely the house of Jahweh, where God is enthroned, i.e. the Jerusalem Temple. Details are given of the structure of the cultic community: Aaronitic priests, Levitical deacons, and the god-fearing, i.e. laymen (cxxxv. 1–3, 19, 20). Even the deeds of God which are described in the main part of the song often have some relationship to the sacred place, to cultic rejoicing and trumpet playing, or there is a reference at the end to the gathering on Zion (xlvii. 6, 9, cf. lxxviii. 68; Exod. xv. 1 ff.). There are dozens of similar examples in other hymns, so that a cultic setting in life cannot be doubted. The Halleluja at the end of Ps. cxlvi and elsewhere (cxxxv?) reveals quite clearly that the song of the singer or choir is taken up by the community at the end in a mighty echo, as we know to have been the case in post-exilic times.[5] Many hymns have been taken up into liturgies (see Ps. xxiv. 1 f., l. 1–5, lxxxi. 2–6, xcv. 1–7).

The cult of ancient Israel was rich in festivals and celebrations. Is it still possible to determine the actual ceremony at which the different hymns were sung? This is the point at which the otherwise excellent compendium by Gunkel/Begrich breaks down: for all hymns are thrown together under the single heading of Israelite festivals. 'Whatever the occasion, the content of what was said varied little.'[6] This opinion is not at all in accordance with traditional Israelite practice, where customs firmly regulated life. It is just as if it were asserted that Christians sung the same hymns at Christmas, Easter and Whitsun. It is indeed possible that the literary type of the hymn can after all be broken down to some extent into those used at different ceremonies. Let us take a look at our three examples.

In Ps. xlvii the particular cultic event is easy to determine. The main section of the hymn, describing God ascending amidst cheers of victory, and sitting upon his throne, is obviously an *accession song* (as are also Ps. xciii, xcvi–xcix). This points to a festival in honour of Jahweh's accession at the Jerusalem autumn festival (Mowinckel), or at least to a festival of particular homage to Jahweh as king (Kraus[7]), which would be connected with the expectation of a theophany.[8] This ceremony will have begun with the cultic community making a procession from the city of

---

[4] Trans. note. The Hebrew rendered as 'sing' in these verses can also be used of 'playing musical instruments'. See Koehler-Baumgartner, *Lexicon in Veteris Testamenti Libros*, 1953, p. 260.

[5] III Macc. vii. 13; I Chron. xvi. 36, cf. Ecclus. l. 18 f.

[6] p. 68.

[7] H.-J. Kraus BKAT[2], 1961.

[8] Gunkel had the strange idea that Jahweh's succession to the throne which is the subject here was an event in the future, an eschatological one, although there is not one reference in the whole of the hymn to the end of time. This interpretation of Gunkel's, which goes quite against his form-critical principles, can only be explained by the unconscious influence of the literary-critical thesis which he inherited, that the composition of the psalms was later linked with prophecy and therefore dependent upon it.

Jerusalem to the temple hill, as described in Ps. xxiv. It was their belief
that as they came within the precincts of the sacred place Jahweh also
arrived at the same moment. So his kingly power was praised in the temple
and in its forecourts. It was Mowinckel who pointed out that this psalm
belonged to this particular celebration,[9] although he went too far in assuming that an accession *festival* took place in Israel, and in fact that the whole
of the Israelite autumn festival was an accession festival. The *ceremony* of
the accession was doubtless only a part of a very extensive celebration.

Ps. cxxxv is a hymn in honour of Israel's salvation history, and will
also have been sung in the temple and its forecourts, though on another
occasion. Here it is not a question of Jahweh assuming kingly power, but a
festival for the saving guidance of Israel through the course of her history.
G. von Rad has shown[10] that Israel regarded the period between the exodus
from Egypt and the entry into Palestinian land as salvation history in its
most eminent sense, and was strongly represented at cultic celebrations
even before the founding of the state. At a later stage this normative
Heilsgeschichte would have been augmented by the history of the earliest
times, and thus in the psalms the creation will have been made to precede
the event in Egypt. The most important events of this period were recited
by priests or other professional speakers, and perhaps even presented in
the form of a ritual drama. The community accompanied the performance
or ended it with a hymn of this kind. Therefore this hymn is set in a
ceremony of remembrance of Israel's salvation.

For Ps. cxlvi, however, it is no longer possible to determine an exact
setting in life. As the information which has come down to us about the
psalms is limited, we have only a scanty and on the whole indirect knowledge of the Israelite cult, and it is by no means always possible to determine
the background of the hymns in detail. With Ps. cxlvi it is even impossible
to make any close definition of the group of hymns to which it belongs. It
is just possible that it is a salvation history hymn which has been altered;
for the main part begins with the creation, and continues with a reference
to the constancy of God, which could well be meant to refer to his continued constancy to the Covenant with Israel. But it is just as easy to
conclude from the reference in verse 10 to God's reign over Zion that it is
a modified accession song, or to believe, with Hans Schmidt (HAT), from
the extended introduction in verses 2–4 that it is part of a festival in remembrance of a particular vow. But these suggestions are purely specu-
lative.

It was Gunkel's view that hymns such as Psalm cxlvi could not have
sprung from a living practice of the cult. This would apply to quite a few
of the examples of this literary type which are to be found in the Psalter.
It seems more likely that the literary type was imitated outside the cult for
personal edification in the form of religious lyrics.[11] Gunkel's idea has

---

[9] *Psalmenstudien*, vol. 2. The long controversy over the succession festival cannot
be discussed in detail here. See Mowinckel PIW I, 106 ff.
[10] Das formgeschichtliche Problem des Hexateuch, BWANT IV, 26, 1938 = GS
9 ff. cf. p. 30 for E.T.
[11] GuB 67.

found wide favour, and it has become common for Old Testament scholars
to vie with each other in discovering as many hymns as possible with no
connection with actual cultic practice. But this inclination could go too
far. It is a natural one for us of the twentieth century who have no affinity
to the cult, but it could well become a 'Protestant' pipe-dream, quite out
of keeping with the ancient Psalter. In face of the present situation in
biblical research it is incontestable that a series of hymns, which includes
Ps. cxxxv, had their place in the cult. The headings also, added in the
post-exilic period, with references to Levitical companies of singers
such as the Korahites in Ps. xlvii, or with the title 'Song for the accompaniment of music', point to cultic usage. Even in the late work of the
Chronicler *all* hymnic passages are ascribed to cultic practice (I Chron.
xvi. 8–36, xxix. 10–12; II Chron. vi. 14 f.; Neh. ix). And it has not yet
been proved that any one hymn in the Old Testament could not fit into
some sort of cultic celebration, or that any hymn shows indisputable signs
of unprofessional composition. Though the idea cannot be ruled out that
some hymns may have had no relation to the cult, it certainly has not yet
been conclusively demonstrated.

C. *History of the Literary Type*

How old is the hymn in Israel? How long did it remain in current use?
What changes did it undergo in its development? These questions can
only be answered by quoting evidence outside the narrow range of our
three examples, for as they belong to different groups of hymns it is not
possible to give them any chronological order.

There are two songs extant from the earlier Israelite period which are
comparable.[12] Firstly, the Miriam song in Exod. xv. 20 f., which according
to its present position was sung directly after the crossing of the Red Sea
by those fleeing from Egypt:

A Sing ye to the Lord,
B for he hath triumphed gloriously;
C The horse and his rider hath he thrown into the sea.

The song is accompanied by timbrels and dances. During it the prophetess
leads the women out (one wonders where to). This short song is so easy to
remember that it is certain to have been sung many times in succession.
Doubtless it was also sung on other occasions. Despite its simplicity—only
parallelismus membrorum, the essential feature of later poetry, is missing—
it is already possible to distinguish the parts which make up the literary
type of the hymn: the invitation to song, the transitional thematic sentence,
and the main section.

The second example, the song of Deborah in Judges v. 2 ff., is longer
and would have arisen perhaps a century later. Parallelismus membrorum
in its ancient, stair-like form, is evident:

---

[12] It is wrong to quote Isa. vi. 3 in connection with the history of the literary type
of the hymn, as Gunkel and Westermann have done. Isa. vi. 3 is a cultic invocation,
perhaps of Egyptian origin, but not a hymn.

A 2. For that the leaders look the lead in Israel, / For that the people
offered themselves willingly, Bless ye the Lord.

   3. Hear, O ye kings; / give ear, O ye princes;
I, even I, will sing / unto the Lord;
I will sing praises to the Lord, / the God of Israel.

C 4. Lord, when thou wentest forth out of Seir, / When thou marchedst
out of the field of Edom,
The earth trembled, / the heavens also dropped, / Yea, the clouds
dropped water.

   5. The mountains flowed . . .

Here even the invitation to song is more elaborate. The main part describes
God's deeds. But the thematic sentence is missing, as in the old Ps. xxix
and civ. It is noteworthy that the song of Deborah has a greater affinity to
many old Babylonian-Assyrian cultic songs than to most of the hymns in
the Psalter. The invitation to song and the main part begin with an infinitive construction ('for that' occurs twice in verse 2, 'when' twice in verse 4),
which is a common construction in Mesopotamian poetry; it is also to be
found in some of the more ancient hymns in the Psalter (cxiv. 1, lxviii. 7).
Also the fact that the singer refers to herself is more in keeping with non-
Israelite psalms.[13] The song therefore reveals that the development of this
literary type was probably influenced by Mesopotamian poetry. This
influence will have reached Israel through the medium of pre-Israelite
Canaan. Moreover the song makes it appear likely that the self-address
form will have been the oldest form of the hymnic introduction. The song
of Deborah is indeed far removed from the classical form of the hymn
which is found in the Psalter. To find the *terminus a quo* for the actual
composition of hymns we should need to go back a good hundred years
before the song of Deborah. This will mean that the form will not have
arisen before the monarchical period, before the time of the Solomonic
temple and the state sanctuaries in Bethel and Dan in the northern kingdom.

Is it possible to calculate when the composition of hymns will have ceased,
i.e. discover the *terminus ad quem*? The books of the Chroniclers give
us a few clues. We have already mentioned that there are parts of the
great compilations which are unmistakeably hymnic; but it is also a fact
that the Chronicler never quotes a hymn in its classical form. Instead the
hymnic passage is always followed by a petition (introduced by 'Now
therefore'), which is not at all in keeping with the style of the hymns in the
the Psalter (I Chron. xxix. 13; II Chron. vi. 16). Where the Psalter is
quoted *in extenso*, a phrase has been expressly added to the quotation to
show that in its present context it is intended as a prayer (I Chron. xvi. 35).
Hence this late stage of the hymnic prayer again shows some similarity to
its ancient Babylonian-Assyrian prototype. In other books of the later
period the hymn's main section is preceded or followed by wisdom
reflections (Ecclus. xxxix. 14b–35, xlii. 15–43, 33; Job. xxxvi. 22–xxxvii.
24, xxxviii f.). By this time, therefore,—400 B.C. at the latest—the literary

---

[13] But examples given in Falkenstein/von Soden begin with the imperative plural.

type was no longer in current use. At least, no more hymns were fashioned in the old style. This makes it possible to date the Psalter and with it the songs quoted above as having been composed between 1000 and 400 B.C. At present this is as far as we can go. There is insufficient material to make out any accurate history of the literary type, as is possible with the Pentateuch narratives. We do not yet know whether the participial clauses in the main part (Ps. cxlvi) belong to the earlier or the later period, or whether they can be accounted for by the particular group of hymns of which they are part. Perhaps the repetition of the call to praise God at the end of the hymn is a late development. These are questions which so far remain unanswered.

D. *Transmission and Redaction History*

As it is not yet possible to outline the history of the literary type, the transmission history of the individual hymns poses us a problem. Ps. xlvii provides us with no basis for an analysis of its transmission history. But Ps. cxlvi reveals that in verse 4, where death is the subject, the words 'on that very day' are a later addition, for they upset the rhythmical balance of the passage. This is an indication of an 'eschatological redaction', to be found in a whole series of psalms (and which was taken further in the Septuagint). We know a bit more about the transmission history of Ps. cxxxv, for passages of a very similar nature crop up in Ps. cxxxvi and cxv. In Ps. cxxxvi we have a repeat of the lines which in Ps. cxxxv constitute the core of the song, principally in the following phrases:

Who smote the firstborn of Egypt
Who smote . . . and slew kings;
Sihon king of the Amorites / And Og king of Bashan . . .
And gave their land for an heritage, / An heritage unto Israel his people . . .

The phraseology is similar because there was probably a fixed wording in salvation history hymns to describe certain events (cf. Deut. xxix. 6; Judges ix. 10). The introduction also follows an established formula, for we also find it in Jer. x. 13:

(When he uttereth his voice, there is a tumult of waters in the heaven,)
and he causeth vapours to ascend from the ends of the earth;
he maketh lightnings for the rain,
and bringeth forth the wind out of his treasuries.

The psalmist is therefore content to describe Israel's saving history mainly in accepted phrases. However, he himself will have worded the invitation to song, the transitional thematic sentence and the conclusion. In these the key word is God's *name*. Both at the beginning and end of the invitation to song, and also at the start of the conclusion (verse 13) the name of the Lord is praised. Indeed, the word Lord occurs no less than fourteen times in A, B and D.

Though the hymn is built around the name of the Lord, verses 15–18 have been revised to include the theme of the worship of idols, the wording of which has been taken from Deut. xxxii. 36 and Ps. cxv. 4–7. Also verse 3 from Ps. cxv has been included:

Our God is in the heavens: / He hath done whatsoever he pleased.

and has been inserted into the beginning of the main section of Ps. cxxxv (verse 6). It is by this means that the transition from the thematic sentence (verses 4 f.) to the main section is achieved. The main section will once have begun with a description of the creation and Jahweh's power over the unruly waters. The relationship of Ps. cxxxv to Ps. cxxxvi is therefore different from its relationship to Ps. cxv. With the first it is a matter of the common use of cultic phrases which were part of the oral tradition, and with Ps. cxv of a literary dependence which arose only later. In Ps. cxxxv therefore we can determine two different stages in its transmission history. This makes us able to discover the great simplicity of what the psalmist is trying to convey: the name of Jahweh gives Israel a more than this-worldly kind of power, and an unconditional obligation. And what Jahweh's name cannot tell us is revealed by a description of the early saving history.

If the analysis of a psalm such as Ps. cxxxv begins with its transmission history—and this is a method which has not yet been used in the commentaries—this will inevitably be followed by a study of its *redaction history*. We have already touched upon the close linguistic connection between it and the following hymn, Ps. cxxxvi. But with the previous hymn also, Ps. cxxxiv, there is an obvious connection with the invitation to song of the hymn we are studying. Hence we must assume a common author.

cxxxiv

Behold, bless ye the Lord,
all ye servants of the Lord,
which by night stand
in the house of the Lord.
Lift up your hands to the sanctuary,
And bless ye the Lord.

cxxxv

Praise ye the name of the Lord;
Praise him, O ye servants of the Lord:
Ye that stand in the house of the Lord,
In the courts of the house of our God.
Praise ye the Lord; for the Lord is good;
Sing praises unto his name; for it is pleasant.

cxxxiv

The Lord bless thee out of Zion.
Even he that made heaven and earth.

cxxxv

Blessed be the Lord out of Zion,
Who dwelleth at Jerusalem.

In cxxxiv servants of the Lord are called upon to *bless* him, and in cxxxv to *praise* him, which they do in the song which follows. In cxxxvi they are called upon to *sing* to him, with the people probably chiming in with the refrain, 'For his mercy endureth for ever'. These three psalms have a strong liturgical link. They will once have belonged to the same setting in life. Together they form the conclusion to the 'Songs of Pilgrimage' (Eissfeldt) which may once have comprised a small book of songs for pilgrims (or may have been composed in the Babylonian exile, looking forward to the return; for cxxxvii ends the series with a gruesome cursing of Babel).[14]

Ps. xlvii is placed in the middle of a group of Korah psalms, Ps. xlii–xlix. The group begins with two psalms of lament, then a royal song (Ps. xlv) which when it was added to the group was perhaps intended to refer to the kingdom of Jahweh. These are followed by hymns extolling Jahweh's glory on Mount Zion (Ps. xlvi), the accession song we have discussed above, and then another song about Zion (Ps. xlviii). The end consists of a reflective wisdom psalm on the frailty of human life and the hope which arises out of communion with God (Ps. xlix). It has yet to be investigated whether these surroundings throw any particular light on Ps. xlvii.

Ps. cxlvi belongs to the Hallelujah group of psalms, cxlvii–cl, which praise the God of Israel in an ever rising crescendo, reaching a climax at the end in Ps. cl, with a call to take up musical instruments. Perhaps these songs are really intended as the crowning conclusion to the Davidic psalms cxxxviii–cxlv (Eissfeldt). This would give Ps. cxlvi the definite role of a transition hymn between songs of praise sung by a single person (Ps. cxlv), to songs by a chorus accompanied by the gathering. The LXX translation shows a further development in Ps. cxlvi. The psalm is ascribed to the prophets Haggai and Zechariah. The other headings also give evidence of this tendency to historicise (vii. 1, xviii. 1, li. 1, etc.). The composition of hymns is linked up with the history of Israel, and they are interpreted in that light.

The redaction history of the psalms has as yet been little investigated. Up till now the main emphasis in form criticism has naturally been on determining the literary type of the individual psalms. Once this has been reasonably well accomplished it should be possible to turn to the redaction history, and to attempt to explain the function of these previously independent cultic songs within their written context, starting with the smaller groups of psalms, such as the Korah psalms, or the Hallelujah psalms. It is not yet clear whether it will be possible to take the study further and to trace the redaction history of the greater complex, i.e. of the five books of psalms as they now stand. It is even possible that these greater complexes arose purely mechanically through the process of bringing together the old collections of psalms, which themselves had been formed simply by bringing together psalms of similar content.

---

[14] However, Westermann considers the 'Songs of Pilgrimage' (and the later song cxix) to be a later insertion and makes cxxxv f. part of the Hallelujah collection cxi–cxviii.

14. THE INDIVIDUAL SONG OF LAMENT, AND THE ORACLE ASSURING THE WORSHIPPER HIS LAMENT HAS BEEN HEARD

J. Begrich = Das priesterliche Heilsorakel, ZAW N.S. 11, 1934, 81–92 = Ges. Studien ThB 21, 1964, 217–231.

Psalm v

For the Chief Musician; with the Nehiloth. A Psalm of David.

A B 1. Give ear to my words, *O Lord*, / Consider my meditation.

2. Hearken unto the voice of my cry, / my King, and my God:
For unto thee do I pray (הִתְפַּלָּל). / 3. O Lord, in the morning
shalt thou hear my voice;
In the morning will I order my prayer unto thee, / and will keep
watch.

D 4. For thou art not a God / that hath pleasure in wickedness:
Evil shall not sojourn with thee.
5. The arrogant shall not / stand in thy sight:
Thou hatest all workers of iniquity. / 6. Thou shalt destroy them
that speak lies:
The Lord abhorreth / the bloodthirsty and deceitful man.

E 7. But as for me, in the multitude of thy lovingkindness / will I
come into thy house:
In thy fear / will I worship toward thy holy temple.
B 8. Lead me, *O Lord*, in thy righteousness / because of mine enemies;
Make thy way plain before my face.

C 9. For there is no faithfulness in their mouth; / Their inward part is
very wickedness:
Their throat is an open sepulchre; / They flatter with their tongue.
B 10. Hold them guilty, *O God*; / Let them fall by their own counsels:
Thrust them out in the multitude of their transgressions; / For
they have rebelled against thee.
11. But let all those that put their trust in thee rejoice, / Let them ever
shout for joy,
because thou defendest them: Let them also that love thy name /
be joyful in thee.
D 12. For thou wilt bless the righteous; / O Lord, thou wilt compass
him with favour as with a shield.

Psalm vi

For the Chief Musician; on stringed instruments, set to the Sheminith. A
Psalm of David.

A B 1. *O Lord*, rebuke me not in thine anger, / Neither chasten me in thy
hot displeasure.

2. Have mercy upon me, *O Lord*; / for I am withered away:
O *Lord*, heal me; /

C   for my bones are sore vexed:
3. My soul is also sore vexed: And thou, *O Lord*, how long?

B   4. Return, *O Lord*, deliver my soul: / Save me for thy lovingkindness'
                                             sake.

D   5. For in death there is no remembrance of thee: / In Sheol who
                                 shall give thee thanks?

C   6. I am weary with my groaning; / Every night make I my bed to
                                       swim;
I water my couch with my tears. / 7. Mine eye wasteth away
                                     because of grief;
It waxeth old because of all mine adversaries.

X   8. Depart from me, all ye workers of iniquity; /
                             for the Lord hath
                           heard the voice of my weeping.
9. The Lord hath heard my supplication; / The Lord will receive my
                           prayer (תְּפִלָּה).

10. All my enemies shall be ashamed and sore vexed; / They shall
                           turn back, they shall be ashamed suddenly.

Jeremiah xv. 15–21

A B 15. *O Lord*, thou knowest: remember me, and visit me, and avenge me
                           of my persecutors;
take me not away in thy longsuffering: know that for thy sake I
                           have suffered reproach.

E   16. Thy words were found, and I did eat them; and thy words were
                           unto me a joy
and the rejoicing of my heart: for I am called by thy name,

A   *O Lord* God of hosts.

C   17. I sat not in the assembly of those that make merry, nor rejoiced:
                           I sat alone because of thy hand;
for thou hast filled me with indignation.
18. Why is my pain perpetual, and my wound incurable, which re-
                           fuseth to be healed?
wilt thou indeed be unto me as a deceitful brook, as waters that
                           fail?

O   19. Therefore thus saith the Lord,
If thou return, then will I bring thee again, that thou mayest stand
                           before me;
and if thou take forth the precious from the vile, thou shalt be as
                           my mouth:
they shall return unto thee, but thou shalt not return unto them.

Q   20. And I will make thee unto this people a fenced brasen wall;
and they shall fight against thee, but they shall not prevail against
                           thee:
for I am with thee to save thee and to deliver thee,
saith the Lord.

Q   21. And I will deliver thee out of the hand of the wicked, and I will
                           redeem thee out of the hand of the terrible.

A literary type which occurs more frequently in the Psalter than the hymn is the *individual song of lamentation*. This is the type on which most people base their conception of the psalm, as a song *ex profundis*. It is also found in the poems of lamentation in the book of Jeremiah, which are wrongly termed 'monologues'. The laments in the book of Jeremiah, of which Jer. xxv has been given as an example, are not to be confused with the book of Lamentations (Threni) which (although indeed not in the Hebrew text, but in the biblical translations) are also attributed to Jeremiah.

A. *Determination of the Literary Type*

Despite much difference in style and expression, these three songs prove to be of the same literary type. They belong to what is known as *Tefillah* in Hebrew (as in vi. 9, or the verb in v. 2). About a third of the psalms are of this type. Here again I do not intend to make an exhaustive study of these three examples, but merely to pick out the characteristics of the type as a whole.

The song always begins with an *invocation to God* (A), which is usually placed right at the beginning, but which occurs at least within the first two verses. The singer is therefore seeking a hearing from the God of Israel. Hence we are now faced with a straightforward prayer to God, which was not the case with the hymn. An Israelite cries out in grave need to his heavenly Lord. This invocation to God is closely linked with a *petition* to him (B), which is often cleverly graded from a general to a particular request. To begin with all that is asked is that the call be heard and the need recognised (Ps. v 'Remember me', Jer. xv). Then divine intervention is entreated, and it is stipulated which form it should take: 'Avenge me . . . take me not away' (Jer. xv); 'Rebuke me not . . . have mercy upon me' (Ps. vi). Finally the point is reached where the particular need is stated: 'Heal me' (Ps. vi). The supplicatory imperative is further strengthened by striking an attitude of entreaty: 'In the morning I will order my prayer unto thee, and keep watch' (Ps. v). Despite an astonishing variance in detail in the openings (A + B) of these psalms they show a very noticeable similarity in style. An individual turns privately to his God in his personal need and sorrow. Unlike the hymn, there is no sign of a community gathering. However, by asking a petition the man conforms to the well-established practice of his time, and therefore indirectly proves himself to be a link in the general transmission of material.

As a rule the motive behind the petition is taken up at a later point in the song, and is expressed in more concrete terms (v. 8, vi. 4). Where the petition crops up again at the end it usually takes the form of a wish extending not so much to the petitioner himself as to his friends or his enemies (v. 10). This type of petition will presumably have grown out of the ancient benediction and curse formulas. They reveal that the petitioner does not confront his God as a completely isolated individual, but that he is very much aware of his relationship to his surroundings. But this the reader only notices at the end of the song, if he notices it at all.

The introductory petition can be followed by a diversity of things.

However, it is most usually followed by a *lament* (C; as in Ps. vi). Though this section is present in all three of the psalms, it has no fixed place. Often it occurs twice (Ps. vi), or it takes up the greater part of the whole song (Jer. xv). It is usually separated from the preceding verses by 'for' (v. 9, vi. 2). Whereas the invocation and the petition are familiar to us in our Christian prayers (although the passionate manner of expression of the Old Testament petition may surprise us), there are other features of the lament which are unfamiliar to us, such as the individual's description of his sore distress. He laments the circumstances he is in (vi. 6), or the machinations of his enemies (v. 9), or the remoteness of God (as in the celebrated introduction to Ps. xxii: 'My God, my. God, why hast thou forsaken me?'). It is unusual for the man praying to infer, as Jeremiah does, that his distress has arisen out of his sacrificial duty to God. In many of the laments the singer places so much emphasis on his personal distress that he seems to have lost sight of the God he is addressing. He expresses himself in extremely plain terms, even to the extent of directly reproaching God. Thus in Ps. vi the singer poses the fearful question: 'And thou, O Lord, how long?' Jeremiah expresses it more critically, reaching a climax of indignation: 'Wilt thou indeed be unto me as a deceitful brook, as waters that fail?' The uninhibited manner of the Israelite's lament to his God, his expression of what he thinks or feels, could shock a man of the West. It alone is enough to refute the age-old preconception of the God of the Old Testament as a despotic master, with men no more than slaves before him.

There is yet another section (D) of the individual lament. Gunkel/ Begrich called this section the *grounds for deliverance*, or the *expression of trust* in God, and where the situation is seen through God's eyes they called it the *grounds for divine intervention*. This section is usually separated from the surrounding parts by an accentuated, 'For thou', or 'As for me', as in the expression of trust in Ps. v. 4: 'For thou art not a God that hath pleasure in wickedness', or again at the end of the same psalm: 'For thou wilt bless the righteous.' God's abhorrence of morally suspect behaviour is appealed to, as is also his historically proved preference for the man who is righteous and loyal to the community. Sometimes this style of presentation is taken so far as to refer to Jahweh in the third person (v. 6); the form of the direct address appears to have been forgotten. The grounds for divine intervention in Ps. vi: 'For in death there is no remembrance of thee', is nothing less than a friendly reminder that if God helps the worshipper to regain his health there will be one more person on earth to spread his fame. Thus God is warned that if anything happened to the worshipper this could be to the detriment of his name. But on the other hand there is hidden consolation here: God takes account of every single person who praises his name on earth.

A variation, direct or indirect, of the grounds for deliverance is the *protestation of innocence* (E), in which the worshipper describes his irreproachable past. Jeremiah's words are particularly suggestive of those of a prophet: 'Thy words were found, and I did eat them; and thy words were unto me a joy.' The passage is given particular emphasis by the invocation at the end: 'O Lord, God of hosts.' Perhaps Ps. v. 7 is also intended as a protestation of innocence: 'But as for me, in the multitude of thy lovingkindness will I come into thy house.' God's lovingkindness (חֶסֶד) is his loyalty to the covenant, by which he favours the righteous. The worshipper is giving himself out to be righteous and pious by calling upon this loyalty.

Some psalms of lament end with the *expression of certainty that the prayer will be heard* (X). This is expressed in a tone of confidence which is sharply at variance with that of the preceding petition, lament, and desire for deliverance. This must be the result of a radical change of mood, for previously the song was an expression of complaint and despair; now it is one of uncategorical assurance. It is difficult to see the reason for this. Begrich explained it thus[1]: the setting in life of the psalm of lament will have been a sanctuary; it will have been answered by an authorised cultic speaker, either a priest or a prophet, with an assurance to the worshipper in the form of an *oracle* (O—S) that his prayer will be heard and that salvation will follow. Unfortunately the Psalter does not contain any direct versions of such an oracle, because it will not have been the business of the singer of the lament. The lament is obviously not sung by an authorised speaker of God's word. Therefore there is no mention of God's judgment, which will presumably have followed a lament in the temple as a matter of course. This can be assumed from the assurances of God's help which have luckily survived in the poems of lamentation in the book of Jeremiah, and which have been included because in his role of a prophet Jeremiah was able to be both worshipper and receiver of the oracle at one and the same time. There are twenty-four oracles of a similar nature in Deutero-Isaiah. Nevertheless the psalms do give hints of such oracles. The worshipper in Ps. v 'keeps watch' for a divine answer (verse 3): what could this mean other than a judgment by the priest or cultic prophet? To the worshipper it is a matter of an assurance of God's approval, which can also be withheld. Also God's blessing upon the righteous in verse 12, a guarantee of divine approval, could be anticipating this act. The connection between the lament and the oracle can be seen even more clearly from the expression of certainty that the prayer will be heard. Here an explicit acceptance of the prayer is quite clearly referred to (vi. 9; in other songs of lament it is even expressly stated that 'thou hast answered me' (xxii. 21)). A mere revolution in feeling on the part of the worshipper is not enough to explain such unexpected statements at the end of these songs of lamentation.

The oracle has its own special structure. It is not clear whether the introduction in Jeremiah, 'Thus saith the Lord', is part of the oracle itself. It is not present in other lamentations in Jeremiah, but often occurs in his

---

[1] The song of lament was a form which was at first probably only used by the king. But later it was 'democratised', i.e. it came to be used by everyone. Sometimes it is difficult to determine whether it is the king praying in a psalm, or a private individual using expressions associated with royalty. For instance, entry into the temple, v. 5, 7 (and the hope of an oracle v. 3, 1) is a royal prerogative. Many historians therefore consider all individual songs of lament to have been sung by the king. See M. Bič, *Studies in the History of Religions* IV, 1959, 316–32.

sayings about the future (ii. 2, 5, iv. 3, 27, etc.). It seems therefore that it belongs rather to general prophetic speech than to the oracle itself. Also the phrase at the end, 'Thus saith the Lord', is more in the style of a prophecy than an oracle. But the *assurance of help* (Q) is an essential part of the oracle. Here the worshipper is promised an end to his distress, which clearly refers to the preceding song of lamentation. When Jeremiah complains that he has been persecuted and humiliated by his enemies, God's answer is that 'I will make thee unto this people a fenced brazen wall'. The same theme often returns a second time, as in Jeremiah xv. 21: 'I will deliver thee out of the hand of the wicked.' God is always 'I' in such expressions of divine intervention, and there is always a reference to the special circumstances of the person addressed. Closely linked to this is a look into the near future, i.e. at the results of this divine intervention (R): Jeremiah's enemies will continue to oppose him, but in vain. Moreover the oracle contains a justification arising out of the special relationship existing between God and the man praying (S), i.e. a *general assurance of salvation*. Once again we are brought up against the amazing wealth of cultic forms in ancient Israel, and the remarkable talent with which the pious Israelite gave expression to his personal sentiments and hopes within those firmly fixed forms.

Although the sections which make up the individual lament are always divided from one another and constitute separate units of meaning, there is no hint of aesthetic purism. To the psalmists the three important elements, petition, lament and grounds for deliverance, are indivisible. Therefore thoughts of deliverance can crop up in a petition, by a reference to Jahweh's faithfulness to the community, his forbearance, or his anger. Or the petition could contain a reference to the wickedness of the worshipper's enemies, or to his languishing condition, thus anticipating the lament itself (v. 8, vi. 1–4; Jer. xv. 15). Such an interplay of themes is not really surprising, for the song is after all a unit. But what is surprising is that as a rule the sections are clearly definable and are consistently maintained.

B. *Setting in Life*

Gunkel revealed that the individual song of lamentation, as well as the hymn, was of cultic origin. This is particularly evident in Ps. v. The worshipper prostrates himself before Jahweh's holy temple (verse 7), or will do so as soon as his song has been heard. Moreover in the early morning he will 'order' his prayer. The Hebrew word ערך is a technical cultic term referring to the stacking of logs and pieces of meat on the altar as a burnt offering (Lev. i. 7 f., 12; vi. 6). The individual lament is therefore associated with a burnt offering, and this is substantiated by references in other psalms. Ps. vi (and also Jer. xv) gives no further hint of its setting in life, but this is quite understandable in so short a song, and proves nothing either one way or the other. Nevertheless its heading, 'For the Chief Musician; on stringed instruments', which was added later, presumably links up the song with the Jerusalem temple, and the oracle which the song reveals as following it makes it likely that this was indeed its original setting. This setting in life differs from that of the hymn in that the individual lament was not part of the public services of the temple, but was rather a private act of a casual nature. Driven by need, the worshipper can choose any day to go to the temple, taking a sacrifice with him. There he can ask a priest to perform an act of lament in his name.

The immediate motive behind the lament could be illness, which the worshipper fears will kill him (Ps. vi). This illness could be considered by the worshipper to have some fundamental cause, such as a sin that he has committed,[2] and which has excited Jahweh's anger; he therefore asks for mercy. Or the motive could lie in the intrigues of his enemies. These are mentioned conspicuously often (Ps. v; Jer. xv), and there is little that exegesis of the psalms has brought to light about them. Some think they refer to post-exilic differences between a pious but poor group of people and a more influential group superior to them and which is indifferent to religion. Others consider the enemies to be national ones, external enemies of Israel and therefore of the individual Israelite. Mowinckel takes this theory further (as for example in Ps. vi[3]) and assumes them to be sorcerers who practise witchcraft and bring about evils such as illness. Finally Hans Schmidt (HAT) maintains that they are part of legal procedure, in which the enemies appear as the opposing party (as in Ps. v, where the enemy has offended the worshipper with their mouth, verse 9).

Although Gunkel proved that the origin of these psalms was cultic, he put forward the view that many of them had long lost their association with the cult. He does not agree with Mowinckel's interpretation that all individual laments are cultic. Ps. vi mentions the poet's bed and his couch, so Gunkel concludes it must have been composed in his own house: 'Mowinckel has doubted whether it was as customary as it appears to compose poems so frequently on a bed of pain. But who does not know that in a night of torment and fear of death it is natural to look for eternal consolation, and that these circumstances provoke a man to produce verse if his talent lies that way?' [4] But this argument appears to be more in keeping with the Christian way of life of the nineteenth century. What everyone 'knows' today could be essentially different to what was known in Palestinian antiquity. Is it possible to imagine that in the cramped Israelite huts, where man and beast slept in one room, and moreover where a man who was ill was regarded with suspicion, and even condemned, by his family, and where the narrow alleyways made it possible for the neighbours to hear every word, that a man would give voice to song in the middle of the night? It seems more probable that of his sleepless nights at home the worshipper in Ps. vi would have talked in the temple. Or it is even possible to conclude that he was so confined to his bed that friends carried him into the sanctuary! On the other hand it is questionable whether any Israelite layman could get up and sing a song in such a place as the shrine of Jerusalem. Post-exilic headings assign many individual laments to a choir of singers. It is possible therefore that the laments were sung by an authorised singer on behalf of the worshipper.

[2] At the basis of this is the conviction that action is able to influence fate, and of the indissoluble link between sin and disaster.
[3] Mowinckel, PIW II, 6.
[4] GuB 182.

However Gunkel is right in saying that in the individual lament its cultic source is less plain than in the hymn. Sacred places and sacrifice are relatively rarely mentioned. Some songs of lament even convey the impression that they were not sung on Zion or at the temple at all, such as Ps. xlii–xliii, where the psalmist thinks back longingly on a previous pilgrimage to the temple: 'From the land of Jordan and the Hermons ... do I remember thee' (xlii. 6). He hopes that one day he will be able to return to the 'holy hill'.[5] And in Ps. lxi the singer cries out 'from the end of the earth' (verse 2).[6] Thus some songs of lament could have been sung at quite a distance from the cult or sacrifice; but it seems they will not have been sung by the ordinary citizen, but here also by a professional singer, for although in narrative passages of the Old Testament there is an occasional prayer of lament which is said in a profane place, these are always *in prose*, even when uttered by a king (II Sam. xxiv. 10, 17; II Kings xx. 2 f.) or a prophet (I Kings xix. 4). The David narrative of II Sam. vii. 18 ff. shows moreover that whenever possible one went to 'sit before the Lord' to pray, i.e. to a sanctuary. The only *poetic* exceptions would be the laments in Jeremiah, but even they could belong to the temple. Even the prayers of the sailors in Jonah i. 14, or the prayer in Neh. i. 5–11 are composed in prose (cf. Tob. iii; Judith ix, xiii. 4 f.). Only at a later period do we meet with poetic songs of lamentation in the style of the psalms performed outside a sacred place (Prayer of Manasses; Job ix. 27–x. 22, xiii. 23–xiv. 22; Ecclus. xxii. 27–xxiii. 6); but here the literary type has undergone a considerable change, and it is questionable whether these songs still come under the category of the individual song of lamentation.

C. *History of the Literary Type*

After a study of the psalms of lamentation, it is a surprise to find that personal petitions and laments occur frequently in the earlier narratives of the Old Testament, although they are always quite separate from each other. The simplest form of the lament is found in the mouth of Rebekah (Gen. xxv. 22): 'If it be so, wherefore do I live?' And the narrator continues significantly, 'And she went to inquire of the Lord'. Lament and oracle therefore belong together. It is the same with Moses in Exod. v. 22 f.; Joshua vii. 7 f.; and with Samson in Judges xv. 18. These laments cannot really be called prayers. But with the petition it is different.

When Samson summons the last of his strength to pull down the pillars of the hall of the Philistines, he cries, 'O Lord God, remember me, I pray thee, / and strengthen me, I pray thee, only this once'. Abraham's servant prayed at length (Gen. xxiv. 12), so did Jacob (Gen. xxxii. 10 ff), and also David (II Sam. xv. 31). These petitions all have an *invocation to God* at

---

[5] Moreover a man who was severely ill would not have been allowed in the temple, cf. II Sam. v. 8.

[6] The argument that some individual laments appear to reject 'the cult' is shallow (Ps. xlii, li, lxix), and must be rejected once and for all. Even in those places where the sacrifices are reduced in prominence in favour of the song itself it is only a matter of a shift within the cult. The *cultic* song achieves a greater significance when set up in comparison with the sacrifice, cf. Mowinckel PIW II, 21 ff.

the beginning, in the same style as in the later individual lament. Also the gradual rise from the general 'remember me' to the particular 'strengthen me only this once' is already present. The petition is also different from the lament in that it already attempts a parallelism of expression. However, it does not seem to expect an answer in the form of an oracle. The fact that in the early Old Testament writings the lament and the petition are consistently separate from each other refutes Begrich's strange theory (which he expressed in reference to Heiler's phenomenological thesis) that 'wherever a man raises his hands in prayer, his prayer is made up of the same components and he employs them in the same order'.[7]

It is therefore a matter of interest that in the Psalter the link between the lament and petition is assumed as a matter of course. The problem becomes more involved, but easier to understand, when we find the same pattern in Babylonian psalms as we do in the Israelite individual lament.[8] The psalms of Mesopotamia comprise a variety of literary types, and we have two examples of the prayers of individuals: a late Sumerian song for reassurance, and an Akkadian prayer of entreaty from the middle of the second millennium. The latter is described in Falkenstein/von Soden: 'The hymnic invocation to God is followed by praises of him, which as a rule are followed by a lament for the worshipper's distress; and then after a transitional formula there is always a petition and finally a thanksgiving and blessing formula.'[9]

A prayer of entreaty to Nergal runs as follows[10]:

A   Most mighty, ever noble lord / first-born of Nunamnir,
     First and foremost of Anunnaku / Lord of the fight,
     Child of Kutushar / the great queen,
     Nergal, most powerful of all the gods / darling of Ninmenna!
     You are glorious, the heavens in all their pureness / are your dwelling-place;
     In the underworld (also) / you have no rival.
     Next to Ea in the gathering of the gods / your counsel is eminent;
     With Sin you survey the heavens / the universe.
     Your father Ellil gave you the black-headed people / everything living,
     Shakkan's beasts, on foot or on wing / he delivered up to you.
C   I, Assurbanipal (or NN, son of NN) / thy servant:
     Lack of favour by god and goddess / has been my lot,
     So that loss(es) and ruin / have visited my house.
     I call and you do not answer / I am made sleepless.
D   Because you, my lord, are full of pity / I have sought your divinity;
     Because you are full of forgiveness / I turn to you;
     Because you used to regard me (with friendliness) / I look into your countenance;
     Because you are compassionate / I place myself before you.

---

[7] GuB 261.

[8] Richly informative, though classified more under motifs than on form-critical lines, G. Widengren, *The Accadian and Hebrew Psalms of Lamentation as Religious Documents*, Diss. Uppsala, 1936.

[9] p. 47.

[10] Falkenstein/von Soden, pp. 313 f.; AOT, pp. 262 f.

B   Look at me trustfully / hear my call,
    Your wrathful heart / approach me in peace.
    Absolve my sins / my mistakes and my crime;
    The deep disinclination your divinity feels toward me / must be
                                        assuaged forthwith!
    God and Goddess, who have been provoked, turning impatiently from
                        me in displeasure / renew your friendliness to me:
F   (Then) I will glorify your great doings / (and) pay you homage.[11]

It is easy to see the differences and similarities between this and the Old
Testament literary type. Here also the singer begins with an invocation,
but this time it is a lengthy one. The reader has the impression that the
prayer's reception depends upon the extent to which the gods are flattered
at the beginning.[12] Therefore compliments are heaped upon them, with a
further description of their glory: 'You are glorious, the heavens in all
their pureness ... '. Then the lament follows, corresponding with section C
of the Old Testament examples. The worshipper begins by introducing
himself by name, and the whole passage is usually shorter and remains
closer to the established pattern than in Israel. Then this is followed by an
expression of trust as the grounds for deliverance (D). The petition comes
only at the end, progressing from the general request, 'Hear my call', to the
particular, 'Absolve my sins'. The conclusion consists of a vow by the
worshipper to praise his god. Though this is missing in the Old Testament
individual laments which have been used above as examples, it can be
found at other points in the Old Testaments (Ps. xxvii. 6, liv. 6, lvi. 12). It
is also sometimes missing in Babylonian compositions.

What does this tell us of the history of the literary type? We can see that
the Old Testament psalm bears a closer affinity to the Babylonian prayer of
entreaty than to the early Old Testament prose versions of the separate
lament or petition. The development of the Old Testament individual
lament will therefore have been influenced by the Babylonian examples,
which preceded it by some centuries. This would not have come about by
any conscious effort on the part of Israelite poets to emulate the Babylonian, but probably through the medium of pre-Israelite Canaan, of whose
psalms we know nothing. However, the Israelites would not have been so
receptive if their own prose laments and petitions had not provided a
basis for the skilled composition of the later individual song of lament.
When the cult of Jahweh was adopted many changes took place. The
merely eulogistic description of the gods' glory was dropped, and with it
the mythological aspects of the hymn. The invocation to song came as a
rule to consist only of the Lord's name and a reference to the relationship
between him and the one praying: 'my King and my God' (Ps. v. 2). 'The
Israelite song of lament is able to conquer the profound distance between
God and man in a way in which the Babylonian song of entreaty had not
wholly managed' (Begrich[12A]).

[11] Translated from the German. The Babylonian Text: L. W. King, Babylonian
Magic and Sorcery, Nr. 27, 1–24.
[12] But cf. Widengren 42 f.
[12A] ZAW 1928, pp. 251 and 238–43.

When did the Israelite song of lamentation, influenced by Canaanite examples, achieve its present form? Presumably in Jerusalem, when the temple of Solomon was built, for many of the individual laments are particularly associated with Zion (v. 7; cf. the Jerusalem cultic term, 'Lord, God of hosts', in Jer. xv. 16). Also the later title, 'Psalm of David', which heads many of these psalms, could perhaps mean 'of the Davidic state sanctuary', and were therefore used in the cult on Zion. In any case there is no trace of a song of lament before Solomon's time. This type of literature therefore arose at the same time as that of the hymn, i.e. at the beginning of the monarchical period. This shows the tremendous influence of the new cultic centre on the transformation and expansion of the Jahweh religion and the faith of the Israelites. The poetic talent it produced is far in advance of that which is evident in the Babylonian prototypes.

How long was the literary type in current use? Gunkel/Begrich have demonstrated that it had died out by the time of the psalms of Solomon in the first century before Christ. Westermann has shown in even greater detail that post-exilic prayers are far removed from the psalm form.[13] It appears therefore that the literary type died out quite early on in the post-exilic period, and earlier than the hymn, for the Chroniclers' writings, despite their love of song, do not contain a single individual lament.

But this only means that no further individual laments were composed. It does not mean that those already in existence disappeared or became forgotten. Many were preserved, but were carried over into another setting in life. They were taken up into books of psalms, and were used as psalms in synagogue services. With this we come to the redaction history.

D. *Transmission and Redaction History*

The individual laments which have been quoted above give no clue to the changes they underwent during the period they were in current use. And up till now no evidence has been found in other individual laments for a history of their transmission.

There is a little more evidence for a redaction history. Ps. v and vi belong to the first collection of the Davidic psalms, comprising Ps. iii–xli. This psalter begins with a series of individual laments (Ps. iii–vii), as does the second Davidic psalter (Ps. li ff.). This position could well have had some significance for the compiler.[14] Jer. xv. 15–21 is juxtaposed to another individual lament (verses 10 f.), and is moreover bound up with national laments uttered by Jeremiah, for which he received an answer from God (xiv. 1–xv. 4 and also ix). Hence the context shows Jeremiah pledging himself to his people. This is then followed by his lament over their thanklessness, which is brought out all the more sharply by the knowledge

---

[13] Even the two examples Add. Dan. i (Song of the Three Holy Children) and Add. Esther xiv. 3–19, which Westermann brings within the literary type of the psalm, have already been much changed. Moreover in both cases it is more a matter of the related literary type of the national lament; only in the second case is an individual protestation of innocence appended.

[14] Bič (see above, p. 175 n. 1) considers Pss. iii–xli to be a coherent accession liturgy. Although his justifications for this thesis are unconvincing, they do raise the question of whether iii–xli were later interpreted as a messianic psalter.

of what he has just done for them. Not much more can be said about
the redaction history of the passage until the structure of the book of
Jeremiah has been analysed in greater detail. Is it possible that this individual lament was once closely connected to others in the same book (xi. 18–
23, xii. 1–6, xvii. 12–18, xviii. 8–23, xx. 7–18)? At any rate these poems
will not have been included when Jeremiah's words were first written
down in the original 'roll', which according to xxxvi. 2, 32 contained words
against Judah, Jerusalem and all the nations; for a song of lamentation
would hardly fit in with such prophecies of disaster.[15]

[15] The two laments of Jeremiah in xv. 10 and xv. 15–18 with God's answer,
addressed presumably to the people, have relevance in this context (also xiv. 1 ff.).
For the redaction history see E. Gerstennberger : Jeremiah's Complaints, JBL 82,
1963, 393–408 (an extremely shrewd analysis).

Section Three: From the Prophetic Writings

The form-critical definition of prophetic narratives was begun by O. Plöger: Die Prophetengeschichten der Samuel- und Königsbücher, Diss. Greifswald 1937. The study of prophetic sayings began with Gunkel, chiefly in the chapter: Die Propheten als Schriftsteller und Dichter, in GrPro, pp. XXXIV–LXX. J. Lindblom: Die literarische Gattung der prophetischen Literatur, UUÅ 1924, Teologi 1, made a more comprehensive comparison with non-Israelite revelation literature. C. Westermann: Grundformen prophetischer Rede, BEvTh 31, ¹1960, ²1964 made a thorough study of the prophecy of disaster, E.T. *Basic Forms of Prophetic Speech*, 1967 (Philadelphia, Westminster Press). Important individual analyses by L. Koehler: Deutero-jesaja stilkritisch untersucht BZAW 37, 1923; H. W. Wolff: Die Begründungen der prophetischen Heils- und Unheilssprüche, ZAW 52, 1934, 1 ff.; R. B. Y. Scott: The Literary Structure of Isaiah's Oracles, in *Studies in Old Testament Prophecy*, Festschrift for T. H. Robinson, 1950, 175–86; R. Rendtorff: Botenformel und Botenspruch, ZAW 74, 1962, 165–177.

15. AHAZIAH'S FALL (II Kings i)

[1 And Moab rebelled against Israel after the death of Ahab.]
2 And Ahaziah fell down through the lattice in his upper chamber
that was in Samaria, and was sick:
and he sent messengers, and said unto them,
Go, inquire of Baalzebub the god of Ekron whether I shall recover
of this sickness.

3 But (the angel of) the Lord said to Elijah the Tishbite,

PO   Arise, go up to meet the messengers of the king of Samaria, and say
unto them,
I   Is it because there is no God in Israel, that ye go to inquire of
Baalzebub the god of Ekron?
KA 4 *Now therefore* (לָכֵן) *thus saith the Lord,*
I   Thou shalt not come down from the bed whither thou art gone up,
III   *but* (כִּי) shall surely die.

And Elijah departed.
5 And the messengers returned unto him, and he said unto them,
Why is it that ye are returned?
6 And they said unto him,
There came up a man to meet us, and said unto us,
Go, turn again unto the king that sent you, and say unto him,
KA   *Thus saith the Lord,*
I   Is it because there is no God in Israel, that thou sendest to inquire
of Baalzebub the god of Ekron?
II   *therefore*
thou shalt not come down from the bed whither thou art gone up,
III   *but* shall surely die.
7 And he said unto them,
What manner of man was he which came up to meet you, and
told you these words?

8 And they answered him,
> He was an hairy man, and girt with a girdle of leather about his
>> loins.

And he said,
> It is Elijah the Tishbite.

9 Then the king sent unto him a captain of fifty with his fifty.
And he went up to him: and behold, he sat on the top of the hill.
And he spake unto him,

KA   O man of God, the king hath said, Come down.

10 And Elijah answered and said to the captain of fifty,
> If I be a man of God, let fire come down from heaven, and con-
>> sume thee and thy fifty.

And there came down fire from heaven, and consumed him and
> his fifty.

11 And again he sent unto him another captain of fifty with his fifty.
And he answered and said unto him,
> O man of God, thus hath the king said, Come down quickly.

12 And Elijah answered and saith unto them,
> If I be a man of God, let fire come down from heaven, and
>> consume thee and thy fifty,

And the fire of God came down from heaven, and consumed him
> and his fifty.

13 And again he sent the captain of a third fifty with his fifty.
And the third captain of the fifty went up, and came and fell on his
knees before Elijah, and besought him, and said unto him,
> O man of God, I pray thee, let my life, and the life of these fifty
>> thy servants, be precious in thy sight.

14 Behold, there came down fire from heaven, and consumed the two
former captains of fifty with their fifties: but now let my life be
> precious in thy sight.

15 And (the angel of) the Lord said unto Elijah,
> Go down with him: be not afraid of him.

And he arose, and went down with him unto the king.

16 And he said unto him,

KA   *Thus saith the Lord,*

I   *Forasmuch as* (יַעַן אֲשֶׁר) thou hast sent messengers to inquire of
Baalzebub the god of Ekron, is it because there is no God in Israel
> to inquire of his word?

II   *therefore*
thou shalt not come down from the bed whither thou art gone up,

III   *but* shall surely die.

17 So he died *according to the word of the Lord* which Elijah had spoken.
[And Jehoram began to reign in his stead.]

A. *Legends of the Prophets*

Apart from the introductory and final sentences we have here an isolated
unit intelligible in itself. This very lively piece proves to be rather a series
of dramatic dialogues than a running narrative. More than half the text is
dialogue. Compared with the earlier saga, it is obvious that this story about
one of the prophets was composed during the second stage of the early

Israelite art of narrative, in the *elaborated style*,[1] and in fact shows quite a development in this style. The human and divine utterances are even more obviously the decisive element in the story than they were in the saga. External happenings are merely contributory. The elaborated style is also indicated by the subtly rising crescendo brought about by the repetition of one theme: first of all Elijah informs the king's messengers of Jahweh's word, then they in their turn inform the king, and then Elijah informs the king himself. But the writer consciously varies the theme. The crucial sentence: 'Is it because there is no God in Israel ... to inquire of Baalzebub the god of Ekron? Thou shalt not come down from the bed whither thou art gone up, but shalt surely die', does in fact occur each time, as does the statement, 'Thus saith the Lord'. But the position of the sentences is changed slightly, and the statement of the facts is fitted to the particular situation. First of all it is 'that ye go', then 'that thou sendest', and lastly 'forasmuch as thou hast sent'. The soldiers' departure to Elijah is also reported several times, but each time the captain's interchange with him varies. The first said, 'The king hath said', limiting his command to the one imperative. The second emphasises the imperative by saying, '*Thus* hath the king said'. The last speaks with complete courtesy, even submission. Elijah's response is annihilating, and becomes increasingly brief. He starts by including a 'now'. This is lacking in the second speech, and on the third occasion he does not even speak. After Elijah's speech there is first talk of a fire, then of a fire of God from heaven. The narrator has therefore gone to particular trouble to vary the repetitions for the sake of his climax, though not forgetting what must remain for the effect of the whole.

As in the earlier saga, the introduction to the story is brief. It consists of only one sentence, as in the story of the ancestress of Israel. The story also ends with one sentence, immediately after the climax has been reached in a poetic speech. Yet the middle part of the story is very different from that of the older literary types. Here the world is neither seen in terms of the family, nor is there any question of glorifying one's forebears, or of cool combat, as in the heroic saga. Neither does it primarily concern constitutional or national changes, as in historical writing (this only in the introductory and concluding sentences which were added later). What is the point of the tale? Does it concern the king? If so, the lengthy treatment given to Elijah's encounters with the three captains would be superfluous. Is Elijah the main interest? He does indeed play an important part, but not as an individual: we know less about what he himself feels than we did about Abraham in the earlier saga. In fact, the story is hinged on the prophetic and divine utterance. The narrator is obviously attempting to bring out the exact correspondence between what is ordained and what follows. Thus in the second scene the angel begins by saying, 'Arise, go up and meet the messengers of the king', which is promptly followed by, 'And Elijah departed'. And when Elijah is cursorily commanded by the first two captains to come down, he answers, 'Let fire come down from heaven and consume thee and thy fifty'. Both times this is immediately followed by a bald statement that fire did come down from heaven and consumed them.

[1] See above, pp. 126, 139.

At the end of the scene the angel commands, 'Go down', and immediately
it is reported that Elijah went down. But the clearest indication of the
relation between word and deed comes at the end, when it is said, 'And he
died according to the word of the Lord, which Elijah had spoken'. That
this is all intentional is made clear by the beginning where the king's
command is *not* stated to have been followed by its performance, although
the messengers obviously obeyed. Also after the third captain's petition to
Elijah the narrator avoids showing Elijah as one who attends to human
utterance and complies with it. True, he does comply, but only after the
angel had given direct authority from God. Therefore the basic element
underlying the story is the conviction that the prophetic utterance, whether
expressly of divine origin, or spoken out of human initiative, is effective;
that it becomes reality shortly after it is uttered.

The same correspondence between speech and happening prevails in
other narratives about Elijah, and also Elisha.[2] It is not merely a characteristic of the individual story, but an element in the structure of the literary type as a whole. The literary type is that of *legends of the prophets*, in
which the prophet is bearer of God's authoritative word, or, in other places,
is a man marked out by God to be the intercessor between God and his
people. The Hebrew term has unfortunately been lost.[3]

What is the setting in life? Just as the medieval legend was evolved in the
seclusion of the monastery or by the knighthood, and was imbued with the
ideals characteristic of these walks of life, so the legends of the prophets
will have been created by the disciples of the prophets. This is particularly
evident in the Elisha stories,[4] where the ethical standards of a particular
social group are very marked. The Old Testament type disappeared, with
its setting in life, in the post-exilic period.

B. *The Literary Type*

As no study has yet been made of the changes undergone by the legend of the
prophets, we must content ourselves here with a few observations to give us
some basis for a transmission history. About 1000 B.C., i.e., at the beginning
of the monarchical period, men calling themselves prophets (Nabi) are first
heard of, either in ecstatic groups (e.g. I Sam. x), or as individuals (Nathan
at the court of David). It is not clear what relationship they have to the more
ancient seers in the books of Samuel, or to the mysterious men of God of the
preconstitutional period (Judges vi, xiii). Here it need only be said that the
first legends can be traced back to shortly after the prophets first step into the
historical limelight, such as in the basis of the stories about Ahijah the Shilonite

---

[2] I Kings xvii. 3+5, 9+10, 13 f.+15 f.; xviii. 1+2, 8+16; xix. 15+19, 20+21;
II Kings ii. 21 f., iv. 42–44.
[3] Gunkel classifies these Elijah narratives still under sagas, and considered legends
to have arisen only in the post-exilic period. This meant that it was difficult for him
to make any clear distinction between the different literary types of the saga. In
Elias, Jahve und Baal 1906 he completely dispensed with any closer definition (as
did Gressmann SAT II 1, ²1921) and talked simply of sagas, though he did distinguish legendary additions (II Kings i. 5 ff.). In 1931 he classified the narratives
about Elijah under historical sagas (RGG² V, 53 f.) which he saw as great models
of the prophetic tradition. The correct classification under *legends* is to be found in
G. Fohrer = Elia, AThANT 31, 1957, ²1968.
[4] von Rad, *Theology* II, pp. 25 f.

(I Kings xi. 29 ff., xiv. 1 ff.), or in the penetrating story about the man of God in Bethel (I Kings xiii). The person of Samuel was also made the subject of legends (I Sam. xv, xix. 18 ff.). Even the figures of Moses and Abraham were taken into legends; indeed, the Elohistic version of the saga about Israel's ancestress [5] has much in it that is strongly characteristic of this literary type. The story reveals just as much about imparting God's word to a non-Israelite king and the power of the prophet as intercessor as it does about this one event out of the life of the patriarch. God's word and his acts always play a decisive part in these legends. They point to the irresistible power of the prophetic calling through the 'spiritual fervour' (רוּחַ). They are always reports about the prophets by the disciples of the prophets, i.e. independent reports, and not reports by the prophets themselves. Legends seem to have been particularly common in the prophetic circles around Elisha, and II Kings tells us much about these circles. These people will presumably have also been familiar with stories about Elijah, Samuel and Moses. Then with the fall of Jerusalem in 587 the literary type disappeared (see below).

C. *Transmission History*

Even before form-critical exegesis it was recognised that II Kings 1 had originally been made out of two independent stories: the Ahaziah-Elijah episode (verses 2–8, 16 f.), and the meeting between Elijah and the 'captains of the king' (verses 9–15). The first story is complete in itself and does not need the second. It depicts a different Elijah, one who suddenly appears and just as suddenly disappears once his message has been delivered. In the second story he is enthroned imposingly upon the top of a hill and the captains have to seek him out.

The Ahaziah-Elijah legend is exciting. 'Despite its brevity and simplicity it is of unrivalled beauty . . . for in no other place is the mysterious element in Elijah's nature expressed with such modesty. This effect is created by the prophet always remaining in the background of the story' (Gressmann).[6] The main theme is clear: an Israelite can only ask Jahweh and his prophets for an oracle. He must not turn to foreign gods. If he does so a prophet will oppose him, even though he be a king, as Elijah did Ahaziah. In this text disaster is announced twice to the king: at the beginning through the agency of the messengers, and at the end by the prophet himself. As the prophet says nothing at the end which the king has not already heard, this scene will have been a later addition added to intensify the climax when the first legend was linked up to the second. The angel of the Lord (verses 3, 15) must also be a later addition, for in all other places Jahweh speaks to the older prophets direct. Only in post-exilic times did an angel appear as intermediary between God and his prophets (e.g. in the night visions of Zechariah).

The second legend, where Elijah deals with the captains, is a relatively late composition, for here the king is nameless, and Elijah is addressed as 'man of God'. Both these facts correspond with a later style; and the address 'man of God' occurs again only in the later narrative of I Kings xvii. 17–24. Otherwise he is always referred to as Nabi (prophet), which is not the case

---

[5] See above, pp. 123, 128–30.
[6] In the first edition of SAT II 1, 1910, p. 281.

with Elisha. Also the conspicuous manner in which the miracle occurs is
more characteristic of the Elisha than of the Elijah legends (cf. II Kings
vi. 8–23). This legend is therefore of later origin, added to show the correct
way to encounter a prophet, and also how a prophet wields his authority.
It may have been instigated by the word play on man of God אִישׁ הָאֱלֹהִים
and fire of God אֵשׁ אֱלֹהִים. It is conceivable that it was never an independent legend, but merely an off-shoot of the older legend of verses
2–8.[7a]

Is there anything historical about the two legends? This is not a question
which is normally applicable to the literary type of the legend as a whole;
but now that we have an outline of the transmission history some facts
emerge which are of interest to the historian. What we have said above
proves the second legend to have no historical foundation. There is nothing
in it about the life history of Elijah. But the story is not completely
unhistorical, as might at first be supposed. It has its own historical framework, which provides us with important information, not about the period
it refers to—the time of Elijah—but about the period of its origin, supposedly that of Elisha, or afterwards. It gives us no specific information
about the central figure of the story, but about those who transmitted the
story. It brings out quite clearly, and in terms which are historically correct,
the feeling of superiority which a man of God and his prophetic circle felt
when faced with representatives of the military authority. The calling of
even one prophet cannot be invalidated by three times fifty soldiers.
Moreover the legend tells us much about the speech forms of that time.
These will be discussed below.

The earlier legend is of greater historical interest. It provides us with
social-historical evidence about the prophetic guilds which transmitted
such stories. These people will most certainly have worn a dress befitting
their profession like Elijah's in this narrative: a fur coat and a leather belt.
And like him they would have opposed the royal house of the Omrides
in the ninth century when it flirted with the foreign cult of Baal. Thus
the same theme of a hostile meeting between the prophet and the reigning
king of Israel crops up many times in other legends of the same period
(I Kings xvii. 1 ff., xviii. 1 ff., xxi; II Kings ix). But here it is possible to
perceive a far stronger influence of the historical Elijah. Only Elijah himself could have emerged so suddenly, would have had the power of
suggestion to impress the king's messengers as he did. These events must
have actually happened, though it is not possible to glean anything further
from the individual aspects of the passage. The prophecy of disaster is
announced three times, each time in a slightly different form. What was
the oldest form? With this question we have reached the point of con-
jecturing what part of the story is historical; and this is a question to which
there is no longer an answer.

[7a] Plöger differentiated between the literary type of the two, the first as a narrative
of the prophetic word, and the second as a narrative of prophetic action. In fact
there is a difference; but even in Elijah's meeting with the captains it is the *word*
which brings about the miracle (the fire of God).

D. *Official Speech between Those of Different Standing, and the Messenger Formula*

II Kings 1 is not only an excellent example of the complex literary type of the legend, but it also contains many component literary types. Before we consider the most important, the prophecy of disaster to the individual, it would be useful to take a brief look at the way the characters in the narrative speak to each other. Of course it is obvious that the Hebrew narrator will have rendered the speeches in a much shortened form, but nevertheless he can be assumed to have retained the essential characteristics of the speech forms. In fact, these will have been brought out even more sharply by having been condensed. Unfortunately the literary types of the official forms of speech in the Old Testament have not yet been analysed, so that the following can only be a preliminary investigation.

At the beginning the king commands his servants, 'Go, inquire of Baalzebub the god of Ekron whether I shall recover of this sickness'. Presumably the king will have instructed his messengers in far greater detail, telling them, for instance, what to take as a gift for the priest or the cultic prophet at the temple of Ekron. But the beginning, with 'Go', and a second instructing imperative, together with the indication of the place and the people to go to, are characteristics of many *speeches by a man of high station to a servant* whom he is entrusting with a duty. This is obviously the form in which a messenger is commissioned (cf. Gen. xlv. 9; II Kings xviii. 19), and is merely one of many forms of commissioning those of lower rank.[7] When the king despatches the captains, the narrator will have imagined the king to have said each time, 'Go, fetch Elijah . . .'. The commanding tone with which such a message was authorised obviously befits the high station of the speaker. When a messenger returns, he is received in a similar fashion with the curt question, 'Why is it that ye are returned?' 'What manner of man was he?' When Elijah appears unannounced the king receives him in a similar fashion with a question in reproach (I Kings xviii. 17, xxi. 20); and Elisha the man of God addresses the prophets under him in much the same manner (II Kings ii. 18).

An example of *how a man of lower station addresses his superior* when compelled to do so is given in verses 13 f., where a layman addresses the prophet. He does not begin with a command, but with a title, 'Man of God'. He then adds a petition, not in the imperative, but in the jussive, with another moderating particle. Then he makes a reference to the situation, introducing it by 'Behold' הִנֵּה, expressing it carefully in an involved series of sentences, reminiscent of parallelismus membrorum. Only then does he get to the heart of the matter: 'But now . . .' וְעַתָּה; but he does not dare to mention it directly, and falls back unwittingly on another plea for his own person (cf. II Kings ii. 16, vi. 1).

When a messenger comes to deliver his message he begins with, 'Thus saith' (*kôh 'āmar*), followed by the sender's name, as did the two captains in

---

[7] Beginning with two imperatives: v. 11; I Kings xvii. 13; II Kings iv. 3, ix. 17, cf. I Kings xviii. 5, 40.

verses 9 and 11.[8] This *messenger formula* (ko-amar-formula = KA) legitimises the speaker and compels the hearer to accept the words he utters as coming from the sender of the message. It could be said to have its parallel in the official stamp on a letter today. If the man addressed is of lower station than the sender, the message will usually consist of imperatives: 'Come down', bid the captains (verse 9, cf. verse 11; I Kings ii. 30; cf. II Kings xviii. 28 ff.). In other places, however, it consists of a question in reproach or scorn (as at the beginning of Judges xi. 12; II Kings xviii. 19). When an underling is directly before the king, he is addressed in just the same way. It is thus clear that the king's daily intercourse with his subjects is extended beyond his immediate surroundings by the use of messenger formulas. The sender of the message is brought as near to the recipient of it, and speaks to him in just the same tone, as if the two were face to face.[9]

There is a more extensive form of the messenger formula not covered by this chapter, which operates with more than the *legitimising formula*, 'Thus saith NN', imperatives and questions. As it is important for an understanding of the type of prophetic speech which we shall shortly be discussing, we shall quote an example used by Westermann. Num. xxii. 5 f. contains a message from the Moabite king Balak to the seer Balaam (It is a message to a man of equal standing, not to one bound in obedience):

	5	And he sent messengers unto Balaam . . . saying,
I		Behold, there is a people come out of Egypt: / behold, they cover the face of the earth, / and they abide over against me:
II	6	come now therefore, I pray thee, / curse me these people;
III		for they are too mighty for me:
(II)		peradventure I shall prevail, that we smay smite them, / and that I may drive them out of the land:
III		for I know that he whom thou blessedst is blessed, / and he who thou cursest is cursed.

This is a highly formal message, which even calls for *parallelismus membrorum*. Here also there are two imperatives. They are to be understood to authorise the message, and they constitute the core of the matter. But before this there is a long *section indicating the present situation*, a situation which urgently needs to be remedied.[10] Finally, after the actual message has been delivered, there is a third section which Westerman calls the motive clause, but which could be more accurately described as the *concluding characterisation*. Usually the recipient of the message is characterised, his abilities extolled or disparaged. (Cf. II Kings xviii. 29, 32). Or it can characterise an opponent: 'They are too mighty for me.'

---

[8] I Kings xx. 2 f., 5; II Kings ii. 30, xix. 3. In II Kings i the usual כֹּה־אָמַר הַמֶּלֶךְ is not used the first time, but דִּבֶּר in its place; this will have been intended to provide variation within the narrative.

[9] The English translation 'thus saith' is in the present, although the Hebrew is in the perfect ('amar). However the Hebrew perfect does not in this case refer back to a particular point in time when the originator of the message first spoke to the messenger alone. Here the perfect is intended to express the absolute validity of the pronouncement. Thus it can only be used by a man of superior or of equal rank.

[10] Cf. Gen. xlv. 9, xxii. 4 f; I Kings xx. 5; II Kings xiv. 9. The indication of the prevailing situation can also take the form of a mocking or reproachful question as in Judges xi. 12; II Kings xviii. 19, 33 (where the statement is placed after).

E. *Prophecy of Disaster to the Individual*

The core of II Kings 1 is a prophetic saying to the king of Israel, delivered quite deliberately three times, so that it is forcibly impressed upon the hearer. What form does this saying take? Since Koehler (and Lindblom) it has been recognised that this prophecy has an affinity with the form of the message. It is still undecided whether the prophets borrowed more than the legitimising formula, 'Thus saith the Lord (kô 'āmar jahwe)'[11] from the messenger formula, which was then commonly used in diplomatic circles. It is therefore best to start by considering the prophecy of disaster to the individual as an isolated type. What Elijah tells the king is what he was instructed to tell him by (the angel of) the Lord in verse 3: 'Arise, go up to meet the messengers . . . and say to them.' This corresponds exactly with the style of the message, as is evident from the discussion above. There should be no doubt about this. But it should not be too quickly assumed that the prophet's position was that of a special messenger, or that his profession was that of messenger. Anyone can be authorised as messengers of the Lord, as for instance the messengers of the king, to whom Elijah simply passes on the words of the Lord, using these men as intermediaries: 'Go, turn again to the king . . . and say unto him' (verse 6). It is further obvious that being authorised as a messenger is only one of the many duties of a servant, just as it is of a prophet. Exactly the same formula, with the two imperatives, crops up in situations which do not call for a message but merely another duty, as in verse 15: 'Go down with him: be not afraid of him.' This is a speech by the divine power which concerns one man personally, and is not intended to be passed on. Scott rightly terms this a *private oracle*, as distinct from the public oracle; hence the abbreviation PO in the text above.

What the prophet has to transmit is of course important. Gunkel saw that it fell into two parts, an introductory exposition of the situation, which in prophecies of disaster consists of severe rebukes and which Gunkel terms the *diatribe* (I), and a following main section which gives notice of the disaster which will be brought about by Jahweh, which Gunkel terms the *threat* (II). The diatribe reproves the man addressed, stating that his position is no longer tenable in the eyes of God, and that the fault lies only with him. Here the Israelite king has turned in his need to a foreign god, thus sacrificing the exclusiveness of his relationship to God. Each time the words are addressed to the recipient directly. Thus in II Kings 1 it is adapted to fit each scene. For the messengers it runs: 'Is there no God in Israel, *that ye go* to inquire of Baalzebub?' But when the prophet addresses the king, he says: 'Forasmuch *as thou hast sent* messengers to inquire of Baalzebub the god of Ekron, is it because there is no God in Israel to

---

[11] F. Baumgärtel (*Verbannung und Heimkehr*, Festschrift W. Rudolph, 1961, pp. 20–23) is doubtful about the connection between 'Thus saith the Lord' and the messenger formula, because the prophetic formula is very often extended to include certain titles in Jahweh's honour, e.g. 'Thus said the Lord Sabaoth'. But the inclusion of certain titles is found just as much in the mouths of royal messengers, e.g. II Kings xviii. 19, and is therefore by no means unknown in the messenger formula.

inquire of his word?' And when the diatribe reaches the king through the mouth of his messengers the wording is different yet again (verse 6). The prophetic guilds, which transmitted such legends and sayings, would not have understood the prophet's diatribe to be verbally inspired, but merely as the prophet's own words. He could give it his own inflexion. Lately it has been asked whether this section was intended to be understood as included in the prophetic saying. It could well be of purely human origin, a reflection by the prophet which he voluntarily appended to the divine word.[12] This view could be substantiated by the fact that in the early prophets (before Jeremiah), the legitimising formula, 'Thus saith the Lord', was as a rule only placed after the diatribe, as in verses 4, 16 (Amos vii. 17 etc.). Indeed there are cases even in earlier times when the formula was placed right before the saying as a whole, as in verse 6 (because it is not the prophet himself who is speaking, but an intermediary at second hand?); cf. I Kings xiv. 7, xx. 28, 42.

Westermann objected to the term diatribe on the grounds that it only makes sense when it refers to an independent literary type, but not when it refers to one part of a greater whole. Moreover a diatribe can only be pronounced to a person directly; it cannot be done through an intermediary, as here. These arguments do not take us very far. With regard to the second objection, it should be remembered that the message was delivered to a subordinate, and corresponds exactly with the style of an official communication. The messenger speaks just as his master would have done had he been present himself.[13] But Westermann was right in saying that the term diatribe is not always a suitable description of the first part of the prophecy. It would be better to call it 'indication of the situation'.

The second section, generally called the *threat*, consists of one very distinctive sentence, formed out of an unconditional negative (לֹא) and an imperfect. This is a combination in the Hebrew which in divine speeches can take the place of the modern negative imperative. It announces a future happening which is already founded in the present. The king is already lying ill on his bed, and the threat proclaims this to be final: he will lie there till he dies. The threat is linked to the section preceding it, the diatribe, or indication of the situation, by the word 'therefore', for the

[12] Von Rad, *Theology* II, pp. 70 ff. H. W. Wolff, Die Begründungen der prophetischen Heils- und Unheilssprüche ZAW 52, 1934, 1 ff. speaks of a 'passage of prophetic reflection', p. 6. 'From the message he receives the prophet can deduce the nature of his commitment. In this he is aided by his observation of the events and his knowledge of the popular state of mind', p. 17.

[13] Westermann, 148 f. therefore suggests, with Wolff (following an earlier attempt by Gunkel), calling the section formally entitled 'motive clause' the more objective 'accusation'. But without doubt this would be even worse. It is true that the first term is not only too formal, but also makes no recognition of the temporal connection between the first and second sections (present—future); but the second term only encourages the mistaken idea that the prophet is using a legal literary type (even though Westermann does state that the term accusation should be understood in a wider sense than a merely legal one). Westermann is right in seeing the diatribe as 'basically a purified and domesticated cursing or condemnation'. This hardly applies to our present-day languages, but could well have done to the Hebrew and the prophetic sayings—despite Westermann's protest. One need only think of Shimei's diatribe in II Sam. xvi. 7 and its consequences. For a prophetic diatribe see II Kings ii. 24.

disaster which God has prepared for the man concerned is the continuation on a divine level of the action which had precipitated it. Ahaziah
turns to the god Baal who descends into the underworld, returning regularly to the earth. What happens to Ahaziah has thus a particular relevance,
with death as well as with revival. The king sees the connection with the
second; but the prophet probably sees the connection with the dying god
as the approach of death. This part of the prophecy remains word for word
the same on each of the three occasions it is uttered, unlike the diatribe.
Therefore to the prophetic guilds, who tell the story, this reference to the
future is much more verbally inspired than the beginning section. Whereas
today a speech about a future happening is considered to be less certain
than one about the present, here it seems to be the other way round. This
is in accordance with the fact that the early prophets mostly utter the
messenger formula before this second section.

Westermann also criticised the use of the term threat. The word threat
does not imply any realisation of what is threatened. A threat is conditional;
it does not follow unconditionally that the disaster will occur, which is what
the prophet intended to say. 'For instance, when the enemy threatens to use
poison gas in a war, this is not the same as announcing its use.' This argument is compelling.[14] Westermann therefore suggests a better term, the
announcement of disaster. The expression is weaker, it is true, but more
accurate. However, Westermann goes further than this, and frequently talks
of a *judgment*, thus reaching uncertain ground; for it cannot be proved that
the prophets saw the disaster which they prophesied as the ruling of a divine
court of justice, with judgment following a contest with the accused. It is
true that the image of legal proceedings does sometimes occur, and indeed
there are even real prophetic lawsuits (Hos. ii. 4 ff.; Isa. i. 2 f., etc.),
but it is dangerous to classify all prophecies of disaster under this
heading.[15] It is better to call Part II the *prediction of disaster*. Only thus is it
made clear that in it (within the framework of the complete literary type of
the prophecy) future events are not only announced but also hailed, in a
specifically prophetic manner.

The prophecy of disaster given in this chapter has a third section,
introduced usually by 'for', or 'but' (כִּי), ending the prophecy powerfully
with the statement, '(thou) shall surely die'. This is the section termed by
Gunkel the justifying, or motive clause, which he put on a parallel with

[14] Though the further argument, that the prophet is a messenger, but that it is
difficult for a messenger to convey a threat for this must be conveyed directly, is less
convincing. The Israelite would think differently on this point. See above.

[15] Here it is very evident what happens when instead of 'diatribe' the term
'accusation' is used. Reference to 'profane' parallels proves fallacious. Of the three
examples brought forward by Westermann, I Kings xxi. 10 has little in common
with a profane legal proceeding; moreover at this point the narrative is very com-
pressed and mentions only the 'false witness', giving no introduction to the accusation. But the two other passages, Jer. xxvi. 11 and Dan. iii. 12, prove to be of a
quite different form than that claimed by Westermann. They show—as was to be
expected—that an accusation before a court begins by addressing a forum of judges,
and talks about the accused in the third person, and not directly to him. H. Graf
Reventlow, Wächter über Israel, BZAW 82, 1962, p. 65, emphasises even more
strongly that prophecies of disaster as well of salvation 'take the form of a legal
proceeding, in which the divine judge is represented by his agents, the prophets,
who in his name pronounce the divine-judicial verdict'. But such far-reaching
conclusions can scarcely be founded on the three or four passages from Ezekiel
which Reventlow quotes.

14

the 'justifying' diatribe at the beginning. In this case it is uncertain why this section should occur a second time: 'It often also happens that the prophets, in their carelessness about any exact arrangement of their material, go from threat to diatribe and then back to threat again',[16] so that here the switch to and fro would have occurred the other way round. Gunkel's followers have taken up this idea. But has the end exactly the same sense as the beginning? Surely this supposition is based on too crude a translation of the particle כִּי. It need not always be taken as the beginning of a motive clause. And also it is surely significant that here the section *after* the prediction of disaster is introduced by 'for' (כִּי), whereas the diatribe at the beginning, i.e. *before* the prediction, always has a different introductory word (usually יַעַן אֲשֶׁר).[17] In the present instance the sentence, 'Thou shalt surely die' is no motive for the impending disaster, but rather a summing up, also of the present situation: 'You are mortally injured and shall remain so'. To an Israelite the king's extreme illness has already brought him within the sphere of death.[18] Once in this sphere he is condemned for ever, for his idolatry has joined him to it insolubly. The cult of Baal and death are the same in the end. Therefore it is suggested that this concluding section (III) be called the *concluding characterisation*, thus avoiding the weak expression 'motive clause', which is so open to misinterpretation. This conclusion, as in the message passing between two men, can characterise either the recipient of the message or, at other places, the sender: 'The Lord hath spoken it', it is asserted in I Kings xiv. 11, cf. xii. 24; also such a sentence does not provide a *motive* for the disaster which is about to occur, but gives it added power by reference to who has caused it.

Is the prophecy of disaster intended to be in prose? It is perhaps possible to discern the rudiments of a synthetic parallelismus membrorum in the prediction: 'Thou shalt not come down / from the bed / whither thou hast gone up'. But this is merely speculation. It is as easy to support Fohrer's view that it is a short verse strophe.[19] To discuss the details of the history of the literary type it would be necessary to call upon other examples. We therefore lay this question aside.

F. Redaction History

The two legends, with their component literary types, the prophecy of disaster and official speech, were probably already connected at the oral stage of transmission. Then one day the whole narrative was written down together with other Elijah stories. We have no knowledge of when this could have been. As the passage now stands it is part of the Deuteronomistic historical writing, which extends from Deuteronomy itself to II Kings, and whose outline and main themes have been magnificently

---

[16] GrPro LXII.
[17] Verse 16; I Kings xiv. 7, xx. 28, 36. The יַעַן אֲשֶׁר clause in I Kings xi. 33 is placed after because of the particular circumstances involved.
[18] C. Barth, *Die Errettung vom Tode in den individuellen Klage- und Dankliedern des Alten Testamentes*, 1947.
[19] ZAW 66, 1954, p. 233.

analysed by Noth.[20] The legends of the prophets were inserted by putting a redactional bracket around them in the form of sentences at the beginning and at the end:

And Moab rebelled against Israel after the death of Ahab.
And Jehoram began to reign in his stead.

The first sentence reappears almost word for word in II Kings iii. 5, and the second has a connection with iii. 1. Logically they both belong to the third chapter. The writer used the two sentences also in chapter 1 presumably in order to bring the prophecy of disaster announced to Ahaziah within the context of national history. The rebellion of Moab after Ahab's death could not be curbed because Ahaziah's illness prevented him from taking action against the enemy, and his illness was connected with his idolatry. In this way national history is presented from the viewpoint of sin and guilt. At the same time it is made very clear that the direction taken by Israel's history was just as much influenced by the prophets as by the kings. Hence the complex literary type which II Kings 1 formerly comprised was taken up into a greater historical work, and became a mere component literary type. The redaction history of the chapter does not end with the Deuteronomistic writing, for there are considerable differences in the Septuagint version.

16. LEGENDS

Dibelius: *From Tradition to Gospel*, p. 104–132; 1934 (London, Nicholson & Watson; New York, Scribner). Bultmann: *The History of the Synoptic Tradition*, p. 244–307, 1963 (Oxford, Blackwell; New York, Harper & Row). Eissfeldt: *The Old Testament: An Introduction*, p. 42–47, 1965 (Oxford, Blackwell; New York, Harper & Row).

To describe the narratives of the prophets as legends[1] will produce in some an even stronger reaction than when we spoke of biblical sagas. In particular the assertion that the stories of the nativity and the empty tomb are legends has produced much unrest in the Christian churches recently, and has brought forth considerable protest from fundamentalists. It is not the place to go into this controversy, which has revealed a regrettable lack of ability on the part of the protesters to view the biblical writings historically, when these are after all so decidedly historical. But also the 'modern' theologians who are under fire are by no means entirely without blame. Only too often they also lack a genuine sense of the historical, so that they are subject to extreme theories, and often use the term legend in a depreciatory sense. This has meant that it has become generally believed that nothing in the Bible has been reliably reported. A form-critical analysis will bring things into perspective for both sides.

[20] Noth, ÜGS.
[1] The English *legend* has a wider meaning, and includes that of the German saga. The German term *legend* corresponds to the *devotional legend* or *edificatory legend*. Bentzen, *Introduction* I, p. 233, n. 4.

A. *Political Legends and Cult Legends*

The term *legenda*, i.e. 'what is read', first arose in medieval monasteries to describe sacred stories which were read aloud during mealtimes. When the European Renaissance rejected everything associated with the 'Dark Ages' which preceded it the term fell into disrepute. In modern linguistic usage the word means narratives, press reports and political tracts which, though based on real events, are of a 'legendary' nature. They are the result of certain party interests, and are therefore biased. A well-known *political legend* is that of the 'stab-in-the-back', i.e. the assertion that in the first World War the defeat of the German Army was entirely the result of a stab-in-the-back, administered by certain groups on the home front. If biblical narratives are classified along these lines under the term legend, then the biblical writers would have ignored, or at least have distorted, the historical facts, out of a biased religious party interest, and against their better judgment. Naturally there is no suggestion of this in a sober form-critical analysis.[2] The biblical writers were one and all concerned—and their beliefs led them to be so—to depict historical reality and to bring out its significance. They wrote in the form of legends for other reasons than because of a one-sided understanding of the material they were handling. Their manner of expression has absolutely no connection with that of legends which reflect a political bias.

There is another use of the term legend which we must consider: that of the religious *cult legend*.[3] These are legends which were read out at ancient cultic ceremonies, or rather, the proclamation of sacred history (*hieros logos*). Thus the legend of the cult is part of a liturgy and is concerned with mythical or historical events which for the cultic community are fundamental to their belief. Of this kind is the Babylonian 'creation epic', *Enuma elisch*, text for the fourth day of the New Year festival, and thus a cult legend. Paul's narrative of the Last Supper in I Cor. xi. 23-25 is a cult legend in this sense. Also the Exodus-Settlement tradition in the Pentateuch and the description of the Sinai covenant in Exod. xx-xxiv will be based on cult legends.[4] However, these legends have little in common with the kind of edificatory legend we are about to consider, which includes the legends of the prophets. Only an incomplete understanding of the cult of the ancient world could lead one to suppose that the recitation of sacred history at a ceremony was for the purposes of edification. In all religions of the ancient world the cult was more in the nature of 'creative drama',[5] and the celebration of a remote event through *hieros logos* was

[2] To see Old Testament legends as derived from the 'propagandist interest of the personnel concerned in the cult' could only be the result of a present-day preconception. Eissfeldt, *Introduction*, p. 45.

[3] BHH II, 1022.

[4] The covenant formularies described in section 3 do not only include the proclamation of apodictic prohibitions but also of the saving history in the form of cult legends.

[5] Unfortunately in New Testament criticism neither Bultmann nor Dibelius have produced a clear idea of the cult. Dibelius talks of the 'aetiological cult legend', thus combining it with another literary type, the aetiological cult saga, which, although it is associated with the origin and development of cultic customs, was not proclaimed in a ceremony as *hieros logos*. This is a very important point.

to re-live that period of the past, and to link the present with the tremendous force which had inspired that earlier divine event. But we
cannot consider this in detail here. It is with a third use of the term legend
that we are concerned, which has considerably greater affinity to the original
medieval meaning of *legenda* than those two we have mentioned above.

B. *The Legend as the Expression of a Particular Way of Thinking*

The medieval term legend is used in form criticism to describe narratives
about the prophets, and also legends about martyrs, nativity legends, and
legends of the apostles. Dibelius groups all these under the heading of
'personal legends', because it is on these that the worship of saints is based.
But it is questionable whether this term is the right one. The narrative
about Ahaziah's fall is certainly intended to inculcate respect for the words
of the prophet, but not to encourage the worship of Elijah. And even the
apocryphal legends of the apostles are not concerned with the motif of
'miraculous self-deliverance' (Dibelius), but with revealing the power
possessed by God, which the reader can rely upon. And the collective
term 'biographical legends', which Bultmann suggests, is even less
appropriate. Both these form critics have a too biased approach to the
subject, and their reflections remain superficial. It is understandable that
the use of the term has been badly received by conservative Christians.

Legends are, like historical writing, the result of a particular way of
thinking (*Geistesbeschäftigung*) but unlike historical writing are not intended
to reproduce events as they occurred or to make them follow an imposed
chain of motivation. Jolles provided a fresh approach to this subject in his
book *Einfache Formen*.[6] He begins with the medieval Christian legend,
which concerns saints, men who are holy because of their virtue. A description of the trials which such virtue undergoes, such as in the story of St
George and the Dragon, is not a description of real events. The saint does
not exist for himself alone but for the community which tells the story. It is
not the sequence of his life which is important, but those moments in his
life in which the good in him is realised. Therefore the legend belongs to
particular sociological groups and to the ideals of their stations: knighthood, for instance, as with St George, or, particularly frequently, monastic
life. What is transmitted about a saint is intended to stimulate those who
hear to emulate him. It is those who look for standards on the path of
virtue who link up the legend with historical persons, for 'we can have no
sure criterion of virtue unless it is depicted in measurable, intelligible and
tangible terms' (Jolles). The figure of the hero then becomes a model for
imitation.

The legend of St George is a verbal picture of those evils with which
knights of the Occident were confronted. It has nothing to do with any
particular point of view. This type of legend died out with the Middle
Ages.[7]

---

[6] [2]1956 (Halle), pp. 19–49; [2]1958 (Darmstadt), pp. 21–61.
[7] Jolles, *Einfache Formen*, sees a modern equivalent in press reports of sportsmen
attempting as yet unattained goals.

There is obviously a sharp difference between the medieval legend and the Old Testament legends about the prophets. Whereas the medieval legend aimed to display the merits of a particular virtue, the Old Testament legend directs attention to the divine authority with which the prophet is endowed, and to whom every person not similarly endowed must submit. Yet the term legend is still the best we can do with the language at our disposal to describe these Old Testament stories; for here also, as in the medieval examples, the story is not really concerned with the biographical details of the hero's life, but involves the hearer directly in what happens. The tale is told in order to edify. It is a matter of obedience and of trust in one's God, who reveals himself *indirectly* through the word or the action uttered or performed by the prophet.[8] In the legend God no longer appears in person, as he did in the saga. The situations in which Elijah or Elisha appear have a typical character, just as those of the saint have also. This is the basis on which the story rests, heavily stylised and standardised. The contrast between good and bad is brought out sharply: on the one hand Elijah, strong in his faith in his god, on the other the idolatrous king. The two unbelieving captains are contrasted with the third, who is a believer.

With the legends of martyrs a new literary type arose in the late Israelite period. The Daniel legends (Dan. i–vi) represent an early stage in its development. These are concerned with God's hidden presence in the adversities experienced in a world which is hostile to Israel and her God; it is in fact through persecution that a man can the better approach his God, provided he remains true to the Jerusalem temple and the precepts laid down by his fathers. In the Jesus legends, to which in particular the synoptic miracles of healing and nature miracles belong,[9] God's power is revealed through the unique person of Jesus. And in the legends of the apostles it is shown how the bearer of the Easter message and the apostolic doctrine is given strength by his heavenly Father. They call for trust in the apostolic proclamation.

Seen from the limited viewpoint of the attitude of mind (*Geistesbeschäftigung*) which produced the saga, it could be said that the legend has a very grey look about it; but this would be disregarding the main principle behind the story, by which the world is seen in terms of what is good or bad. Certainly compared with the national saga there is a marked lack of colour and humour, but then this is intentional. Even important characters are nameless, such as the captains. The places where the events occur are of no importance. It is not made clear where Elijah met the messengers, and on the top of which hill he confronted the captains. In these aspects the legend and the saga are utterly opposed. When place names are given in legends—such as Samaria or Ekron in II Kings i—they have a strong symbolic significance, for the good or for the bad. Also the plane of events i.e. the setting of the essential elements of the story, differs from that of the

---

[8] In the legend God does not appear directly to people as he did in the Genesis sagas.

[9] Dibelius and Bultmann separate the miracle stories from the legends, which is hardly correct.

saga. Although it is true that in the later, elaborated syle of the Israelite saga (see section 12) the exchange of words was important, what was really decisive was always the action, the defeat or the success (which sometimes holds good 'up to the present day'). Human endeavour in the saga was always presented in terms of two opposites: wise or foolish, brave or cowardly. But in the legend what is decisive is the attitudes of the religious or the irreligious man, with the opposites of belief or unbelief, virtue or vice. Unlike historical writing legends, like sagas, include *miracles*. However, the miracles depicted in legends are of a different kind to those found in sagas. Whereas in the saga the miracle is part of the flow of events and is described in detail, stage by stage, in the legend it usually occurs suddenly and unexpectedly, breaking into the natural course of events. Hence not many details can be given. We are told twice of the miraculous fire from heaven in II Kings i, but we have no description of its coming. (In the language forms also there are considerable differences between sagas and legends, but as yet this has been scarcely analysed.)

Both the legend and the saga are concerned with God's action on earth. Both look beyond the ordinary connection of earthly events and show *how God is at work within these events*. Historical writing was not able to do this, being concerned only with the human level of failure or of success, and merely accepting the fact that God influenced this (see the transmission of David's succession to the throne, II Sam. ix ff.). However, sagas and legends are also concerned with *how* God influences events, the saga more with the external, objective story, and the legend more with the internal, subjective aspects of it. Thus both ways of thinking play an essential part in the biblical writings. Divine revelation and divine action should not only be expressed in the language of metaphysics, for this has no connection with history. Sagas and legends, therefore, do not conflict with the general link between biblical faith and history, but on the contrary emphasise it. Although we no longer possess a conception of the world which produced sagas and legends, if Christian theology is to remain Christian it must maintain contact with the driving motive underlying biblical sagas and legends.

The term legend is therefore much disliked by believing Christians, because they fear that to use it is to deny the historicity of divine revelation, which is part of their faith. It is indeed vital for the Christian faith, unlike all other religions, that it should be based on historical facts. But the historical foundation of Old and New Testament history is by no means called in question by the form-critical determination of literary types. That Jesus appeared to his disciples and later followers after his death, or that they were convinced of his physical resurrection (I Cor. xv) is not doubted when it is disputed whether the narrative about the discovery of the empty tomb in Mark xvi is a legend or not. And the facts that Jesus was born of Mary, came of a poor background, and grew up in Nazareth still stand, even though it is determined that the Lucan pre-history is legendary, and it is not quite certain whether Jesus was born in Bethlehem or was of the house of David. And Elijah's historical opposition to the royal house of Israel is just as little affected by the legendary nature of II

Kings i. But we must emphasise yet again that the judgment implied by the use of the term legend is a purely literary one, and says nothing either one way or the other about the historicity of the events.[10] This can only be judged after an appraisal of the transmission history of the narrative in question.

17. THE YOKE OF THE KING OF BABYLON (Jer. xxviii)

On the literary types in the book of Jeremiah H. Wildberger: *Jahwewort und prophetische Rede bei Jeremia*, 1942; on the redaction history S. Mowinckel: Zur Composition des Buches Jeremia, SNVAO 1913 No. 5.

1 And it came to pass in the same year, in (the beginning of) the reign of Zedekiah king of Judah, in the fourth year, in the fifth month, that Hananiah the son of Azzur the prophet, which was of Gibeon, spake unto me in the house of the Lord, in the presence of the priests and of the people, saying,

KA 2 *Thus speaketh the Lord* of hosts, the God of Israel, saying,
I   I have broken the yoke of the king of Babylon.
II   3   Within two full years will I bring again (participle) into this place all the vessels of the Lord's house, that Nebuchadnezzar king of Babylon took away from this place, and carried them to Babylon:
     4   and I will bring again (participle) to this place Jeconiah the son of Jehoiakim, king of Judah, with all the captives of Judah, that went to Babylon, *saith the Lord*:
III   for I will break the yoke of the king of Babylon.
     5 Then the prophet Jeremiah said unto the prophet Hananiah in the presence of the priests, and in the presence of all the people that stood in the house of the Lord, 6. even the prophet Jeremiah said, Amen: the Lord do so:
          the Lord perform thy words which thou hast prophesied, to bring again the vessels of the Lord's house, and all them of the captivity, from Babylon unto this place.
     7   Nevertheless hear thou now this word that I speak in thine ears, and in the ears of all the people:
     8   The prophets that have been before me and before thee of old prophesied against many countries, and against great kingdoms, of war, and of evil, and of pestilence.
     9   The prophet which prophesieth peace, when the word of the prophet shall come to pass, then shall the prophet be known, that the Lord hath truly sent him.
    10 Then Hananiah the prophet took the bar off the prophet Jeremiah's neck, and brake it.
    11 And Hananiah spake in the presence of all the people, saying,
KA   *Thus saith the Lord:*
          Even so will I break the yoke of Nebuchadnezzar king of Babylon within two full years from off the neck of all the nations.
          And the prophet Jeremiah went his way.

[10] Dibelius ThR, 1929, pp. 204 f. and *From Tradition to Gospel*, p. 108. Bultmann is more sceptical, *Tradition*, p. 245, n. 1.

12 Then the word of the Lord came unto Jeremiah, after that Hananiah the prophet had broken the bar from off the neck of the prophet Jeremiah, saying,

PO 13 Go, and tell Hananiah, saying,

KA *Thus saith the Lord:*

I Thou hast broken the bars of wood; but thou shalt make in their stead bars of iron.

KA 14 For *thus saith the Lord* of hosts, the God of Israel:

II I have put a yoke of iron upon the neck of all these nations, thàt they may serve Nebuchadnezzar king of Babylon; and they shall serve him: and I have given him the beasts of the field also.

15 Then said the prophet Jeremiah unto Hananiah the prophet,

AA *Hear now,* Hananiah,

I the Lord hath not sent thee; but thou makedst this people to trust in a lie.

KA 16 Therefore *thus saith the Lord.*

II Behold, I will send thee away (participle) from off the face of the earth: this year shalt thou die,

III because thou hast spoken rebellion against the Lord.

17 So Hananiah the prophet died the same year in the seventh month.

A. *Legends and Biography of the Prophets*

Jer. xxviii is also a legend of the prophets. It is similar to the narratives about Elijah in that the speeches take up far more of the story than do the descriptive parts. The speeches in fact contain all the essential happenings, and what is reported in the descriptive passages is merely the consequence of what was said in the speeches. The central theme of the legend of the prophets is the prophet as bearer of God's word; we are very little concerned with the complex course of his life. As in the earlier legends, here also God's word is realised at the end, in absolute accordance with what was said and occurred. However, despite these similarities with the earlier legends, the literary type has now undergone a change. Jeremiah lived two hundred years after Elijah. During that period stories about the prophets did not retain a fixed form because prophecy itself did not remain the same. The legends have become historically condensed. Elaborations, which had been common in earlier narratives and which were sometimes still present in the legends about Elijah, and particularly about Elisha, have completely disappeared. It is not that the story is any less exciting. But the final unravelling of the entangled state of affairs is less clear-cut than when Elijah confronted the king in his idolatry. The conflict has entered the realm of thought. Previously the contrasts between truth and falsehood, and between obedience to God's will and an arbitrary act of remonstrance, both characteristics of the legend, were very clearly depicted. By the time of Jeremiah it is not so straightforward: one of Jahweh's prophets confronts another (also in chapter xxix), or the defenders of the Promised Land oppose Jeremiah, who calls for surrender and submissiveness in face of foreign domination (chapter xxxvi–xxxviii).

The change extends also to the form of the story. A date is now given at the beginning, possibly an accurate one (verses 1, 17), and this is usual in the Jeremiah legends (and also as far back as Isa. xxxvi–xxxix). Details are also given of the scene of the event, and there is mention of witnesses to it. Hananiah is the son of a certain Azzur, and comes from Gibeon. Jeremiah met him in the house of Jahweh, the Jerusalem temple, on a particular occasion at which the priests and all the people were present (verse 1). He spoke before this gathering (verse 5). Details of this sort were not given in the earlier legends about the prophets, where there was a tendency to standardise. The essential characteristics of the legend recede into the background. The literary type has now come close to historical writing. The medieval term legend is now even less suitable than it was for the Elijah legends, but there is no better term available. For the hearer is still encouraged to emulate Jeremiah, and still to respect Jahweh's word, however unpredictable its coming may be. Details of time and place were not added by the narrator to demonstrate his inventiveness, but in an attempt to place the event, so that by now there is a tendency to make it historical. Obviously the details render the coming of Yahweh's Word easier to grasp.

There is a new aspect to the story in that it concerns a saying by the 'true' prophet, Jeremiah, with a description of his receiving his instructions from Jahweh, expressed in the distinctive *formula for receiving God's word*: 'The word of the Lord came unto Jeremiah.' This expression is often used in Jeremiah and the later prophets. In the older legends the narrator of the story still retained some freedom at this point; e.g. II Kings i. 3: 'But (the angel of) the Lord said to Elijah', or in verse 15 'And (the angel of) the Lord said unto Elijah.' And it was also possible to have the prophet speak without indicating the source of what he said; 'And Elijah the Tishbite . . . said unto Ahab' (I Kings xvii. 1). However, occasionally the formula for receiving God's word was also used in these earlier narratives (I Kings xvii. 2, xviii. 1, xxi. 17); but this could perhaps be explained as an addition by later redactors.

The term 'formula for receiving God's word' (*Wortempfangsformel*) was adopted by Reventlow.[1] It shows that the notion of God's Word has assumed a more fixed form. God no longer addresses each prophet individually. His message is now subject to the objective hypostasis of *dabar*, so that it comes to the prophet always in the same form. Zimmerli suggests the term 'word event formula' (*Wortereignisformel*),[2] which although it emphasises that something really happens might nevertheless give the impression that it describes a merely momentary event. The prophet does not mean that the word takes place at that one moment, and then vanishes, but that the word remains in existence from then on as a real active force. Thus Mowinckel interprets the Hebrew expression as, 'The Word of Jahweh became active reality for NN.'[3]

This reference to the happening of the word is followed by a *private oracle* authorising the messenger, with two imperatives, as in the books of

[1] ZThK 58, 1961, p. 274: H. Wildberger, *Jahwewort und prophetische Rede bei Jeremia*, 1942, calls it a 'revelation formula' (*Revelationsformel*), p. 49.
[2] *Ezechiel* (BK), pp. 88–90.
[3] *Die Erkenntnis Gottes bei den Propheten*, 1941, p. 19; cf. von Rad. *Theology* II, pp. 80 f.

the Kings: 'Go, and tell . . .'. Nothing has changed here. But with this we come to aspects of this tale which belong to the component literary type of the prophetic saying, which will be discussed below.

In ascertaining the literary type it is important to take a look at the general context of the passage. In verse 10 there is a reference to a wooden yoke which Jeremiah bears, and which was torn from him and broken by his colleague Hananiah. The chapter has not prepared us for this incident; there was no earlier reference to the yoke. Yet the previous chapter refers to it: 'Thus saith the Lord to me: Make thee bonds and bars, and put them upon thy neck' (xxvii. 2). Then it goes on to say that the yoke Jeremiah took upon himself symbolises the rule of the Babylonian king over the peoples of the Near East. This is a *symbolic action, or sign* on the part of the prophet, and a number of similar actions by the prophets are reported. Its significance was the same as that of a prophecy: it proclaimed—visibly— the inevitable future, and also heralded the event. Jeremiah's act in chapter xxvii is symbolical, just as Hananiah's action is also symbolical when in a display of strength he takes the yoke off Jeremiah and breaks it. In our legend both actions with the yoke are moments of release accompanying what is proclaimed. Both Hananiah's and Jeremiah's words revolve around the object of the yoke, and with it the authority of the Babylonian king. But the yoke is not mentioned at the beginning of the narrative. Does this mean that chapters xxvii and xxviii always belonged together, and that the tacitly accepted division between them, which makes our narrative an independent unit, should not be there? This is Weiser's conclusion (ATD), who sees the two chapters as always belonging together. However, Rudolph (HAT) points out that chapter xxvii is a personal report by Jeremiah, in which he speaks in the first person, and that chapter xxviii is an independent report about Jeremiah, told by someone else. He therefore assumes the link between the two chapters to be secondary and that between 1a and 1b of chapter xxviii there was once a longer description of Jeremiah's yoke which was left out when the two chapters were later combined.

It is not easy to come to a conclusion about this, because of the individual nature of the Jeremiah legends; for it appears that these were not collected by the prophet's disciples, as in the case of the books of Kings, to be used for oral transmission. Jeremiah did not have a circle of disciples around him, as did the older prophets, or at least we never hear anything about them. There was only one man with him: Baruch, who was apparently no prophet, but a scribe. The book often states that he wrote down sayings at the dictation of Jeremiah, which he later read out on occasions (xxxvi. 4, 32; xlv. 1). So it has long been very reasonably assumed that the collection of Jeremiah narratives in the second half of the book (chapters xix f., xxvi (xxvii) xxviii f., xxxiv, xxxvi–xlv, li, lix ff.) was composed by Baruch. It does not immediately concern us here whether it was Baruch or another anonymous contemporary of Jeremiah who wrote them down. Whoever did so composed the first *biography of a prophet*. Thus the general context of the story proves it to have been always a part of a greater complex literary type. But we must hasten to qualify the term biography, which is a modern one. The narrator does not set out to portray the course of an interesting man's life, but the fate of a prophet and his sayings, and as the result of his sayings. He does not begin with his birth and his youth, but deals only with the latter part of his life: with his sorrows and persecution. The end of the prophets' effective ministry could be said to become itself a single symbolic action. The result of this is the first biography composed in Israel. From the literary as well as the theological viewpoint it cannot be over-praised. The reader is surprised by the empathy in this account of the life of the master and friend, and also by the sophisticated manner of presentation, which occasionally reveals an acute psychological insight. Despite the short sentences the whole agony of a man racked by internal conflict—for such was Jeremiah—is eloquently presented. This is the report of an eye witness who is completely reliable. There is therefore no problem about the historicity of the story: it happened just as it is reported.

Chapter xxviii has therefore never been an independent unit. It was conceived as a component literary type within the new literary type of the biography. Nevertheless it is odd that the talented 'Baruch' reported the events in which Jeremiah took part, including the Hananiah episode, always in relatively isolated sections, creating an impression that they are independent of each other. But to a form critic this is not surprising. As there was no such thing as 'biography', Baruch adapted the current literary type of the legend about the prophets to his own ends. Thus by connecting up a whole series of legends he created a new form. The literary type of the legend of the prophets reached its end. It became only the foundation of a new construction. In fact, after Baruch no legends about the prophets were written. (Only in late-Israelite times do stories appear which could be termed legends, such as that of Jonah, the Daniel stories and the Book of the Martyrdom of Isaiah, but they have little in common with the old legends.)

What is the setting in life of the 'Baruch' narrative? Whom was he writing for? According to the text (chapter xliii f.) Baruch finally settled in Egypt with Jeremiah. The book will have been written there, presumably for a small group of refugees who, despite all the difficulties of their situation, still believed in the word of the prophet and derived encouragement from hearing about him.

The Baruch narrative is however only the final version in the history of the transmission of these traditions. We have shown above how chapter xxviii (perhaps at a later stage) was linked to chapter xxvii. Doubtless the two chapters once had a closer connection to chapter xxix, as is evident from a use of language common to all three. They are also linked by the same theme, for they all describe encounters with false prophets.[4] Then finally chapters xxvii–xxix, with the rest of the Baruch biography, were built into the larger unit of the book of Jeremiah as it now stands. At this point the single sections of the biography were (again) separated and shuffled about. This was easy to accomplish as Baruch had used the legends as a model, putting together relatively independent units. Thus chapter xxviii became part of the section (chapters xxvi–xxxv) on the prophecies of salvation for Judah and Israel. For

---

[4] Rudolph (HAT) supposes that chapters xxvii–xxix could once even have been a separate polemical work against a suspect prophetic movement of the exile period.

the final redactors the prophecies of disaster, including the encounter between Jeremiah and Hananiah, will have been intermediate points within the framework of the prophecies of salvation in xxvii. 22, xxix. 10–14, xxxii. In the sayings of Jeremiah the emphasis will then have been laid upon the yoke of the king of Babylon, whose sway over the nations will no longer have been seen in purely negative terms by the redactors. To them it would have been a purely intermediary stage on the way to final salvation (as in Dan. ii, iv–vii). Thus the chapter has won a new emphasis, although it is hardly possible to make out details of this.

B. *Prophecy of Disaster to the Individual*

There are several literary types of prophetic speech in Jeremiah xxviii. In it the prophecy of disaster to the individual is interwoven with a prophecy of disaster to the nation in verses 13–16; but it is easy to determine the difference between them. The prophecy to the individual again finds its source in a private oracle in the form of a message with two imperatives (verse 13a), which conforms with the pattern set by the books of Kings. The actual prophecy of disaster to the rival prophet does not begin until verse 15, with the phrase, 'Hear now, Hananiah'. This section is new to us, for it was not present in II Kings i. It is an *appeal for attention* (AA), which after Amos is often found before a diatribe.[5]

The diatribe (indication of the situation, I) again presents the position as one requiring remedy and intervention by Jahweh. Hananiah has not only taken a false commission upon himself but has deceived the people into believing a false sign. Thus the nation is endangered, and is only saved by a prediction of disaster (II, v. 16) introduced by the messenger formula (כֹּה אָמַר יהוה = KA formula). The people are freed from the danger occasioned by Hananiah by the latter's banishment, indeed with his sudden death. The prediction of disaster (II) begins with an indication that Jahweh will positively intervene: 'Behold, I will send thee away from off the face of the earth.' This sentence links the threat fast to the diatribe, where it was said that Jahweh had not *sent* Hananiah. The first and second part of this prophecy of disaster are therefore linked together by word play. This was a device much loved by the prophets; in II Kings i there was a play on the words 'man of God' and 'fire of God', אִישׁ הָאֱלֹהִים and אֵשׁ אֱלֹהִים.

This seems an artificial device to us today, but to the Israelites it had great significance. To them the word and the object it represented belonged essentially together; it appears that the sound of a word was not a matter which could be settled at the discretion of the speaker, but was called for by the thing represented. Therefore any phonetic similarity between two words was the result of a fundamental connection between the two things. Although Hananiah had not been sent by Jahweh, by making a false prophecy of salvation in verses 2–4 he in fact called down a real action by Jahweh. This action concerned him personally, crushingly: he was sent to his death. The announcement of God's action begins with, 'Behold', and

---

[5] This expression is used by Zimmerli in *Ezechiel* (BK), p. 288. Lindblom spoke of a 'sermon formula' (*Predigtformel*); von Rabenau, WZ Halle V, p. 678 of a 'herald's summons' (*Heroldsruf*).

is followed by a participial clause announcing Jahweh's personal intervention. This is the ancient custom in any group of prophecies of disaster
to the individual (II Sam. xii. 11; I Kings xi. 31, xiv. 10). Adjoined to
this is a further sentence announcing how this would affect the man
concerned. He is the subject of what follows: 'This year thou shalt die.'
(It is the same in the three other examples just mentioned.) At the end,
true to form, there is the concluding characterisation (III), in this case of
the recipient, Hananiah: 'Because thou hast spoken rebellion.' Thus
Hananiah is deprived of his life and the people are freed of the threat
which he has posed.

C. *Prophecy of Disaster to the Nation*

The prophecy to Hananiah conforms to the familiar pattern of the prophecy of disaster to individuals, but a second prophecy of disaster is
embodied in this narrative, in the shape of the speech by Jahweh in
verses 13–16, this time directed at the whole of Israel, indeed, at 'all these
nations'. However, the diatribe preceding it (statement of the situation, I)
still only concerns the Hananiah aspect of the story: 'Thou hast broken the
bars of wood; but thou shalt make in their stead bars of iron.' Essentially
this is not a diatribe, even less an accusation (as Westermann asserts), but
rather a straightforward statement by the speaker. There is a reference to
the present state of things. The wooden yoke which Jeremiah has long been
wearing whenever he is in public as a symbol of the sad future of his
people was broken by Hananiah in the flush of his own prophetic certainty.
Jeremiah recognises the action, though with qualifications. This display
of power has rendered the symbol of the yoke void. But then there follows
an obscure word, the sense of which we can no longer discover (even the
Greek translation made no sense of it, for at this point the text has been
changed): by his action Hananiah has invoked an even greater, unshatter-
able yoke, perhaps from Jahweh himself. Human remonstrance against
God's expressed will is not merely ineffectual: its result is paradoxical, for
it provokes an even harsher act of retaliation from God. This must be
roughly the sense of the passage. Jeremiah simply accepts it. Therefore
this passage is not really a diatribe *for Hananiah*, though he also is addressed,
but it concerns all those listening. It is really an introduction to a *prophecy
of disaster to the nation* (II).

> For *thus saith the Lord* of Hosts, the God of Israel:
> I have put a yoke of iron upon the neck of all these nations, that they may
> serve Nebuchadnezzar king of Babylon; and they shall serve him: and I
> have given him the beasts of the field also.

Here also the prediction refers not only to how God will intervene but also
to how those concerned will react. However, this time the end reflects the
beginning in that *God* is mentioned again: 'and I have given him
the beasts of the field also'. God's intervention is expressed with
particular force. The disaster is not announced by means of a nominal
clause with 'Behold' and a following participle, but by means of a sentence

in the perfect, with the object preceding the verb. Although Israel is not mentioned at all, this is indeed a prophecy of disaster to the nation, for it must be remembered that the text of the prophecy will have been changed when it was linked to chapter xxvii, and that the expression 'all these nations' refers back to xxvii. 3, where the nations are named as those of Edom, Moab, Ammon, and the people of Tyre and Zidon. When Jeremiah called Hananiah to account in the presence of all the people, he would have stated more clearly what he meant. But this does not mean that Jeremiah originally cited Israel itself: the prophets loved to use veiled language when referring to those involved in destruction wrought by God. Yet the audience would not have doubted that Jeremiah was announcing a 'threat' to their own nation, however it was worded originally. Thus the term prophecy of disaster to the nation is justified.

The prophecy of disaster to the nation is given a particular quality by the title accorded to Jahweh at the beginning of the messenger formula (KA): 'The Lord of Hosts' was a ceremonial title of dignity used in the Jerusalem temple. To this is added the ancient name 'God of Israel'.[6] It is also given particular prominence by the fact that it is furnished with two messenger formulas, one before the prediction of disaster as well as one before the diatribe. Yet the basic structure of the prophecy has not changed. A prophecy of disaster to the nation is no literary type in itself, but merely a part of the general literary type of the prophecy of disaster. At one point this passage is an exception to the rule, for there is no concluding characterisation at the end; but this will have been the result of the link with the second prophecy of disaster to Hananiah. In all other prophecies of disaster to the nation the concluding characterisation is an integral part (e.g. vi. 13).

D. *Prophecy of Salvation*

In the midst of these prophecies of disaster by Jeremiah there is a prophetic speech by Hananiah promising salvation. It is conspicuously similar in form to the literary types used by Jeremiah and is easy to confuse with them. Hananiah also begins with the messenger formula (KA), 'Thus saith the Lord' (verse 11), using a more extended form of it in verse 2. His prophecy of salvation begins with an *indication of the change which has taken place* (I): Jahweh has broken the yoke of the king of Babylon. God has already made the decision, and the political pressure put upon the Syrian-Palestinian peoples by the great Babylonian power has already ceased. Thus the way is now open for fresh intervention by Jahweh, announced in the form of a participial clause, similar grammatically to verse 16. The main section, the *prediction of salvation, or the promise* (II), has three versions of the same word combination: '(Un)to (from) this place', and twice: 'I (will) bring again'. This repetition is intended to give greater effect to the pronouncement. It does not disturb the flow of the narrative,

[6] Our passage does not suffice to prove it a general rule that prophecies of disaster to the nation always contain the more elaborate messenger formula, whereas individual prophecies of disaster only 'Thus saith the Lord'. It has yet to be discovered when the simple formula is used and when the more elaborate one.

for in fact it has been very cleverly inserted, at the beginning, in the middle, and at the end. The promise is concluded by a reference to the whisper of Jahweh (נְאֻם יְהֹוָה 'saith the Lord'). We have not encountered this expression before, but Jeremiah himself uses it, as will shortly be seen. The third section, the concluding characterisation, we have already met in verse 16, 'For I will break the yoke', and in II Kings i. This ties up with the reference at the beginning to the changed state of things. In fact, it is the same word for word, except for a small but significant difference: at the beginning it was the perfect tense, but here it is in the imperfect. What in heaven is considered to have happened is seen on earth as not yet having taken place, as still in the future. Although on the face of it Hananiah's saying conforms in style to the customary prophecy—all three sections are present: indication of the present situation, prediction, concluding characterisation—in fact it is only a superficial similarity, for the first and third sections prophesy also, and it is only the force of the literary type which separates the two from the middle section.

The literary type of the *prophecy of salvation* is easier to analyse when it is compared with one of Jeremiah's prophecies. Here is his speech to King Zedekiah from xxxiv. 4:

AA Yet hear the word of the Lord, O Zedekiah, king of Judah :
KA *Thus saith the Lord* concerning thee,
II Thou shalt not die by the sword ; thou shalt die in peace ;
    And with the burnings of thy fathers, the former which were before thee,
    So shall they make a burning for thee ; and they shall lament thee, saying Ah Lord !
III for I have spoken the word, saith the Lord.

It is easy to see the relationship to the saying by Hananiah and the conformity to the general pattern of the prophecies of both salvation and disaster. Both can be preceded by the *appeal for attention* (AA) (cf. xxviii. 15). The prophecy itself is basically in three parts: indication of the situation, prediction, and concluding characterisation. The first part appears to be lacking in chapter xxxiv only because the situation had already been sufficiently well indicated in the preceding prophecy of disaster (verse 2 f.).

The expression, 'Saith the Lord' (*whisper of Jahweh* נְאֻם יְהֹוָה), therefore crops up at the end of a Jeremiah prophecy also. It is not used in the Elijah or Elisha stories, but on the other hand very frequently in Jeremiah, usually as a concluding formula, as in xxviii. 4; and not only as the conclusion to an isolated unit, but also after a section of the narrative, most frequently after the prediction (also as in xxviii. 4). The expression is certain to have originated and to have been used independently of the messenger formula, to which it is to a certain extent opposed. But the changes it underwent are still unclear, as is its exact significance.[7]

As in xxxiv. 3 f., all Jeremiah's prophecies will most certainly have been *poetical* when they were delivered orally. It was through being written down and through later versions (which to some extent are missing in the Septuagint) that they became prose.

[7] See back as early as the seer's saying in Num. xxiv. 3f., but also II Sam. xxiii. 1.

E. *The Reception of a Prophecy*

Amen: the Lord do so: the Lord perform thy words which thou hast prophesied, to bring again the vessels of the Lord's house, and all them of the captivity, from Babylon unto this place.

By using the words, 'unto this place', Jeremiah is quite definitely echoing Hananiah's words. How is his speech to be understood? Is Jeremiah being ironical, or does he in fact endorse what his opponent has said? The form-critical interpretation of what he means is of vital importance for the sense of the whole narrative and for the relationship between the two prophets. In fact, in verse 5 Jeremiah uses the word, 'Amen', a word which has come to him direct from Jahweh, so that it appears therefore that he is sincere in what he says. This conclusion is confirmed by I Kings i. 36, where Benaiah accepts a commission as messenger of his king with the words, 'Amen: the Lord, the God of my lord the king, say so too. As the Lord hath been with my lord the king, even so be he with Solomon.'

This conforms strikingly with the style of Jeremiah's words. The word 'Amen', is used when someone positively accepts a commission or a message. It is fitting that he should also append a request for benediction, whose content has some relation to what has just been said. Jeremiah is therefore positively accepting Hananiah's prophecy; after all, it corresponds with his own desires, for he too hopes for the salvation of the nation. Jeremiah therefore reckons that it is possible that Hananiah is the bearer of a genuine message from God. But at that moment he lacks inspiration, so although he cannot discover anything *against* Hananiah's words, on the other hand he cannot support Hananiah utterly wholeheartedly; and this determines the remainder of the story.

F. *Reflection by the Prophet Himself*

In verse 7 however Jeremiah begins anew with the words, 'Nevertheless hear thou this word that I speak in thine ears, and in the ears of all the people'. This is the appeal for attention (AA), which usually introduces a prophecy (verse 15). But here it is a reflection by Jeremiah himself, and he continues by saying that although a prophecy of disaster must be believed immediately, a prophecy of salvation must be seen to have been accomplished before it can be believed. The long introduction shows that Jeremiah is carefully following a particular style in his speech, but it is impossible to say with certainty which literary type lies hidden here, for there are insufficient examples for comparison.

It is not even certain whether these lines do in fact originate with Jeremiah himself. They could be explained as the result of the redaction history; for it is surprising to find Jeremiah using the image of an age-old succession of prophets of disaster. On the other hand, it is quite possible to imagine it coming from the later Deuteronomistic revisers, whose hand is apparent in other places in Jeremiah (cf. the Deuteronomistic passages II Kings xvii. 13, 23 and earlier, Deut. xviii. 5 f.).[8]

G. *The Pronouncement Accompanying a Symbolic Action*

In the text Hananiah speaks once again, in verse 11, though more briefly, when he makes a symbolic action by tearing the wooden yoke from Jeremiah's back and shattering it. After a messenger formula (KA) he says, 'Even so will I break the yoke of Nebuchadnezzar . . . within two full years.' This same style, with an explanatory sentence preceded by a messenger formula and an adverb of comparison, is also used by Jeremiah when he smashes the potter's vessel (chapter xix. 11, cf. xiii. 8–11, li. 64). Both these are symbolic actions; but it is true that in Hananiah's utterance this style is not employed throughout.

Thus this one chapter from Jeremiah reveals the complexity of the language used by the prophets. The most important of its literary types demand a still closer investigation.

18. HISTORY OF THE LITERARY TYPE OF THE PROPHECY

A. *The Structure of the Prophecy of Disaster*

As a sequel to Sections 15 and 17, a comparison of II Kings i and Jeremiah xxviii will bring out the basic structure of the prophecies of disaster and salvation[1], and also to some extent reveal the changes which took place within this literary type. To begin with it is essential that the structure of prophetic sayings be studied first from the *narratives* about the prophets, and not from the *speech passages* in the great books of the prophets; for these last contain long complexes of speech in which it is extraordinarily difficult to define the limits of a unit, because the writer has often left out the introductory and concluding sentences when he took the individual sayings out of

---

[8] E. Osswald, *Falsche Prophetie im AT*, SgV 237, 1962, p. 19, maintains that this passage was a later addition. She also considers verses 5 f. to have been added later, though this is less likely; an amen of this nature would never be added later to a prophet's speech.

[1] In the first edition the *prediction* (*Weissagung*) of salvation or disaster was termed the *Ankündigung* (*announcement*), and *Weissagung* was used to denote the literary type of the prophecy as a whole. However this implied that the whole was concerned only with a pronouncement about the future, but in fact this holds true only for the middle section. Hence in this second edition *Weissagung* is used in its sense of prediction to describe only Part II of the literary type. The restriction in the meaning of the word makes it possible to apply more accurately to the Old Testament the dogmatic-theological term *Weissagung* (*prophecy*), as opposed to *Erfüllung* (*fulfilment*). At the same time it makes it possible to give a specific term to the very particular manner in which a prophecy not only predicts the future but also, by means of the power conveyed by the word, hails it. The term *Profezeiung*, when used for the literary type which is described here, has the advantage of formality and does not imply a too hasty interpretation (as, for instance, 'message' does), and because in fact it is this literary type which is particularly characteristic of the pre-exilic prophets. The form-critical use of the term naturally assumes that not every prophetic speech takes the form of a prophecy, for the prophets now and then use speech forms other than that which is described in this chapter, such as the disputation (*Streitgespräch*), lawsuit (*Gerichtsrede*), etc.

the oral tradition. This was to prevent a too frequent repetition of formulas. Thus sometimes the messenger formula (KA) is completely lacking for several chapters of sayings on end, because the writer will have considered these to have been tacitly understood from the title of the book. It should give no grounds for the assumption that the prophet was able to utter his prophecy without the messenger formula. The diatribe also is often absent from the beginning of a prophecy, because the big complexes were mainly concerned with pronouncements about the future. On the other hand the narrative sections and the legends retain much more of the original presentation of a prophetic utterance, although here also it is likely that the material has been slightly condensed. Once the nature of the prophetic saying has been grasped from the narrative sections, it is then easy to analyse the sections which consist only of sayings.

The structure of the literary type of the prophecy of disaster did not change between the time of Elijah and that of Jeremiah. In Jer. xxviii there is no fundamental difference between prophecies of disaster to the *nation*, which first appear at the time of Amos, and those to the *individual*.[2] We have no definite examples of the literary type after the post-exilic period.

As a rule these prophecies of disaster consist of three parts:

1. *Indication of the situation' or Diatribe.* Here the religious, social or political situation is set out, and also the relationship between God and those for whom the prophecy is intended. The cause is a particularly pressing situation calling for remedy, either for the good or for the bad. If the diatribe is very formal, it begins with, 'Forasmuch as . . .' (יַעַן אֲשֶׁר) II Kings i. 16, cf. Jer. xxix. 25, 31, etc.). If the prophet is particularly indignant, he begins with a question in reproach, as in II Kings i. 3, 6. If he has had time to let the matter mature in his mind the diatribe can then consist of a brief statement, as in Jer. xxviii. 13, 15, cf. xxxvi. 29.

2. *Prediction of Disaster, or Threat.* The main point is (a) usually contained in a brief sentence in the negative with the verb in the imperfect, e.g. 'Thou shalt not come down from the bed whither thou art gone up' in II Kings i. 4 (Jer. xxxvi. 30, xxii. 11, 18). This is surprising to anyone well acquainted with grammatical forms of this kind, because the prophets are expected to use a special prophetic perfect which is intended to express their certainty about the event which is to take place. But a perfect is never used at this central point of the prophecy so far as I know. This form could be termed the *apodictic prediction* because of its affinity in form to certain Old Testament commandments.[3] (b) The prediction can also be expressed by means of a participial clause, of which Jahweh is the subject and which is usually introduced by, 'Behold, (I)', which is a *presentative*, or demonstrative particle, whose function is to present an idea to the mind. This participial clause is always placed at the beginning of the prediction and describes the sudden intervention by God by which the untenable present state of things described in the diatribe will be radically altered. A further sentence, with those affected as the subject,

---

[2] Hempel suggests that the national prophecy of disaster arose out of the prophecy of disaster to the king, and that it therefore reflects 'a great sociological process'; 'in place of the word to the king as representative of his people arose the threat against the people themselves' (ThLZ 87, 1962, col. 205).

[3] See above, p. 192.

describes the consequences of this intervention, i.e. the new situation, as in the speech against Hananiah in xxviii. 16. This construction is much used in Jeremiah (xxxii. 28, xxxiv. 22, xxxv. 17, xliii. 10, xliv. 30), but it was already well established then (I Sam. iii. 11; II Sam. xii. 11; I Kings xiv. 10).[4] It is suggested that these cases should be termed the *prediction with a presentative*.[5] In Jeremiah both forms are used together, with the participial construction placed first (xxxiv. 2 f., xliv. 26). The transition[6] from I to II is often achieved by means of לָכֵן 'therefore'.[7]

The prediction of disaster, the second section, always comprises the real substance of the prophecy. A good example from the Jeremiah narratives which shows this is xxvi. 18, where the elders of Judah know a prophecy apparently from oral tradition, which can be found in detail in the book of Micah iii. 9–12. But they quote a shortened form: they know only the prediction. It follows that for general purposes the prediction is the essential section of a prophecy.

3. *The concluding characterisation*, either of those affected by the prophecy (II Kings i. 4) or of the sender (Jer. xxviii. 4). Not much more need be said about it. It usually begins with 'for', or 'but' (כִּי).[8] The characterisation is the shortest part of the saying, rounding off the prophecy. It also shows that the words of the prophets are not in the least intended to be 'irrational'; indeed, this 'motive clause' is intended to be entirely 'rational'.

These three sections are usually accompanied by the *Ko-amar formula* (KA), usually called the messenger formula. It is placed either before I (II Kings i. 16), or before II (II Kings i. 4, 6; Jer. xxvii. 16); after Jeremiah it frequently appeared at both places (Jer. xxviii. 13 f.), and in the

---

[4] At a more ancient period sometimes הִנֵּה was used at this point, with another subject, e.g. I Kings xiii. 2, xx. 35.

[5] הִנֵּה as a presentative in J. Blau, VT IX, 1959, 130 ff. A particular kind of announcement with a presentative is when it begins with הִנְנִי אֵלֶיךָ; see P. Humbert, *Opuscules d'un Hébraïsant*, Mémoires de l'Univers. de Neuchâtel 26, 1958, 44–53. Humbert shows that sentences with such a presentative usually follow *waw* with the perfect as 'stern rebukes' (p. 49); and this does not only apply to the particular kind which he discusses.

[6] The prediction is sometimes bound up with the diatribe in a very special fashion. Wolff rightly emphasises how much the prophets are concerned to show that the future action by God (the prediction) is a necessary result of the present (the diatribe). The diatribe is intended to make the impending happening, i.e. the divine action, intelligible. (Such an attempt might be difficult to reconcile with the firm Protestant belief that God's Word must be 'simply accepted' without question.)

[7] *La-ken* = 'upon my word'; F. J. Goldbaum, JNES 23, 1964, 132–5.

[8] The introductory particles play a notable part in the arrangement of the prophecy: יַעַן אֲשֶׁר before the indication of the situation I, כֹּה before the KA formula, לָכֵן before the prediction II or the KA formula, הִנֵּה before the subject matter of the prediction, כִּי before the concluding characterisation. J. Muilenburg has studied the important placing of particles in the Hebrew language in HUCA XXXII, 1961: 'Among the Hebrew particles there is one group that plays a distinctive lexical and rhetorical role. They are the signals and signposts of language, markers on the way of the sentence or poem or narrative, guides to the progress of words, arrows directing what is being spoken to its destination. . . . The intended meaning becomes alive and dynamic in the ways that the particles are employed' (p. 135).

early prophetic period usually before II (the prediction). Why it was not always placed at the beginning of the prophecy is still a mystery. At the beginning, however, there is always the *appeal for attention* (AA, שְׁמַע or plural), which was used after the time of Amos (Amos vii. 16; Jer. xxviii. 15).

Where the prophet refers back to a prophecy of disaster which he had announced earlier, he uses a fixed framework. He tells of a preceding *private oracle*, by which he had received authorisation. Usually it runs, 'Go, and say unto him (II Kings i. 3, 6, 15). At a later period—and frequently in Jeremiah (see above, p. 202) this was preceded by the *formula for receiving God's word*: 'The word of the Lord came unto . . .'.

B. *The Structure of the Prophecy of Salvation*

The prophecy of salvation also usually includes the *Ko-amar formula* (messenger formula); it can be placed before both I and II (Jer. xxxii. 14 f., xxxv. 18 f.; II Kings iii. 16 f.), or only before I (Jer. xxviii. 2, xxxii. 36), earlier also only before II (I Kings xvii. 14, xi. 31; Isa. vii. 7). The prophecy can begin with an *appeal for attention* (Jer. xxxiv. 4). If the prophet describes how he came to be authorised for this particular duty, he refers to a private oracle which told him what to do (Isa. vii. 3 f.) and uses—after the time of Jeremiah—the *formula for receiving God's word* (Jer. xxxiii. 1). Just as for the prophecy of disaster, for the prophecy of salvation there is also a fixed framework.

The two passages given in Section 17, Jer. xxviii. 2–4 and xxxiv. 4 f., provide us with quite enough material to show that the prophecy of salvation and the prophecy of disaster are basically similar in construction.

1. To begin with the situation is sketched in; not however with a diatribe, nor with a question in reproach, but by means of a statement (as in xxviii. 2, but also xxxiv. 12, cf. xxxii. 36 and earlier, I Kings xxi. 29, II Kings xx. 5). The involved introductory phrase, 'Forasmuch as' (יַעַן אֲשֶׁר) is also to be found in prophecies of salvation (Jer. xxxv. 16). Often this section is in the form of an exhortation, e.g. xxxiii. 3: 'Call upon me, and I will answer thee . . .'. Other examples (xxix. 5–7; Isa. vii. 4 ff.; I Kings xi. 31; II Kings iii. 16, iv. 43). It has therefore been thought that a prophecy of salvation always began with what is fundamentally an exhortation, but there is no doubt that this is inaccurate. The exhortation is by no means so established a part of the prophecy of salvation as the diatribe is of the prophecy of disaster. It is only one special instance of the section in general: the *indication of the present situation*. If an exhortation is placed at the beginning, the section following it often begins with 'For', followed by a messenger formula (Jer. xxxii. 15, xxxiii. 4, xxix. 8; I Kings xi. 31, xvii. 14; II Kings iii. 17). When this is so there is usually no characterisation at the end.

2. *Prediction of salvation, or promise.* This corresponds with its parallel in the prophecy of disaster in so far as the sentence containing the core of the matter is again (*a*) in the imperfect, followed usually by a negative predicate, i.e. of 'apodictic' construction, such as Jer. xxxiv. 4 f. (xxxv. 19),

or (b) it is a participial nominative clause (Jer. xxviii. 3) which usually begins with 'Behold, I', i.e. a presentative (Jer. xxxii. 37, xxxiii. 6). Both these constructions are an ancient part of the promise also. A genitive imperfect can be found as early as I Kings xvii. 14; II Kings iii. 17; Isa. vii. 7; and 'Behold, I' with the following participle as early as I Kings xi. 31, and II Kings xx. 5.[9] The transition from I to II is achieved by 'therefore' (Jer. xxxv. 19).

3. The *concluding characterisation* refers in both our examples, Jer. xxviii. 4 and xxxiv. 5, to the sender, the one who has authorised the message and is also the cause of what will happen. This is also the case in Jer. xxxii. 44 and xxxix. 18 (the last passage also characterises the recipient). This section is often missing in the prophecies of salvation of the earlier prophets (e.g. I Kings xvii. 14); but this could be because it has been left out at a later stage by narrators.[10] The prophet would have taken it for granted that any future salvation—contrary to any future disaster—would be the result of divine compassion and not of human merit, so that logically a conclusion could characterise only God.

The literary type of the prophecy prevailed up until the post-exilic period and still appears in the prophets Haggai and Zachariah, though by this time there are clear signs of disintegration. Exhortation predominates. The messenger formula and the formula 'saith the Lord' crop up so often that prophecies are bespattered with them. This can be seen from the prophecy of salvation in Haggai ii. 3–9 to Zerubbabel and the rest of the people:

Who is left among you that saw this house (the temple) in its former glory?
And how do ye see it now? is it not in your eyes as nothing?
Yet now be strong, O Zerubbabel, saith the Lord;
and be strong, O Joshua, son of Jehozadak, the high priest;
and be strong, all ye people of the land, saith the Lord, and work:
for I am with you, saith the Lord of hosts,
according to the word that I covenanted with you when ye came out of
Egypt,
and my spirit abode among you: fear ye not.
For thus saith the Lord of hosts: Yet once, it is a little while,
and I will shake the heavens, and the earth, and the sea, and the dry land;

---

[9] P. Humbert, La formule hébraïque en *hineni* suivi d'un participe, Revue des Etudes Juives 97, 1934, 58–64. Opuscules (see App. 5) 54–59 points out that this formula—apart from rare exceptions—is only used when God is the subject. It is only occasionally and untypically used in a message between two men (Num. xxiv. 14; I Kings v. 19). Humbert is of the opinion that it came from ancient cultic oracles, but this is unlikely as it has been found that the formula is mainly used in announcements of disaster (85 out of the 125 times). This could mean that it was only later that it found its way into the literary type of the prophecy of salvation. At any rate it emphasises a sudden, direct intervention by God, as against the negative imperfect form which gives the impression of an action developing over a period of time. Did the presentative announcement first arise in the representation of a vision? הִנֵּה is often used at the start of the description of a vision (Amos vii. 1, 4, 7; Jer. xxiv. 1, etc.).

[10] In I Kings xx. 13, 28 the third section is transformed into a 'saying of self-attestation' (*Erweiswort*), see W. Zimmerli, *Das Wort des göttlichen Selbsterweises (Erweiswort), eine prophetische Gattung*; in Mélanges bibliques rédigés en l'honneur de A. Robert 1957.

and I will shake all nations, and the desirable things of all nations shall
come,
and I will fill this house with glory, saith the Lord of hosts.
The silver is mine, and the gold is mine, saith the Lord of hosts.
The latter glory of this house shall be greater than the former, saith the
Lord of hosts:
and in this place will I give peace, saith the Lord of hosts.
In the Chronicles the prophecy shows an even greater change.

It is difficult to decide whether the prophecies of salvation and disaster
should be considered as separate literary types or merely as two variants
of the general literary type of the prophecy, for the boundary between
two literary types can be very indeterminate, particularly if they share a
common setting in life. It is therefore not surprising to find some prophecies which predict salvation as well as disaster, or which switch from one
to the other (I Kings xii. 24; Jer. xxxviii. 17 ff., xlii. 2 ff.; also the Mari
prophecies). It therefore remains an open matter whether they are to be
considered separately or together. The Israelite placed all these sayings
under the one heading, 'The (not even *a*) Word of Jahweh' (דְּבַר יהוה). The
word 'prophecy' (Weissagung) should be reserved in Old Testament
exegesis for those units which correspond to the construction of the
prophecies of disaster and salvation described above. Not every pronouncement by a prophet is a prophecy in this sense.

C. *Parallels outside Israel*

The literary type of the prophecy is not to be found in the literature of the
pre-monarchical period in Israel. On the other hand excavations in the
ancient Euphrates town of Mari have produced tablets in cuneiform writing
dating from the middle of the second millenium before Christ, which
contain elements of the later Old Testament prophecy and its use of the
literary type of the prophecy. A letter from a state governor to king Zimrilim of Mari[11] gives the report of a man dreaming on his knees in the
temple of the god Dagan:

I Why do not the messengers of Zimrilim remain constantly with me?
 And why does he not report to me (about everything)?
 Otherwise a long while ago I should have
 Delivered the chiefs of the Benjaminites into the hands of Zimrilim.
PO Go now! I have sent you (or, I send you). You will say the following to
Zimrilim:
II Send your messengers to me and report to me fully
 Then I will toss the rods of the Benjaminites
 Into a fish basket and place them before you.[12]

The similarity in construction to the Old Testament literary type is
unmistakeable. Here also there is first a reference to the present situation

---

[11] N. von Soden = *Verkündigung des Gotteswillens durch prophetisches Wort in den
altbabylonischen Briefen aus Mâri*, Welt des Orients 1950, 397–403.
[12] Translated from the German.

(I), and then an indication of future developments (II). Between these there is something resembling a private oracle (PO), but here it is part of the official proclamation. The chief difference between this and Old Testament usage is that there is no legitimising messenger formula, although it would have had some relevance in an official exchange of letters with Mari (ANET, pp. 482 f.). The constant use in the Old Testament of the *Ko-amar formula* emphasises the distance between prophet and God. The prophet is the conveyor of the divine word. God is not (or no longer) mysteriously in him. A further important difference is that in the Mari prophecy salvation and disaster are interlocked. Both are of a limited nature, dependent upon the decision of man. The Old Testament prophecy of the pre-exilic period allows much less significance to human decision (or looks back upon it as something made long ago which cannot be altered); salvation and disaster are sharply divided from each other, and achieve the level of irrevocable divine action. The history of the literary type of the prophecy gives us important information about the way in which the uniqueness of Israel's concept of God had developed over the course of time.

D. *Comparison with the Message*

What do we find if we compare the prophecies of disaster and salvation, i.e. the 'message' from God to man, and the message which passes between two men? It has been shown above [13] that the full pronouncement of a messenger, communicating a message between two equals, consists of the following sections:

> Messenger formula
> Indication of the pressing situation
> The wish of the sender (often in the imperative)
> Concluding characterisation

Let us compare this with the pre-exilic prophecy:

Prophecy of salvation	*Prophecy of disaster*
Indication of the pressing situation (sometimes an exhortation)	Diatribe
Messenger formula (*Ko-amar*)	Messenger formula
Prediction of salvation	Prediction of disaster
(Concluding characterisation)	(Concluding characterisation)

Is the prophecy therefore a prophetic message? Do the prophets act here as authorised messengers, heralds of their God, where possibly God's *kingly* rank is emphasised, as in human terms it is principally the king who sends out messengers? It must be borne in mind that the prophets are never expressly referred to as messengers of God. A messenger who genuinely comes from God must be a divine being, such as the 'angel of the Lord', who in fact is called a messenger מַלְאָךְ in the Hebrew.[14] And as to the content, 'Threat, exhortation and promise certainly do not normally play a part when a messenger is authorised.'[15] Therefore despite the fact that they

[13] See page 189 f.

[14] The only passage—of later origin—where perhaps a prophet is described as מַלְאָךְ is Mal. iii. 1.

[15] Rendtorff 166.

both fall into three sections this does not mean that they must both be examples of the same literary type. It is true that there is a great similarity between them, to the extent that occasionally the message between men takes on an elevated language and uses parallelismus membrorum. In these cases the message is composed in the same way as the prophetic sayings, which also appear to occupy a middle point between formal poetry and prose.

A closer comparison reveals that despite their affinities the prophecy and the message passing between two men are indeed separate things. However, the *messenger formula* is in fact common to both: 'Thus saith NN.' But this formula (KA) is a relatively independent section within the prophecy: it can change its position, or even appear twice (Jer. xxviii. 13 f). It also crops up in other prophetic literary types which have nothing in common with the style of the prophecy, e.g. the pronouncement accompanying a symbolic action (Jer. xxviii. 11). The position of the messenger formula is quite different in the earlier prophecies and in the message. In the latter it is normally placed at the beginning, and in the former it is normally placed between the first and second sections. Also, at least in the prophecy of disaster, the first section is not only a general indication of the situation but is also a diatribe, referring to the offence which has been committed, and this is the form it has taken since the beginning of prophecy. The middle sections differ most: whereas in the message this section gives notice of the particular wish or command of the sender, in the prophecy it announces a future event, and one which is set into motion by the sender himself.[16] This future event is expressed either by a participial clause preceded by a presentative: 'Behold, I', or an apodictic negative sentence in the imperfect, which implies that 'it will not happen', in both prophecies of disaster and salvation. Neither of these constructions is used in the message. It would be interesting to see whether the concluding characterisation also shows typical differences.

How can we explain the relationship and also the differences between the two? Obviously the message between men had some influence on the formation of the literary type of the prophecy. This could only have occurred by means of a change in the conception of God. By the time of the later prophets God no longer speaks directly to the people concerned, as he did in the Genesis sagas, but sends a prophet as intermediary. But it appears that other forces were active in the development of the literary type of the prophecy of which we no longer have any exact knowledge and which transformed the pattern of the message. The middle section was completely different right from the start.[17] Perhaps it originated from an old saying by a seer (Num. xxiii. 9, 20). Thus it has always been more than a message placed in the mouth of the prophet by God: it is an independent literary type.

The history of the prophecies of disaster and salvation reveals that after the time of Jeremiah the messenger formula came to head the unit (xxviii. 2), or to appear twice (xxviii. 13 f.). Is this the result of the influence of the message passing between men, or must we consider it to be a change in the prophetic way of thinking, by which more and more prophetic thoughts came to be thought of as inspired, even including the reflection on the situation of those concerned (the diatribe)?

E. *Setting in Life*

Where does the literary type of the prophecy belong? It is used by Elijah, Jeremiah, but also by Hananiah. The prophet of salvation therefore uses

[16] With the command in Part II the Mari prophecy has a closer affinity to the message between two persons than with the Old Testament literary type of the prophecy.

[17] H. Graf Reventlow, Wächter über Israel, BZAW 82, 1962, sees the prophecy announced by a prophet to have arisen out of cultic benediction and curse rites (on the basis of a comparison of passages from Ezekiel with Lev. xxvi).

the same literary type as that 'prophet of disaster', Jeremiah. This is a point of consequence in any evaluation of the false prophets in the Old Testament. It also brings out the continuity between the writing prophets and the older prophecies of an Elijah or Elisha. Thus the reform prophets, despite objections against a superficial prophetic practice, have a very strong link with the Nabis of earlier times. Form-critically it shows how very much even a man of such individuality as Jeremiah is bound by the linguistic usage and doctrine which he inherits. Despite the prophets' emotional eccentricities (impressively brought out by Gunkel) they conform very much to the prevailing customs and linguistic usage of their day. This is a bond which we must interpret very differently from Gunkel: it is quite obvious that it does not detract from the greatness of these men. All important figures in the history of God and the world are not alienated from their time and their language, but are even more involved than the average man.

The prophecy is not formal literature, but intended for oral pronouncement. This is apparent enough from the legends of the prophets. But also the brevity and austerity of construction can only be explained by such a setting in life. Moreover the sayings themselves give a clear indication of this setting in the frequent appeal for attention at the beginning: 'Hear the word . . .', which is obviously directed at the listener rather than the reader.

Where were these prophecies proclaimed? Elijah's prophecy in II Kings i took place in the king's palace, even when it came to the king indirectly, through the mouths of intermediaries. However, Hananiah spoke in the temple at Jerusalem on a ceremonial occasion at which the priests and the people were present, taking part in some cultic event. Jeremiah's answering prophecy will have been pronounced in the same place, for it is directed at a wide audience and it is therefore probable that a mass of people were present then also. This observation touches upon a point of controversy in form-critical research today, for the next question is: do Hananiah and Jeremiah speak as private individuals, making use of an opportunity before or after the ceremony and before the people had dispersed to quickly announce their prophecies? Or, and this alternative has considerable consequences, do both prophets make their appearance in the middle of a cultic ceremony; do they therefore have an established position in the liturgy of their day? Are they, in their capacity as prophets, also temple functionaries? In short, are they cultic prophets? Discussion of this point is still continuing, so that all we can do here is to refer to it briefly. Meanwhile the Elijah legends go so far as to indicate that a prophecy was also pronounced outside a cultic place, and in fact usually was so. Is it possible that the custom changed during the time of the writing prophets?[18]

A point which has a bearing on cultic prophecy is the relationship of the prophets to Israelite divine law. It is recognised that the Decalogue and other series of commandments originated as part of a cultic event. It happens that some prophecies of disaster upbraid an infringement of these

---

[18] The inspiration for the thesis that prophecy was bound up entirely with the cult came from S. Mowinckel: *Psalmenstudien* III, 1923, E.T. *The Psalms in Israel's Worship*, 1962 (Oxford, Blackwell; Nashville, Abingdon Press). A survey of present-day problems in von Rad, *Theology* II.

laws in the diatribe. Elijah's question to Ahaziah: 'Is it because there is no God in Israel?' when Ahaziah goes to inquire of Baalzebub the god of Ekron, calls to mind the first commandment of the Decalogue: Thou shalt have none other gods before me. In Amos also there are many similar connections to be found between prophecies of disaster and apodictic commandments. It has yet to be seen whether it is possible to deduce from these connections whether the prophets had the official duty of upholding the divine law. It would be very difficult to postulate a connection between the prophecy of disaster to the nation in Jeremiah xxviii and the cultic commandments, especially as verse 14 states that the yoke of Nebuchadnezzar is not over Israel alone but over all nations. (It would be necessary to suppose an offence by all the nations against the Israelite divine law.) Neither can the prophecy of disaster to Hananiah, reproaching him for lying and deceiving the people, be explained in these terms. Hananiah acted in good conscience, and his offence, that he had not recognised the signs of the times, is to a certain extent an 'objective' one, so that it cannot be simply traced back to a commandment. Thus this is a point which is still open to investigation. (The connection between the prophet's prophecies and the ancient divine law could best be explained after a closer examination of the sentences in the negative imperfect in the prediction, followed by a comparison with the old commandments.)

However, the public pronouncement of a prophecy is only the second setting in life. It did not originate at that moment. In fact, II Kings i and Jer. xxviii show with absolute clarity that the public oracle is preceded by a *private oracle*, which the prophet receives when he is alone with his God. Strictly speaking, a private oracle involves a public oracle, at least in its main features. But to determine the difference between them more clearly it is advisable to call those words which come to the prophet personally the private oracle. This is the point at which the prophet usually receives his instructions. Once he has received them, he goes to the place and the people concerned. Thus it was that in Jer. xxviii the prophet was rendered almost speechless in a public place, for he had not yet received God's word. All that he could do was to accept the prophecy of his rival. An attempt has been made by Gunkel and others after him to look into the phenomenon of the prophet's reception of God's word, i.e. at the inspiration behind the prophecy.[19] The point at which to start from is therefore not the literary type of the prophecy, but that of the account of a vision. This is a subject we cannot pursue here. We can only say that a final analysis of the phenomenon has not yet been made. For instance, it is not clear in our present context whether the prophet actually received the prophecy in articulated words, or whether he heard unarticulated voices which he translated into words himself. All that can be stated with certainty is that the word was not received in the stillness of mystical absorption, but was associated with a physical ecstasy which shook the prophets' being. Such ecstasies were attributed to 'spiritual fervour' (רוּחַ). (This was so with Elijah and also with Ezekiel.)

[19] Survey of the literature up to that point in von Rad, *Theology* II, 99–119.

The sayings of the prophets did not of course remain only for oral pronouncement. First they were collected orally by the prophet's disciples and formed into series of sayings, with or without an accompanying narrative, and soon afterwards they were written down. It appears that a whole school of disciples was formed around Isaiah, and perhaps also around other prophets. It was the duty of these groups to transmit a reliable version of the words of the master. It was the same with Elisha, to whose circle of adherents the Elijah stories will also have belonged.[20] (But in Jeremiah we hear nothing of such a group. Only Baruch is with him. Therefore the mass of the Jeremiah sayings must be considered not to have gone through a long period of oral transmission.) When written down the units not only changed their literary type, from that of the prophecy to that of the book of the prophets, but also their setting in life. The prophetic speeches will then have only been read to those who believed in the word of the prophet, and no longer to an uninitiated gathering of people. Thus a third setting in life was reached. Such groups seem to have been formed particularly after the destruction of Jerusalem, in Palestine and the Babylonian exile; but we know very little about this.

These examples from the prophetic writings have revealed a number of independent prophetic literary types: legends of the prophets, prophecies of disaster and salvation, pronouncements accompanying a symbolic action. An attempt has been made to bring out the characteristics of a type, so that the reader will have some basis for recognising it in other contexts. Of course this does not mean that all prophetic literary types have been covered, for important examples such as the lawsuit,[21] or the woe-song discovered by Westermann[22] (which must not be confused with a diatribe), or the account of a vision, have remained unconsidered for reasons of space. The reader should not suppose that there is only one genuine prophetic literary type. An analysis of the prophetic literary types is arduous because their form has been much obscured by later revisions. Nevertheless it is this that will give us the key to prophetic language and to the theological mystery of prophecy, which is as problematic as it is important. Without a form-critical basis exegesis of the prophetic language inevitably loses itself in pure speculation.

[20] For the nature of such schools see Mowinckel, *Prophecy*.

[21] The few extant prophetic lawsuits have been placed by the redactors (of their own predilection) at the beginning of the prophetic books: Isa. i. 2 f.; Jer. ii. 4–12; Hos. ii. 4–15; iv. 1–10, etc. They have had a large role in exegetical discussion since H. B. Huffmon, The Covenant Lawsuit in the Prophets, JBL 78, 1959, inferred from some parts of them a process against the *infringement of the covenant formular* (see above, section 2C). Cf. J. Harvey, B 43, 1962, 172–96, and G. E. Wright, *Festschrift for J. Muilenburg*, 1962, 26–67. Yet it must be emphasised that the rare literary type of the prophetic lawsuit by no means justifies interpreting the very frequently used literary type of the prophecy as Jahweh's judicial word.

[22] Pp. 136–40.

INDEX OF BIBLICAL REFERENCES

INDEX OF BIBLICAL LITERARY TYPES
AND THEIR ELEMENTS